The Competitive Advan
Market Multinationals

Multinationals from Brazil, Russia, India and China, known as the BRIC countries, are a new and powerful force in global competition and are challenging the incumbency of much older global companies from the developed world. Emerging market multinational enterprises (EMNEs) now account for a quarter of foreign investment in the world, are a prolific source of innovation and make almost one in three cross-border acquisitions globally. Despite this, traditional theories of international business do not provide a satisfactory explanation of their behaviour or performance. The authors of this book shine new light on the rise of EMNEs and how they have built a competitive advantage through innovation, novel configurations of their international value chains and the acquisition of companies overseas. Any manager, policy maker or researcher who wishes to understand the emergence of this new breed of multinational will find this book an invaluable resource.

PETER J. WILLIAMSON is Professor of International Management at Judge Business School, University of Cambridge. He also consults on global strategy, mergers and acquisitions (M&A) and Chinese business, and serves as non-executive director of several companies spanning financial services through to green energy.

RAVI RAMAMURTI is Distinguished Professor of International Business and Strategy and Director of the Center for Emerging Markets, Northeastern University, Boston. His previous publications include *Emerging Multinationals in Emerging Markets* (Cambridge University Press, 2009).

AFONSO FLEURY is a professor in the Production Engineering Department at the University of São Paulo. He is also a consultant to Brazilian public and private firms as well as subsidiaries of multinationals. His previous publications include *Brazilian Multinationals: Competences for Internationalization* (Cambridge University Press, 2011).

MARIA TEREZA LEME FLEURY is Dean of the School of Business Administration at Fundação Getulio Vargas in São Paulo. Her previous publications include *Brazilian Multinationals: Competences for Internationalization* (Cambridge University Press, 2011).

The Competitive Advantage of Emerging Market Multinationals

Edited by

PETER J. WILLIAMSON, RAVI RAMAMURTI,
AFONSO FLEURY AND MARIA TEREZA LEME
FLEURY

CAMBRIDGE
UNIVERSITY PRESS

CAMBRIDGE UNIVERSITY PRESS
Cambridge, New York, Melbourne, Madrid, Cape Town,
Singapore, São Paulo, Delhi, Mexico City

Cambridge University Press
The Edinburgh Building, Cambridge CB2 8RU, UK

Published in the United States of America by
Cambridge University Press, New York

www.cambridge.org
Information on this title: www.cambridge.org/9781107659414

© Cambridge University Press 2013

First published 2013

Printed and bound in the United Kingdom by the MPG Books Group

A catalogue record for this publication is available from the British Library

Library of Congress Cataloguing in Publication data

The competitive advantage of emerging market multinationals / Edited by Peter J.
    Williamson, Ravi Ramamurti, Afonso Fleury and Maria Tereza Leme Fleury.
      pages   cm
    ISBN 978-1-107-03255-2 (Hardback) – ISBN 978-1-107-65941-4 (Paperback)
    1. International business enterprises–Developing countries. 2. Competition,
International. I. Williamson, Peter J., editor of compilation.   II. Ramamurti, Ravi,
editor of compilation.   III. Fleury, Afonso Carlos Corrêa, 1947– editor of compilation.
IV. Fleury, Maria Tereza Leme, editor of compilation.
    HD2932.C65 2013
    338.8′891724–dc23

2012036020

ISBN 978-1-107-03255-2 Hardback
ISBN 978-1-107-65941-4 Paperback

Contents

List of figures   *page* viii

List of tables   x

Notes on contributors   xii

Acknowledgements   xxiv

Introduction   1
Peter J. Williamson, Ravi Ramamurti, Afonso Fleury
and Maria Tereza Leme Fleury

Part I   Innovation and competitive advantage

1   Innovation by Brazilian EMNEs   11
Moacir de Miranda Oliveira Junior, Felipe Mendes Borini
and Afonso Fleury

2   Innovation by Russian EMNEs   29
Sergey Filippov and Alexander Settles

3   Innovation by Indian EMNEs   46
Nikhil Celly, Jaideep Prabhu and Venkat Subramanian

4   Innovation by Chinese EMNEs   64
Peter J. Williamson and Eden Yin

Commentaries on Part I

(I.i)   The contribution of innovation to EMNEs'
competitive advantage   81
Bridgette Sullivan-Taylor

(I.ii)   Innovation in emerging markets and the rise of
emerging market MNEs   89
Ram Mudambi

**Part II   Value-chain configuration and competitive
advantage**

5   Value-chain configurations of Brazilian EMNEs   97
*Afonso Fleury, Maria Tereza Leme Fleury and Felipe
Mendes Borini*

6   Value-chain configurations of Russian EMNEs   116
Valery S. Katkalo and Andrey G. Medvedev

7   Value-chain configurations of Indian EMNEs   132
Suma Athreye

8   Value-chain configurations of Chinese EMNEs   149
Kaimei Wang and Yongjiang Shi

Commentaries on Part II

(II.i)   How emerging market multinational enterprises
upgrade capabilities using value-chain configuration in
advanced economies   174
Alvaro Cuervo-Cazurra

(II.ii)   Value-chain configurations of emerging country
multinationals   180
Jagjit Singh Srai

**Part III   Mergers and acquisitions and competitive
advantage**

9   Cross-border M&A and competitive advantage
of Brazilian EMNEs   191
Alvaro B. Cyrino and Erika P. Barcellos

10   Cross-border M&A and competitive advantage
of Russian EMNEs   220
Kalman Kalotay and Andrei Panibratov

11 Cross-border M&A and competitive advantage of
Indian EMNEs 239
Ravi Ramamurti

12 Cross-border M&A and competitive advantage of
Chinese EMNEs 260
Peter J. Williamson and Anand P. Raman

Commentaries on Part III

(III.i) Cross-border M&A by the new multinationals:
different reasons to 'go global' 278
Simon Collinson

(III.ii) Cross-border acquisitions by EMNEs 284
Ravi Sarathy

Conclusion: rethinking the implications of EMNEs' rise 290
*Peter J. Williamson, Ravi Ramamurti, Afonso Fleury
and Maria Tereza Leme Fleury*

References 319
Index 340

List of figures

3.1 Models for the innovation–internationalisation
process of Indian firms *page 50*

5.1 The distinct VCC shapes for developed vs. emerging
country MNEs 108

6.1 The 'value role–company size' matrix 122

8.1 Manufacturing system evolution matrix and
key drivers 152

8.2 Company A's internationalisation process 157

8.3 Three aspects to identify overseas individual factory
development path 168

9.1 Number of transactions and total reported values.
Outbound M&A from Brazilian companies 196

9.2 Geographic location of the foreign acquisition
targets, 1990–2010 (% of total transactions) 200

9.A1 Exchange rates (monthly average) 219

10.1 FDI outflows and cross-border M&A purchases of
Russia, 1992–2009 ($ million) 224

10.2 Share of Russia in world FDI outflows and
cross-border M&A purchases, 1992–2009 (%) 227

10.3 Cross-border M&A purchases of Russia by industry,
1992–2009 (%) 228

10.4 Cross-border M&A purchases of Russia, top ten
target countries, 1992–2009 ($ million) 229

11.1 Determinants of international competitiveness of
emerging market firms: CSA–GSA–FSA framework 240

11.2 Relationship between internationalisation strategy
and FSA exploitation or exploration 254

12.1 The evolution of Chinese EMNEs' M&A activity in
aggregate (value of foreign acquisitions, $ billion) 260

12.2 Chinese EMNEs' M&A activity by sector (value of
foreign acquisitions, top four sectors, $ billion) 261

12.3 The 'double handspring' strategy of EMNEs' M&A   275
C.1 Competitive advantage through internationalisation   293
C.2 Determinants of international competitiveness of
     emerging market firms: CSA–GSA–FSA framework   308

List of tables

2.1 Investment in R&D by Russian companies:
global look *page* 36
2.2 Interplay between internationalisation and innovation 38
3.1 Key points for three phases of innovation in
Indian firms 61
4.1 Capabilities underpinning innovation by
Chinese EMEs 77
5.1 Regional location of the activities of Brazilian
multinationals 101
5.2 Distribution of Brazilian multinationals according
to industry 102
5.3 The TNI of Brazilian multinationals 102
5.4 The structure of activities performed in Brazilian
subsidiaries 111
5.5 The structure of preferences for the set up of VCC 111
6.1 Internationalisation determinants for Russian MNCs 125
7.1 Nature of outward greenfield projects over developed
and developing countries, 1990–9 143
8.1 Identification of research gaps 153
8.2 Case companies studied for their manufacturing
internationalisation 155
8.3 CRT TV import duties from China, Vietnam and
Thailand to Asian countries (%) 162
8.4 A changing evolution of overseas factories' market
focus after the acquisition 164
8.5 Four tasks of TTE post-acquisition integration 165
8.6 TTE sales volume and forecast of CRT televisions in
Asia, 2005–10 (units) 165
8.7 The development of Company B's overseas factories
before and after the acquisition 167

8.8 Match between international manufacturing strategy
and four dimensions 172
II.1 EMNE strategies for global reconfiguration of the
value chain in advanced economies 176
II.2 Description of internationalisation investment motives 182
9.1 Number and value of transactions ($m): outbound
cross-border M&A from Brazilian companies 195
9.2 Outward FDI and foreign acquisitions of Brazilian
companies 197
9.3 The twenty main Brazilian cross-border acquirers 198
9.4 Percentage of controlling power targeted by the
acquiring company 200
9.5 Generic strategic groups and drivers of foreign
acquisition 207
9.A1 Mode of entry versus motivations to internationalise 211
9.A2 Mode of entry versus competitive advantages 215
10.1 Russian OFDI to 'Western' and 'Eastern' economies,
2007–9 ($ million and %) 222
10.2 Number of foreign acquisitions, greenfield projects
and strategic alliances initiated by Russian companies,
2000–10 226
10.3 Cross-border M&A mega-deals (over $1 billion) by
Russian MNEs, 2004–10 230
11.A1 International acquisitions over $100m by Indian
firms, 2008–2010 (in descending order of value) 256
III.1 Dominant patterns in cross-border M&A across the
BRIC economies 279

Notes on contributors

SUMA ATHREYE is Professor of International Strategy at Brunel Business School and Founding Director of the Centre on International Business and Strategy in Emerging Markets at Brunel University. Her research focuses on internationalisation and its impact on technology management in developed and in emerging economies. Some of her well-cited publications are on knowledge markets and the growth of international licensing, foreign investment into India, the growth of the Cambridge high-tech cluster, the software and pharmaceutical industries in India and the internationalisation of Chinese and Indian firms. She has won several grants for her research, which has also been recognised by national and international media.

ERIKA P. BARCELLOS is an associate professor at Fundação Dom Cabral, Brazil. She is specialised in the fields of strategic management and international business, having coordinated executive education programmes related to innovation and internationalisation of emerging market companies. She has published in leading journals such as the *International Journal of Emerging Markets* and the *International Journal of Human Resource Management,* and has written several case studies and book chapters in those fields. Erika has a BSc in Civil Engineering from the Federal University of Minas Gerais, an MSc in Business Administration from the University of Sao Paulo (USP) and an MBA with high honours from Boston University.

FELIPE MENDES BORINI is an associate professor at Escola Superior de Propaganda e Marketing (ESPM-SP), Brazil. He has a PhD in Business Administration from USP and a masters degree from Pontifical Catholic University of Sao Paulo, Brazil. He is chief editor of *Internext*, a scientific journal of international business in Brazil. His research interests are strategies and innovations of foreign subsidiaries, transference of reverse innovation and strategies of enterprises from and on emerging markets.

NIKHIL CELLY is an assistant professor of strategy and international business in the School of Business, University of Hong Kong. His research examines the global restructuring strategies of multinational enterprises (MNEs), in particular acquisitions, downsizing and downscoping. He is also studying the internationalisation capabilities of firms in the emerging economies of India and China as they globalise. He has interviewed firms in Canada, the US, China and India for his research, and also written several teaching cases on international strategy. Nikhil teaches courses on strategic management and global business at undergraduate and MBA levels. He has a PhD in General Management from the Richard Ivey School of Business, University of Western Ontario, an MSc in Electrical Engineering from the University of Rochester and a BEng in Electronics and Communications from the University of Delhi.

SIMON COLLINSON is Dean and Professor of International Business and Innovation at Birmingham Business School, University of Birmingham, and sits on the governing body of the Economic and Social Research Council (ESRC) and the Council of the British Academy of Management. He was previously at Warwick Business School, where he held the posts of Deputy Dean and Associate Dean (MBAs). His current research is on innovation and competitiveness in emerging economies, with a particular focus on China. He is the Guangbiao Visiting Professor at Zhejiang University in Hangzhou and works more broadly with multinational firms and UK government agencies on China-related issues. Another research focus is complexity and performance. Working with the Simplicity Partnership, Simon has developed ways to help firms simplify their organisation structures and corporate strategies to concentrate more effectively on adding value. He has published in numerous journals, and is also co-author of the Financial Times/Pearson *International Business* textbook with Alan Rugman. His research has recently featured on BBC Radio 4 and in the *Sunday Times*, the *New Statesman* and *US News & World Report*.

ALVARO CUERVO-CAZURRA is an associate professor of international business and strategy at Northeastern University. He studies the internationalisation of firms, with a special interest in developing country multinational firms. He also analyses governance issues, with a special interest in corruption in international business. His research appears in leading academic journals, such as *Academy of Management Journal, Journal of International Business Studies, Strategic Management Journal* and *Research Policy,* and in several edited books. He is the reviewing editor of *Journal of International Business Studies* and serves on the editorial boards of other leading journals, such as *Strategic Management Journal, Global Strategy Journal, Organization Studies* and *Journal of World Business.* His geographical area of expertise is Latin America. He has done fieldwork in Argentina, Brazil, Chile, Costa Rica, Mexico, Nicaragua, Spain and the US. Alvaro teaches courses on global strategy and sustainability at undergraduate, masters, executive and PhD levels. He received a PhD from the Massachusetts Institute of Technology (MIT) and another from the University of Salamanca.

ALVARO B. CYRINO is currently Vice-dean of EBAPE-Fundação Getúlio Vargas, Brazil. He has a BSc in Business and Public Administration from the Federal University of the State of Paraná, Brazil, a Diplôme d'Études Approfondies from the Université de Technologie de Compiègne, France and a PhD in Business Administration from the École de Hautes Études Commerciales (HEC), France, with a major on strategy. He has worked in executive positions at universities, in the public sector and in private companies, including international assignments. As a consultant in the field of strategic management and international business, he has been working for major Brazilian companies. His current research interests include the field of strategy, with an emphasis on the resource-based view, and the field international business, where he has concentrated on the internationalisation process of companies from emerging markets.

SERGEY FILIPPOV is an assistant professor of innovation management at the Delft University of Technology. In 2009 he successfully completed a PhD programme in the Economics and Policy Studies of Technical Change and earned his PhD degree. Sergey Filippov holds an MA in the Management of the European Metropolitan Region from Erasmus University, Rotterdam and an Executive Master's degree in International and European Relations and Management from the University of Amsterdam. His academic interests are diverse and include corporate innovation strategies, technology management, globalisation of innovation and the presence in Europe of multinational companies from emerging economies. He has published widely, including international refereed journals and books, and has been invited as a speaker to a variety of European and international conferences, workshops and training programmes.

AFONSO FLEURY is a professor in the area of work, technology and organisation at the University of São Paulo. He was a research fellow at the Institute of Development Studies in the UK, Tokyo Institute of Technology, École Nationale des Ponts et Chaussés in France and the Institute for Manufacturing at Cambridge University, UK, and elaborated research projects for both Brazilian and international organisations. He is currently engaged in research on international manufacturing and operations, and coordinates a large project for the Centre for Technology Policy and Management at USP on the internationalisation of firms from Brazil, China, India, Russia and other emerging economies. His latest book is *Brazilian Multinationals: Competences for Internationalization* (Cambridge University Press, 2011). He is associate editor of the *Journal of Manufacturing Technology Management* and regional editor of *Operations Management Research*.

MARIA TEREZA LEME FLEURY teaches in the area of human resources management. She is the Dean of the School of Business Administration of Fundação Getulio Vargas, São Paulo, and former Dean of the School of Economics, Business Administration and Accountancy at the University of São Paulo. She has published several books and papers on strategy and competence management, internationalisation of emerging countries' firms, human resources management, management of organisational culture and labour relations. Her latest book is *Brazilian Multinationals: Competences for Internationalization* (Cambridge University Press, 2011). She is on the board of the Business Association for Latin America Studies (BALAS) of the Scientific Committee of Euromed Marseille, France, and on the editorial boards of the *International Journal of Human Resources Management* and other Brazilian and Latin American journals.

KALMAN KALOTAY is Economic Affairs Officer at the Division on Investment and Enterprise of the United Nations Conference on Trade and Development (UNCTAD). He has been a member of UNCTAD's *World Investment Report* team since 1996. Since 2009 he has also been part of the UNCTAD group preparing the *Investment Policy Reviews* for individual countries. He also served as associate (1996–2003) and deputy editor (2003–4) of UNCTAD's *Transnational Corporations* journal. Previously, he studied economic cooperation among developing countries at the UNCTAD secretariat (1990–6). Before joining the UN, he taught international economics at the Budapest University of Economic Sciences and Public Administration (currently Corvinus University of Budapest), Hungary (1983–90). He holds a PhD in International Economics from the same university. His work and publications have focused mainly on foreign direct investment and multinational enterprises in, and from, economies in transition.

VALERY S. KATKALO is Vice-Rector of St. Petersburg University (SPbU) and Dean of the Graduate School of Management (GSOM). Professor Katkalo was one of the founders (1993) of the GSOM at SPbU, where he has been Dean since 1997. Under his leadership GSOM became the Russian member of CEMS (an alliance of business schools and multinational companies) and the Partnership in International Management (PIM). It received international accreditations from the Association of MBAs and the European Foundation for Management Development (EFMD) Programme Accreditation System (EPAS). By EdUniversal ranking it is the most internationally recognised Russian business school and (as of 2010) ranked as the number two business school in Eastern Europe. Professor Katkalo's research focuses on evolution of strategic management theory, network organisations and advances in management education. He is the founder and chief editor of the *Russian Management Journal*. He is a member of EFMD Board of Trustees, CEMS Strategic Board, EPAS Accreditation Committee, and of several boards for Russian and international universities.

ANDREY G. MEDVEDEV is Professor of Strategic and International Management at Graduate School of Management, St. Petersburg University. Professor Medvedev's research and teaching interests lie in the sphere of international business strategies and management at multinational enterprises, including selection of foreign operations modes. In 1992–6, he was among the first Russian scholars to establish new education programmes, such as MBAs and programmes in international management, in several Russian universities and business schools. Since 1992, he has been Visiting Professor in these areas at business schools in Finland, France, Italy, Latvia, Sweden, Switzerland and the UK, including such leading institutions as Henley Management College (UK), Aalto University School of Economics (Helsinki) and University of St. Gallen (Switzerland). Professor Medvedev is a member of the CEMS faculty group in Global Strategy. He is the winner of several case study writing contests organised by Stockholm School of Economics, Central and East European Management Development Association (CEEMAN) and Russian Association of Business Education (RABE).

RAM MUDAMBI is Professor and Perelman Senior Research Fellow at the Fox School of Business, Temple University, Philadelphia. He is Visiting Professor at the Centre for Strategic Management and Globalization (SMG), Copenhagen Business School, and at the University of Reading, UK. He is a lifetime fellow of the Academy of the University of Messina, an honorary professor at the Centre of International Business, University of Leeds (CIBUL) and a member of the advisory council of the University of Bradford Centre in International Business (BCIB). He is an associate editor of the *Global Strategy Journal* and the Book Review Editor of the *Journal of International Business Studies*. He serves on the editorial boards of various management journals. He has published over sixty refereed articles and six books. His work has appeared in *Strategic Management Journal, Strategic Entrepreneurship Journal, Journal of International Business Studies, Journal of Political Economy* and *Journal of Economic Geography*, among others.

MOACIR DE MIRANDA OLIVEIRA JUNIOR is an associate professor at the Business Administration Department of USP. He was a visiting researcher at the Judge Business School, University of Cambridge. His current research interests are related to the internationalisation strategy of Brazilian firms and also to the strategic role of the subsidiaries of foreign multinational corporations in Brazil. He has published in several international refereed journals and books. He is also a director of the Latin American Chapter of the Academy of International Business (AIB-LAT) and was the coordinator in Brazil of the Global Call Center Research Project (GCCRP). As a consultant in the field of strategic management and international business, he has been working for major Brazilian companies.

ANDREI PANIBRATOV is an associate professor at the Graduate School of Management, Saint Petersburg State University, Russia. He holds a Doctor of Sciences in Economics from Moscow State University of Management (2006), an MBA from the University of Wales (1999) and a PhD in Economics from St. Petersburg State University (1998). He has visited conferences and professors' training programmes at Haas School of Business, University of California at Berkeley, Texas A&M University, HEC (France), Aalto University School of Management, Fundação Dom Cabral, European Case Clearing House (ECCH) and World Association for Case Method Research and Application (WACRA). He has participated in consulting and research projects for the World Bank, University of Manchester Institute of Science and Technology (UMIST), Lappeenranta University of Technology School of Business and Tampere University of Technology, as well as other European and Russian companies. His research and teaching interests include Western multinational enterprises' strategy for Russia, internationalisation of Russian firms, marketing decisions when moving abroad, outward foreign direct investment from Russia and Russian multinationals.

JAIDEEP PRABHU is Jawaharlal Nehru Professor of Indian Business and Enterprise, and Director of the Centre for India and Global Business at Judge Business School, University of Cambridge. He has a BTech degree from the Indian Institute of Technology (IIT) Delhi, and a PhD from the University of Southern California. Jaideep's research interests are in marketing, innovation, strategy and international business. His current research is mainly on the globalisation of innovation, and the role of emerging economies in this process. He has published in and is on the editorial board of leading international journals such as the *Journal of Marketing* and the *International Journal of Research in Marketing*. He has consulted for the UK government's Department of Trade and Industry and has taught and consulted with executives. He has appeared on BBC News24 and Bloomberg BusinessWeek, and his work has been profiled in *BusinessWeek*, *The Economic Times*, *The Economist*, *The Financial Times*, *Le Monde*, *MIT Sloan Management Review*, *The New York Times* and *The Times*.

RAVI RAMAMURTI is Distinguished Professor of International Business and Strategy and Director of the Center for Emerging Markets at

Northeastern University, Boston. He is a Fellow of the Academy of International Business (AIB). Professor Ramamurti obtained his BSc (Physics) from Delhi University, his MBA from the Indian Institute of Management, Ahmedabad, and his Doctor of Business Administration (DBA) from Harvard Business School. He has been a visiting professor at Harvard Business School, MIT's Sloan School of Management, Tufts University's Fletcher School and the Wharton School. Professor Ramamurti's research and consulting have focused on firms operating in, or from, emerging economies. He has served in leadership roles in the Academy of Management's International Management Division and been involved with the AIB for three decades. He serves on the editorial boards of several international journals. His recent books include *The Future of FDI and the MNE* (Emerald, 2011) and *Emerging Multinationals in Emerging Markets* (Cambridge University Press, 2009). Professor Ramamurti has done research in or consulted with firms and governments in more than twenty emerging economies.

ANAND P. RAMAN is Editor At Large at the Harvard Business Review Group, based in Boston. An economist by training and a business journalist by profession, his areas of interest include globalisation, strategy, operations and the history and future of management. He has been a business journalist and editor on two continents for over twenty years, and has headed newspapers, business magazines and web-based media operations. After completing the Harvard Business School's Advanced Management Program in 2000, Anand joined the *Harvard Business Review* in July 2001, where he still works as a primary editor and oversees HBR's twelve global editions. A member of the World Economic Forum (WEF)'s Global Advisory Council on emerging multi-nationals, Anand has presented papers at the annual meetings of the Strategic Management Society and the Society for Operations and Production Management, and spoken at several conferences in Asia and the US. Anand has edited five McKinsey Award-winning articles, and in 1992 he received India's Sanskriti Award for Outstanding Contribution to Journalism.

RAVI SARATHY gained his PhD in International Business at the University of Michigan and his MS at Northwestern University, US. Professor Sarathy's major research and teaching interests are in international business and global strategy, industrial policy, global infrastructure and the airline and computer software industries. Before joining the College of Business Administration faculty there, Professor Sarathy held a Leonore Annenberg Teaching Fellowship (LATF) from Tufts University and consulted and taught in Brazil. He was a Fulbright scholar and held the Fulbright-Flad Chair in Strategic Management at the Technical University of Lisbon in the Spring of 1996. Professor Sarathy has been a visiting professor at HEC, France; Bocconi University in Milan, Italy; Monash University in Melbourne, Australia; the University of Michigan; and at the Fletcher School of Law and Diplomacy, Tufts University. Professor Sarathy is also a Certified Management Accountant (CMA).

ALEXANDER SETTLES has been at the Higher School of Economics at the National Research University in Russia for six years as a visiting professor, is Deputy Director of the Corporate Governance Center and a lecturer in the Department of General and Strategic Management. He teaches courses in corporate governance, international management, corporate social responsibility and new venture creation. His research interests are corporate governance of Russian and other emerging market firms, outward foreign direct investment, cross-cultural management practices, corporate strategies and organisational design. In 2005–6 he was a Fulbright Scholar in Russia and continues to serve on the Fulbright Commission in Russia as well as participating in the selection process for the Muskie Program. Prior to coming to the Higher School of Economics, he worked at the University of Delaware. He has served as a consultant to the World Bank Institute, the Organization for Economic Cooperation and Development (OECD) and the Center for International Private Enterprise.

YONGJIANG SHI is a university lecturer of industrial systems in the Engineering Department, and Research Director of the Centre for International Manufacturing in the Institute for Manufacturing, Cambridge University. He has been studying management of international manufacturing network and supply chain for about fifteen years. His recent research interests have covered global manufacturing strategy, network system design, technology transfer and emerging Chinese manufacturing companies. He is working on several research projects: a global manufacturing virtual network (GMVN) to develop new manufacturing architecture for collaborative manufacturing network between companies; post-mergers and acquisitions (M&A) integration to help companies achieve synergy; emerging nations' multinational corporations development; and different countries' culture characteristics and their impacts on global supply network development.

JAGJIT SINGH SRAI is Head of the Institute for Manufacturing (IfM) Centre for International Manufacturing. Jag's main research and practice interests are in the areas of international manufacturing and supply networks. Current research areas include supply-chain mapping and value-chain analysis, operations integration of multiorganisational manufacturing and service networks and the development of new forms of supply network that support emerging industries. As part of the 'research-into-practice' activities of the Centre, recent industrial engagements span many sectors and include application of supply-chain mapping and value-chain analysis approaches. Before joining Cambridge University, Jag's previous roles have been in industry as a manufacturing and supply-chain director of a multinational (multiregional) operation, technical director of a national business and other senior management positions, with over seventeen years' industrial experience in a variety of front-line manufacturing and supply-chain operational roles. He is a Chartered Engineer and a Fellow of the Institute for Chemical Engineers.

VENKAT SUBRAMANIAN is an assistant professor in strategy at the University of Hong Kong School of Business, Hong Kong, and at the Vlerick Leuven Gent Management School in Belgium. He was a research fellow in strategy and international management at the Catholic University of Leuven, Belgium and a research associate in strategy and finance at INSEAD, France, before going on to complete a PhD in management at the Solvay Business School, Université Libre de Bruxelles, Belgium. He has published in leading academic and practitioner journals and in the business press, on topics of strategy and international business. He has advised start-ups in Europe and Asia, and is currently conducting a project on the global competition of emerging market companies into other fast-growing markets.

BRIDGETTE SULLIVAN-TAYLOR is Research Director of Strategy, Organisational Learning and Resilience (SOLAR). Her research interests include understanding strategic thinking and acting in different international business contexts. Her current research investigates global uncertainties, risk and developing organisational resilience in the face of global threats and extreme threats and events; and inter- and intra-organisational learning and international innovation transfer. Her research has informed practitioners, think tanks and UK government policy through publications and other dissemination events at Westminster. Her PhD examined the implementation of strategic change in a global service organisation, a UK airline. This research investigated the characteristics of a global strategy and the factors that impact upon the diffusion of the strategy across the organisation's global network. Bridgette has previously held positions in the private sector and academic appointments in New Zealand, the UK and Europe, and has received a number of Outstanding MBA Teaching Awards.

KAIMEI WANG gained her PhD at the Centre for International Manufacturing, Institute for Manufacturing, Cambridge University. During the doctorate research, she focused on the research of manufacturing internationalisation strategy and processes of Chinese multinational corporations. After graduation, she joined an automotive manufacturer and is currently responsible for strategic planning and business development of the after-sales supply-chain network.

PETER J. WILLIAMSON is Professor of International Management at Judge Business School and a fellow of Jesus College, University of Cambridge. Peter divides his time between research and consulting on global strategy, M&A and innovation and as non-executive director of several companies spanning information technology (IT) through to green energy. He holds a PhD in Business Economics from Harvard and has held professorships at London Business School, Harvard Business School and INSEAD (in Singapore). Peter has worked with companies in China since 1983 and co-authored *Dragons at Your Door: How Chinese Cost Innovation is Disrupting Global Competition* (2007). His article 'Is your innovation process global?' (*MIT-Sloan Management Review*) received a MIT–Sloan–Price Waterhouse Coopers Award honouring articles that have contributed most to the enhancement of management practice.

EDEN YIN is a senior lecturer in marketing and a fellow of St Edmund's College, Cambridge. He holds a BSc from Jilin University, an MA from West Virginia University and a PhD from the University of Southern California. He is a member of the American Marketing Association, Institute for Operations Research and Management Sciences (INFORMS), Academy of International Business (AIB) and Academy of Marketing Science. He has taught both undergraduates and graduates, as well as business executives, in the US, the UK, China, Australia, Finland, Denmark, Brazil and Argentina. Eden Yin taught strategic marketing at the University of Southern California and principles of marketing and internet marketing at the Loyola Marymount University in Los Angeles, prior to joining Cambridge Judge Business School.

Acknowledgements

We would like to thank all those who participated in the international conference: 'Re-Assessing Emerging Market Multinationals' Evolving Competitive Advantage' held in Cambridge, UK, on 25–7 March 2011, for their valuable ideas and contributions to the lively debate that provided the foundation for this book, along with the conference hosts, the University of Cambridge, Judge Business School and Jesus College, and the co-sponsors, Fundação Getulio Vargas, Universidade de Sao Paulo and Northeastern University.

Peter Williamson conveys his thanks to the International Institute for the Study of Cross-Border Investment and M&A (XBMA) for its financial and research support of the project. Afonso and Maria Tereza Leme Fleury would like to express their thanks to Fundação de Amparo a Pesquisa do Estado de Sao Paulo (FAPESP) and Conselho Nacional de Desenvolvimento Cientifico e Tecnologico (CNPq) for their support of the research that contributed to this book. Ravi Ramamurti would like to thank the Liberty Mutual Foundation and the US Department of Education for their support of Northeastern University's Center for Emerging Markets, which co-sponsored the research project leading to this volume. He would like to dedicate this volume to his late Dean, Thomas E. Moore, whose dynamic leadership made Northeastern a particularly enjoyable and productive place to work from 2004–10.

Introduction

PETER J. WILLIAMSON,
RAVI RAMAMURTI, AFONSO FLEURY AND
MARIA TEREZA LEME FLEURY

Until recently, when the question 'what are the competitive advantages of multinationals from emerging economies in the global market?' was posed to either academics or Western executives it typically elicited a simple response: 'None'. To the extent that these firms from emerging economies were winning market share abroad, this was explained by the fortuitous access to so called 'country-specific advantages' (CSAs) such as a pool of low-cost labour in their home base (Rugman and Verbeke, 2001). Their success was viewed as a legacy of their birth. They were generally thought to lack ownership of the rich stocks of proprietary, intangible assets that theory argued was required for multinationals to be an efficient organisational form (Caves, 1986). Dunning (2001) termed the benefits of these intangible assets 'ownership advantages' – a term chosen to emphasise the idea that the transaction costs involved in transferring these assets (and hence their associated advantages) across borders using market mechanisms are higher than the costs of transferring them internally within an organisation under the same ownership. Without these intangible assets there was no reason why their products and resources should not be exchanged internationally through trade in an open market. According to a strict interpretation of this theory, therefore, the existence of emerging market multinational enterprises (EMNEs) must simply be the result of market distortions such as trade barriers or government support.

This received wisdom has begun to look increasingly implausible because EMNEs have continued to expand globally, in many cases successfully taking market share from multinationals headquartered in developed market multinational economies (DMNEs) that benefit from global capabilities and networks built over many decades (Verma *et al.*, 2011). These EMNE's have also invested directly in building their subsidiaries overseas, both in the developing and developed world. According to the United Nations Conference on Trade and Development (UNCTAD) World Investment Report (2011), almost

25 per cent of all global foreign direct investment (FDI) in 2010 emanated from emerging economies, which accounted for six of the top-twenty investing countries. As a result, a number of EMNEs now have configurations of different value-generating activities that span the globe. Huawei, now the world's second-largest supplier of telecoms equipment by revenue, has operations in over 140 countries. Its twenty-three-country global research and development (R&D) network now includes centres in France, Germany, India, Italy, Russia, Sweden and the UK. The Brazilian company Vale, meanwhile, has mining operations in Bahrain, Belgium, Canada, France, Norway and the US. It also has 150 minerals exploration and R&D projects underway in twenty-one countries spanning three continents.

Meanwhile EMNEs have been the source of innovations that they have deployed across the world such as: the development of ultra-deep water, 'pre-salt' oil production technology by Petrobras, now being deployed in Africa, the Middle East and the Gulf of Mexico; Moscow-headquartered Kaspersky Lab, which has developed sophisticated anti-virus software supplied to leading global corporations such as Microsoft, IBM and Cisco and has offices in China, France, Germany, India, Japan, the Netherlands, Poland, Romania, South Korea, Sweden, the UK and the US; and Indian firms such as Wipro and Infosys that pioneered innovative, global business models to deliver information technology services.

EMNEs have also been increasingly active in the market for cross-border mergers and acquisitions (M&A): in 2011 they accounted for 29 per cent of global cross-border acquisitions by value according to UNCTAD. These investments would not be economically rational, nor profitable for shareholders, if EMNEs were relying solely on home-country advantages that were available to all their competitors or could be efficiently transferred internationally via arms-length market transactions. In the case of cross-border M&A, it might be that EMNEs are seeking to acquire the resources they lack to be competitive globally (Bresman *et al.*, 1999; Forsgren, 2002). But this explanation leaves unanswered the question of whether EMNEs are able to out-bid their established multinational rivals in the global market for corporate control and still make such acquisitions profitable (Gubbi *et al.*, 2009).

Given that EMNEs are rapidly becoming important players on the global stage and that traditional theories seem to provide, at best, an incomplete explanation of their behaviour and performance

(Girod and Bellin, 2011; Ramamurti, 2012), it is opportune to take a new look at the sources of competitive advantage enjoyed by EMNEs. That is the goal of this book. In the chapters that follow we will seek to reassess the roots, the evolution and the current extent of EMNEs' competitive advantages and the role that internationalisation has potentially played in building and strengthening these advantages. This work builds on the seminal book by Ramamurti and Singh (2009a) that explored the competitive advantage of EMNEs primarily from the standpoint of the country-specific advantages these firms had harnessed, and another by Fleury and Fleury (2011), which thoroughly examined the foundations of internationalisation by Brazilian firms.

Through our reassessment we also hope to shed further light on a number of fundamental questions that the rise of EMNEs poses for the theory and practice of international business. Perhaps the most basic and far-reaching of these questions is whether the behaviour of EMNEs and their impacts on global competition require a new theory, or whether what we observe can be explained by adapting existing models of how multinationals evolve and compete.

The roots of much of the existing theory can be traced back to the experience of firms, primarily from Europe and the US, who began their international expansion in the nineteenth century (Wilkins, 1970; Chandler, 1980). This experience shaped the concept of multinationals as 'arbitragers' as well as establishing the idea that national country of origin was a primary force shaping the way particular multinationals evolved. International business researchers studying multinational firms that expanded their networks following the second world war also contributed key assumptions on which subsequent theories have been built (Wilkins, 1974). These included the idea of FDI moving 'advantages' (Hymer, 1976) from more developed markets to less developed ones (often driven by barriers to trade and government policies to promote import substitution) and the role of maturation of technologies and products along a lifecycle as a primary determinant of location (Vernon, 1966). These early, post-war studies were largely based on samples of US firms – perhaps not surprisingly, as the US accounted for an estimated 85 per cent of global FDI between 1945 and 1960 (Jones, 2005: 7).

It is clear, therefore, that our theories about the emergence of multi-nationals and the drivers of FDI have been shaped by a rather particular set of national and historical contexts (even if these influences are seldom acknowledged or perhaps even recognised). If these contexts differ in important ways from the environment that prevails today then we might expect the EMNEs of the twenty-first century to behave differently and achieve different results from multinational firms that expanded their international reach and competitiveness in earlier eras.

In fact, there are at least five reasons why we might expect existing theory to be less than perfectly applicable as a tool for understanding the current expansion of EMNEs and their sources of competitive advantage.

First, we might expect that the strategies adopted by firms expanding internationally in today's environment that is already highly globally integrated to differ from the one riven with protectionist barriers and impediments to the flow of capital and products across the world on which much of the existing theoretical concepts have been based. The higher level of global integration, more advanced communication technologies and freer flows of everything from capital to information across the world, might be expected to influence the potential strategies followed by companies as they seek to become globally competitive.

Second, the way in which a firm develops from a national player to become a multinational might be expected to progress through a cycle. In comparing EMNEs with DMNEs and looking for similarities and differences, therefore, we need to compare companies at the same stage in their cycle of development; not mature multinational companies with those in the early stages of their development cycle (Ramamurti, 2009b: 419–20).

Third, EMNEs do not seem to follow the pattern of the product life cycle theory (Vernon, 1966) that postulates that products move from developed to developing countries as the product matures. EMNEs often shift products, processes and know-how from the developing or emerging economies to developed markets.

Fourth, EMNEs do not always seem to expand their international operations incrementally starting with regions with low psychic distance from their home market to regions with higher psychic distance (Vahlne and Wiedersheim-Paul, 1973; Zaheer, 1995). Instead, they often appear to establish subsidiaries or make acquisitions in locations with high psychic distance from their home base. This may reflect a fifth difference from established theory: that EMNEs appear to emphasise the role of internationalisation as a means to access new locational advantages rather than to exploit ownership advantages.

Yet prevailing theories suggest that strategies based purely on exploration will not be competitive against incumbent multinationals that have existing ownership advantages (Dunning, 2001) because the latter can already transfer them around the world more efficiently than the newcomers.

These differences between the current environment and the context that shaped much of our existing theory, along with observations about the rise of EMNEs and the nature of their international expansion that seem paradoxical when viewed through established theoretical lenses, at least requires us to reassess the explanatory power of existing theories.

With the growing number of economies now being classified as 'emerging' or 'growth' economies, and the multitude of potential sources of competitive advantage, the goal of understanding the competitive advantages of EMNEs risks becoming a Herculean task. In order to keep it within tractable bounds we have decided to focus our core analysis on multinationals venturing abroad from the four largest emerging economies: Brazil, Russia, India and China – dubbed by Jim O'Neill of Goldman Sachs the 'BRICs'. In drawing conclusions from studying the BRICs in the final chapter we will seek to examine the implications and applicability of our findings to the non-BRIC emerging economies. We also decided to concentrate on three, inter-related potential contributors to competitive advantage: the innovation capabilities of EMNEs; the way in which they have sought to access and combine different resources and strengths by locating different activities in different geographies (their 'value-chain configurations'); and the role of cross-border M&A in helping EMNEs to access complementary resources and learning that can be integrated with their existing capabilities to build new sources of competitive advantage.

Clearly this list of potential contributors to EMNEs' competitive advantages is by no means exhaustive. In the course of our examination we have sought to understand other sources of competitive advantage from which EMNEs might be benefitting – especially those non-traditional firm-specific advantages (FSAs) suggested in existing literature such as the ability to unlock latent demand in low-end segments (Prahalad, 2005), or capabilities in dealing with weak institutions and infrastructure (Morck *et al.*, 2008; Cuervo-Cazurra and Genc, 2008). Where possible, we have also considered how CSAs, both from the firm's country of origin and from the locations where they have established subsidiaries, have contributed to the creation of competitive advantages within EMNEs. Where appropriate we have considered the effects of other factors such as economies of scale, home and host government policies, market power, branding, institutional context and governance. We believe that by focusing on innovation, value-chain configuration and M&A and their interactions as the key channels through which EMNEs develop their competitive advantage, we have adopted a framework within which many and varied contributors to EMNEs' competitive strength can be fruitfully explored.

Within the framework we seek to examine not only the 'raw materials' from which EMNEs create competitive advantages, but also the processes they have adopted to build those advantages. These processes include the key role of their absorptive capacity (Cohen and Levinthal, 1990) and EMNEs' use of dynamic capabilities to convert their domestic CSAs and resources accessed abroad into competitive advantages (Teece *et al.*, 1997). For example: How have Chinese MNEs used acquisitions to acquire new technologies or R&D capabilities that came to be combined with their internal product and process design and manufacturing capabilities to create new sources of competitive advantage? How have Russian MNEs configured their value chains to leverage the natural resource endowments in the home country? How have Indian MNEs absorbed host-country knowledge and adapted their innovative business models to gain competitive advantage in other emerging markets? How have Brazilian firms transferred production competences from overseas subsidiaries to headquarters to improve their competitive advantage both at home and abroad?

The remainder of the book is organised as follows. In Part I, four chapters are devoted to the question of how (and to what extent) innovation capabilities have contributed to the competitive advantages in global markets among multinational firms emerging from Brazil, Russia, India and China respectively. For the purposes of the analysis in this section we have consciously adopted a broad definition of 'innovation' that goes beyond technological break-throughs to include business model innovation, novel improvements in the price/performance ratio of product offerings, and innovations in management systems and processes, etc. This reflects our belief that commentators in the past have risked overlooking some of the most important innovations that are providing EMNEs with competitive advantage by focusing too narrowly on advanced technology, R&D spending or patent registrations as the measures of innovation. Part I concludes with two commentaries, each of which seeks to compare and contrast the findings for innovation as a source of EMNEs' competitive advantage across the four countries and suggest conceptual frameworks that might shed light on the commonalities and divergences observed.

In Part II, four further chapters explore the ways in which EMNEs have configured their value chains so as to span different locations in ways that enable them to exploit their existing competitive advantages as well as to access new resources and knowledge that can be used to create new types of competitive advantage. Thus EMNEs may establish subsidiaries (or other types of presence such as joint ventures, alliances, or equity stakes) in other locations so as to access resources including finance, technology and knowledge, natural resources, customer intelligence, or brands that can be used to enhance the competitive advantage of their companies in global markets. One of the interesting features of EMNEs' strategies here, compared with their cousins from developed economies, is that they are much less likely to fully relocate production or other core operations overseas. Instead they are apt to build value-creating activities such as R&D or marketing overseas – these were the very activities that DMNEs were last to relocate offshore (if they do so at all). Again, Part II concludes with two commentaries that compare and contrast the value-chain configurations of multinationals from the four BRIC countries examined in this section and aim to develop a conceptual framework that helps to explain the different roles of value-configuration strategies in contributing to EMNEs' evolving competitive advantages.

Part III examines the role of offshore M&A in providing access to resources and knowledge that can be combined with EMNEs' home-based resources and capabilities to extend existing sources of competitive advantage and create new ones. A key area of investigation here is whether EMNEs are using offshore M&A in ways that are any different from DMNEs; specifically, our intuition from anecdotal evidence and existing research (Gubbi, 2009; Guillén and Garcia-Canal, 2009) was that offshore M&A by DMNEs is of the market-seeking type (buying a 'market position' as described by Haspeslagh and Jemison, 1990), while in the case of EMNEs it is more likely to be of the strategic-asset-seeking type (i.e., to gain rapid access to competences such as R&D or marketing). Where EMNEs acquired substantial market share positions in foreign markets, meanwhile, we hypothesised that their strategy might be to attempt to drive further global consolidation in industries considered mature in developed markets. Again the concluding commentaries that act as a 'book-end' to this section compare and contrast the evidence from across the four BRIC countries and propose a theoretical framework to better understand the role of cross-border M&A in helping EMNEs build their global competitive advantage, including complementing and enhancing their existing innovation capabilities and adding additional 'pieces of the jigsaw' that help them move towards their desired international value-chain configurations.

In the concluding chapter of the book we step back to review the overall evidence on how EMNE's are using globalisation not only to exploit their existing advantages, but also to explore the world for new learning and capabilities that they can combine with their existing experience to evolve novel and powerful types of advantage to compete in global markets.

We then explore some of the similarities and differences between EMNEs from the different BRIC countries in terms of the role CSAs have played, the industries on which they have focused and the sources of competitive advantage on which they have built. This allows us to revisit the role of critical factors such as knowledge flows and learning, government policy, industry maturity and the global market environment in the shape and pace of EMNE's emergence. In discussing these factors we tackle the question of whether, in the light of what we have observed from this in-depth study of the emergence of EMNEs from the BRIC countries, we need to revise, adapt or perhaps more fundamentally renew established theories of how and why companies internationalise.

Comparing the similarities and differences between EMNEs from different BRIC countries also paves the way for an assessment of the implications our findings might have for the multinationals that are now starting to venture forth from other emerging economies in Asia, the Middle East, Latin America and Africa beyond the BRICs. Finally we conclude our discussion by drawing out some of the implications for managers and policy makers – both those concerned with developing successful strategies through which EMNEs can continue to strengthen their competitiveness and global reach, and those whose remit is to work out how developed economies and DMNEs need to respond to prosper as the new phenomenon of EMNEs continues to develop apace.

PART I

Innovation and competitive advantage

1 | *Innovation by Brazilian EMNEs*

MOACIR DE MIRANDA OLIVEIRA JUNIOR,
FELIPE MENDES BORINI AND AFONSO
FLEURY

Innovation in Brazil

Brazil is not considered a good performer when it comes to innovation. The observation is not wrong but it is also not correct. Brazil is not well ranked in specialised lists which evaluate the performance of the country as a whole according to the traditional indicators: investment in research and development (R&D) and number of patents. However, Brazilian firms are internationalising successfully and innovations play an important role in their strategies.

The approach to innovation adopted by Brazilian companies takes on a perspective different from the traditional scientific research leading to technological break-through, so much appreciated in developed countries. In this chapter, we will show that other approaches to innovation are being developed by Brazilian multi-nationals in order to gain competitive advantage.

We will show that these approaches are the result of a series of factors and circumstances involving: the evolution of the country's social and political environment that affected organisational culture and entrepreneurship; the obliviousness of the national innovation system; the unfolding of economic development policies that prescribed areas where local companies could grow in the face of competition from the subsidiaries of foreign multinationals; and, finally, the competences and resources which supported the strategies of Brazilian multinationals to compete in the international markets.

The shaping and posture towards innovation in Brazil

Until the 1930s, Brazil was essentially an agricultural country. Then, an import substitution industrialisation policy was implemented and Brazil began to build its infrastructure and basic inputs industry; that was done mainly through state-owned enterprises acquiring turn-key projects and licensing technology. During the second world war period, imports and foreign direct investment (FDI) were drastically reduced, thus allowing the development of local consumer goods and capital goods industries that supplied the gap in Brazilian domestic markets.

In the 1950s, aiming to accelerate industrialisation, Brazil attracted foreign multinationals to drive the process, especially in high-tech industries, while Brazilian private firms settled in traditional sectors (timber, paper, furniture, textiles, food, beverages, publishing and printing, among others). As Vernon (1966) predicted, the subsidiaries of foreign multinationals became essentially manufacturers of products already standardised in the developed countries; their role did not include innovation of any sort.

In the 1960s, Brazil saw the rise of the military regime. Five-year plans for national development as well as for scientific and techno-logical development were implemented. It was a period marked by investment in sectors linked to 'sovereignty and national security', leading to the creation of companies related to the defence and aero-space industries; Embraer was founded in 1969. Brazilian companies grew significantly, especially in capital goods and engineering services. The petrochemical industry was developed according to a tripartite model involving state capital, local private equity and foreign partners (as technology suppliers). In that period, the development of local technological capabilities was stimulated; however, the relative import-ance of subsidiaries of foreign multinationals was intensified.

The 1980s was the 'lost decade', a period of inflation, trade imbal-ance and low growth. The reliance on five-year plans ended and the exhaustion of the imports substitution industrialisation model led to the opening of local markets in 1991.

Therefore, until the late 1980s, the business environment was char-acterised by a large internal market, heavily influenced by decisions of government policy marked by discontinuity and inconsistency. Those conditions shaped entrepreneurs dependent on local institutions, with a 'parochial' mindset, avoiding risk and detached from the international landscape. Those features greatly jeopardised the development of their competitive strengths; innovation, in particular, was not part of the critical success factors.

In the early 1990s, the government redefined the country's competi-tive system. To control inflation, bank accounts were frozen, which had a brutal impact on demand, especially for unessential goods. Many industries had to rediscover their markets and establish new strategies. In addition, the government introduced a number of major policy initiatives, established a timetable for a progressive reduction of import duties, abruptly slashed subsidies and introduced a privatisation programme in order to expose Brazilian industry to stronger competition. From 1994 to 2001, the Brazilian government, following the Washington Consensus, assumed that 'the best industrial policy is no industrial policy; the markets will select the winners'.

In those turbulent conditions, importing became far easier and the foreign multinationals profited from the lack of repertoire of local firms to increase presence of their subsidiaries, mainly through acquisitions. Traditional Brazilian industrial groups and leading firms disappeared; important state-owned enterprises were fully privatised. In practice, what happened was a Darwinian process: only those firms that had become internationally competitive were able to prosper.

However, despite Brazil's new-found political and financial stability, words such as disorder, uncertainty, attrition and fluidity are still employed to describe the business environment, meaning a set of unique obstacles that make it harder to do business in Brazil than in other countries. Brazil still ranks badly in the competitiveness rankings: the World Economic Forum (WEF, 2010) classifies Brazil as 58th, behind China (27th), Chile (30th), India (51st) and Costa Rica (56th).

Under those circumstances, Brazilian companies adopted a distinctive approach to strategising: 'they prepare for golden opportunities by managing smartly during the comparative calm of business as usual (active waiting). When a golden opportunity or "sudden death" threat emerges, managers must have the courage to declare the main effort and concentrate resources to seize the moment' (Sull and Escobari, 2004; Sull, 2005). Therefore, Brazilian leading firms developed a specific strategic approach due to the influence of local enablers and constraints.

At the operations level, a remarkable upgrading has been observed since the early 1990s with the hybridisation of the Japanese Production Model (JPM). At that moment in time, when leading firms self imposed the target to reach the productivity and quality levels found in global leaders, the JPM became their chief source of inspiration. Its dissemination was led by subsidiaries of foreign multinationals as well as local enterprises such as Petrobras, Vale, Gerdau and WEG, among others.

Therefore, competences in operations were upgraded and firms established strategies based on operational excellence.

Under those circumstances, it becomes evident why the Brazilian approach to innovation is different from those of developed countries, even though the ambiguity still remains among policy makers. As Erber (2004) asserts, 'From the beginning of the nineties to the present the Brazilian economy was ruled by a specific view of the process of economic development, which emphasised the role of technical progress as a means to achieving fast and stable economic growth. Nonetheless, the degree of endogenous technical innovation [as measured by traditional indicators] in Brazil remains very low.' Historically, the country's investments in R&D as a percentage of gross domestic product (GDP, adjusted for purchasing power parity, PPP) remains at 1 per cent, although a slight trend upwards has been observed in recent years. According to Innova-Latino (2011), the share of global investment in R&D in Brazilian enterprises in the period 1996–2007 remained level at 1.5 per cent, while that of Indian enterprises increased from 1.4 per cent to 1.8 per cent, and that of Chinese enterprises jumped from 2 per cent to 9 per cent.

However, Brazil is considered to be an innovating country if other types of measure are taken into consideration. According to the article 'Tapping the world's innovation hot spots' (Kao, 2009), Brazil ranks 12th, trailing Australia (10th) and Denmark (11th), but ahead of France (14th), China (17th) and Russia (19th). Under that scenario, Brazilian multinationals have found their own approach to innovation profiting from other sources of inspiration, as we shall see next.

The types of innovation prioritised by Brazilian firms

Brazilian firms are much more concerned with process rather than product innovations. On the other hand, their repertoire includes specific types of innovation that may be classified as: commodity innovations, sustainable innovations, business models innovations, bottom-of-the-pyramid innovations and reverse innovations.

Starting with commodity innovations, a renowned Brazilian economist recently wrote that it seems 'indelicate to name certain products as commodity', in the sense of commodities being homogeneous products, interchangeable with other products of the same type, indistinguishable in regards to origin, because some incorporate a great amount of knowledge and technology into them. Brazilian multinationals operating in the resources-based industries and produ-cing 'commodities' invest heavily in R&D activities, keep strong ties with local and foreign universities and research centres and own a significant number of patents. In this chapter, we will focus on Petrobras, although Vale could also be used as an example. The case of Embrapa, the Brazilian agricultural research corporation cited by *The Economist* (2010) as being responsible for 'the Brazilian agricul-tural miracle', will also be mentioned.

The second type of innovation relates to sustainability issues. Brazil occupies a privileged position when it comes to natural resources, biodiversity and clean energy; some Brazilian multinationals are explor-ing that potential to develop sustainable innovations. We will analyse two cases: Natura, a cosmetics producer which fully adopted the triple bottom line principles and incorporates them in the formulation of its strategy and business model, and Braskem, that developed the 'Green Polymer Project' as part of its strategy to access renewable raw material sources in line with the company's vision of sustainability.

Bottom-of-the-pyramid (BOP) innovations, or frugal innovations, should also be more easily achieved by emerging country firms. However, in Brazil, native firms seem to be less concerned with this type of innovation than foreign subsidiaries. Actually, the Brazilian BOP innovators are in the services sector: Casas Bahia 5 and Banco Postal are the most representative cases, but none of them has gone international (Prahalad, 2005). We will present the cases of Caboclo sandals and Odebrecht's operations in Africa.

Business models innovation as a competitive advantage is something already incorporated in the managerial literature and media; for example, it is one of the criteria used by *Business Week* when selecting the most innovative companies. However, one has to recognise that the development of business models is strongly influenced by the local business environment (Fleury and Fleury, 2011). Therefore, Brazilian firms are formulating business models differently from other countries. We will present two cases: Embraer and Gerdau; their distinct innova-tive and competitive business models reveal different features and circumstances of the Brazilian business environment.

Finally, there are reverse innovations, meaning innovations that are developed in foreign countries by subsidiaries of Brazilian multi-nationals. The application of reverse innovations is justified by two factors: marketing (access to markets, understanding and responding to local needs and increasing proximity to customers) and those relating to technology (recruiting qualified staff, access to foreign talent and differentiated technologies) (Chiesa, 1995). In order to discuss how Brazilian multinationals are doing reverse innovation, e.g. using their subsidiaries to innovate, we will briefly present four cases: Sabo, WEG, Embrapa and SMAR.

Brazilian multinationals building competitive advantages through innovation

Commodity innovation

Commodity innovation is a quantum leap from process innovation. Process innovation is usually associated with investments in new plant and equipment, in order for firms to gain in terms of productivity, material utilisation, quality and reliability, as well as to enhance the capacity to manufacture new products. It is also said that the danger associated with process innovation is that any competitor could easily follow suit, removing the initial advantage gained from the investment. However, commodity innovation means new ways of obtaining products that are standard or slightly commoditised, not easily imitable and provide the innovator with a strong competitive advantage. Petrobras is a good example.

Petrobras (PB) was founded in 1953 with the mission to refine oil as efficiently as possible in refineries that were built for it on a turn-key basis by foreign engineering firms. It was essentially a time of learning by doing. In 1966, Petrobras' research and development centre (known as Cenpes) was located next to the Federal University of Rio de Janeiro, and played a fundamental role in lending support to PB's strategies, especially during the design phase and implementation of the second and third petrochemical poles. Cenpes' role was leveraged during the oil crises in the 1970s, when the Brazilian energy matrix was redefined to accommodate the then newborn Proalcool Program.

But the area in which PB was most innovative is in exploration. When the 1970s' oil crisis erupted, PB increased the efforts to guarantee supply inland and in foreign countries, starting in Colombia in 1972. In 1976 and 1978, PB made two major discoveries in Iraq, and others followed. In the 1980s, PB discovered oil in the deep waters of the Campos Basin, near Rio de Janeiro. At that time, existing technologies were able to pump oil from a water depth of as much as 120 metres. From this point on, PB began developing its own technology, exceeding depths of 500 metres around 1990, when it won the Offshore Technology Conference Prize. By 1999, it had reached a depth of 1,853 metres, still in the Campos Basin. PB's latest discoveries are concentrated in ultra-deep waters, more than 5,000 metres below sea level, and under a 2,000-metre layer of salt. This so-called 'pre-salt' layer contains light oil, of which the recoverable volume is estimated at some 5 to 8 billion barrels. Its exploitation poses technological challenges that are unprecedented in the oil industry.

PB's technological developments resulted in its taking out around 1,000 patents and brought internationalisation advantages in their wake. Currently, one of PB's strengths in operations outside the Southern Cone, in places such as Africa, the Middle East and the Gulf of Mexico, consists of taking advantage of its proprietary competence and technologies as a competitive differential.

Another area of PB involvement is biofuel, as evidenced by the establishment, in July 2008, of Petrobras Biocombustivel, a PB subsidiary in charge of developing projects for the production and management of ethanol and biodiesel. The company created a business model based on a policy of partnering with international firms that have access to markets, for export purposes, and with Brazilian ethanol producers already active in this sector. For instance, through its acquisition of the Okinawa refinery in Japan in 2007, PB started to supply the Asian market with ethanol. This initiative is part of the effort to comply with environmental pollution reduction targets. With a presence in twenty-eight countries, Petrobras aims to be among the top five integrated energy companies in the world by 2020.

Other Brazilian multinationals like AmBev, Companhia Siderurgica Nacional (CSN), JBS-Friboi, Vale and Votorantim Cement and Metals also derive their competitive advantages from producing better and cheaper, revealing distinctive competences in process development and innovation.

Product innovation

The evolution of both the local business environment and the competitive environment reinforced the timid positioning of Brazilian enterprises in regards to product innovation. For example, Brazil has had some innovative experiences in the automobile industry, like the Romi-Isetta in the 1950s, a compact car similar to the Tata Nano, and the Gurgel-Itaipu, an electric car in the 1980s, as well as in the electronics industry, where Gradiente stood up as a national leader until the 1990s. However, the lack of institutional support and the pressure exerted by the multinationals through their lobbies, among other factors, made those ventures more difficult than usual and they failed. Although several initiatives and programmes to reverse that trend have been established since the mid-1990s, the number of firms able to compete based on product innovations is still incipient. We will highlight two cases: Alpargatas and Tigre.

Tigre started out in 1941 as a producer of combs. At the end of the 1950s, when the company had already made considerable progress, with an extensive range of extruded and injected plastic products, it invested in a project that was innovative for its time: PVC tubes and connections for hydraulic installations.

In the construction industry, soil and climate conditions influence design and the materials used; commercialisation conditions influence success due to the enormous market fragmentation. That creates a specific microcosm favouring innovative behaviour, and that was true for Tigre. As a regional pioneer in regards to hydraulic installations, Tigre assumed a comfortable leadership position in the Brazilian market and led the internationalisation, having set up a greenfield plant in Paraguay in 1977, where it has an 80 per cent market share.

Foreign competition chased Tigre in Brazil with the arrival of the Swiss company Amanco which already operated in other Latin American countries. From 1997 on, Tigre intensified its internationalisation efforts, establishing factories in Chile, Argentina, Bolivia, Peru, Ecuador, Colombia and the US. In the competition for the Latin American markets, Tigre prevailed and Amanco was later sold to the Mexican group Mexichem. In the US, Tigre sells innovative products using the local brand Drain, Waste and Vent (DWV).

Turning to the case of Alpargatas and its key brand Havaianas, the case starts with a Scottish immigrant establishing a factory in 1907 to produce a rather primitive type of footwear made with raw rope and light canvas. Alpargatas developed a more sophisticated product line and replaced the previously mentioned footwear in the 1960s, launching a very simple sandal assembled from two pieces injected with plastic, called Havaianas; it had tremendous success in the local market. Later, Alpargatas enhanced their product lines and became a contractor to marketers such as Mizuno and Timberland.

In the 1990s, Alpargatas invested further to differentiate Havaianas, shifting the product's image from a low-cost product to a higher added value product. Marketing segmentation, focused campaigns, product customisation and commercialisation strategies were developed and implemented: Havaianas became fashionable. Internationalisation followed with the aim of conquering higher-income consumers in the advanced countries, starting with Italy and France. Fancy and expensive models were prepared by Swarovski and H Stern (a Brazilian jeweller), and showrooms were assembled at Saks and Galerie Lafayette. Currently, Havaianas are manufactured in Brazil, Argentina and Uruguay and sold in eighty countries through operations managed from seven offices in different locations. Thus, to achieve success, Havaianas combines innovations in product and processes (the most important secret being the formulation of the plastic components) with innovations in marketing and distribution.

The two cases are clearly quite distinct from the world's most-renowned product innovators, especially those in the technologically advanced industries. However, it reveals the markets where Brazilian firms can be product innovators: fashionable goods and products which have regional markets.

Sustainable innovation

Social and environmental responsibility has become a powerful instrument to win over conscientious consumers in markets like the US and Europe. That is especially true for companies located in countries with rich biodiversity such as Brazil.

Braskem is the petrochemical arm of the Odebrecht Group, established in 1944 as a service provider for the petrochemical industry. Odebrecht grew to become one of the world's biggest heavy engineering and construction services providers based on a distinct business model, Odebrecht entrepreneurial technology (OET).

Odebrecht moved into petrochemicals in the 2000s. Braskem was created as the merger of six companies and thirteen plants in different regions of Brazil. Due to the distinct nature of the business and the need to integrate different organisational cultures and operating systems, Braskem had to adapt OET, but the basic principles remained. Concurrently, to achieve the operational targets, Braskem adopted operational excellence programmes and benchmarked the best performers in the industry worldwide. Braskem started with bulk type of production and is gradually moving to a customer-oriented strategy, where customer relationships and technology competences play a key role, to produce higher value-added products. Braskem developed the Green Polymer project for a biodegradable plastic as part of its strategy to access competitive renewable raw material sources (sugar cane) in line with the company's vision of sustainability. It inaugurated the first green plant in 2011 and plans to expand the project to other countries. Recently, both Dow and Monsanto announced their plans to produce green plastics.

Natura is a cosmetics producer that invests about 3 per cent of net sales in R&D, process improvement and joint projects, with research institutions in Brazil, France, Italy and the US. The firm admits that its success depends largely on the ability to innovate continually to face global competitors like L'Oreal and its subsidiary, Body Shop. To cope with that challenge, Natura decided to focus on differentiated products to facilitate their entry into the European market, named the Ekos line and based on the country's natural assets: perfume essences of pitch-white, a tree of the Amazon forest, liquid soaps based on guarana, a fruit from the Amazon, and so on.

Its vice presidency for innovation employs around 300 people in six departments: makeup; skincare; hair care and bath; fragrance; advanced technology concept (TCA); and management of information, knowledge and quality. Natura invests more than $2 million per year in market research to identify trends in consumer preferences and behaviour. Its technology acquisition plan is based on permanent monitoring of patents and technical literature; a set of sixty key words, updated yearly, is used to search several databanks (Yu and Tromboni, 2002).

Moreover, what is distinctive about Natura is its full commitment to the triple bottom line principle: the firm incorporates it in the formulation of its strategy and business model. Natura has developed sustainable supply chains in Brazil and that, as part of its internationalisation strategy, is one of its major challenges: to have local sustainable chains which comply to its ecologically correct operating principles.

Business model innovation

For Santos, Spector and Van der Heyden (2009) business models are not equivalent to business strategies: 'A business strategy is specified by the answers to three questions: what is the offer, who are the customers, and how is the offer produced and delivered to the customers? It is the how question that subsumes the firm's choice of business model. Organisations can have essentially the same product or service offer (the what), aim for the same market segment (the who), and do so with different business models (the how).' Therefore, even if products and markets are the same, firms might develop competitive advantage by innovating in terms of business models. We will analyse two Brazilian multinationals that have created competitive advantages through innovative business models: Embraer (risk partnering) and Gerdau (strategy execution).

The history of Embraer dates back to 1941, when the Ministry of Aeronautics was created, and to 1950, when Brazil's Technological Aeronautics Institute (ITA) was established. In 1962, a study showing that the number of Brazilian towns served by air carriers was dropping noticeably, and that no aircraft then produced met the technical and financial requirements for efficient operation, sparked the initiative for the creation of Embraer, in 1969, as a state-owned enterprise. Embraer's first product, a ten to twenty-seat regional aircraft, was a success in the foreign markets as well.

In the early 1990s, two things then occurred concomitantly: the development of a new regional jet, and the privatisation process. Once it was privatised, there was a radical shift in the way it did business, thanks to an injection of financial and market competences, so that market pull became its driver instead of technology push. The new business model, put in place for the 45-seat regional jet, involved risk partnerships with four foreign suppliers from Chile, Spain, Belgium and the US. This model was innovative not only because it was based on a global supply network, but because it combined partnering and risk sharing.

For its next product, Embraer improved the business model. In the aeronautical industry, a new aircraft has to be sold before the production system is put in place. Embraer undertook to deliver the product to its first buyer 38 months after the order was placed, when the usual was 60 months. To achieve this target, Embraer developed and implemented an innovative project management model that integrated 400 engineers from 16 firms in several countries, with 600 engineers in Brazil. The number of risk partners increased to 11, including large traditional multinationals, such as Kawasaki (Japan) and Latecoere (France). Moreover, partnering firms assumed responsibility for the technical specifications and detailing of sub-projects, while Embraer remained in charge of detailing clients' needs, the general project specifications, the structure sub-projects, the integration of all the systems and the final assembling. This organisational model was unprecedented anywhere in the world and was later emulated by other firms in the aeronautical and other industries as well.

Although Embraer competes in a sophisticated global industry it cannot be considered a R&D intensive company; technically, Embraer is an 'integrator', a firm specialised in integrating complex product systems (Prencipe *et al.*, 2003). Its innovative business model was competently developed to become a competitive advantage that the markets gradually acknowledged.

The Gerdau Group is the thirteenth largest steel producer in the world, according to the Iron and Steel International Institute, and the leader in America in the production of long steel for the construction industry. It is ranked as one of the most internationalised Brazilian firms. It was founded in 1901 as a nails producer and, back in 1948, the firm acquired a steel mill, thus expanding its product offerings for the construction industry. Thereafter, Gerdau expanded its business throughout Brazil by means of acquisitions and organic growth.

What is different and innovative at Gerdau is what might be called 'strategy execution in competitive timing' (Sull and Escobari, 2004). In the 1980s, Gerdau entered into an international technical service agreement with Funabashi Steel and Nippon Steel, embracing the Japanese production method as the basis of its organisational process. Moreover, Gerdau assumed the role of developer of management techniques derived from the Japanese management principles. In the hybridisation process that followed, the Japanese features were blended with the Brazilian ones, resulting in a winner model. The Gerdau Business System (GBS) is a document similar in nature to the Toyota Production System, conveying the firm's mission and values, in addition to formalising its best administrative and operating practices. It covers sixteen macro-processes, ranging from marketing and sales to social responsibility, and each macro-process has a global manager.

Gerdau's business model is based around regional, vertically integrated operations, whose activities range from collecting and processing scrap metal to the distribution of products, which are generally manufactured in accordance with end clients' customised projects. This strategy, which has implications in terms of transportation and freight costs, was initially developed in Brazil and then transferred to the US given the geographical extent of both territories.

Gerdau grew abroad primarily through acquisitions, and subsequently by expanding the businesses it acquired. Joint ventures have also played a major role in its development. One of Gerdau's latest acquisitions was Chaparral, an icon of the American steel industry in the 1990s.

AmBev, a Brazilian brewery that merged with Interbrew to create InBev in 2004, and then acquired Anheuser-Busch in 2009 to become the world's largest producer, is another example of Brazilian companies basing their internationalisation strategy on getting the timing of acquisitions right. Behind the cases of Gerdau and AmBev – and a couple of others – lies the figure of Vicente Falconi, a renowned Brazilian management guru. Falconi was the first Brazilian to get in touch with the Japanese in the 1980s, and has acted as an important bridge between the two countries since that time. He has consulted for a large number of Brazilian multinationals.

Bottom-of-the-pyramid innovation

Performing at the base of the pyramid is a great challenge for developed country multinationals and a great opportunity for emerging country multinationals. For the latter, the opportunity comes from their embeddedness in environments where the informal economy and institutional gaps prevail (London and Hart, 2004; Khanna and Palepu, 2010). In principle, these multinationals can exploit the potential of these environments more easily than developed country multinationals that have to learn how the systems work in these markets; they should be able to create value-added innovations based on the social pyramid, or apply the experience at the base of the pyramid to explore the base of the pyramid of other countries.

An example is Caboclo, an enterprise that commercialises sandals handmade by an artisans' cooperative in the north of Brazil, using recycled tires and raw leather. It is a company dedicated to products manufactured in Brazil by underserved communities, using the base of the pyramid to sell their products abroad. In other words, the company uses fair trade, which favours production at household scale and guarantees a fair wage to its producers.

Another way to exploit innovation at the base of the pyramid is to bring the capabilities created in the country to meet the base of the pyramid in foreign countries. An example is the work of Odebrecht, currently one of the twentieth largest engineering firms in the world.

Even though it operates in the US and Europe, Odebrecht learnt how to do business in markets that are particularly turbulent. In all cases, its business model, founded in Odebrecht Entrepreneurial Technology, provided the guidelines for consistent and efficient performance. In particular, when the contractors are governments of emerging or underdeveloped countries, the objective is to build sustainable development.

For example, in Angola, the company operates in infrastructure, real estate, energy, bioenergy, mining, agribusiness and special projects. Since 2007, Odebrecht has been responsible for the revitalisation project covering maintenance works, urban sanitation and support to improve traffic in the main roads. The company is also responsible for managing the food distribution network of the Angolan government. In that partnership, Odebrecht has the task of organising the logistics of twenty-nine stores and two distribution centres in eighteen provinces.

There are other cases of bottom-of-the-pyramid innovations such as Casas Bahia and Banco Postal, a partnership between Empresa de Correios e Telegrafos (Brazilian Post Offices) and Banco Bradesco, Brazil's largest private bank, which turned post offices into banking service centres. However, these initiatives are still confined to within the country's borders.

Reverse innovation

Reverse innovation, which is becoming increasingly important to maintaining the competitiveness of multinationals from developed countries, is still more critical for the competitiveness of emerging markets multinationals. That is because, unlike the emerging multinational that is able to internationalise and exploit pre-existing advantages, emerging country multinationals internationalise in search of new capabilities (Mathews, 2006). In other words, the emerging country multinational needs to do the best of their subsidiaries much faster than the traditional multinationals (Borini *et al.*, 2009).

To achieve that aim and do reverse innovation efficiently there are three alternatives:

(a) acquisition of innovative firms in foreign countries;
(b) insertion in global production and research networks; and
(c) deliberate strategy of seeking innovation and knowledge abroad.

In the last decade, acquiring abroad surpassed other modes of entry for Brazilian firms. For some of those firms, the purpose of internationalising involved doing reverse innovation from the start. The most emblematic case is Sabo. The company produces sealing systems for the automotive industry. In the 1980s, Sabo became a certified supplier for GM in Brazil and was thus able to supply Opel's factories in Europe. In the 1990s, Sabo acquired two firms in Argentina and one in Europe (Kaco). One of the important factors in Sabo's decision was the fact that Kaco had developed distinctive competences in R&D, which included strong links with German universities.

After the acquisition, Sabo was upgraded, becoming a joint developer within the auto industry. After Kaco's acquisition, a shift in the origin of Sabo's patents to Germany was observed, where three of the four centres of innovation are located (Nascimento, 2009). Those innovations lead to greater competitiveness in the global markets, but they are also triggered by demands from Brazil, where Sabo supplies the global automakers installed in the country.

Another example is WEG, currently one of the three largest electric motor manufacturers in the world. In the last decade WEG has expanded internationally by investing in the acquisition of manufacturing units: one in Argentina, one in Mexico, one in Portugal and one in China; it has a presence in over 100 countries. The Portuguese subsidiary meant a shift in its innovative activities, because it develops and manufactures higher added value products to be utilised in areas where the risk of explosions is high. The development of that product line remained abroad because products commercialised in Europe must have the certification labels of European laboratories (Moura, 2007).

A second way in which Brazilian multinationals are developing innovations abroad is through global research networks. Embrapa, the Brazilian agricultural research corporation, is a research institution dedicated to the development of knowledge in tropical agriculture. It has 9,000 employees, of whom 2,215 are researchers: 18 per cent with a master's degree, 74 per cent with a PhD and 8 per cent with a post-doctorate qualification. The company's budget for 2011 is close to $2 billion. The company is now involved in 'virtual laboratories' (Labex), where Brazilian scientists work on the premises of similar institutions in foreign countries. Embrapa's researchers share resources and expert-ise with colleagues from the US, Europe and South Korea. For example, in a US Labex, innovations generated a clean bill of health to the entire swine population in Brazil. Studies are also being made to support the actions of low-carbon farming for the sustainable manage-ment of agricultural soils.

The third alternative concerns Brazilian multinationals which have decided to establish innovation centres in foreign countries in search of innovations that are difficult develop at home. SMAR is a supplier of industrial automation equipment for the sugar and ethanol industry. Its internationalisation began in 1980 to the US and later to Europe. The company has R&D labs and manufacturing facilities in New York and Houston in the US, twenty patents and over forty requests in progress in the United States Patent and Trademark Office. Its internationalisation strategy was driven by technological innovations, developed for appli-cations in Brazil. The global demand for industrial automation created a clientele for SMAR, mostly in developing countries (Stefanovitz and Nagano, 2006). Currently over 30 per cent of its production is sold on the international market through offices in several countries.

Some of the technologies developed in the US R&D centres were transferred to Brazil where they are assembled to suit the requirements of local customers. SMAR is also managing global projects jointly developed by headquarters and subsidiaries. In those projects, the headquarters appoint local staff to support subsidiary team while the subsidiary appoints the project coordinator (Silveira, 2008).

Other Brazilian multinationals, like Suzano, have invested following that same strategy: acquiring R&D labs in foreign countries aiming to do reverse innovation.

The Brazilian way to innovate

The previously mentioned cases provide relevant evidence of Brazilian multinationals' approach to innovation. To conclude, we must ask:

- is it different from other countries? What are the reasons for the differences?
- are Brazilian multinationals trying to catch-up? Is it a matter of time?
- does it create sustainable competitive advantages?

The answer to the first question is that the Brazilian approach to innovation is idiosyncratic, local conditions being the most important factors in shaping it. The arguments of 'co-evolution', i.e. the influence of local institutions on technological development, and path dependence, in the sense of historical patterns of technological development playing a central role in determining the pace of future technological change, play a central role in the explanatory model.

The second question requires further elaboration. For some authors, 'innovative capabilities at basic, intermediate, and/or high-intermediate levels for different technological functions [is] a pre-condition for attaining research-based and patenting capabilities at the international knowledge frontier' (Figueiredo, 2007). It is implicit that Brazilian multinationals would then be following the steps of the incumbents.

However, the evidence might also be interpreted as Brazilian firms assuming that they will never catch up in technology because their rate of capability building is slower than the technological frontier. Brazilian firms would then be adopting another route where technological capability is a qualifier, not an order winner, and innovation relates to transforming country-specific advantages (CSAs) into firm-specific advantages (FSAs) mainly.

The notion of qualifiers and order winners is due to Hill (1989); it refers to the process of how capabilities are converted into competitive advantage and market success. Technology as a qualifier means that the firm displays the basic capabilities required to get into or stay in a market. Technology as order winner means that it is the technology that will win the bid or customer's purchase; in this case, firms must be technologically more advanced than their competitors. Brazilian firms assuming technology as a qualifier is justified by many factors, especially the non-stimulating local environment, where economic, industrial, technological and scientific policies are inconsistent among them, discontinuous over time and never technology-oriented. The entrepreneurial mindset, that remains risk averse, and the weak national innovation system also contribute to that outcome.

In those circumstances, Brazilian multinationals are innovating through the transformation of CSAs into FSAs to create order winners. The different types of innovation described in the previous sections provide sound evidence. Perhaps that should not be considered as idiosyncrasy because innovation seems to be country specific. For example, the US emphasises individual entrepreneurship and technology break-through; Japan relies on collectivism and technological fusion (Kodama, 1985). Similarly, Brazilian multinationals' innovativeness is associated with competitive advantages emanating from the Brazilian culture and resources and disadvantages associated with local institutions.

The remaining question regards sustainability over time. In principle the answer is yes, those type of innovations will provide competitive advantage in the foreseeable future because they require systemic innovation approaches to supply the world with basic inputs produced in compliance with environmental and social responsibility criteria, consumer products produced under the sustainability principles and other specific products for which, due to specific historical reasons, the country produced competitive multinationals.

2 | *Innovation by Russian EMNEs*

SERGEY FILIPPOV AND ALEXANDER
SETTLES

Introduction

Russian firms face a clear quandary in terms of innovation and value creation due to their inability to effectively create new applications based on the rich human resource base inherited from the Soviet past. Unlike countries like China, India, Brazil, Singapore, Taiwan and other emerging markets, Russia lacks the economic incentive scheme to translate new discoveries into viable products and services. The tradition of a high level of concentration of research activities in specialised public and private research and development (R&D) centres separates new technology developments from market forces and customer needs. According to a recent OECD Innovation Policy Review (2011) Russia still suffers from a system where innovation is not firm-specific and the lack of competition undermines the economic incentives for innovation. Russia also faces an ageing cohort of scientists and increasing global competition for both innovation and talent, and lacks market orientation in firm-level innovation investments. In this chapter we explore how Russian multinational corporations (MNCs) address their innovation needs, provide an overview of how they operate within the Russian innovation system and examine case studies of Russian firms which have broken out of the bounds of their domestic system and utilised innovation-driven strategies in their firm-level internationalisation.

Innovation is universally recognised as a competitive advantage and a key driver of growth of multinational companies. Presently, innovation is not limited to Western multinationals, emerging multinational companies are realising the strategic value of innovation too. Among emerging multinationals, Russian companies represent an interesting case. Russia inherited the Soviet science and technology (S&T) complex that enjoyed success in many technological domains. However, the institutional collapse after the break-up of the Soviet Union had a

29

profound effect on innovation, science and technology. Since the early 2000s the Russian economy has been widely acknowledged to be dependent on natural resource production. Exports of hydrocarbons and other natural resources make up to 80 per cent of all Russian exports. The major emerging Russian multinational companies primarily operate in the natural resources sectors. Diversification of the national economy has become a top priority for the Russian political leadership. The former Russian president, Dmitry Medvedev, has repeatedly called for the 'modernisation' of Russia's economy and appealed to Russian companies to design and implement innovation strategies.

Despite the general interest in this topic and its relevance, the role and place of innovation in emerging Russian multinationals remain under-researched (with some exceptions, e.g. Podmetina *et al.*, 2009). The objective of this chapter is to fill this gap and to describe how Russian emerging multinationals have developed innovation policies and practices. We seek to explore the nexus between innovation and internationalisation of Russian companies. More broadly, we aim to reflect upon whether innovation represents a firm-specific advantage – competitive advantage for Russian emerging multinationals. The conventional wisdom about emerging multinationals – especially those from Russia – is that they fail to innovate even with the extensive state support of state corporations, scientific institutes and now technology parks. The key variable missing in the Russian equation falls in the translation of advances in discovery into successful commercialisation. An unpacking of the innovation process (McCann and Mudambi, 2005) indicates that the translation of scientific advance into innovation requires the competence of commercialisation in R&D managers. Russian multinationals have been so far unable to create firm-level advantage in commercialisation and fall far behind others from emerging markets such as India and China.

Innovation capability is often measured by patenting activity; however in the Russian context patents do not always provide meaningful representations of innovation process, as the efficiency of R&D measured by patents is low. Other standard measures of innovation are not always readily available in Russia. Therefore, the paper relies on secondary data and anecdotal evidence.

The chapter is structured as follows: we first set the context for innovation by providing a macro-view of Russia, the strategic intentions of the government's policies and innovation practices in

Russian (domestic) companies. We then examine the interplay between innovation and internationalisation. Finally, we provide critical reflections and conclusions.

Context: innovation in Russia

Macro-view and public policy

The Soviet leadership regarded the S&T complex as a matter of national priority. Soviet S&T was particularly crucial for the defence sector, and innovation was assessed from a technological, not economic perspective. Therefore, it is unsurprising that the situation in other sectors of the Soviet economy was rather disappointing. The command economy was inherently resistant to innovation. Introduction of innovation and new technologies would lead to (short-term) disruption of the existing structure. Disruptive technologies were not suited to the Soviet model and were actively discouraged. Because Soviet enterprise directors were not interested in profit maximisation, innovation and following reorganisation were considered as a burden.

The transition to a market economy has not improved the situation, and even worsened it in many respects. While elimination of the command economy was a necessary condition for resistance to innovation to disappear, it was not a sufficient one (Berliner, 1988). In the volatile transitional environment of the 1990s, innovation receded into the background. Most enterprises were struggling for survival in the new economic conditions, and innovation was perceived as luxury, a risky investment which would pay off in the long term. The situation has not radically changed in the 2000s.

The potential for technology and innovation to drive Russia's productivity growth is severely limited by several factors, such as a weak regulatory environment, weak intellectual property rights protection, low levels of collaboration between public and private sectors and inadequate technological infrastructure. The institutional framework for innovation favours large prestige processes that are institutionally and politically driven, and the Russian Academy of Science at times hindered developing business science networks while also resisting international engagement, including a widespread rejection of the use of English in scientific work. The private sector remains reluctant to engage in innovation and the innovation that has been engaged in has been in part driven by government policy and funding. Apart from the aforementioned problems, the fundamental issue is the structure of the Russian economy. It is heavily dominated by extractive and energy industries where the potential for innovation is constrained. In contrast, R&D-intensive sectors such as biotechnologies and electronics are under-developed.

The problem is recognised by the Russian leadership and the utmost attention is given at the top political level. The Governmental Commission on High Technologies and Innovations was established in 2007, and since March 2010 it has been headed by the then prime minister, Vladimir Putin. Two years later, in May 2009, the Commission for Modernisation of and Technological Development of Russian Economy was established, headed by the then president, Medvedev. The Russian government started to allocate funding to innovation through a number of state corporations, such as Rosnano (nano-technologies), Rosatom (nuclear technologies) and Rostekhnologii (high-tech industrial products for civilian and military purposes). In February 2011 the Russian government presented a draft of the National Innovation Strategy 2020. It aims to increase the number of Russian companies conducting technological innovations by up to 40–50 per cent, and for Russia to reach some 5–10 per cent of the global market of high-tech products and services.

The landmark project of Dmitry Medvedev is the Skolkovo innovation centre, a planned high-tech business area to be built near Moscow which is meant to become Russia's Silicon Valley. The site is intended to be an ultra-modern complex created to encourage technology-based companies and start-ups. The objectives are to stimulate Russian innovation systems by creating a springboard to globalise Russian businesses, localise international R&D activities, facilitate development of new high-tech businesses, products and services and to attract foreign talents.

Despite all the energetic actions undertaken by the Russian political leadership, the actual situation remains disappointing. A vivid indication is a session of the Presidential Commission for Modernisation and Technological Development held on 31 January 2011. At the beginning of 2010, Medvedev requested the top management of large state-owned companies to design innovation programmes and increase funding of innovation. As it turned out, only one-third of companies had designed such programmes, let alone increased funding.

At the session, the then president regretted poor progress in modernisation, in spite of massive investment. 'Today we have investment and money, though not huge, for innovations projects, but still have practically no innovations', Medvedev stated. 'There are very few high-tech products which could compete at the world market', he emphasised, and named companies performing badly in terms of innovation:

There is another issue I would particularly like to address: almost none of the state-owned companies have people among their top executives specifically responsible for innovation ... I won't name companies that are doing better right now, but I will name the companies whose R&D spending is very low . . . These include Rosneft, IDGC Holding, Sovkomflot and Aeroflot . . . it's just unacceptable. Corporations must dramatically increase R&D spending; moreover, they must work together with research centres, and this should also be an obvious step. (Medvedev, 2011)

It shows that the heritage of the Soviet administrative style is still dominant, at least in relation to state-owned corporations. In these companies innovation is something not driven by market forces but enforced administratively, while the company management perceives it as a burden. In contrast, private companies may indeed realise the value of innovation. However, in the current climate of unstable business environment and institutional weaknesses, innovation might be too risky, requiring long-term efforts and strategic orientation. The Russian MNCs have not been able to translate Soviet S&T legacy into innovation due to lack of a proper institutional arrangement, a well-functioning economic regime within a competitive market place, and a general failure to develop competence in R&D management. In perhaps a similar manner to late period Soviet enterprises, Russian MNCs have been incentivised by the Russian government to over-pursue high-technology to maintain the Soviet legacy, while missing out on the low-technology innovations that would meet consumer demand in the Russian economy.

Innovation in Russian companies and comparison with other BRIC economies

Research and development activities in Russia primarily occur in state-owned or state-financed R&D institutions, while innovation in Russia tends to be concentrated in large companies, possessing sufficient financial, human and intellectual resources for it. The strategic value of innovation and R&D in large Russian companies has been realised only recently. This phenomenon has been of limited relevance in Russia in the period of economic transition in the 1990s, when the economy was characterised by low investments in R&D. The main goals of most companies at that period were acquisition of state assets in controversial deals, struggle for a market share, corporate restructuring and consolidation. Investment in R&D did not generate immediate profits and therefore was considered uneconomical.

There are a minority of Russian firms that engaged in the development of international research networks as a means to enhance their innovation activities and absorptive capacity and to utilise their inventions. Many Russian companies started their internationalisation in the 2000s. While outward foreign direct investment (FDI) was recorded since the early 1990s, it was more 'capital flight' rather than distinctively designed internationalisation strategies and establishment of a network of overseas subsidiaries. Roughly at the same time, many large Russian companies showed a growing interest in financing R&D and creation of in-house R&D departments. International growth of some firms was strongly biased towards the former Soviet republics of the Commonwealth of Independent States (CIS) or Eastern European countries, yet other emerging Russian multinationals started investing in all regions (Asia, Africa and Latin America) and particularly advanced economies of Western Europe and North America. It is expected that access to Western technologies and know-how has become a distinctive driver of this expansion.

Vahtra (2010) aims to depict the scope and potential impact of outward R&D-related FDI by Russian companies. The study concludes that the evidence of R&D investments by Russian companies remains notably scarce. One of the explanations is that many emerging Russian multinationals are concentrated in the low-tech and natural resource-based industries, and the share of high-tech sectors in the Russian economy is marginal. Specifically, only a few financial–industrial conglomerates account for significant R&D-related FDI. Moreover, even this small share of R&D-related FDI does not always prove to be successful. Skolkovo Research (2009) identifies 'unsatisfactory knowledge transfer' as one of the six key operational challenges faced by Russian multinationals.

Managers of Russian multinationals recognise the importance of innovation. Innovation here is understood broadly and may mean any management, operation or production technology or technique adopted to improve efficiency of the firm. In this manner, Russian managers are no different from their BRIC counterparts (BRIC stands for Brazil, Russia, India and China). A survey among executives on the role of innovation in emerging economies of Brazil, China and India conducted by the Boston Consulting Group (BCG) delivered the same findings. Among the main conclusions are that innovation is becoming a priority in emerging economies, and companies' willingness to spend on innovation and their satisfaction with the return on innovation spending are inching higher (BCG, 2010). The actual numbers of R&D expenditures are in contrast with these intentions, however. Russian multinationals have fallen behind in terms of R&D expenditures in comparison to multinationals of other BRIC economies. In our analysis we rely on the R&D Scoreboard annually published by the UK's Department for Business Innovation and Skills (Table 2.1).

Among the top 1,000 to 1,400 (depending on the year) global companies rated in the Scoreboard with the highest R&D investments, Russia is consistently represented by only one company – Gazprom. Among others, the carmaker AvtoVAZ, oil and gas producer Lukoil and the micro-electronics company Sitronics are also included. In total, the amount of R&D investment by Russian firms in the Scoreboard increased from £132.6 million in 2005/06 to £683.2 million in 2009/ 10. Likewise, there has been an upward trend in expenses as a proportion of operating profit. Nevertheless, performance remains disappointing if measured in terms of R&D intensity (R&D as a proportion of sales), which remains at 0.5–0.6 per cent. In 2009/10, this indicator stood at 3.6 per cent on average for all companies in the Scoreboard. An explanation might be that Russian companies such as Gazprom and Lukoil operate in low R&D-intensive sectors as such.

Comparison with other emerging multinationals (from BRIC economies) is illustrative. Judged by the amount of companies in the Scoreboard and the sum of their R&D investment, there is a continuous upward trend. Chinese companies are leading – in 2009/10, the sixteen largest R&D spenders invested more than £4.5 billion. Chinese multinationals virtually doubled their R&D investment compared to 2008/09. Against the background of other BRIC companies, performance of Russian companies is disappointing as they are clearly lagging behind.

Table 2.1 *Investment in R&D by Russian companies: global look*

	2005/06	2006/07	2007/08	2008/09	2009/10
Number of global companies in the Scoreboard	1,250	1,250	1,400	1,000	1,000
Russian companies in the Scoreboard	Gazprom	Gazprom	Gazprom AvtoVAZ Sitronics	Gazprom Lukoil	Gazprom AvtoVAZ Lukoil
Total R&D investment, £ m	132.63	254.70	367.82	520.54	683.16
as % of sales	0.5	0.6	0.7	0.3	0.6
as % of operating profit	1.4	1.6	2.2	1.4	2.8
R&D investment per employee, £000	0.3	0.6	0.6	0.9	1.1
Memorandum (number of companies and total R&D investment)					
Brazil	3	3	5	3	6
	448.02	674.81	983.48	1,546.11	1,263.99
China	5	7	9	12	16
	608.87	765.66	991.91	2,411.73	4,595.84
India	3	7	15	7	12
	155.08	268.17	751.94	721.59	1,066.02

Source: compiled from respective annual editions of the R&D scoreboard published by the UK's Department for Business Innovation and Skills.

One of many possible explanations, as mentioned above, is sectoral R&D intensity and the position of emerging multinationals in global value chains. For instance, many Chinese manufacturing companies have progressively moved from original equipment manufacturing (OEM) to original design manufacturing (ODM) to original brand manufacturing (OBM). In this evolutionary journey the role of innovation and investments in R&D is vital. Likewise, many Indian multinationals operate in information technology (IT) and pharmaceutical sectors where demand for innovation is crucial. Many Russian companies active in low-tech resource-based sectors do not face the need to invest in innovation heavily. Innovation is certainly possible in low-tech sectors; innovation in Brazil's biofuel sector is an excellent example. In Russia, product and service innovation is mainly in the early stages of imitation in the service industries, and reverse engineering in home electronics and consumer durables. Yet, there are hardly any examples of break-through innovations in Russia's low-tech sectors.

Interplay of innovation and internationalisation

In this section we aim to examine the interaction between internationalisation of Russian companies and the role of innovation in it. Russian firms have adopted internationalisation strategies to overcome their domestic market limitations especially in institutions and competition policy and to break the managerial framework that limits effect commercialisation. The literature has shown that technological resources can significantly influence the internationalisation and international activities of firms (Brock and Jaffe, 2008). The interplay between internationalisation and innovation has been raised by several scholars. Saarenketo *et al.* (2004) argues that internationalisation is compulsory for firms in some high-tech sectors that have only a few potential domestic clients. In line with this, Kafouros *et al.* (2008) claim that firms need to be sufficiently present in several markets to capture the fruits of innovation. In other words, internationalisation is seen as a necessary condition for innovation. Other authors, such as Kyläheiko *et al.* (2010), position innovation and internationalisation as a trade-off, and classify firms according to their degrees of internationalisation and innovation.

Considering the specific context of internationalisation of Russian companies, two types of this process can be identified – 'domestic' and

Table 2.2 *Interplay between internationalisation and innovation*

	'Domestic' internationalisation (to neighbouring markets/CIS)	'Global' internationalisation (to the West)
Innovation-driven	Russian companies possess advanced technological competences and offer new innovative solutions in less advanced markets (innovation is not necessarily 'new to the world')	Russian companies internationalise globally using innovation as a source of competitive advantage
Innovation-seeking	Russian companies internationalise by seeking innovation and technological competences in nearby markets	Russian companies internationalise to acquire innovation and knowledge abroad, and compensate for the weaknesses of the Russian national innovation system

'global' internationalisations. The former means entering nearby (less advanced) markets such as CIS countries. In contrast, the latter implies internationalisation to more advanced Western markets. In terms of the role of innovation in internationalisation, we identify two types – innovation-driven and innovation-seeking internationalisation. The first type means internationalisation underpinned by strong ownership advantages in innovation. In turn, the second type means obtaining access to innovation as a strategic motive of internationalisation. These approaches are summarised in Table 2.2.

Below, we briefly explain each of these approaches; however, in line with our research objective, the focus is on innovation-driven internationalisation. In other words, we seek to analyse the role of innovation as a driving force behind internationalisation of some Russian companies.

Innovation-driven internationalisation

'Domestic' innovation-driven internationalisation

'Domestic' innovation-driven internationalisation can be observed in CIS countries. Russian companies internationalise using products and services not necessarily new to the global market, yet new to the host country. Russian firms in the mobile telephony industry have been very successful implementing the *local optimiser* strategy (Ramamurti and Singh, 2008) of creating services for low and middle income customers both in Russia and the CIS states.

Mobile telephony is a rapidly changing high-tech industry with demanding customers. The markets are heavily regulated with substantial barriers to entry that must be overcome through relationships with government regulators. Russian mobile phone operators have been able to partner with handset providers and producers of the cellular network technology to provide competitive networks to meet the cutting edge technology demands of its customers while providing a service at a reasonable cost for low to medium income customers. The expansion of Russian telecoms companies VimpleCom, MTS and Megafon into the 'near abroad' and frontier markets has involved a successful strategy of applying technology solutions developed in the Russian market to these emerging and frontier markets. VimpleCom during the 2000s entered markets in Russia, Ukraine, Kazakhstan, Uzbekistan, Tajikistan, Georgia, Armenia and Kyrgyzstan, as well as Vietnam and Cambodia. MTS has similar operations in Ukraine, Uzbekistan, Turkmenistan and Armenia, and Megafon in Tajikistan, Abkhazia and South Ossetia.

CIS countries may be used as a testing ground for new innovative products or services before they are offered on a wider scale in the home country. For example, in April 2006 a Belarusian subsidiary of MTS (part of Sistema JSFC), in partnership with Siemens, launched a trial area of a 3G communication network in the capital, Minsk. As the trial proved to be successful, MTS announced the launch of 3G in its home market, Russia, in the second half of 2008 and early 2009 (in partnership with Ericsson). Similarly, with its launch in Ukraine in 2007, MTS became the first operator in the CIS region to offer Blackberry enterprise services to its subscribers. MTS had launched similar services in Russia in 2008.

It should be noted that the expertise, technology and innovation that drove the expansion of Russian telecoms companies to the CIS countries were originally developed in collaboration with Western partners. For MTS and VimpelCom, foreign expertise in the telecoms sector has become indispensable for performance improvements, and they have chosen alliances and partnerships with foreign companies as a way to access the latest technologies. Both MTS and VimpelCom entered in to partnerships with Ericsson and other leading technology companies. Strategic alliances and partnerships serve as means for Russian firms to access technology know-how of developed market firms at a time when these firms do not have the internal R&D capacities to create their own technology advances.

'Global' innovation-driven internationalisation

Global innovation-driven internationalisation is inherent to most Western multinationals, entering foreign markets using their competitive advantages that can be a unique technology or know-how. Most Russian multinationals operate in the resource-based and low-tech sectors, and hence this scenario is hardly applicable. However, several examples can be found in the IT sector.

Russian firms that have expanded into Western markets in search of innovation resources are engaging in the practice of 'global' internationalisation as a means to rebalance their competitive resources and to gain access to R&D and know-how to absorb new technologies. An example of this strategy is Sitronics, a Russian company involved in telecoms, IT, system integration and consulting and the development and production of microelectronics. Sitronics is part of the Russian conglomerate Sistema, which was established through the merger of a privatised, former state-owned research institute and the Czech manufacturer of telecoms equipment and software STROM Telecom. This born global firm established in 2002 has been focused on the Eastern European, Eurasian and developing country markets. The firm invests heavily in R&D and out of 10,000 employees approximately 3,500 work directly on R&D activities. Its network of R&D facilities connects Russian and Ukrainian specialists with Czech, Slovak and Greek facilities. Sitronics capitalises on the unused and low-cost research capacity in Russian and Ukrainian research centres and, through private ownership and the use of modern management techniques, has been able to reorganise the innovation system within the firm. By combining research activities in Russia and international development and production activities, Sitronics has been able to overcome the institutional weakness to innovate in the Russian market.

Sistema, Russia's leading consumer-focused technology group, began establishing R&D centres in each of its main businesses in 2006. The centres are to engage in the development and introduction of new technologies for the operating companies in their business areas. On the corporate level, Sistema has created a Department for Innovation Projects to identify and coordinate priority R&D projects for each business area and the corporation as a whole. This office will maintain a single database of ongoing innovation projects and house a special service to ensure the corporation's intellectual property rights are protected in Russia and internationally. In 2006, the strategy was successfully implemented in the telecoms business area, where all R&D centres were unified in a single structure, Intellect Telecom. In 2007 Intellect Telecom focused on developing R&D and technical strategies and solutions for products and services for Sistema's telecoms companies. Also during 2007, a concept was developed for the creation of an R&D centre for the Radar and Space business (Sistema, 2010).

Kaspersky Lab is a Russian computer security company, founded in 1997, offering anti-virus, anti-spyware, anti-spam and anti-intrusion products. The company was founded with virtually zero investments, and now Kaspersky Lab is a privately held company headquartered in Moscow with regional offices in India, Germany, France, the Netherlands, the UK, Poland, Romania, Sweden, Japan, China, South Korea and the US. It provides anti-virus software for leading global corporations such as Microsoft, IBM and Cisco. Further, in 2010, it released technology that protects mobile devices without straining their batteries, ingeniously spreading the power burden throughout a cluster of phones that share the security system.

Another example, also in the IT sector, is ABBYY, a software company that provides optical character recognition, document capture and language software for both PC and mobile devices. The company is headquartered in Moscow and distributes its products worldwide. Its development history is virtually identical to the Silicon Valley model for advanced technology companies. A group of students at the Moscow Institute of Physics and Technology, one of the Russia's leading research universities, got together to form a software company led by its current chairman David Yang. Their first product was Russian–English dictionary software Lingvo in 1989. Since then the company has grown by producing an ever-wider range of products. Today, ABBYY is a leading provider of document conversion, data capture and linguistic technologies, in over 130 markets worldwide. It has over 900 employees in several offices across the world – Russia, Ukraine, Cyprus, Germany, the UK, the US, Japan and Taiwan.

Innovation-seeking internationalisation

'Global' innovation-seeking internationalisation

'Global' innovation-seeking internationalisation is a distinctive and very common strategy. Russian companies internationalise into advanced markets with the strategic intention to acquire advanced technology and know-how. In mature industries such as metals and mining emerging market firms can be viewed as *global-consolidators* (Ramamurti and Singh, 2008) that leverage their low-cost production firm-specific advantages (FSAs) to acquire assets internationally. These firms have been able to utilise what Ramamurti and Singh (2008) refer to as 'production and operational excellence' and 'privileged access to resources and markets' to compete effectively with Western multi-nationals. In the case of Russian firms that fit these criteria, such as major metals firms Evraz Group, Novolipetsk Steel, RUSAL, Servestal and NLMK, they have made international investments to consolidate production and build market share, open up new markets and acquire new technology assets.

Considering the engineering sector, the large Russian conglomerate, the Renova Group, acquired two Swiss engineering companies. Both investments are particularly important as they offer Renova access to new technologies that may be used on the Russian market. The first acquisition was the Swiss engineering company Sulzer AG. Sulzer's activities include machinery, equipment, surface technology and thermal turbo machinery. Another asset is the Swiss company OC Oerlikon, the leader in the market of semiconductor and vacuum technologies, manufacturing of textile machinery and data storage technologies. Besides, the company develops innovation technologies in outer space exploration, solar energy, laser and nanotechnologies.

'Domestic' innovation-seeking internationalisation

A somewhat less common scenario in relation to the nearby markets is the 'domestic' innovation-seeking internationalisation, whereby Russian companies start internationalisation from entering nearby markets and obtaining domestic innovative firms. Because generally the nearest markets possess lower technological capabilities than in the home base, Russian companies would rarely employ such strategy. This, however, cannot be completely ruled out. Many Russian companies have sought to reestablish the value chains that were spread across the CIS countries after these were broken up with the collapse of the Soviet Union. In this respect, the drive of Russian companies into CIS countries can be explained not only by efficiency-seeking motives, but also by asset-seeking ones. Russian multinationals acquire former state-owned research institutes and construction bureaux, and integrate these foreign R&D divisions in their corporate networks.

Innovation and competitive advantage of Russian multinationals

Emerging Russian multinationals face significant competition both in their home markets and when they venture abroad. Developing firm-specific advantages that are based on the country-specific advantages of S&T and high levels of education has been difficult for Russian firms. Of particular difficulty is the funnelling and conversion process of translating scientific advances into successfully commercialised innovations. There are high performing firms that have adopted inter-nationalisation strategies to create these firm-specific advantages. Depending on their sectoral, ownership and other characteristics, companies may choose any (or several) of these four generic scenarios of the interplay between internationalisation and innovation.

As it seems, large companies in manufacturing sectors tend to rely on foreign technology and know-how, and one of the motives of foreign expansion is access to this advanced expertise.

The focus of our research, however, is on innovation-driven inter-nationalisation. We find very few examples of Russian companies successfully using innovation to build competitive advantage and expand overseas. Many of these companies are start-ups in the infor-mation and communications technology (ICT) sector that have grown organically and expanded internationally, using the Soviet heritage in exact sciences (physics, mathematics) as a basis.

As for traditional resource-based companies, although innovation is articulated as a key priority, there is little evidence of development and implementation of new innovative processes and technologies.

Analysis and conclusions

This chapter examined internationalisation of emerging Russian multi-nationals in conjunction with innovation and technology. Russia has a rich history and legacy of break-through inventions and science and technology but a troubled history with entrepreneurship and innovation. However, with the collapse of the Soviet Union and command economy, the S&T sector suffered substantial (financial, human and intellectual) losses. Along with the collapse of the Soviet system the creation of the institutional framework and entrepreneurial incentives for value-creating entrepreneurial activities was lacking. Besides, the fragmentation of the S&T sector itself, as well as its disconnection from business, poses a great challenge for Russian firms. Russia's potential country-specific advantage in science and technology is not easily transferred to internationalising companies.

Most Russian multinational companies operate in resource-based, low-tech sectors where the need for innovation and new product development is limited. Innovation in low-tech industry primarily takes the form of concrete problem-solving, according to customer requirements and within certain pre-defined budget constraints, that can be viewed as incremental innovation. Overall, innovation in these companies is rarely perceived as a source of competitive advantage.

In certain industries there are clear advantages that Russian firms can gain through innovations that they have developed to overcome weak institutions, operating in an economy that only recently joined the World Trade Organisation (WTO), geographic distances and climatic conditions, and other cultural factors of the Russian business environment. These innovations that have given Russian firms significant competitive advantage in their home market have been able to be extended in other emerging markets with similar institutions or business environments. In the telecoms and natural resource sectors Russian multinationals have been able to tap into this ability to conduct 'reverse innovation' to be competitive against Western multinationals. It should be noted that the 'innovations' created by Russian multinationals are not always viewed as positive as their firm-specific advantages may be related to how well they can influence government decisions, clear their goods through customs, reduce the cost of labour, etc.

Despite many good examples, innovative performance of most Russian companies, including multinationals, remains poor. In fact, in terms of S&T and innovation, the Russian case is substantially different from other BRIC economies. Russia (Soviet Union) used to enjoy a leading position in the S&T domain, on par with the US and other leading economies. The collapse of the Soviet Union and the transition to a market economy has led to virtual demise of the S&T sector. Presently, Russian companies face difficulties capitalising on this Soviet

S&T heritage, and Russia is moving away from the global technological frontier. As for Brazil, India and China, transition of these countries to the rank of 'emerging economies' has been coupled with substantial investments in S&T and R&D. The example of China is particularly illustrative in this respect.

The world does not witness the emergence of a Russian Apple or Microsoft, despite the existing human talent (and technological and engineering expertise). However, the world does witness the emergence of technological companies established by Russians, but not in Russia. The example of the Russian computer scientist Sergey Brin, co-founder of Google, is remarkable. In other words, the Soviet/Russian education system (in exact sciences) might be good at producing talent, but the current business climate does not offer creative conditions for its utilisation.

What prevents Russian firms from being more innovative and competing globally using innovation as a competitive advantage? We may conclude that the problem is not on the supply side (education, talent, entrepreneurs), but in the process of commercialisation. Many good innovative ideas remain only concepts because companies fail to commercialise them, and use them as a source of competitive advantage to compete globally. Weak institutional environment, endemic corruption, ineffective implementation of the rule of law, excessive governmental intervention in the economy and similar factors remain an insurmountable barrier to successful commercialisation of innovative ideas.

Russian political leadership acknowledges this major problem. The Russian president has consistently expressed the need to modernise the Russian economy and to diversify it away from reliance on commodities. Similarly, state-owned corporations are instructed to design and fund innovation programmes. The issue is that innovation cannot be enforced from the top of the political system, it must be embraced by businesses themselves. This is not yet the case in Russia.

3 | *Innovation by Indian EMNEs*

NIKHIL CELLY, JAIDEEP PRABHU AND
VENKAT SUBRAMANIAN

Introduction

In 2010, there were fifty-six Indian firms in the *Fortune Global 1000*. These included firms like Sun Pharmaceutical with revenues of slightly less than $1 billion, to Infosys and Tata Consultancy Services (TCS) with market values of roughly $30 billion, and Indian Oil with revenues of about $50 billion.[1] Most of these firms now have operations overseas. Some, such as the Tata Group, have more than 57 per cent of their revenues coming from abroad. In this chapter, we examine the links between Indian firms' internationalisation and their innovation capabilities over the last two decades. We also discuss the implications of these recent trends for developments in Indian firms' innovation and internationalisation in the future.

The innovation and internationalisation process of Indian firms has been dynamic, with both elements changing qualitatively and quantitatively over the last two decades. We identify three broad phases in this process: an initial phase (which roughly covers the 1990s) and two subsequent phases (which together roughly cover the 2000s). These phases correspond to the changing institutional landscape in India (and overseas). For instance, in India, the 1990s was a period of opening up of the economy following several decades of import substitution and tight internal controls. Thus, Indian firms in the 1990s were still constrained in what they could do internally but were even more constrained in terms of what they could do outside the country.

We structure our discussion of these three phases around the following questions:

(1) What were the innovation capabilities of Indian MNEs in each of these phases?

---

[1] Source: http://en.wikipedia.org/wiki/List_of_companies_of_India.

(2) How did Indian firms use these innovation capabilities to internationalise, both to other emerging markets as well as to developed markets?

We then answer the following questions:

(3) What is the applicability of the model that comes out of the analysis of the two questions above, both with respect to firms going from emerging markets (EMs) to emerging markets as well as firms going from emerging markets to developed markets (DMs)?
(4) What conclusions can be drawn about the competitive advantage of Indian MNEs arising from innovation?
(5) What will the still-evolving third phase of innovation and internationalisation look like for Indian MNEs in the years to come?

Innovation by Indian firms has been driven and determined by a mix of institutional, industry and firm-level factors. As the economic and institutional environment has evolved, the competitive dynamics across a range of industries have changed. Specifically, the emphasis that firms have placed on innovation versus internationalisation, and the nature of the relationship between the two, has changed over time. While there have been distinct cases of companies using India-specific factors to compete in international markets, such as the well-known and widely recognised success of Indian information technology (IT) and business process outsourcing (BPO) firms, there have been an equal number of cases driven by other types of relationships between innovation and internationalisation which we outline below.

To structure our analysis, we look at three distinct though overlapping phases of innovation and internationalisation of Indian firms.

Phase One (1990–2000): arbitrage-based internationalisation

The first phase of Indian internationalisation, roughly corresponding to the 1990s, marks a starting point in terms of the development of the innovation capabilities of Indian MNEs. The overall thrust of such innovation involved the arbitrage of a low cost base in India. The penetration of international markets was based on the trading of entrepreneurial skills. Such internationalisation was largely focused on markets that at the time were categorised as transitional or developing – such as the ex-Soviet bloc, Africa and South-East Asia. To gain a better understanding of why this was the preferred method of internationalisation, we examine the context, both in India and overseas, and the type of firm-level innovation that leveraged this context.

The Indian context, in the 1990s, consisted of groups of largely oligopolistic firms, particularly family-owned business groups, across a range of industries. Such an outcome was due to a specific approach to a managed market economy that the Indian government had pursued for the preceding decades. Specifically: the government allocated licenses to firms to undertake a specific industrial activity, and the focus of government policy was (a) import substitution across a range of products, such as consumer goods and medicines and (b) to manage 'destructive' competitive forces (Luce, 2008).

At the same time, a large number of industry sectors had also been 'reserved' for small- and medium-sized enterprises – this was termed as the 'license raj', wherein the state was involved in micro-managing the management decisions of private firms (Das, 2002; Luce, 2008). The 1990s marked a period when new institutional arrangements were being devised and slowly implemented. Regulatory barriers were removed across a range of industries, so that new, and sometimes foreign, competition could enter. For example, beverage giants Pepsi and Coca Cola entered the Indian market in this period, after a gap of nearly two decades, while some automakers such as Ford also made limited entry with a few models. At the same time, nevertheless, old institutional practices, built over decades of the license raj, were still intact in many aspects, such as foreign exchange and foreign ownership restrictions. The transition provided particular challenges for many firms, as they needed to make sense of and respond to changing institutional and industry conditions in terms of the direction and magnitude of such changes.

As the economy liberalised in the 1990s, and as new institutional conditions evolved, some firms, particularly the more entrepreneurial ones, tended to aggressively initiate international expansion. Many of these were from emerging industries such as IT. Such an approach used a combination of factor-based arbitrage and entrepreneurship that matched supply in India with demand in overseas markets.

The demand from overseas markets came from changes that had occurred there in the 1990s. New markets emerged following the end of the cold war and the collapse of the Soviet Bloc, as well as from growth in Africa. Institutional infrastructure in many of these countries was just beginning to be established, and industry conditions were also being opened up to new competition. In other words, there were similarities between conditions in the Indian context and some of these overseas markets, in terms of the direction of change in institutional and industry conditions.

The theoretical explanation for this pattern of innovation and internationalisation lies in institutional theory which suggests that the firm's ability to exploit or improve its capabilities abroad may vary, depending upon the institutional contexts in which it invests. Kostova (1996) was one of the early researchers to recognise these challenges and termed the construct 'institutional distance' to tap into the extent of similarity or dissimilarity between the regulatory, cognitive and normative institutions of countries. The institutional environment, in particular, affects various aspects of firms' operations and thus its competitive advantage in the host country. Regulatory, normative and cognitive factors can affect various aspects of firms' activities and ways of competing in the host country (Xu and Shenkar, 2002).

Emerging countries are characterised by a lack of the soft infrastructure that makes markets work efficiently (Khanna and Palepu, 2006: 62). This infrastructure includes intermediaries such as market researchers, supply-chain partners, rating agencies and media, regulatory systems and contract-enforcing mechanisms. Thus emerging countries are characterised by 'institutional voids' that make it difficult for companies to access capital or talent, to invest in R&D or build global brands. Emerging country firms or local firms can exploit these voids to compete with multinational enterprises (MNEs) from developed countries that lack experience of operating in these institutional settings (Khanna and Palepu, 2006).

Thus emerging market firms that have learned to compete in institutional environments characterised by weak institutions and institutional voids may be better positioned to compete in other emerging markets with similar environments. This logic underlies the concept of institutional arbitrage. Hall and Soskice (2001) define institutional arbitrage as follows: 'multinational enterprises may shift particular activities to other nations in order to secure the advantages that the institutional frameworks of their political economies offer for pursuing those activities' (Hall and Soskice, 2001: 57). Thus gaps in the host institutional environment or an unfavourable institutional environment may be offset by taking advantage of institutional arbitrage.

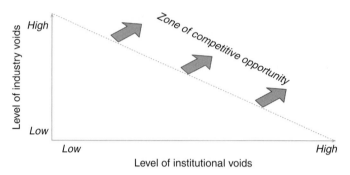

Figure 3.1 Models for the innovation–internationalisation process of Indian firms

In summary, institutional theory concepts suggest that emerging market firms may benefit from engaging in institutional arbitrage in other emerging markets (Figure 3.1).

In addition, industry conditions in many of the still 'emerging' and mostly 'transitional' markets were also evolving in the 1990s. In many emerging markets, industry structures were less well developed and less competitive than in developed markets. For instance, supplier networks and related industry infrastructure were less well developed. Product innovation was less aggressively practiced, and incumbents tended to coexist in terms of sharing the overall market. At the extreme, entire industries or important segments of industries were undeveloped. In other cases, industries had homogenous product offerings, with little segmentation or differentiation to address the unique demands of customer sub-segments.

In such a context, firms from other emerging markets that have relatively advanced domestic markets in terms of product innovation and competitive intensity were likely to find such under-developed markets and industries attractive for entry. These firms could bring assets that they had developed in their domestic markets, and that had value, i.e. fit, in specific emerging or developing economies. These assets and capabilities could be unique, in the sense that Western competitors may not have the same accumulated set of relevant capabilities. Thus, penetration of particular segments was potentially easier. Figure 3.1 reflects this idea that emerging market firms may find attractive opportunities under specific institutional and industry conditions.

For Indian firms, relative success in addressing such new demands in the 1990s was to a large extent based on their use and leveraging of various kinds of innovation. Some of these were product-based, mostly in low-end consumer goods, garments and medicines, namely 'the four Ts': tea, toothpaste, t-shirts and tablets. Major rationale for such innovations were those based on exploiting factor differentials, in terms of both cost and quality, between India and the host markets. Other types of product-based innovations were also seen on a limited scale. For instance, automobiles and trucks were exported to other developing markets, particularly those in Africa that had similar infrastructure conditions as in India. They also had similar institutional conditions, particularly in the rigour of product certification and quality expectations, as well as price points that the local host market could afford. In these conditions, while there was some latent demand, the Indian firms had the appropriate product portfolio at the price points that would open up the market for them. Similarly, Indian firms, specifically trading houses, were major providers of certain basic consumer goods to the Russian market, in the post-communist 1990s. Institutional conditions for many of these consumer goods were still being formed, in terms of product certification, while industry conditions meant that many such products were suddenly unavailable as supply chains collapsed together with purchasing power. Indian firms then moved to provide such basic consumer goods at prices that were attractive to a population that suffered a rapid loss of purchasing power, following the collapse of the Soviet system.

A second type of innovation, once again based on factor differentials, also emerged in this period of the 1990s. These were essentially processes that were done at a lower cost and sometimes higher productivity than in overseas markets. Such process innovations primarily enabled the IT sector to develop and thrive, and also involved the trend of 'body-shopping' that arbitraged low cost-based skills between home and host markets. The market focus of such innovating firms, however, was different from the product-based types – the primary focus here was the developed markets rather than other 'developing' or 'emerging' or 'transitional' markets.

A final type of innovation that emerged in this period was innovation in business models. Firms were able to develop unique value propositions based on distinctive value chains, both inside and outside the firm. An interesting case is that of the diamond industry globally. Typically centred in the Belgian port city of Antwerp, the industry became increasingly dominated by the Indian diaspora from the 1990s.

These Indian firms, typically family owned and managed, provided a unique business model of intermediary services between diamond supply and demand. Sourcing rough diamonds from Botswana, and from Southern Africa, they moved these diamonds to the western Indian city of Surat, and then used highly skilled and low-cost artisans to polish and sell the finished product to global buyers. In other words, the business model was based on providing a unique link between different value-chain players in Africa, India and Belgium.

This initial first phase of internationalisation and innovation was thus characterised by some common elements: innovation based on labour or factor arbitrage, entrepreneurial skills that drove the ambition to enter and succeed in international markets, a focus on developing or emerging or transition economies (with the exception of IT firms that primarily focused on developed market clients) and arbitraging to a limited extent on institutional and industry conditions. However, there was still a range of restrictions imposed by regulation and the firm-level capabilities. For example, restrictions on foreign exchange and hence overseas investments were still prevalent, along with redundant inefficiencies built up during the decades of the license raj. These barriers made market-seeking innovations relatively few, and with even more limited cases of success in international markets. In the second phase, however, innovation picked up, and the further opening up and liberalisation of the Indian economy meant that internationalisation had a different character. We elaborate on this below.

Phase Two (2000 to 2005): innovation for the Indian market

The second phase of our analysis broadly corresponds to the years 2000 to 2005. In the first phase, Indian firms were still emerging out of a protected environment and the sense of entitlement that entry barriers created by regulation conferred. However, through the 1990s, as the Indian economy became liberalised and a different set of institutional conditions set in, Indian firms developed towards operating in more competitive conditions. In 2000–5, then, innovation trajectories and firms' focus shifted from the transient advantages afforded by labour and cost arbitrage as both the environments and firms' strategies changed.

While there were some uncertainties in Phase One on whether the opening up of the Indian economy was going to be transient, during

Phase Two it became increasingly clear that the liberalisation process was largely irreversible. The philosophy of the Indian state in managing the Indian economy had clearly changed from active participation to providing the context within which private firms could grow and prosper. Further, many restrictions, such as those on capital and foreign exchange transactions, were relaxed, as the Indian economy gradually became more integrated with the global economy. Hence, M&A emerged as a viable strategy for Indian firms looking to gain globally competitive innovative capabilities.

Competitive conditions, too, became more intense across a range of industries, as more were opened up to both domestic and foreign competition. Many Indian firms radically restructured in the late 1990s and early 2000s, as they shed peripheral businesses and increased focus (Luce, 2008). While in the past, the philosophy of many Indian firms, and business groups in particular, was that 'we can do anything and everything', the philosophy in the 2000s became more focused within sometimes related fields (for instance, oil, gas and refining for the Reliance Group, or the industry sector approach of the Birla Group).

As Indian companies became more efficient and as new firms entered, the Indian economy as a whole started to pick up speed. Economic growth in the 2000s put India on the world map, and made it one of the more attractive emerging markets, along with the other BRICs (BRICs stands for Brazil, Russia, India and China). This offered opportunities not only for foreign firms, but also for local firms to enter new segments of the Indian market and develop new ways of competing. That is, the domestic market became a primary target, but competition from local and overseas firms meant that Indian firms had to learn new ways of competing.

A combination of competitive pressure and market opportunity motivated some Indian firms to move up the innovation value chain and gain more access to resources and markets. This in turn pushed many firms to seek new ways of competing from those that were solely based on labour or cost arbitrage (as in Phase One). Indian firms now had more confidence in their ability to compete not only with domestic competitors, but also increasingly with multinational firms. All this in turn had implications for how they chose to do innovation whether with products, processes or business models.

In terms of product innovation, firms in the pharmaceutical industry began to go beyond generic drugs based on a low-cost advantage, towards developing new molecular entities in biotech including biosimilars. Such moves involved more research intensive activities, instead of primarily manufacturing activities. For instance, market leader Biocon increasingly invested in research and development (R&D) to move to a more innovation-based model, and also extended into partnerships with Western players such as Pfizer for insulin biosimilars (Enright and Subramanian, 2008). This was a process that was begun in the early 2000s, following India's signing up to the trade-related intellectual property rights (TRIPS) regime, when many pharmaceutical firms in India initiated forays into innovation as a way to reduce dependence on the imitation-based model practised for the previous two decades.[2] In general, while in the 1990s a majority of the Indian pharmaceutical industry was focused on bulk drugs, the early 2000s saw an increased focus on prescription drugs for the domestic market. Prescription drugs commanded higher margins, but required increased investment in R&D as well as marketing and distribution. Overall, while the R&D investments in the pharmaceutical industry in the1980s and 1990s were done with public funds, the 2000s increasingly saw investments by private firms (Saranga and Banker, 2009).

In terms of process innovation, it is instructive to see how IT firms evolved in Phase Two. Indian IT firms tried to integrate vertically by seeking industry-specific knowledge, such as banking or insurance, and developing some consulting expertise to go along with their back-end IT services. The IT firms' major customers were in the developed markets of North America, Europe and Japan. However, these firms were not always successful as they ended up competing with IT majors such as Accenture or IBM, among others. The foreign MNEs had developed client relationships, a key entry barrier, and were also increasingly moving their back-office services to India. While competition was one factor, many firms in the IT industry, used to rapid growth in their traditional service offerings, had little motivation, and hence had some inertia in shifting their focus from one based on labour-cost arbitrage to one based on knowledge.

The more interesting evolution was the increasing focus on business model innovation, particularly in services. Consider the case of Bharti

---

[2] The Indian Patent Act 1999, was an effort to make the previous legislation, the Indian Patent Act 1970, TRIPS complaint. TRIPS was established in 1994, and later became part of the World Trade Organisation (WTO) accession agreement.

Airtel – a leading telecoms player in India. It had developed a specific model for providing mobile phone services in India. It had focused its activities on marketing, brand building, pricing and billing instead of the actual provision of the technology. By outsourcing many of the technology-related activities such as developing and managing network equipment as well as some of the back-office IT activities such as customer data, it was able to reduce capital expenditures. This enabled the firm to focus on the customer side, and offer some of the lowest prices globally to customers, thus driving rapid market growth. In fact, together with other leading players such as Reliance Telecom, Bharti Airtel was able to bring mobile phone access to the vast interiors of India, where having a telephone had been a luxury in the past. To a large extent, this was made possible by value propositions that were oriented towards price points that combined low call rates with low-cost phones that made mobile telephony affordable to a large number of rural customers.

As the Indian economy gathered pace, many Western multinationals that were still holding back in the 1990s entered the Indian market with significant commitments. To be able to compete in this qualitatively different environment (compared to Phase One), some Indian firms felt the need to focus their resources on succeeding in the domestic market. The emphasis was now increasingly on innovation, but many firms lacked capabilities, particularly in technology. Selective acquisitions by companies primarily in engineering, such as by the wind-power company Suzlon and moulding company Bharat Forge, often played the role of enhancing the capability profile of the Indian firms in their ability to compete in the domestic market. Indian firms' horizons also started expanding beyond their domestic markets, and domestic strategies became increasingly integrated with these firms' global strategies.

There were some limited efforts to internationalise home-grown innovations in Phase Two. Some firms tried out international entry on a relatively small scale. For example, Mahindra and Mahindra launched their off-road vehicles in some African countries, while Tata Motors began to sell their trucks in some African and South American countries. However, these efforts were limited, and were largely driven by the forces of competition in domestic markets. Internationalisation and innovation in Phase Two had a qualitatively different character to Phase One; these became more asset- and capability-seeking rather than market seeking in Phase Two. This was because the focus was increasingly on the rapidly growing domestic market, and assets were being built up to drive innovation to compete in the domestic market primarily.

Overall, from a focus on cost-based arbitrage advantages in Phase One, the focus in Phase Two shifted increasingly towards competing on innovation capabilities. Such a shift involved different skills sets and knowledge bases than those involved in Phase One.

Phase Three (2005 to 2010): leveraging innovation into international markets

While Phase Two saw an emphasis on innovation as a way of gaining competitive advantage, particularly in the domestic market, Phase Three saw a greater focus on internationalisation as well – particularly the search for new markets. During much of the first decade of the 2000s, institutionally, many of the developing or transitional economies such as China, Russia, Brazil and Africa made moves towards improving investment conditions and establishing new legal and institutional conditions. While their application and rigour were not always uniform, the opening of these markets, particularly large markets like China and Russia, offered great opportunities for multinationals, both from developed and emerging markets. While large- and medium-sized developing and emerging countries moved to a new market philosophy and industrial structure, many industries were still opening up or emerging, especially in services and healthcare. At the same time, institutional environments, too, were still evolving, and were similar to conditions in India. For instance, anti-trust and foreign exchange regulations were still being put in place in countries such as Russia and China, as these countries addressed issues of macro-economic policy along with currency regimes and privatisation policies (Goldman, 2003).

In terms of product innovation, in industries such as automobiles, local players like Tata Motors and Mahindra and Mahindra, after launching successful products in the Indian market, moved more aggressively into markets in Africa, South America, China and even the US. Their products included trucks from Tata to off-road and farm vehicles from Mahindra and Mahindra. These were based on their established success in the domestic market being exported to overseas markets where industry and institutional conditions allowed for market penetration.

In terms of process innovations, pharmaceutical firms increasingly targeted their biosimilars to overseas markets. In addition many IT firms morphed into business process outsourcing firms, as they took on ever more types of processes for their overseas clients.

But the more interesting and probably profound development in innovation for international markets came in the form of applying unique business models that were first developed for the Indian market, and then subsequently adapted for the overseas market. Many of these were interestingly in services rather than products, the latter being typically considered to be the strength of firms from emerging markets such as China and based on low cost arbitrage. In contrast, service-based internationalisation was based on innovation, and particularly innovation in business models.

Take again the case of Bharti Airtel. In the second half of the 2000s, the company started internationalising into neighbouring markets like Bangladesh where it invested $500 million. Bharti Airtel later bought the African assets of Zain Communications, a Kuwait-based telecoms firm in 2010. In effect, what Bharti Airtel was trying to do was to apply its business model (i.e. its price-focused outsourcing of capital-intensive parts of the activity chain and system) to markets that it believed it could compete in – where there were some industry and institutional conditions that were still evolving. Similarly, after having gained a reputation for quality at low cost in medical services, Indian healthcare providers started expanding their scale-driven business model into some South-East Asian countries, such as Thailand, Vietnam and even Singapore. For example, Fortis Healthcare, a major Indian healthcare provider, expanded its footprint by buying into the assets of a cancer hospital in Singapore, with the objective of implementing the scale-sensitive business model that it had developed in Indian conditions, as well as gaining new capabilities from the advanced medical infrastructure in Singapore.[3]

In other industries, such as diamonds, the Indian entrepreneurs who had increasingly dominated cutting and trading, moved up the value chain and started offering a wider range of services such as financing and end-to-end logistics, thus adopting a one-stop business model for their buyers. In the highly visible IT industry, the model moved

[3] See www.business-standard.com/india/news/qa-malvinder-mohan-singh-fortis-healthcare/426504.

towards what was called a 'global delivery model' where clients' needs were served with a combination of assets on site at the client's location, in addition to the Indian company's assets and capabilities in India, and sometimes in other parts of the world (such as China). In other words, in a number of industries, what was increasingly becoming innovative was not the product or the process, but the business model itself that was often rolled out in India, scaled, and then applied to particular overseas markets that had the right industry and institutional conditions needed.

Boundary conditions, limits and challenges

We see that Indian firms' use of innovation capabilities to successfully internationalise rested on two main choices. First, the choice of location (emerging market or developed market, and then which country in particular) and second the adaptation or adoption of existing or new business models. Successful Indian MNEs were able to find a fit between the home country (India) and host country institutional and industry conditions. They were able to leverage their internally developed innovative capabilities to fit these markets (e.g. Indian pharmaceutical firms in Russia in the 1990s; IT firms into developed markets).

The institution-based view argues that firms develop resources to respond and compete in their home environments, including their institutional conditions (Peng *et al.*, 2009). Emerging market firms faced with institutional voids end up developing 'specific' resources and capabilities to compete in such environments. These institutionally adapted resources and developed capabilities including innovation capabilities then drive the firm's strategies at home and abroad (Cuervo-Cazurra *et al.*, 2011). Similarly, industry conditions, too, drive firms to develop resources and create strategies that help them serve customer needs and interact with competitors and counter the strategies of competitors within the norms and regulations of the institutional environment.

Thus Indian MNEs who first entered other emerging markets and less developed markets benefited from the resources, capabilities and strategies developed in India. They were at a competitive advantage over firms from developed markets that did not have the experience of developing complementary or primary resources in their home countries to counter institutional and industry voids. Further, Indian

MNEs were at a slightly advanced stage of development compared with firms from some emerging markets like Russia and others in specific industries. Emerging market MNEs can save on the learning cost of developing resources because they already have such experience at home, and may even be able to transfer some of the resources already developed to the new host country. Creative application of prior strategies that worked in their home markets may also allow these emerging market firms to identify unique segments of demand within an already functioning industry or an entirely new industry category altogether.

The second and particularly the third phase of internationalisation coincided with developments in both the institutional and industry environment in India. Pro-market reforms reduced institutional voids with the liberalisation of markets and improvements in governance (Cuervo-Cazurra and Dau, 2009).The opening up of the Indian economy both forced and enabled Indian firms to become more competitive by being able to access more capital, invest in new resources and upgrade existing resources through greater investments in R&D, training and assets. Thus, Indian MNEs developed greater capabilities leading to higher levels of innovation. Further, Indian firms were also forced to go overseas in search of technology and learning to compete both with Indian firms at home and MNEs in their home markets. This springboard action (Luo and Tung, 2007) further developed their innovation capabilities. As they moved up the value chain, Indian firms were better positioned to compete not only in emerging markets that had developed further, but also in key industries in developed markets.

Despite these successes, Indian MNEs still had some limitations, however. In some developed markets, Indian firms lacked competitiveness or faced tougher institutional environments than at home and were thus unable to compete (for example, the pharmaceutical industry's expansion in the US has not been as successful as those into emerging markets, where Indian firms have often run into trouble with regulatory bodies such as the US Food and Drug Administration). There were also challenges in specific industries in specific emerging markets. For example, Indian pharmaceutical firms faced tough competition from Western firms and regulations favouring local Chinese companies in China. Several Indian firms that had entered China in the early 2000s were forced to scale back efforts in 2009–11.

Conclusions: lessons learned and the way ahead

Innovation and internationalisation by Indian firms has changed significantly over the last two decades (see Table 3.1). In this time, continued development in India has removed some institutional voids, though not all. Further, Indian MNEs have evolved and are no longer solely reliant on their domestic markets. Some, such as the Tata group, now generate more revenue from overseas markets than from their home market. This also applies to several pharmaceutical firms. Such firms increasingly resemble international players, competing in India and abroad. As the competitive and institutional context, both in India and outside, has changed, firms have adjusted their strategies to compete in newer ways.

Indian firms' strategies on innovation and internationalisation have become increasingly complex and increasingly involve a mix of asset-seeking and market-seeking rationales. Several leading Indian firms are now listed overseas and are able to access international capital. They have established R&D centres of excellence in developed markets. Learning from these experiences (both successful and unsuccessful), Indian firms are now engaging in higher technology innovation both in India and overseas with a view to targeting the high end of developed markets. For example, Suzlon, the Indian alternative energy firm, started off in 1995 with basic technology to counter soaring power costs and the infrequent availability of power in the Indian state of Gujarat. It is now the world's third-largest wind power equipment manufacturer. It has R&D centres in Belgium, Denmark, Germany, India and the Netherlands, and manufacturing facilities on three continents. India is now also a hub for small cars, and Chennai is referred to as the Detroit of South Asia.[4] Pharmaceutical firms such as Dr Reddy's and Ranbaxy have led the way in drug discovery and acquiring patents in the US. India is also increasingly a global hub for drug research and development and for clinical trials.[5] Further, Indian firms are using innovation capabilities to invest in other emerging markets to both develop these markets as well as to expand the scale and scope of their operations. For example, Infosys and Wipro have

---

[4] *Wall Street Journal*, 8 July 2010, available at http://online.wsj.com/article/SB10001424052748704111704575354853980451636.html.
[5] 6 July 2011, available at http://clinuity.com/blog/2011/07/india-emerging-as-hub-for-clinical-trials-says-assocham.

Table 3.1 Key points for three phases of innovation in Indian firms

	Phase One: the 1990s	Phase Two: the first half of the 2000s	Phase Three: the second half of the 2000s
Overall	Low cost, trade entrepreneurial skill as innovation, to other EMs (e.g. Soviet bloc, Africa, South-East Asia, e.g. Birla to Thailand and Malaysia; Mittal to Kazakhstan and Indonesia)	Moving up the innovation value chain, primarily focusing on the Indian market, selective internationalisation – both market seeking and asset seeking to be better able to compete domestically	Leveraging business model innovation from India to other EMs (China, Africa, Eastern Europe, Latin America) but also to some DMs both to leverage existing innovation capabilities but also to acquire these capabilities (e.g. Suzlon in Europe; Dr Reddy's; Tata's in UK)
Indian context	Expertise from five decades of import substitution in low-cost, high volume (e.g. generics and auto but also consumer goods); low cost, mostly using labour or some other kind of arbitrage; entrepreneurial skill: lots of small- and medium-sized firms, but mostly trade; innovation was mostly about matching supply and demand	Institutional development; acceleration of opening of the Indian economy; macro-economic growth; new firms entering old and new industries; increased and substantial foreign competition; relaxation on joint venture investments; relaxation of capital and foreign exchange controls	Increasing local and foreign competition; experience in competing with innovation; more institutional evolution, more access to capital; accelerating macro-economic growth; relative improvements in infrastructure
External context	Institutional conditions and cultural issues, how governments operated; industry immaturity: some market opportunities (e.g. Soviet Bloc countries, Africa); similarity in markets (low incomes) and supply and related infrastructure	Opening up of new markets; institutional development; access to domestic markets and assets by foreign firms	Liberalisation in many markets; economic crisis; protectionism in some markets; institutional evolution, industry immaturity and evolution

Table 3.1 (*cont.*)

	Phase One: the 1990s	Phase Two: the first half of the 2000s	Phase Three: the second half of the 2000s
Product innovation	Generics; low-end consumer goods: 4Ts namely tea, toothpaste, T-shirts and tablets, autos etc.	From generics to biomsimilars; autos/ vehicles for Indian market; services (healthcare, banking, etc.) for Indian market (e.g. Mahindra and Mahindra tractors in Africa; Tata trucks in Africa/South America)	From generic drugs to new molecular entities to biotech including biosimilars (e.g. Biocon has a licensing deal with Pfizer to do insulin biosimilars; statins) (e.g. Mahindra and Mahindra tractors in China, Africa, US; Tata trucks into more EMs)
Process innovation	Business process outsourcing, body-shopping, IT	IT firms taking more activities; innovating in biotechnology (drug discovery – biosimilars)	IT firms going into verticals, consulting, global delivery models, cross-country product development processes (Dr Reddy's; Suzlon)
Business model innovation	Diamond industry: getting rough diamonds from Botswana, South-East Asia and Australia to Surat and then using highly skilled and low-cost artisans to polish and then sell to global buyers: Africa, India, Belgium	Telecoms (Bharti Airtel); healthcare, autos, banking – reconfiguring the activity chain and system; cost innovation and market generating prices, primarily focused on domestic markets	For services not just products – e.g. mobile telephony Bharti Airtel going to Africa; healthcare going to Thailand/South-East Asia; diamond industry moving to high value-added, e.g. to higher value diamonds, bigger diamond pieces plus services such as financing with one stop shop etc.

established software development centres in Shanghai and Chengdu, China, while Aurobindo Pharmaceutical has set up production and manufacturing facilities in Datun, China.

The typical process followed by these firms, particularly those that focus on business model innovation, was to first develop and fine-tune the innovation in India, and then to adapt it to specific industry and institutional conditions overseas. While still in the early stages, such approaches have made it possible for domestic and international strategies to become more integrated. As the Indian economy continues to integrate with the global economy, not only in terms of products and markets, but also institutionally, this trend is likely to increase. Given India's recent emergence as a global player, Indian firms may begin to focus on identified areas of excellence and continue to build capabilities here instead of spreading into other sectors. Indian firms may also begin to add manufacturing innovation instead of services innovation to complete the value chain of activities in these key industries.

However, global expansion also comes with pitfalls – accessing international capital may reduce the cost of capital but exposes firms to international regulatory pressures and more rigorous standards of corporate governance. Indian firms' ability to manage across borders is still nascent when compared with that of Western multinationals – specifically in attracting and motivating foreign talent, understanding overseas cultures, customers and competitive conditions and adjusting levels of integration and responsiveness dynamically across time, geographies, products and activities. It is also unclear how some of the recent large-scale acquisitions will perform: how will Bharti Airtel fare in Africa, and how successful will the Jaguar and Land Rover acquisitions prove to be for Tata over time? Either way, the next few years promise to be significant ones in the development of Indian firms' internationalisation and innovation efforts.

4 Innovation by Chinese EMNEs

PETER J. WILLIAMSON AND EDEN YIN

Introduction

Traditionally, Chinese firms have often been considered as 'low cost' and 'me-too' players, lacking adequate innovative capability to create competitive advantage beyond their ability to produce low-cost products or low cost–low quality substitutes for those of their much more advanced Western peers. However, in recent years, contrary to this characterisation, more and more Chinese firms have begun to emerge as strong global contestants, and in some cases new leaders, in particular product lines and segments in the global market. One of the most publicised examples is Huawei Technologies, which specialises in designing and manufacturing telecoms equipment and routers. It has now surpassed all of the established telecoms equipment suppliers except Ericsson in global market share and profits, and in routers is now directly challenging the global market leadership of Cisco, long regarded as the flagship enterprise in the sector. In the personal computer (PC) business, meanwhile, Lenovo overtook Acer, Dell and HP in the third quarter of 2012 to become the world's largest PC maker, as forecast by Lenovo group chairman Liu Chuanzhi.

Although the achievements of these companies are perhaps the most widely known, they are hardly alone. In fact, today there are quite a significant number of Chinese firms that have successfully established themselves among the global market leaders in a variety of industries. Already by the late 2000s, Zeng and Williamson (2007) identified a list of strong global players from China including: Wanxiang Group in automotive components and systems; Galanz, a leading maker of microwave ovens; and Shanghai Zhenhua Port Machinery, a top crane manufacturer; among others. Four years on, more and more firms from China are emerging as formidable challengers of their once much more advanced Western rivals. But not only are Chinese firms gaining share in the global market, they are also becoming more and more innovative. Haier, Lenovo, China Mobile, BYD and others, for example, were ranked among the top fifty most innovative companies by *Business Week* magazine last year.

In this chapter we explore the role of innovation in helping Chinese emerging multinationals move beyond the position of unambitious copy-cats or timid subcontractors to Western brands. Macro-level evidence such as the rapid growth in patents both applied for and granted by Chinese firms in China and abroad suggests innovation is playing a key role in the changing competitive advantage of Chinese firms in the global market. According to recent data, China now leads the world in patent activity and the Chinese government continues to promote policies that are aimed at transforming 'Made in China' into 'Invented in China'.[1] We find that innovation has played a significant role in allowing Chinese companies to transform country-specific advantages (CSAs) such as low labour costs and rapid growth in market demand into firm-specific, competitive advantages (FSAs; Williamson and Yin, 2009). In building this new layer of competitive advantage, however, Chinese firms have often taken extended, non-traditional approaches to innovation that go far beyond pure technological progress.

Redefining innovation

Much of the publicity around innovation focuses on fundamental break-throughs and Nobel-prize-winning research. Of course managers also recognise the value of so called 'incremental innovations' – those that involve relatively minor changes in technology and deliver a small increment to customer value, but can pay off if scaled up to sufficient volume (Diet Coke and Gillette's multi-blade 'Fusion' razor are classic examples; see Chandy and Tellis, 1988). They are also well aware that more often than not, the lion's share of the value of new ideas, products, services and processes is captured by those who find innovative ways to commercialise, standardise and engineer these inventions for the mass market. But even here we are used to associating innovation with adding value – more functionality, more

---

[1] See http://thomsonreuters.com/content/news_ideas/articles/science/china-leads-the-world.

features, and entirely new products and services – for which we expect customers to pay a price premium.

In studying the types of innovation that have contributed to the ability of successful Chinese multinationals to win share in the global market, however, we have observed a much broader range of innovations at work. These include five main types:

First, *cost innovation*: reengineering the cost structure in novel ways to offer customers adequate quality and similar or higher value for less cost (Zeng and Williamson, 2007). Second, *application innovation*: finding innovative applications for existing technologies or products. Third, *business model innovation*: the idea of changing one of the four core components of the business model (customer value proposition, profit formula, key resources or new processes) but with a twist – adjusting those aspects that can be changed quickly and at minimal cost, and sometimes, reconfiguring the traditional value chain to achieve extreme flexibility and agility. Fourth, *shanzhai* (which translates as village fortress) *innovation*, stemming from a hybrid innovative approach that combines both product and process innovations to produce more versatile and cheaper alternatives to the mainstream, existing products. Finally, *technological innovation*, which focuses on technological break-throughs and increasing sophistication and features as described above.

Models of innovation adopted by Chinese firms

As Prahalad and Mashelkar (2010) observed, most innovation initiatives by established multinationals are built on the assumptions of affluence and abundance. The predominant innovation model adopted by incumbent multinationals, therefore, starts with scientific research (the 'R' in R&D), followed by creating economically viable products that embody the science ('development'), then the creation of prototype, which, if successful, is followed by scaling up and volume manufacture of final products. It is a costly and time-consuming process, which often involves many millions of dollars of investment and years of sustained efforts. For the winning, break-through products that emerge, the rewards for the innovators can be huge and sustained, including potential first-mover advantages that create or underpin market leadership. The 'wastage rates' associated with investments in the pursuit of fundamental technological innovation, however, are frequently high because the probability of break-through technological change is, almost by definition, likely to be low.

To date, participating in the quest for break-through, technological innovation has looked either unattractive or impractical for the vast majority of Chinese firms. Even among the largest Chinese companies, most lack a solid base of proprietary technology on which to build and the staff and processes necessary to conduct basic research. Smaller players and most private companies in China also lack the capital to make long-term, risky investments in R&D. As a result, most Chinese companies – even emerging Chinese multinationals – have tended to concentrate their efforts on other types of innovation listed above. In understanding how this innovation focus has contributed to the competitive advantage of globalising Chinese firms and how their competitive advantage might evolve in the future, each element of this broader set of innovation initiatives deserves brief comment in turn.

Cost innovation – creating high quality with low cost

The idea of innovation efforts focused primarily on reducing cost while maintaining quality – on producing cheaper products and offering similar functionality at better value for money – might seem unorthodox. Some might even regard it as business suicide: why invest in R&D and innovation to sell tomorrow's products at lower prices than prevail today? But perhaps this kind of innovation can offer an important source of competitive advantage in a global market where 'value-for-money' segments are growing rapidly, driven by two trends. First is the shift towards developing-country markets as the engine of growth in global demand. Recent estimates by global accounting firm, Ernst & Young, for example, suggest that 70 per cent of world growth over the next cycle will come from emerging markets.[2] In order to access the potential demand growth in these emerging markets, where income levels are relatively low, offering exceptional value-for-money will be critical. The capability for cost innovation, therefore, is a very promising source of competitive advantage. Moreover, even in the most developed countries, the value-for-money segment of customers is

---

[2] See www.ey.com/GL/en/Issues/Business-environment/Six-global-trends-shaping-the-business-world – Emerging markets increase their global power (accessed 24 July 2011).

expanding due to the 2008 financial crisis and the resulting economic recession. Even before the slump, many consumers were finding it difficult to meet their aspirations for improved living standards: the median wage rate for workers in the US, for example, was stuck at the same level in real terms as it had reached in 1972.[3] To access these potential customers by delivering better value for money, cost innovation capabilities will also be key.

Cost innovation involves creative ways of reengineering products or processes to eliminate things that do not add value (or value that consumers are willing to pay for). The Chinese battery maker, BYD, is a good example. Observing that the high cost of lithium ion (Li-Ion) batteries (at the time costing $40 each) was preventing their use in mainstream products, BYD focused their innovation efforts on reducing costs without compromising performance. Their R&D tried to find a way to replace some of the most expensive materials used in Li-Ion rechargeable batteries with cheaper substitutes. BYD also worked on reengineering the production process. It figured out how to make batteries at ambient temperature and humidity, avoiding the necessity to construct and maintain expensive 'dry rooms' in the plant. These moves resulted in costs falling by 45 per cent, taking the cost for each battery down to just $12.

These advances resulted in a value-for-money revolution that saw Li-Ion batteries replace their lower-performance nickel cadmium (NiCad) predecessors in volume applications. As BYD hopped from volume segment to segment, costs fell further, allowing it to notch up global battery market shares of 75 per cent in cordless phones, 38 per cent in toys, 30 per cent in power tools and 28 per cent in mobile phones.

Guangzhou Cranes Corporation (GCC) followed a similar path, focusing its innovation this time on eliminating redundancy in its products and removing unnecessary steps from the production process. Prevailing industry practice, for example, was to secure metal joints by welding both sides of adjoining plates. GCC focused its R&D and engineering staff on redesigning the joints so that equivalent strength could be achieved with a single weld, thereby cutting both cost and production time (a critical consideration for buyers often faced with tight construction schedules).

---

[3] Source: Economic Report of the President, 2012, Washington DC, US Government Printing Office, Table B- 47, 374.

Application innovation – creating new applications of an existing technology

Application innovation refers to innovation that is new in terms of its application, but not its technology. In other words, it involves creating a new application for an existing product or technology. The classic example is the humble sandwich: neither the bread nor the meat filling was new. Instead, the great innovation, credited to John Montagu, Fourth Earl of Sandwich back in the eighteenth century, was in combining the two. In many companies such repurposing would not be graced with the term 'innovation' at all. Because they rely on proven technology, however, application innovations often require less investment and generate faster payoffs compared with entirely new inventions.

Success in application innovation begins with lateral thinking that seemed to come naturally to many of the Chinese companies we studied – perhaps because Chinese philosophy starts from a view of the world as an inter-connected whole, focusing more on similarities, connections and relations rather than on differences, division and idiosyncrasy of its component parts. As a result, application innovation was more common and also appeared to be more highly valued among Chinese corporate innovators than among similar, incumbent multinationals.

This kind of thinking was behind the application innovation that has helped Antas Chemical Company in China's Guangdong province rapidly win share in the global market for sealants used in the construction industry. Builders have traditionally used acrylic-acid-based products to seal the frames of exterior doors and windows. These products are reliable once dry, but if rain hits the construction site within the first twenty-four hours after acrylics have been applied their performance is substantially impaired. This problem was typically solved by deploying a high-cost product manufactured using silicone as an alternative in critical applications.

Antas was not a supplier to the building industry but was well established in the business of selling the sealants used in shipping containers – a highly demanding environment for waterproofing. Its butane-based sealants not only offered better long-term performance and were waterproof the instant they were applied, they also had lower production costs. Their innovative idea of reformulating and repackaging the butane-technology sealants for easy use in the construction industry only looks obvious with hindsight. Because the supply chains to these user industries had remained proverbial 'silos', no one had seen the potential before Antas made the leap.

Another variant of application innovation is to combine existing, even mature, technologies for a new purpose. Take the example of Broad, a privately owned Chinese innovator in energy-efficient air conditioners based in Changsha in Hunan Province. The company was formed with capital of just $3,000 in 1988, but its founder Zhang Yue had an innovative idea: instead of powering an air conditioner with expensive electricity, why not use waste heat or natural gas to generate cool air directly? The technologies for conversion of heat, either wasted by power stations and boilers, or produced by combusting natural gas, were well established. But no one had applied them to large-scale commercial air conditioning plants of the type used in skyscrapers or airport terminals. Broad's innovation was to do just that. Over the years of applying existing technology in new ways it has succeeded in developing air conditioning systems that reduce energy consumption by up to 80 per cent compared with conventional systems powered by electricity – with huge savings in both cost and greenhouse gas emissions. Today its products are installed in over sixty countries, including massive installations that cool Bangkok's airport and the Expo 2010 pavilions. Broad is the number one supplier of this 'green' technology to the US and Europe as well as China.

All of these types of application innovation share characteristics that are particularly attractive as a way of building competitive advantage in serving value-conscious customers both in the fast-growing emerging markets and at the mid- to lower-end of developed markets where profit margins tend to be lower. This is because application innovation economises on investment, reduces risk and speeds up payback by leveraging existing, proven technologies.

Business model innovation – creating new ways of doing business with extreme flexibility

Some of the world's most competitively successful innovations have stemmed from novel ideas that did not involve changes in the underlying technologies, products or services at all. Instead, they involved innovative redesign of the business model by which value was created and delivered to customers. Low-cost airlines such as South West Airlines or Britain's Easyjet are classic examples. They share the same aircraft technology as the legacy carriers and offer the same fundamental utility – 'get from A to B safely and quickly'. But they deploy a business model that breaks all the traditional norms: flying only point-to-point routes rather than through hubs, standardising fleets, eliminating frills, charging separately for everything from food to baggage, employing multiskilled staff that check you in and then become your flight attendants and so on.

A recent survey suggests that more than 50 per cent of executives think this kind of business model innovation will become an even more important ingredient for success than product or service innovation (Johnson *et al.*, 2008). But the same study also indicates that no more than 10 per cent of the money invested in innovation by global companies is directed at coming up with new business models. Part of the reason for the apparent contradiction seems to be that business model innovation is viewed as requiring the kind of wholesale organisational transformation that few companies have succeeded in achieving quickly.

Among Chinese companies, however, our research suggests that business model innovation is widely pursued in the quest for competitive advantage. Rather than turning the organisation upside down, Chinese companies tend to focus on fewer simple and well-targeted innovations in the way things are done, that can still have the potential to transform accepted business models.

Take the case of Tencent, the Chinese company that runs the country's largest social networking and instant messaging service. Over the past decade Tencent built up its core business with the simple idea of allowing subscribers to route short messages from their computers direct to the mobile phones of China Mobile's customers, for a fee of 10 Chinese Yuan (around $1.50) per month. The service was immensely popular: Tencent's customer base grew to almost 500 million active accounts.[4] Then came Tencent's next business model innovation: it used its links between PCs and the mobile network to allow its customers to play on-line games for free. By eliminating the need to download the software onto a gaming console, the problem of counterfeiting that had dissuaded many of its US and Japanese rivals from entering the market simply disappeared.

Instead of charging for downloads of the gaming software, Tencent collected revenue from the exploding number of gamers by selling them

---

[4] *The Economist*, 'Networked Networks', 17 April 2010, Asian Print Edition, p. 67.

digital add-ons such as virtual weapons and clothing. It now sells virtual extras ranging from digital wallpaper to picture frames to augment all its base services. With revenue growing at 60 per cent per annum, its market capitalisation has exceded $37 billion. It is now seeking to extend this business model overseas, initially through a 10 per cent stake in one of Russia's leading Internet companies, Digital Sky Technologies, that itself holds stakes in both Facebook and Zynsa.

It is not only in high-tech, digital businesses, however, that a focus on coming up with simple but powerful business model innovations is helping Chinese companies build competitive advantage. We also observed it in the more mundane business of industrial paint. Recall the application innovator, Antas Chemical, which deployed waterproof adhesive technology from shipping containers in the building industry. The paints division of Antas has also been an innovator – this time by introducing a novel business model. When Antas sales representatives visited industrial customers, they started to regularly receive requests to set up a recycling system to remove the mounting piles of empty paint cans taking up valuable space at the end of their production lines. The problem was that Antas could not see how to make recycling of cans pay. Their solution turned out to be even simpler: reengineer the business model by installing tanks at the customer sites, and take over the responsibility of timely cleaning and resupply with new colours to satisfy customers' changing production runs.

Another example of Chinese firms' business model innovation is a group of firms based in the most populous city of Zhejiang Province, Wenzhou. Over the years, Wenzhou has produced a number of firms that are now leaders, such as Delixi Group and DongYi, in a number of global value chains including power supply, electronic equipment and shoes. Delixi, established in 1984, for example, is now one of the largest privately owned enterprises in China specialised in the manufacturing of electric power transmission equipment, such as high and low voltage switchgear sets. An important part of its value proposition is its ability to offer customers choice of a wide variety of product specifications, totalling some 30,000 alternatives, to suit particular applications more closely than the more restricted product range offered by its competitors.

Key to Delixi's ability to deliver this wide variety of specifications is the flexibility it has achieved by dividing its value chain down into micro-components and activities. Each activity is undertaken by a number of small, family-owned firms that are specialist, but also agile.

By flexibly recombining the activities and outputs of this wide network of suppliers, Delixi is able to vary the specifications in ways that would be difficult for a single, vertically integrated operation.

Normally high costs of coordination constrain the competitiveness of this kind of highly fragmented business model. But the 'Wenzhou business model' used by companies like Delixi has been able to reduce these costs dramatically by making use of a combination of proximity and kinship ties. First, the firms in one particular village specialise in the same activity, competing and cooperating simultaneously. This provides a downward pressure on costs while providing easy scalability and agility. Second, because the combination of all these specialist villages in Wenzhou can deliver almost all the components that Delixi needs, communication costs are kept down through collocation and familiarity.

What we observe among Chinese firms, therefore, is profitable business model innovation that does not involve a company in the long battle of attrition so often associated with root-and-branch organisational change. Instead, their innovation is to pinpoint a few critical, but simple innovations in the business model that can increase return on investment and cut the payback period.

Shanzhai innovation – improving over counterfeits at an extreme speed

This category of innovation is perhaps seen as most controversial, especially in the West, because it has evolved from the long line of Chinese firms that specialised in making counterfeits of well-known products and brands. As unacceptable as this practice may be, over successive cycles it has allowed some of the firms involved to develop a formidable set of capabilities of three types. First, they have improved their technological skills enabling them to focus more on high-tech or technology-based products such as consumer electronics, telecoms products and even cars (including copies of top brands such as Mercedes-Benz and BMW produced in northern China). Second, they have graduated from making an inferior version of the original products to developing the counterfeited versions that actually offer additional, improved features or benefits. Third, they are able to bring the counterfeited products to the market extremely quickly – sometimes even overtaking the roll-out schedule of the original manufacturers. These firms are nicknamed 'shanzhai' ('village fortress') in Chinese, implying they are outlaws hiding away when making their products.

Being secret operations, these companies are naturally difficult to research. But one such company that we have been able to identify is SciPhone, which specialises in producing counterfeited iPhones, branded as 'Dream G2'. Their products look very similar to the iPhone and their basic functionality is sufficient to satisfy the needs of lower-end Chinese consumers. But they also offer unique features that the original iPhones do not even provide, such as the multiple SIM cards, better photo quality, a large set of foreign language options, rugged metal casing and so on. These shanzhai smart phones have been extremely popular among mid- and lower-tier customers due to their versatility, resilience and lower price points.

These shanzhai firms are often established by experienced engineers and executives who have worked for mainstream mobile phone producers, such as Nokia, Motorola, Samsung and so on for years. They have deep understanding of the technological and manufacturing processes of mobile phones and therefore are able to use a combination of product and process innovations to create a new breed of phones that out-perform leading brands in terms of functionality desired by Chinese lower-end customers. Their process innovation, meanwhile, lies mainly in speed of delivery by reengineering the design and manufacturing processes to achieve exceptional reductions in time to market.

Despite the obvious limitations of shanzhai innovation as a strategy for international expansion, the experience gained by these firms and their unique capabilities in serving low-end markets and moving at exceptional speed may provide an interesting foundation to rapidly build new players that leave counterfeiting behind and become future players in the mainstream global market.

Technological innovation – following the footsteps of incumbent multinationals but improving on established processes

Perhaps not surprisingly, there are also some firms in China that follow a more orthodox approach to innovation, based on trying to achieve significant technological advances. Given the importance and growth of the value-for-money, price-competitive market in China, severe gaps in the infrastructure for protection of intellectual property and lack of experience in basic R&D, these firms are certainly a small minority. They are the ambitious few that aspire to be global leaders in technological innovation; they accept that there are few shortcuts or easy ways, and hence are willing to invest heavily in fundamental R&D. Among these companies, Huawei Technologies and Wanhua Polyurethane are prime examples of successful implementation of this strategy. Both companies have achieved impressive market share in the foreign markets, including those of the most developed economies.

Despite adopting the more traditional route of technological innovation, however, these firms tend to focus on technological break-throughs that will result in different customer value propositions than their established global competitors. In telecoms switches, for example, Huawei focused efforts on replacing hardware components with more sophisticated software in its products, making them extremely robust and simple to operate, and reducing the amount of maintenance and technical expertise that had to be undertaken on-site. These qualities immediately made the products attractive to telecoms operators in emerging markets.

As it turns out, the use of technological advances to reduce operating complexity and maintenance also turned out to be attractive to customers in developed economies facing high labour costs and delays in getting service personnel on-site in congested cities. Huawei has thus benefited globally from directing its technological innovation towards redefining the customer value proposition, rather than simply increasing the technical capabilities of the equipment per se.

Sustainability of the innovation advantage pursued by Chinese firms

The discussion above has presented evidence that emerging Chinese multinationals are relying on more than just low Chinese factor costs in order to compete and that innovation, defined broadly, has made a significant contribution to their enhanced competitiveness. In order to provide sustainable competitive advantage in the global market, the innovations pursued by emerging Chinese multinationals not only have to profitably create additional value for customers, but they also need to be difficult for global competitors to imitate. This depends importantly on those kinds of innovations requiring unique capabilities that are slow and costly to build.

Table 4.1 sets out some of the key capabilities required to achieve three of the main types of innovation we observed among emerging Chinese multinationals above: cost innovation; application innovation; and business model innovation. We have not analysed shanzhai innovation separately because it is primarily a context that has allowed some Chinese firms to develop the capabilities necessary to achieve these three main types of innovation at record speed. Nor have we analysed the capabilities necessary for more traditional technological innovation as these have been well rehearsed in the literature.

First, all three types of innovation require a major change in the mindset for competitors who have traditionally focused on 'block-buster' technological innovation to focus on how to deliver 'more from less' – equal or more value to customers with less cost, investment and time. Such a change is unlikely to be easy because it requires incumbents to shift the focus of engineers and designers who are motivated by inventing products and services that are 'newer, bigger and better' towards reverse engineering, eliminating cost without undermining quality, redeploying existing technologies, or (in the case of business model innovation) achieving break-throughs without changing the core product or service at all. In practice this capability has been emerging in Chinese companies from years of operating under very tight resource constraints, intense price pressure and high demand uncertainty. It is far from clear that it can easily be transplanted into a multinational organisation that has grown up in a resource-rich environment.

In the case of cost innovation, in addition to this new mindset, to be successful companies need to develop new designs and processes that enable costs to be reduced without sacrificing quality or value to consumers. To implement these changes also requires a high level of flexibility to reconfigure resources, organisational structures and processes.

To successfully achieve application innovation the most important capability required to pursue this type of innovation is lateral thinking, combined with a customer-benefit-centric approach to innovation. Application innovation requires firms to constantly ask themselves 'who else may need the benefits offered by our existing technologies?' This 'who' may be in a completely different industry which none the less offers the next big growth opportunity.

Table 4.1 *Capabilities underpinning innovation by Chinese EMEs*

Types of innovations	Capabilities required	Practical approaches
Cost innovation	– Access to low-cost resources – Cost-oriented innovation mindset – Flexibility competency – Combinative competency – Simplification – Parallel processing – 'Good enough' mentality – Regimented work ethic	– Substitute expensive materials with cheap ones – Substitute costly manufacturing processes with low-cost ones – Create flexible manufacturing process – Look for cross-industries economy of scale – Understand the existing process of production – Cut out unnecessary sections and focus on the most vital function – Develop new features based on consumer insights
Application innovation	– Customer benefit-centred mindset – Lateral thinking – Cross-functional collaborative capability	– Identify a group of industries that are similar in terms of the customer benefits sought, e.g. who else also needs it? – Identify a group of industries that may use similar technologies, e.g. where can this be used? – Choose the sizable industry that requires the minimal level of product adaption
Business model innovation	– Proactive attitude towards change – Insights on consumer value proposition – Insights on existing limitations of value proposition – Creative thinking – Extreme level of integration	– Understand the existing consumer value proposition – Augment or enhance the service component of this value proposition – Develop essential infrastructure or resources to deliver this enhanced service-based value proposition

To successfully match the kinds of business model innovations of the type initiated by emerging Chinese multinationals, meanwhile, requires not just designing a new business model, but doing so in ways that do not require a long and painful change management process. The trick is to innovate the business model in ways that extend and leverage much of the existing capability set and culture of the organisation.

All three of these types of innovation, however, suffer from the problem that once a new product or service has been created it is likely to be difficult to protect from imitators. Application innovation, for example, because it does not involve the creation of a new technology, will be inherently difficult to patent. Likewise business model innovation the world over is generally not suitable for protection via traditional intellectual property rights (IPR) tools. The main barrier to its imitation comes from the inability of newcomers to assemble and then coordinate the complex set of inter-related activities that underlie a new business model. The imitability of cost innovation, meanwhile, will depend on the extent to which the mechanisms used to improve cost–value trade-off are obvious by observing the product or service, or whether they depend on underlying processes and capabilities that are much less transparent.

More classic technological innovation, meanwhile is likely to prove easier to protect using traditional IPR tools (witness the large number of patents granted to Huawei around the world) even if they are directed at different value drivers than incumbent competitors.

Innovation models of Chinese firms and global competitiveness

The final question to consider is whether the potential competitive advantages associated with the innovation models pursued by Chinese firms are applicable to profitably winning share in the global market. Applicability has two key dimensions. First is whether a suitable market for the value proposition exists, or can be created, in the foreign market. The second test that an innovation must pass if it is to underpin competitive advantage in the global market is transferability.

Cost innovations will find a fertile market wherever there is a significant proportion of 'value-conscious' customer segments since these innovations improve the trade-off between value and cost faced by buyers. For the reasons explained above these segments can be expected to continue to grow in both emerging and developed markets. Cost innovations will be transferable, meanwhile, so long as they depend on designs and processes that enable costs to be reduced without impairing quality and core functionality, rather than depending purely on low factor costs in China.

Provided a common need exists, application innovation should be applicable globally although its transferability may be impeded by different regulations prevailing in different markets that were designed with a particular technology in mind.

The transferability of business model innovations is perhaps the most complex. The basic architecture of the business model innovation should be easily transferable from one market to another. To be profitable, however, the business model innovation will require a suitable set of factor cost conditions, buyer behaviour and amenable suppliers and partners, as well as competitors whose existing business models offer inferior potential on the dimensions of value and cost. These conditions are likely to vary significantly from market to market around the globe, limiting the transferability of Chinese business model innovation to certain environments.

The Chinese approach to technological innovation, meanwhile, should be readily transferrable to global markets, providing the customer value propositions to which it is aimed are valid among a sufficient number of consumers in the target market.

Conclusions

As Govindarajan and Ramamurti (2011) have indicated, there is a need to rethink how the birth of new breeds of innovation from the emerging markets is impacting the theory and practice of mainstream innovation and internationalisation. They call for research centring on issues such as the types of new innovations emerging markets spawn, the new competitive advantages of emerging market firms and the implications for the new capacities that Western multinationals may need to develop as their established positions come under increasing challenge from EMNEs. In this chapter we have outlined the range of innovation models that emerging Chinese multinationals are adopting and their contribution to creating sustainable competitive advantage for these firms in the global market. A key conclusion is that the leading Chinese firms who aspire to become global players have innovated in a variety of ways that potentially contribute to their competitive advantage in ways that go far beyond pure factor cost advantage in China. Their innovation initiatives cover a wide spectrum from cost innovation, through application and business model innovation, to more traditional technological advances. How much these initiatives will contribute to sustainable competitive advantage in the global market varies according to the ease with which innovations can be imitated by competitors and the applicability and transferability of Chinese innovations to markets abroad. One thing, however, is clear: emerging Chinese multinationals are developing and leveraging innovation capabilities that are becoming an important part of their armoury in the quest to expand their share of global markets.

COMMENTARIES ON PART I

(I.i) The contribution of innovation to EMNEs' competitive advantage

BRIDGETTE SULLIVAN-TAYLOR

New forms of innovation are emerging from the developing economies. This commentary examines the four studies in this section that challenge the conventional view of innovation, and in particular the source, type and nature of innovation commonly found in the developed world. The aim is to help develop a better framework to advance theory and guide future research on the role of innovation in Brazil, Russia, India and China (BRIC).

How context shapes innovation

The authors concur that the development of competitive advantage through innovation is country specific, since the nature and evolution of innovation is often heavily contextualised and each BRIC context poses significant challenges. In this section, we will examine the similarities and differences of the local contexts and their influence on the type of innovation that has emerged and contributed to the international competitive advantage of emerging market multinational enterprises (EMNEs) in BRIC.

Macro: country-level factors

According to Oliveira Jr, Borini and Fleury (Chapter 1), since the 1990s, *Brazil*'s economic development has been dominated by a single view that emphasises the role of technical progress. This orientation towards innovation has emerged from an unstable political and financial context that stabilised in the 1990s through government intervention. This opened up the market and forced this late industrialising nation to catch up by focusing on operational excellence. Despite this, Brazil still has a low level of investment in innovation and poor competitiveness rankings (fifty-eighth in the world). However, it has developed innovative products for the

Brazilian market that have turned out to be attractive in other similar emerging multinational (EM) contexts.

In *Russia*, according to Filippov and Settles (Chapter 2), innovation was constrained by many factors, including a weak regulatory environment that resulted in poor protection for intellectual property (IP) such as patents, low levels of collaboration between public and private sectors and inadequate technology infrastructure. These constraints were exacerbated by the collapse of the Soviet Union, which resulted in its fragmentation and a loss of science and technology know-how. Despite the government's attempt to impose innovation politically, multinational corporations (MNCs) have failed to innovate even with state support for science institutions and technology parks. As a result, potential competitive advantages were not captured and used as the basis for internationalisation.

The *Indian* context differs from the other BRIC countries in many key respects, according to Celly, Prabhu and Subramanian (Chapter 3). Before the 1990s, the market was dominated by groups of largely oligopolistic firms and family-owned businesses across a range of industries. Government regulatory barriers (for certain industries) existed in the form of industrial licences, import restrictions and protectionary measures for small firms. The 1990s saw the liberalisation and opening up of the economy, following several decades of import substitution. Hence, the approach taken by entrepreneurs was factor-based arbitrage that matched supply in India with demand overseas. Indian entrepreneurs were therefore able to identify and target similar EM contexts (Täube *et al.*, 2011), where institutional infrastructure and industry development were similar to India (e.g. the collapse of the Soviet bloc and opening up of the African continent) and which provided significant new market opportunities. More recently economic growth in India has been led and dominated by the service sector, while most of the world manufacturing has been shifting to China (Kumar and Fodea, 2009).

In *China*, according to Williamson and Yin (Chapter 4), the contextual background differs from the other three countries. China is already the world leader in second-generation and process innovation (Breznitz and Murphree, 2011). Traditionally, the emphasis here has been on pure factor cost advantage; value-for-money is important in a price-competitive marketplace where there are severe gaps in the infrastructure, poor protection of intellectual property and a lack of basic research and development (R&D) experience (Garabato, 2009).

Its national model has involved mastering second-generation innovation, including the mixing of established technologies and products to come up with new solutions, plus organisational and process innovation (Breznitz and Murphree, 2011). The rapid growth in patents applied for and granted to Chinese firms in China and abroad suggests innovation is playing a key role in their competitive advantage.

The Chinese government continues to promote policies that are aimed at transforming 'Made in China' into 'Invented in China'. Hence, there is a political belief that mastering 'innovation' is the key to securing long-term economic growth, national welfare and power (Breznitz and Murphree, 2011). Having largely exhausted low-cost-based and investment-intensive economic growth models, China is now searching for the next source of sustained economic growth.

Micro: firm-level factors

Within the macro context, firms in BRIC have developed varying degrees of organisational capability to leverage innovation.

In *Brazil*, foreign firms got an early start in the country but their subsidiaries had limited mergers and acquisitions (M&A) capabilities to innovate for the local market. Local firms were either privatised or faced a Darwinian contest of survival of the fittest. They built up their capabilities in process engineering and production. The business environment was characterised by a large and uneducated internal market that was protected and heavily influenced by discontinuous and inconsistent government policy decisions. Entrepreneurs were believed to have a parochial mind-set, to avoid risk and to be detached from the international landscape; hence, innovation was not considered a key success factor. Brazilian bottom-of-the-pyramid (BOP) firms were found mainly in the service sector and were not focused on internationalisation.

In *Russia*, the macro conditions resulted in the domination of the resource industry and hence R&D was underdeveloped; innovation was not seen as a source of competitive advantage. Furthermore, there was limited capability in successfully translating scientific inventions into innovative products. Unsatisfactory knowledge transfer was a key challenge for Russian MNCs, along with low brand recognition, inappropriate organisational structures and minimal R&D investment. There was also internal resistance to innovation from poorly motivated employees, due to a widespread feeling that innovation was both risky and a luxury.

In *India*, prior to the 1990s, innovation was based mainly on labour–cost arbitrage (Täube *et al.*, 2011). Competitive pressures and market opportunity motivated some firms to move up the innovation value chain and gain more access to resources and markets. Firms sought new and different ways of competing, rather than one based solely on labour or cost arbitrage. Internationalisation was focused on transitional or developing markets or on 'industry voids' where it was difficult for companies to access capital or talent, invest in R&D or build global brands (Garabato, 2009). Another form of innovation was business model innovation, which focused on developing capabilities to compete with foreign MNCs entering India. But market-seeking innovations with patented or branded products were relatively rare.

In *China* low-cost and me-too players that lack the technological capability for basic research have learnt to thrive by focusing on cost innovation and in the process have gained an important advantage over Western organisations. Large Chinese companies lack the proprietary technology or capability to conduct basic research, while smaller private companies lack the capital to make risky long-term investments in R&D. Hence, most Chinese multinationals have tended to concentrate their efforts on other forms of innovation, such as application innovation, business model innovation and *shanzhai* (pirated brands and goods). However, there is recent evidence that some Chinese firms have begun to emerge as global leaders in particular product lines or segments. These firms are moving far beyond their earlier role of copy-cats or subcontractors to Western companies. In this way, some Chinese companies are transforming country-specific advantages (CSA) into firm-specific advantages (FSA).

Implications for theory and future research

Collectively these papers raise questions about our theoretical assumptions and perceptions of EMs and suggest several new lines of further research.

Theoretical issues

The findings indicate that EMs are not all the same, although Western firms often make this assumption, despite the fact that EMs are hardly uniform in the nature and extent of their institutional voids. They all fall short to varying degrees in providing the institutions necessary to support basic business operations (Khanna and Palepu, 1997, 2012). MNC theory also assumes that firms share the same motivations for internationalisation, i.e. to become global players that dominate developed markets. However, the studies in this volume suggest that EM firms often aspire to penetrate other EMs, at least initially. This observation has been echoed by industry analysts: 'now globalisation flows in both directions, and increasingly also from one developing country to another' (Garabato, 2009: 2).

MNC theories also think of innovation in terms of major scientific or technological break-throughs, whereas we see in these studies that small innovations, intended to address local EM issues (e.g. BOP), can also lead on to success at a global level. Western firms risk underestimating the innovation potential of acquisitions in EMs and of the opportunities for two-way learning. MNCs are not traditionally structured for two-way knowledge flows, especially with EM subsidiaries. Large, diversified business groups, with centralised control, remains the dominant form of MNC enterprise throughout most emerging markets (Khanna and Palepu, 2006). EM firms, on the other hand, seem to have the capability to transfer knowledge from one EM to another. This raises the question of what MNCs can learn from EM firms about managing global knowledge flows and organisational learning. Different EM national innovation systems may differ in relation to dealing with and responding to the current global financial and economic crises (Baskaran and Muchie, 2011). Innovation in the context of the worldwide financial recession will look very different from the boom times of the past, when break-through innovations and feature-rich products were valued. However, in recessionary times customers in rich countries become more value conscious, making cost innovation capabilities honed in EMs a powerful competitive advantage.

MNC theory also assumes an automatic ability for organisations to leverage advantage from their acquisitions. However, this is not always possible in EMs, either due to unmotivated staff (Russia) or the shortage of technical skills (China, India).

MNC theory assumes that it is possible to manage intangible assets, IP and knowledge flows within the boundaries of the firm, so that spillovers can be easily managed. However, in practice this has been found to be more difficult in environments characterised by weak institutional contexts, such as EMs. Western companies take for granted a range of institutions that support their business activities, but many of these institutions are absent from other regions of the world (Khanna and Palepu, 1997). The findings suggest that Western firms have struggled to manage their IP in the EM context, while Chinese firms have found managing intangibles too difficult and have retreated to ownership of hard assets. The findings also raise questions about whether acquisitions of low-tech EM firms can actually lead to potential spillovers in high-tech sectors (it has been assumed that they can enhance the technical capabilities of MNCs).

Future research

The country studies raise a number of questions for future research. In *Brazil* there is a call for qualitative longitudinal studies that help identify the transitions from one type of competitive advantage to another. In *Russia*, the interplay between innovation and the internationalisation of companies from EMs is a promising avenue of research. The role and place of innovation in Russian MNEs is currently under-researched. In *India* there is a need for further comparative studies on Indian companies in the BRIC context. Research could investigate how Indian firms have strengthened their generic capabilities by targeting markets at the bottom of the pyramid where they seem to have a competitive edge over developed-country firms (Täube *et al.*, 2011).

The *China* paper calls for a rethink of how new types of innovation from the EMs are impacting the theory and practice of mainstream innovation and internationalisation. There is a need for research on the types of new innovation EMs spawn, the new competitive advantages of EM firms and the implications for the new capacities that Western multinationals may need to develop as their established positions come under increasing challenge from EMNEs.

Overall, there is a need to rethink innovation priorities at the headquarters level of MNCs. The findings suggest that MNCs can increase return on investment (ROI) and shorten payback cycles beyond the old blockbuster innovation mentality. Hence the old views of R&D need to be abandoned to allow fresh innovative thinking via four new approaches: (1) start from the market; (2) seek simplification rather than complexity; (3) approach research constraints as stimuli for creativity; and (4) focus on the possibilities of immediate payback rather than long-term break-throughs.

There is also a need to build on the individual context-specific findings and explore more general knowledge gaps relating to EMs in general. Overall, there is a call for a more coherent and robust international comparative study, starting from the same conceptual and empirical position and using the same unit of analysis, metrics and performance measures across all the BRIC countries. Without this it is difficult to identify coherent longitudinal patterns and establish any basis for a comprehensive comparison that will move the field forward.

If Western companies fail to come up with effective strategies for engaging with emerging markets, they are unlikely to remain competitive (Khanna and Palepu, 2005). Further empirical research could review the field of innovation in the EM context by examining these trends and informing current thinking in this area. Key questions that could be explored include:

- What can the West learn from the BRIC approach to innovation?
- To what extent could cost innovation/incremental innovations such as those emerging from the EMNEs be considered as core innovations?
- Are the innovative features of EMNEs actually features of an industry or of a specific market context?
- To what extent do innovations developed within the context of significant constraints including regulatory, resource, political and managerial resistance and constraint make EM innovations more or less easily transferable to similar EM contexts?
- Could a larger comparative study that compares and contrasts the impact of government interventions be conducted to reveal the extent of the differences across BRIC?

Conclusions

MNC theory was developed from studies of MNCs from developed countries identify overall trends in internationalisation. This has resulted in MNCs that are structured to manage subsidiary activity in a top-down, hierarchical, one-way process orientation, as these large organisations are usually centrally managed and coordinated. However, these findings suggest that local subsidiaries often produce innovations from the bottom of the organisation that need to be captured and transferred across other EM contexts in order to achieve global competitive advantage.

Additionally, in the current global recessionary context, there needs to be a reconceptualisation of innovation towards a low-cost approach. Without this reconsideration of conventional approaches, MNCs will be unable to capture, harness and transfer innovations from their subsidiaries and convert them into international capabilities and competitive advantage in order to compete with EM firms.

(I.ii) Innovation in emerging markets and the rise of emerging market MNEs

RAM MUDAMBI

Introduction

As recently as the late twentieth century the archetypical multinational enterprise (MNE) was a hub and spoke system with the hub located in an advanced market economy, the major nodes located in other advanced economies and the minor nodes located in the rest of world. The main challenge of such an MNE was balancing local responsiveness with global integration (Bartlett and Ghoshal, 1989). By this time, Vernon's (1966) product cycle model was becoming less applicable to finished goods and services, but it was still alive and well for knowledge creation. Innovation was still largely concentrated in advanced market economies and 'exported' to middle and lower income economies.

A key phenomenon of the early twenty-first century is the rise of emerging markets as players in extant global research and development (R&D) networks, as centres for development of new business models and as sources of ground-breaking yet 'frugal' innovations (Govindarajan and Ramamurti, 2011). As part of this trend, we have witnessed the appearance in world markets of competitive multinationals based in these markets (Khanna and Palepu, 1999a, 1999b). There is general agreement that such emerging market multinational enterprises (EMNEs) are becoming more important and that they do not fall into one or even a few easily recognisable categories (Mudambi, 2008; Ramamurti and Singh, 2009a). There is evidence that emerging market firms face significant resource and institutional gaps in their home markets requiring them to develop competencies to cope with these hurdles (Khanna and Palepu, 1999a; Cuervo-Cazurra and Genc, 2011). However, given the specific nature of local contexts (Meyer *et al.*, 2011), it is unclear how these firms translate their locally relevant competencies in order to compete in global industries. Hence, there is much that is not understood about the process whereby EMNEs arise, survive and thrive.

Williamson and Yin (Chapter 4) advance the view that Chinese firms have graduated to parity and even market dominance in many sectors of the world economy based on their innovative capabilities. They present a five-fold taxonomy of Chinese firms' innovative processes. Celly, Prabhu and Subramanian (Chapter 3) assess the development of EMNEs based in India and present a framework of three phases, which they term 'arbitrage-based internationalisation' (1990–2000), 'innovation for the Indian market' (2000–5) and 'leveraging innovation into international markets' (2005–10). Filippov and Settles (Chapter 2) point to the challenges of creating EMNEs in an economy with a world class science and technology base, but a woeful lack of managerial skills and inadequate business services. Along the same lines, Oliveira, Borini and Fleury (Chapter 1) note that the performance of Brazil when measured by traditional innovation indicators is dire; they suggest that this picture emerges due to Brazilian firms' emphasis on hard-to-measure process and business model innovations.

This commentary aims to integrate these contributions within the overarching framework of research in international business and the geography of innovation. In order to do this, it is necessary to understand the changing nature of the global economy as well as the evolution of the role of advanced country MNEs in the global innovation system. In this view, the rise of innovation in emerging markets and the rise of successful EMNEs in the world economy are outcomes based on the same set of factors.

Global value chains – from trade in goods and services to trade in activities

Until the end of the twentieth century, most international trade consisted of goods and services. Improving technology and logistics combined with falling trade barriers made a wider range of locations viable as sites for business. This made it possible to unpackage goods and services into their component value-chain activities, so that today trade is increasingly in these activities or 'tasks' (Mudambi, 2008). The most noticeable aspect of this trend in the popular press is the phenomenon of off-shoring, i.e. the movement of an *activity* to its most globally efficient location. This activity may be housed within a wholly owned subsidiary (captive off-shoring) or outsourced to a local provider in a foreign country (off-shore outsourcing). As the firm configures its global value chain (GVC), off-shoring is a location decision, while outsourcing is a control decision (Mudambi 2008). Over the last two decades, we have witnessed a dramatic change in firms' GVCs with a huge increase in the extent of activities that are outsourced, off-shored or both. Successful GVC orchestration allows MNEs to combine 'the *comparative advantages* of geographic locations with their own resources and competencies to maximise their *competitive advantage*' (Mudambi and Venzin, 2010: 1511, emphasis in original).

Advanced economy MNEs as the spark for change in emerging market economies

Leading MNEs are part and parcel of this trend so that the MNE of the twenty-first century is becoming a multihub organisation (Prahalad and Bhattacharyya, 2008; Mudambi, 2011). This transformation gives rise to a subsidiary challenge of increasing local entrepreneurship and innovation and a concomitant HQ challenge of integrating the diversity of innovative outputs that arise within its far-flung network. This is based on the recognition that the fundamental differences across regions are so large that attempting to coordinate all functions from a single location is impossible. The authority and control delegated to emerging market regional headquarters in firms like General Electric (GE), Philips and Xerox represent nothing less than a new epoch in the organisation of the MNE. For example, while GE runs four global R&D hubs, the one that has the most comprehensive range of research responsibilities (including basic research), with a headcount of 3,800, is the John F. Welch Technology Center (JFWTC) located in Bangalore, India (Ernst and Dubiel, 2009). Some MNEs, like Cisco, have taken this a step further, establishing a parallel global headquarters located in an emerging economy (Kumar, 2010). These trends indicate that the 'competence-creating subsidiary' that generates entirely new technologies and business capabilities for the parent MNE (Cantwell and Mudambi, 2005; 2011) may actually be evolving to achieve a status of parity with the global headquarters (Hedlund, 1986).

Leading MNEs are recognising that the emerging markets that were once regarded merely as markets for adaptations of goods and services designed for advanced economies are changing in fundamental ways. On the demand side, emerging market customers with rising incomes are demanding products that are optimised for their own local environments. On the supply side, the local systems of innovation in emerging markets are growing increasingly sophisticated. This has two important implications. First, they are becoming valuable components of global R&D networks. Second, they are putting forth novel new solutions for local problems that often find larger and more lucrative applications back in advanced market economies (Williamson and Yin, Chapter 4; Celly *et al.*, Chapter 3; Govindarajan and Ramamurti, 2011). The supply side also contains a threat for advanced economy MNEs in the form of new and aggressive EMNEs (Awate *et al.*, 2012).

The genesis and capabilities of EMNEs

There is increasing evidence that many emerging market firms that appear on the world stage as EMNEs first enter GVCs by taking advantage of outsourcing and offshoring by advanced country MNEs. Typically they begin by undertaking standardised low value-added activities that they use to develop capabilities and linkages with global customers and suppliers. They use these low value-added activities as stepping stones to higher value-added activities. The Indian information technology (IT) industry (Patibandla and Petersen, 2002) and the Chinese auto industry (Liu and Tylecote, 2009) as well as evidence for the emerging economies of Central and Eastern Europe (Yang *et al.*, 2008) all support the thesis that numerous successful EMNEs began through interactions with advanced economy MNEs.

EMNEs have achieved leading positions in many of the world's industries, including cement, steel, software, computers and mobile handsets. However, while this is an impressive and laudable achieve-ment, it is important to distinguish between output capabilities and innovation capabilities (Bell and Pavitt, 1993). The former are associated with the ability to use and make adjustments to extant technologies, while the latter are associated with the ability to create and develop entirely new technologies. In this sense, even the most advanced emerging market firms have developed sophisticated output capabilities, but still rely on advanced economy firms to introduce 'next generation' technologies. Indeed, many of their subsidiaries in advanced market economies are set up with explicit knowledge-seeking (learning) mandates, to maintain their output capabilities at the technology frontier. This will inevitably change and perhaps fairly soon, but for the moment all evidence relating to emerging market firms suggests that their capabilities are output-related in terms of Bell and Pavitt's (1993) specifications.

Concluding remarks

The traditional hub-and-spoke advanced economy MNE organisation of the twentieth century is particularly unsuited to leveraging the opportunities and threats in and from emerging markets. This explains in part why MNEs are transferring ever more sophisticated activities to emerging market economies (Mudambi, 2008; Kappen, 2011). Increasing the strategic responsibilities vested in these subsidiaries allows them to fully exploit the opportunities that arise from local embeddedness while still maintaining connectivity within the MNE network. Thus, GE's JFWTC and Microsoft Research India, both in Bangalore, have global mandates and substantial control over the future trajectory of innovation affecting their parent firm's worldwide operations. In other words, they cover both the demand and supply side opportunities in emerging markets.

Using emerging market hubs as means of accessing growing markets as well as tapping rich new resource pools, often results in innovative solutions that have applicability in many locations, including in advanced economies. For example Cummins, the American engineering MNE, developed low-horsepower generators for the Indian market and soon found that it could successfully sell these in Africa, Latin America and the Middle East (Brown and Hagel, 2005). Conversely, Mahindra and Mahindra, an Indian EMNE, found that it could sell its low-horsepower tractors in the US. Microfinance, a business model pioneered by Grameen Bank, a local organisation in Bangladesh, has spread to Brazil and Mexico and is taking off in the poorer neighbourhoods of advanced economies (Hill and Mudambi, 2010).

The contributions of Williamson and Yin (Chapter 4) and of Celly *et al.* (Chapter 3) indicate that several Chinese and Indian EMNES are on their way to developing the capabilities to service their domestic hinterland as well as compete successfully in advanced market economies. By the same token, the contributions of Filippov and Settles (Chapter 2) and Oliveira *et al.* (Chapter 1) suggest that fewer Russian and Brazilian firms have reached this level of maturity. These contributions highlight the diversity in the nature and strategies of EMNEs.

As these developments continue, they challenge international business researchers to develop theory and models to understand the working of multihub MNEs and EMNEs. The hubs in advanced market economies and those in emerging and poor economies have vastly different capabilities and strategic motivations. Ensuring that these hubs do more than merely coexist; that they truly collaborate and create a whole that is more than the sum of the parts, calls for a boundary-spanning function of a higher order.

PART II

Value-chain configuration and competitive advantage

5 | Value-chain configurations of Brazilian EMNEs

AFONSO FLEURY, MARIA TEREZA LEME
FLEURY AND FELIPE MENDES BORINI

International value-chain configuration

The discussion of value-chain configuration (VCC) touches the essence of the phenomenon of multinational companies. A company only becomes multinational because the location of its operations in different countries gives it competitive advantages. At the same time, in order to settle in a foreign country the company has to rely on distinctive competitive advantages relative to both local and international competitors. The international value-chain configuration (IVCC) provides a depiction of the strategy of a multinational company, its achievements, the forces to which it is subject and perhaps also signals its future intentions.

The aim of this chapter is to show how the Brazilian multinationals are configuring their international value chains and how they are managing them to compete in international markets. For that, the primary information is the spatial dispersion of activities: what activities are they doing and where. A second level of information relates to why: what are the reasons that justify the adoption of the configurations observed. The third level relates to how: what strengths are mobilised to move into the international locations? Finally, it is important to assess how the Brazilian multinational companies are managing their international value chains to gain competitiveness.

In addition, the movements of Brazilian multinationals need to be contextualised. After all, as part of the group of late movers, Brazilian multinationals usually settle operations in sites that have previously been occupied by value chains of incumbent multinationals. That is, in principle, internationalisation implies confrontation, not only with local companies but also with other multinationals in destination countries. Consequently, the room for manoeuvre available to multinationals of emerging countries is different.

We address the issue through the application of a competence-based management/competence-based competition approach (Prahalad and Hamel, 1990; Hamel and Heene, 1994, Teece, 2009), by departing from the standpoint that what provides competitive advantage for any firm is the set of organisational competences they develop. For a firm to emerge as a multinational it must rely on a differentiated set of competences when compared to international competitors and, from then on, build a dynamic relationship between the parent company and its value chain for the fast and continuous enhancement of organisational competences, irrespective of location and mode of entry.

The reasons for the choice of the competence-based management/competence-based competition approach are the following: (a) the multinational might be considered as a network of competences geographically dispersed (Rugman and Verbeke, 2001; Knight and Kim, 2009); (b) competence formation at firm level always has a strong relationship with the local environment (Kogut, 1991; De Leo, 1994), which provides differentiation among multinationals originated in different countries; (c) more than seeking to understand the environmental factors that may motivate companies to go international, this approach prioritises the issue of how companies create dynamic capabilities to become internationally competitive (Teece et al. 1997; Teece, 2009); (d) the competence-based competition approach (Prahalad and Hamel, 1990, Hamel and Heene, 1994) which had enormous repercussions in the early 1990s, has resurged as the basis for a large number of studies in recent years (Barney and Clark, 2007; Verbeke, 2009; Teece, 2009); for instance, Verbeke (2009: 84) assumes that 'the notion of core competencies is largely equivalent to the higher-order concept of Firm Specific Advantage'.

The questions that must be addressed are:

- What is the spatial dispersion pattern of Brazilian multinationals' activities and how is it evolving over time?
- What is the competitive advantage that allows emerging multinationals to set their VCCs? and
- How do international operations contribute to the upgrading of competences, leading to greater competitiveness?

We will start with a discussion about the emerging country multinationals' spaces for manoeuvre and how they were configured in the recent past. Then, a brief description of the Brazilian multinationals will precede the analysis of how they are manoeuvring in those spaces and the characteristics of the value chains that they are establishing. We then move to more aggregate type of analysis aiming to disclose the preferences of Brazilian multinationals for the configuration of their value chains and how are they using the potential created by those chains to improve their competitive advantages. These analyses are based on two surveys realised in 2006 and 2010, respectively. In the final section, we highlight the insights and propose some generalisations.

The emerging multinationals' room for manoeuvre: the spatial and temporal dimensions

The literature reveals that after the second world war there were two periods that were especially propitious for the internationalisation of firms. Firms from the advanced industrialised countries, especially the US, led the movement in the first period, in the 1950s and 1960s. The expansion of multinational pioneers took place in a context of global economic recovery in which the installed capacity was less than the demand, allowing the internationalisation processes to occur under conditions of relatively low competitiveness. The pioneering multi-nationals settled subsidiaries that replicated, on a smaller scale, all the functions performed by the companies' headquarters, in a model that Porter (1986a) was latter to call 'multi-domestic'.

The second wave of internationalisation was generated in the 1970s by a different set of contextual factors that favoured the internationalisation of Japanese firms. However, the paths followed by Japanese multinationals were distinct from the pattern identified for the first-movers. Analyses made at the time used terms such as 'catch up' and 'leapfrogging' to refer to the need of new multinationals quickly to achieve levels of productivity and technological capability equivalent to that of global leaders, to not succumb during the internationalisation process (Lee and Lim, 2000). That is, the multinationals of the second wave had to conquer their spaces in global production. For this, they needed to develop distinctive competencies, emerging as champions in nationally competitive schemes organised by governments (Amsden, 1989; Aoki, 1990; Prahalad and Hamel, 1990). The establishment of their IVCC also followed different criteria. For example, since one of the competitive advantages of Japanese companies was their manage-ment model (Schonberger, 1982; Womack *et al.*, 1990), Japanese multinationals prioritised greenfield sites to locate their subsidiaries, aiming to ensure transferability of their management models.

The emergence of those new competitors had profound consequences. At micro level, it demanded that pioneering multinationals restructured to regain their competitive edge (Hayes and Wheelwright, 1984; Bartlett and Ghoshal, 1986). At macro level, developed country governments (re)assessed which industry sectors would be bearers of the future and which belonged to the past. This debate led to the identification of both sunrise and sunset industries (Dertouzos *et al.*, 1989). The latter were to be disregarded as obsolete and the former emerged as a priority, originating what is currently encompassed as knowledge-intensive industries (Mudambi, 2008).

The organisational restructuring process of multinationals involved: the separation and disaggregation of activities; concentration on those activities that fitted with the firm's core competences and offered high value added; and the use of partnering, outsourcing and off-shoring to cover other activities that were required to complete the value chain. This gave rise to the concept of value-chain configuration, meaning that 'most major companies are in the process of fragmenting themselves by examining each piece of their operations and asking how it may be deconstructed. And if deconstructed, in which nation the fragmented function can best be performed' (Contractor *et al.*, 2011: 6).

Those authors recall that, initially, the competitive advantage sought through the configuration and management of value chains was cost reduction. However, with the evolution of the approach and practice, developed country multinationals incorporated new drivers such as better service to clients, creativity and innovation (Contractor *et al.*, 2011: 11).

The third wave of internationalisation has multinationals from the BRICs (Brazil, Russia, India and China) as the main protagonists. As late-movers in the international markets, their movements have to be analysed in relation to the early-movers that have already had or are in the process of establishing their VCCs. In other words, their room for manoeuvre is smaller and to a certain extent shaped by the multinationals that have preceded them. It might be described through four dimensions:

- The spaces left by developed country incumbents moving towards knowledge intensive industries;

- The positions created by incumbents when they establish international supply and distribution chains;
- The new frontiers created by regionalisation and globalisation;
- The positions conquered in internationally competitive markets.

In examining the international expansion of Brazilian multinationals we will analyse the impact of each of these factors. We will also explore the main tactics Brazilan companies used to internationalise their value chains: acquisitions, greenfield investments and joint ventures, as well as off-shoring (which has also been used in a few cases).

The Brazilian multinationals

The general characteristics of the internationalisation of Brazilian companies are the following:

- It took them a long time to internationalise, which took place decades after their creation, like the vast majority of Latin American firms (Cuervo-Cazurra, 2008).
- Their strategies focused initially on Latin American countries, after the establishment of the Mercosur (a trade agreement between Argentina, Brazil, Paraguay, Uruguay and Venezuela); in this way, Brazilian firms profit from geographical closeness and reduce institutional and cultural differences. However, that changed over time. Table 5.1 shows the spatial dispersion of the activities of Brazilian multinationals in the recent past.
- What should be highlighted in Table 5.1 is the growing importance of new frontiers created by globalisation – Asia, Africa and Oceania – to the Brazilian multinationals.

Table 5.1 *Regional location of the activities of Brazilian multinationals*

	Latin A	North A	Europe	Africa	Asia	Oceania
2006	46.91	11.34	20.62	6.7	14.43	0
2007	40.38	14.72	20.00	8.3	16.60	0
2008	46.23	17.31	20.61	10.75	10.75	0.43
2009	52.95	9.18	16.89	5.43	14.66	0.89

Source: Fundação Dom Cabral

Table 5.2 *Distribution of Brazilian multinationals according to industry*

Industry	Number	Examples
Extractive industries	4	Vale (mining), Petrobras (oil and gas)
Basic inputs suppliers	20	Companhia Siderúrgica Nacional and Gerdau (steel), Votorantim (cement) and Braskem (petrochemicals)
Crop and animal production	4	JBS-Friboi, Brazil Foods (Sadia/ Perdigão)
Consumer products	10	AB InBev/Ambev (beverages), Coteminas (textile-apparel)
Construction materials	4	Tigre, Duratex
Components and systems suppliers	17	Sabo (auto parts), Weg (electric equipment)
Complex products assemblers	6	Embraer (aircraft), Marcopolo (buses)
Information Technology	11	CI&T (business intelligence), Stefanini (software), Bematech (hardware)
Engineering Services	4	Odebrecht, Camargo Correa
Other services	17	IBOPE, Griaule Biometrics, Fogo-de-Chao
Total until 2010	**97**	

Source: Fleury and Fleury (2011).

Table 5.3 *The TNI of Brazilian multinationals*

	2009	2008	2007
Most internationalised	0.67	0.68	0.68
Top 23 (average)	0.26	0.28	0.24
Top 40 (average)	0.16	0.17	0.16

Source: Fundação Dom Cabral

- The economic sectors in which Brazilian firms compete internationally include a broad spectrum. Some examples are shown in Table 5.2.
- Finally, it is important to stress that the stage of internationalisation of Brazilian companies is relatively low. Table 5.3 shows their transnationality indices (TNI).

The spaces occupied by Brazilian multinationals

Spaces opened by the movement of developed countries and their companies moving to knowledge intensive industries

For more than a century, Swift was the world's largest meat producer. The firm began in Chicago, in 1875; its growth was due to two technological break-throughs: the refrigerated car, and the first highly coordinated production and distribution network in the world.

Swift had a hegemonic presence in Argentina and Brazil throughout the twentieth century. However, the Brazilian operations were closed down in the early 1990s and, in 2005, the Argentinean operation was sold to JBS-Friboi, a meat company founded by a butcher in Brasilia, in the 1960s. In 2007, JBS-Friboi acquired Swift and Co., as well as Pilgrim's Pride, in North America, thus becoming the world's largest meat producer. The Swift–JBS case exemplifies the cycles that characterise industrial dynamics.

As previously mentioned, the meat industry was classified as a sunset industry in the analyses made in the late 1980s. Sunset industries were the mature, resources-intensive, low-growth industries, like shoes, textiles, steel and others. In contrast, the sunrise industries of the future would be younger, high-growth industries, like computers, consumer electronics, semiconductors and digital equipment. The latter gave rise to the knowledge industry, the knowledge-based industrial systems or creative industries, among other labels. 'Intangible assets are the lifeblood of creative and knowledge-intensive industries, which may be defined as those where value creation is disproportionately based on specialised, non-repetitious activities. These data indicate that such industries will be "fundamental to the creation of wealth in the future"' (Mudambi, 2008: 700). On the other hand, the sunset industries began to be gradually abandoned by incumbents in developed countries, creating opportunities for multinationals from emerging countries.

The case of the meat industry presented in the opening of this section is not exclusive; it happened and it is happening in other sunset industries. In the steel industry, on a smaller scale than India's Mittal and Tata Steel, Brazil's Gerdau and Companhia Siderurgica Nacional (CSN) gained important positions in the North American market through acquisitions. One of the companies acquired by Gerdau is

Chaparral Steel, a firm which was taken as an icon of the resurgence of the American steel industry. The same is happening in the cement industry. Votorantim is conquering markets in North America, following the Cemex example. Braskem has acquired Sunoco Inc and Dow's plants in the US and Europe.

In most of those cases, the acquired company is as large as or larger than the Brazilian parent company. In general, the incumbents lost competitiveness due to managerial and financial difficulties. Thus, the challenge of the Brazilian acquirers is to inject resources and make the turnaround of the acquired company. A study conducted by the Harvard Business School describing the intervention of JBS-Friboi on the newly acquired Swift and Co stresses that 'the company's [JBS'] culture prioritises simplicity, directness, and the absence of internal politics and egos, in operations, prizes efficiency, economies of scale, a lean cost structure, quality and operating as close to full capacity as possible. Led by one of sons of the founder, the intervention aims at "back to basics": management restructuring, getting incentives right, cost-reductions and cost-consciousness, operational improvements and increased productivity' (Bell and Ross, 2008).

Therefore, in the cases where Brazilian multinationals are replacing incumbents, their VCC implies that all organisational functions are performed in the foreign locations. The transfer of competences from headquarters to subsidiaries prioritises production and finance mainly. Depending on the stage of the acquired company, competences related to marketing and research and development (R&D) might remain relevant for the performance of the whole enterprise

Spaces created by multinationals from developed countries to establish global production networks (GPNs)

In the 1980s, influenced by the rise of the Japanese production model as a new best practice, the Brazilian subsidiary of General Motors (GM) began to change the way in which it related with suppliers, introducing new and stringent criteria to select their local suppliers. Sabo, a producer of sealing components, was among the selected ones. By becoming a certified supplier, Sabo was able to compete with other GM suppliers around the world to supply Opel's factories in Europe. However, to fulfil GM's requirements concerning supply followers, Sabo was expected to internationalise. In 1994, Sabo acquired Kako, a German autoparts producer. One of the important factors for Sabo's decision was the fact that Kako had developed distinctive competences in R&D, including strong links with German universities. After the acquisition, Sabo was upgraded, thus becoming a joint developer within the industry, supplying a large number of auto makers, including the top brands like BMW.

The above example illustrates the shift in the way in which pioneering multinationals reorganised their supply chains and the room of manoeuvre that was created for the emerging country multinationals. That is why: 'In many industries outsourcing has made scale an industry asset in the sense that economies of scale can be captured by outsourcing to contract manufacturers who, in the face of competition, pass on the benefits of scale' (Teece, 2009). In this process they create GPNs, involving emerging country firms which, eventually, might themselves become multinationals.

An important contribution to the understanding of GPN was made by Gereffi *et al.*, (2005), who highlight two critical issues: (a) the governance structure, i.e. authority and power relationships that determine how financial, material and human resources are allocated and flow within a chain; and (b) upgrading, meaning that to advance in the international context, companies in emerging countries have to initially join GPNs led by multinationals from developed countries, taking responsibility for activities that the latter are not interested in doing. Bartlett and Ghoshal (2000) observed that the biggest challenge is not to get in, but to climb up the GPN.

The Sabo case presented at the start of this section exemplifies insertion and upgrading in a producer-driven value chain, i.e. in a chain where the governance was exerted by a manufacturing firm like GM. However, there are other cases in buyer-driven value chains, i.e. when the governance is exerted by a commercial firm, not a manufacturing firm. Coteminas is another interesting example, having acquired Springs in the US, to penetrate in the American market with new brands (Wamsutta and Springmaid). In due time, Coteminas kept the high value-adding functions (marketing and R&D) in North Carolina, and transferred production to Mexico.

Therefore, a distinctive feature of emerging multinationals which link into GPNs is the rapid upgrading into higher value-adding activities.

The new frontiers created by regionalisation and globalisation

The North American Free Trade Area (NAFTA), Association of South-East Asian Nations (ASEAN) and African Economic Community (AEC) treaties aimed to integrate regional economies, with a view to increasing intra-regional trade. They are a strong inducement to regional internationalisation. The creation of the Mercosur was, for sure, a landmark in the internationalisation of Brazilian firms; it absorbed 36 per cent of the country's foreign direct investment (FDI) until 2002. The tax regime added to geographic proximity and smaller cultural distance justified the figure.

Data on the foreign operations of Brazilian enterprises in the Mercosur estimate that some 300 subsidiaries that originated from Brazil were set up in Argentina, profiting from the Mercosur tax breaks. This figure includes subsidiaries of Brazilian firms as well as affiliates of local multinational enterprise (MNE) subsidiaries, especially of those in the electromechanical and automotive sectors.

Tigre is a representative of the Brazilian multinationals that have a regional scope. Founded in 1941 as a producer of combs, at the end of the 1950s it invested in a project that was innovative for its time: PVC tubes and connections for hydraulic installations. Tigre developed a business model that was appropriate to the reality of the Brazilian market, which is extremely fragmented: sales occur in small quantities at more than 100,000 outlets spread throughout a territory where access is difficult. Anticipating the internationalisation of Brazilian firms, Tigre established a joint venture in Paraguay in 1977, and currently produces in eight South American countries and in the US. The expansion throughout South America was made through acquisitions, mainly. The subsidiaries might be characterised as local implementers (Birkinshaw and Morrison, 1995); they have productive facilities and the functions required for the localisation of production. Differently, the entry into the US required a joint venture with Drain, Waste and Vent (DWV), a local firm, and a greenfield plant. In the US, Tigre produces and sells its own products under the DWV brand.

Africa is also attracting Brazilian multinationals, especially in infrastructure and natural resources exploitation. The attraction is especially strong in the Portuguese speaking countries, like Angola, where Vale and Odebrecht have huge operations. Notwithstanding, due to the distances (as measured by the framework that identifies cultural, administrative, geographic and economic [CAGE] differences or distances between countries; Ghemawat, 2001), those companies have to implement a complete set of organisational activities and, additionally, include some which deal with the institutional voids characteristic of less developed countries.

Therefore, the shape of the VCC curve adopted by Brazilian multinationals which move to neighbouring Latin American and African countries remains the same: production and logistics are the activities performed at the subsidiaries, while R&D and marketing are kept at the home country.

Spaces occupied in globally competitive markets

Last, but not least, there are Brazilian companies that compete on an equal footing basis with the multinational global leaders. These more prominent cases are the ones most mentioned in studies on multinationals from emerging countries, starting with Dragon Multinationals referenced by Mathews (2006). We will highlight the cases of Embraer and Vale.

Embraer is the third largest producer of aircraft in the world, competing fiercely with Bombardier from Canada. Embraer's VCC is quite peculiar, due to the business model it developed, based on cooperation and risk sharing (Fleury and Fleury, 2011). Embraer is a leading company in decentralised manufacturing where its value chains encompass those of the partnering companies. For example, in the production of the model 170–195, Embraer has eleven risk partners, spread all over the world. These companies supply aircraft modules which are assembled at Embraer's headquarters in Brazil. Each one of those companies is responsible for the specific R&D and marketing activities. Embraer is classified as a systems integrator, according to Prencipe *et al.* (2003) and as a metanational enterprise, according to Doz *et al.* (2001).

Vale is also a world leader operating in the mining industry. Due to the business characteristics, Vale's VCC is radically different from Embraer's. Vale operates in two fronts: the first is extraction and primary transformation, where Vale operates in the US, Bahrain, France, Belgium, Norway and Canada. The second is mineral research, where Vale develops around 150 projects in twenty-one countries located in three continents. In Africa, Vale's investments centre on

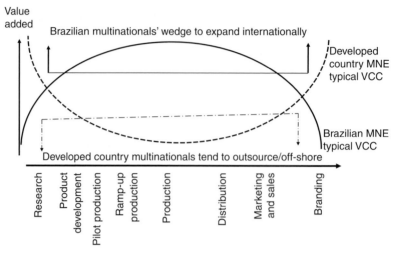

Figure 5.1 The distinct VCC shapes for developed vs. emerging country MNEs

deposits that are closer to the surface, which can be extracted more easily and consequently pose less risk. In mature countries, such as Australia, Canada and Chile, Vale employs cutting-edge technology to discover deeper deposits, besides pursuing partnerships with the firms that hold local mining rights.

The shape of Brazilian multinationals' value chains

In conclusion, Brazilian multinationals' internationalisation process has been broad-ranged, depending on international market entry conditions. In regards to their VCC, unlike developed country multinationals, Brazilian multinationals display a distinctive strategy. Such distinction is shown in Figure 5.1.

Figure 5.1 shows the developed country MNEs' VCC 'smiley' curve in contrast to the typical Brazilian multinationals' VCC. For developed country multinationals, production outsourcing/off-shoring is a long time reality and the actual discussion concerns the off-shoring of high value-adding activities, like R&D (Mudambi, 2008; Contractor *et al.*, 2011).

The curve picturing the Brazilian multinationals has an inverted shape, meaning that their core competences and, consequently, their high value-adding activities are associated with production. Their typical international value chain is represented by production located in foreign countries, mostly in wholly owned plants, and eventually, depending on the characteristics of country and subsidiary, some activities related to R&D, marketing and branding are kept abroad.

The preferences for international location: an aggregated analysis

In the previous section we analysed the way in which Brazilian multinationals configure their value chains under the constraints that are imposed by external circumstances, with an emphasis on the way in which their international competitors are setting their own value chains.

In this section we look at the VCC from another standpoint, namely the choices of Brazilian multinationals for the establishment of their value chains. We considered three factors which could be determinants of the configuration of Brazilian multinationals' value-chain activities: geographic region, the region's level of development and competitive conditions of the country.

(1) Geographic region: Latin America or anywhere else? The assumptions of the Nordic School, as well as Rugman's and Brain's theory of regionalisation (2003), lead us to hypothesise that Brazilian multinationals would show a preference to locate activities in Latin America. Minor cultural and geographic distances would reduce the liability of foreignness and allow cost advantages in operations, logistics and communication, reducing the transaction costs. Therefore, Latin American countries would be preferred in regards to investments and be more likely to receive the full set of value-chain activities than countries in distant regions. For these regions, investments would be more selective and focused on specific activities.

(2) The development stage of host countries: more or less developed than Brazil? Some authors, like Mathews (2006) and Child and Rodrigues (2005), argue that emerging country multinationals locate value-chain activities in developed countries as a way to boost their productive, technological and marketing efficiency, following an asset-seeking strategy in order to increase their competitive advantages. On the other hand, authors like Khanna and Palepu (1999a), Cuervo-Cazurra (2007) and Khanna *et al.* (2010)

admit that emerging country multinationals have a competitive advantage originated from operating in countries where there are institutional voids, and thus prefer to invest in less developed countries where institutional issues are also present: they could gain entry into those locations with ease of adaptation and strength to exploit gaps. That would be true especially if they are compared with multinationals from developed countries.

(3) Competitive conditions of countries: more or less competitive than Brazil? The pioneering studies about emerging country multi-nationals pointed out that they would prefer to move to countries with less competition, because that would bring them competitive advantages (Wells, 1983). However, the opposite may also be true: emerging country multinationals would establish their value chains where they can take advantage of the competitive environment, i.e. factor conditions, support companies, local demand and local competition (Porter, 1990), with learning effects that would result in competitive advantages (Guillen and Garcia-Canal, 2009).

To explore those preferences, we analysed data provided by a survey conducted in 2010–11 involving seventy-six subsidiaries of thirty-six Brazilian multinationals in different economic sectors. We assumed that the structure of each subsidiary could be assembled by five organ-isational activities: production (including manufacturing and logistics), marketing (including marketing, sales and customer relationship management), product/service development (including R&D and engineering), finance and human resources management. In the value-chains approach, the first three are related to value creation and the last two are related to support. Table 5.4 presents the relative participation of distinct types of subsidiaries' structures, thus revealing the shape of their VCCs.

Of the subsidiaries, 92 per cent perform activities directed to finan-cial management and 82 per cent in the human resources management domain.

We analysed the above distribution in regards to the three determinants for choices and preferences previously shown, resulting in Table 5.5.

Despite the limitations of the sample, some observations might be made. First, among the three assumptions, those that best distinguish why a subsidiary carries out a given activity in the international value chain are the region and the stage of the country's development.

Table 5.4 *The structure of activities performed in Brazilian subsidiaries*

Activities performed in the foreign subsidiary	Number	Percentage
Full subsidiaries (production + development + marketing)	32	42
Production plus marketing	9	12
Production plus product development	9	12
Production only	2	3
Product development only	0	0
Marketing only	14	18
Marketing plus product development	10	13
Total	76	100

Table 5.5 *The structure of preferences for the set up of VCC*

Activities performed by the subsidiary	Region	Developnent level	Competition
Full subsidiaries	LA	less	indifferent
Production plus marketing	indifferent	indifferent	indifferent
Production plus product development	indifferent	less	indifferent
Production only	indifferent	less	indifferent
Product development only	–	–	–
Marketing only	other than LA	more	indifferent
Marketing plus product development	LA	more	indifferent

Subsidiaries that perform the full set of activities are preferentially established in Latin America. Latin America is also prioritised in cases where the subsidiary performs basically marketing and product development activities, with production remaining in Brazil. Natura, a cosmetic producer, and Randon, a truck components producer located in the extreme south of the country, a region very close to the other Mercosur countries, are two examples. On the other hand, regions other than Latin America (Europe, North America and Asia) are preferred when the subsidiary performs activities related to marketing only. Havaianas, a producer of beach sandals, is a good example.

Brazilian coffee producers are establishing service chains in Asian countries, to brew coffee exported from Brazil.

Regarding the variable countries' stage of development, Brazilian multinationals, again, prefer to locate their overseas production activities in developing countries. That outcome seems to reinforce the Khanna *et al.* (2010) argument that that choice is related to their capacity to explore institutional voids in the host countries. The Brazilian investments in Africa and the perseverance to operate in unstable Latin American countries like Venezuela and Bolivia, exemplify that trend. On the other hand, when marketing activities are at the core of the internationalisation process, Brazilian multinationals prefer to settle in developed countries, probably to explore richest markets. Those outcomes open room for debate in regards to the applicability of Mathews' argument of the pursuit of knowledge and resources in the case of Brazilian multinationals in general. The choices reveal a distinct strategy, much more conservative in that regard.

Finally, the competitiveness dimension did not bring statistically significant evidences. From the factors that were analysed, infrastructural conditions, and the availability of a specialised workforce, appeared as influential to the choice of location when the subsidiary performs production activities abroad. Similarly, subsidiaries which carry out production activities in conjunction with marketing activities are influenced mostly by market conditions, i.e. high demand and strong competition.

To summarise, Latin America is the preferred location for the configuration of value chains not only for the arguments disclosed by the Nordic School and Rugman's regionalisation theory, but also due to the capacity of Brazilian multinationals to deal with institutional voids. On the other hand, when the investments do not contemplate production activities, other sites are preferred.

Are Brazilian multinationals using their VCCs to increase competitiveness?

The previous sections showed that Brazilian multinationals:

- rely very little on subcontracted off-shoring, as developed country multinationals currently do;
- prefer 'foreign in-house off-shoring' (Contractor *et al.*, 2011: 7) through the operation of foreign subsidiaries.

The question that remains is: how do Brazilian multinationals manage their value chains for the creation of competitive advantages?

The answer to that question requires a longitudinal perspective, looking at the way in which their value chains evolve over time. Following the approach adopted in this paper, we understand that competitive advantages are built from organisational competences (Prahalad and Hamel, 1990; Teece *et al.*, 1997; Teece, 2009). Therefore, the quest is to understand how Brazilian multinationals use their VCC to improve their organisational competences.

With that aim, we compared the outcomes of two surveys about 'Organisational competences and competitive strategies of Brazilian multinationals', the first conducted in 2006 and the second in 2010/2011 respectively.

We assumed that:

(1) every firm has to manage strategically five key competences: production, marketing, product/service development, financial and human resources management;
(2) the way in which value chains are managed aims at upgrading the firm's organisational competences and creates competitive advantages; organisational learning is the key process.

The data analysis showed that in 2006:

- headquarters prioritised the transfer of competences related to production and finance, followed by the marketing and human resources management competences;
- the product and services development competence was the only one whose intensity of transfer was statistically smaller than the other four;
- the transfer of competences from subsidiaries to headquarters presented a very low intensity for the five types of competences.

That suggests that the headquarters were very much concerned in assuming the control of the subsidiaries which, in their turn, were expected to improve their operational and financial performance with minor changes in their product lines.

The picture changed substantially in 2011:

- the transfer of marketing and financial competences from the headquarters to the subsidiaries became more intense, indicating that those areas began to work under a global perspective, centralised at the headquarters;

- the transfer of production competence decreased significantly while the transfer of product/service development increased significantly;
- in the other direction, the transfer of production competences from subsidiaries to headquarters increased significantly, while the transfer intensity of the other four competences remained low.

Therefore, the main change relates to the production competence: subsidiaries seem to have increased their competences in production up to a point that the headquarters consider interesting the reduction of the intensity of the transfer of that competence in their direction.

The growing status of subsidiaries is also revealed by the increasing flows of marketing and finance competences from headquarters to subsidiaries. As to the human resources competence, it stayed level throughout all statistical tests. This competence, considered a local competence in the sense of not being transferable (Rugman and Verbeke, 2001), is still a great challenge for Brazilian multinationals. In regards to the development competence, parent companies increased the intensity of transfer to subsidiaries to make them able to contribute to product and service development in a wider perspective. On the other hand, the reverse transfer increases only for production; the others stay level.

That outcome reveals an imbalance in which the headquarters are teaching their subsidiaries about every competence, but are learning from them only in what concerns the production competence. Therefore, even if Brazilian multinationals are doing their best to extract value from their international operations, the limits of that effort are clear. The learning process seems to be very much focused on the production sphere; the lessons that could be learnt in regards to the other four competences are yet to be better understood.

Conclusions

In their 2008 article on international supply chain development, Srai and Gregory first associate configuration with strategy realisation, and then differentiate between the configuration of the firm and the configuration of the supply network. Later, the authors introduce maturity as a key concept to understand the impact of configuration on performance. After their empirical research they conclude that 'The impact of configuration on performance requires a re-evaluation of maturity models where the link between process maturity and performance will require a configuration context' (Srai and Gregory, 2008: 407).

The concepts utilised by the authors seem highly pertinent to elaborate the final analysis of the Brazilian VCCs. As late-movers in the international markets, Brazilian multinationals are managing the transition between the configuration of the firm and the configuration of the network. That is a strategic challenge but, even though they are immature in international market operations, they seem to be still sticking to the former while gradually learning how to evolve to more open and complex ways of networking.

Brazilian multinationals have a distinct approach in relation to VCC when compared to developed country multinationals. While the latter are adopting a strategy to optimise the use of resources, the Brazilian multinationals' VCCs feature a high level of redundancy. Evidently, that can be attributed to their immaturity, but that does not cover the full spectrum of causations. Another general cause for that is the fact that they seldom exert the governance of global production networks. Only firms which are in governance positions in certain economic sectors where 'design rules' (Baldwin and Clark, 2000) are able to 'fragment themselves and after deconstruction decide in which nation the fragmented function can best be performed', as proposed by Contractor *et al.* (2011).

On the other hand, there are causes that seem to derive from the specific fact that they are Brazilian. Overall, it seems that they are very prudent in their internationalisation strategies. As we have shown, the internationalisation of Brazilian enterprises: (a) aims at replacing incumbents or becoming global followers; (b) would prefer to invest in Latin America due to smaller distances and the possibility of striving in unstable institutional settings; (c) seem to be extremely objective in their investments in the developed countries, through the minimisation of the operational structure of their local subsidiaries; (d) are still learning how to exploit the potential represented by their value-chain configurations.

Under that strategy their approach to the creation of competitive advantage has to be considered in relative terms: they seem to be extremely competitive in the areas where they have chosen to compete.

6 | Value-chain configurations of Russian EMNEs

VALERY S. KATKALO AND ANDREY G.
MEDVEDEV

The dynamic growth of multinational enterprises (MNEs) from emerging economies – mostly from so-called BRIC countries (Brazil, Russia, India and China) – is widely acknowledged as one of the key developments in the global economy in the last fifteen years. Today emerging market multinational enterprises (EMNEs) account for nearly one-tenth of the foreign sales and foreign assets of the top 500 multinationals in the world, compared to only 1–2 per cent in 1995 (UNCTAD, 2010). In the 2000s, the number of companies from emerging economies in the *Fortune Global 500* has more than tripled (from twenty-one to seventy-five).[1] In the new decade, competition between multinationals from developed countries and EMNEs with global aspirations (defined by Boston Consulting Group as 'global challengers') will continue to intensify. This new trend in globalisation of the world economy was reflected recently in booming interest in EMNEs in international business (IB) and strategic management (SM) fields, including publication of several books on the subject (Rugman, 2005; Goldstein, 2007; Casanova, 2009; Larcon, 2009; Ramamurti and Singh, 2009a).

Most of the existing EMNEs literature is either quite descriptive or is based on rather limited arguments in the early theoretical interpretations of foreign expansion of MNEs from emerging economies. Attempts to explain the growth of foreign direct investment (FDI) and reinforcement of EMNEs' positions with country-specific advantages (CSA) come across several difficulties. Reasoning based on CSAs could not suffice the need for our comprehensive understanding of the nature and mechanisms of EMNEs' competitive advantages. On one hand, today (as compared to the second half of the twentieth century) FDI is no longer the only attribute of multinational activities. Cross-border value-adding non-equity arrangements are gaining at least similar strategic importance for MNEs from both developed and emerging

---

[1] See http://money.cnn.com/magazines/fortune/global500/2012/full_list.

economies. On the other hand, firm-specific advantages (FSA) related to a firm's resources and capabilities are increasingly understood as even more critical than the CSA factor to explain evolving competitive advantages of EMNEs. This echoes the recent rise in importance of the business model concept in explaining (sustainable) differences in firms' performances by strategic management scholars. Thus, focusing on organisational forms (i.e. outsourcing structures and production value chains) used by EMNEs might be much more promising than traditional FDI- and CSA-centric approaches to analysis of their phenomena.

Also, there is a certain geographical imbalance in the existing studies of EMNEs. For example, Russian ones received much less attention than Chinese multinationals or 'global Latinas'. Partly this might be explained by the fact that Russian MNEs (RMNEs) were late-comers to the elite of global business, with a relatively small number of 'global challengers' for Russia. However, in 2008–9, Russia was among the top seven investors in the world by FDI outflows (UNCTAD, 2010), and several RMNEs are noticeable global leaders in the oil and gas sector and the metal industry, and a few more are emerging in other sectors. Thus, analysis of business models employed by MNEs from Russia may not only help in understanding these developments but contribute to comparative studies of competitive advantages of MNEs from BRIC countries.

In this chapter we undertake an initial attempt to analyse organisational aspects of RMNEs' competitive advantages, in particular their modes of value chain configuration and subsidiary management. The chapter is organised in five sections. In the first a brief summary of MNE theories and the rational for MNE's activity configuration is presented. In the second, MNE's industrial profile is considered as its strategic dimension. A framework for analysis of MNEs' activities configuration is developed in the third section. Strategic motives for international expansion of RMNEs and value-chain aspects of their FSAs are investigated in the fourth section. The fifth section is devoted to strategic roles of RMNEs' subsidiaries. Concluding remarks follow.

MNE theories and the rationale for MNE's activities configuration

Historically, the first explanations of MNE phenomena were proposed within IB studies. Many IB scholars tried to equate FDI and MNE theories (Caves, 1982; Buckley, 1990; Krugman and Obstfeld,

2006). In his turn, J. Dunning, who formulated the eclectic paradigm of FDI in the 1970s, emphasises that we cannot use FDI theories to explain strategic decisions in MNEs: 'the eclectic paradigm of international production is not (and has never purported to be) an explanation of the transnational or multinational *firm*' (Dunning, 2000). Among circumstances which limit the use of eclectic paradigm, Dunning mentions reconfiguration of MNEs' assets, clustering of firms and formation of industrial networks (Dunning, 1995).

Though investing in host countries is an obvious feature of an MNE, this mode of foreign operations is not the only one accessible to firms. Divisions of MNEs undertake operations of foreign trade, sign licensing agreements, create strategic alliances with foreign partners and participate in carrying out joint projects. That is why, synchronously with theoretical consideration of FDI, scholars are studying the nature of multinational firms, aiming at creation of the 'theory of MNEs' (Pitelis and Sugden, 2000) and analysing empirical data on MNEs' activities (Rugman and Verbeke, 2008). Teece (2009) put forward a proposal to form the 'MNE theory' by adding conclusions made within a resource-based concept to IB-theory (in particular, the eclectic paradigm).

Researchers of MNEs distinguish between the two groups of factors predetermining firms' competitive advantages: those caused by CSA and those with FSA. A CSA results from political, legal, economic, financial, cultural and labour qualification factors as well as access to natural resources. Some interesting observations on CSAs in emerging countries are presented in Ramamurti (2009b). In turn, FDI phenomena could be explained partly by the fact that the firm relies on internalisation advantage in order to realise its FSA which is defined as a unique capability proprietary to the firm. An FSA may be based on product or process technology, knowledge, managerial and logistic skills, marketing skills and brand names and the firm's ability to operate in emerging markets or within a multidomestic environment. Ramamurti (2009b) treats state support of some firms in emerging countries as an FSA for those firms as well.

As a tool to classify MNEs' strategies, Rugman (2005) proposed the CSA/FSA matrix where the focus is made on interactions of CSAs and FSAs with taking into account their relative strengths and weaknesses. In his paper devoted to analysis of MNEs from emerging countries (mainly from Asia), Rugman (2009) investigated CSAs and FSAs of these MNEs by applying the CSA/FSA matrix. The cell of the CSA/FSA matrix, characterised by a 'strong CSA–weak FSA' mix, generally indicates a place of resource-based and/or mature, internationally oriented firms producing a commodity-type product. Obviously, all Russian large MNEs operating in mining, oil and gas, metal-processing industries are in this cell. As for a 'strong FSA–weak CSA' combination, respective firms are usually differentiated firms with high-level marketing and customisation and strong brands. For such firms, home-country CSAs are not essential for their effectiveness. Such firms are uncommon among the large Russian MNEs.

According to Goldstein (2007), strategic management theory provides a useful complement to Dunning's ownership location internalisation (OLI) framework (Dunning, 1988) in understanding the activities of contemporary MNEs. Ramamurti (2009a) states that IB-theory could explain a lot about EMNEs, but not everything of interest to managers and policy makers. Gui (2010) proposed that although in the past multinational activities and FDI have been often used as synonyms, this assimilation appears today increasingly inaccurate.

MNEs' industrial profile as a strategic dimension

A wide use of SM-concepts in management of MNEs has led to implementation of the third element in the system of decision-making on firms' foreign operations, in addition to the country of operations and the firm itself, namely the industry (or *strategic business area*). Taking into account characteristics of an industry acts as an important factor in formulation of a foreign expansion strategy. First of all, it is necessary to distinguish multidomestic and global industries which differ in the degree of national responsiveness. The patterns of competition in multidomestic and global industries were described in Porter (1986b). Grant (2008) adds two more types of industries to the two, namely sheltered industries (where there is practically no internationalisation) and trading industries (where internationalisation does not need FDI). Today Russian MNEs are represented mainly in global and trading industries.

To explain strategic alternatives of MNEs from emerging countries one may use the 'integration – responsiveness' framework (Prahalad and Doz, 1987). Large Russian MNEs pursue more often either a global or a transnational strategy, characterised by rather ramified value chains where operations conducted in different countries are tightly integrated.

Based on research results achieved in SM studies, we can argue that the choice of a foreign operation mode by firms should be defined not only by knowledge about the target country accumulated at the given stage of the firm's internationalisation (through the learning process), but also by a whole set of strategic factors. It means that foreign operation mode selection has to support the chosen strategic alternative (Hill *et al.*, 1990; Cullen and Parboteeah, 2005; Lasserre 2007). Among the factors influencing the choice of foreign operation mode, we could mention the firm's strategic goals, its resources and capabilities, regulation in the target country and political risks, nature of its product and the market (industrial environment and industrial risks), geographical and cultural 'distance' and need for control over foreign operations. For example, by implementing its corporate internationalisation strategy, Gasprom uses a diversified set of foreign business operations: exports of raw materials, processing on a tolling basis, establishing joint ventures with foreign partners, participation in large infrastructural projects and direct investment in manufacturing facilities abroad.

The limited number of sectors where Russian MNEs operate confirms that the industry factor has direct influence on opportunities of Russian firms to expand internationally and on foreign expansion modes used by Russian firms. Different levels of development in various sectors in the national economy strongly predetermine their net outward investment positions. Therefore, the model of investment development path (Dunning, 2000) cannot explain dynamics and directions of FDI flows being applied to the Russian economy as a whole. In Russia, particular sectors are at different stages of the investment development cycle.

For this reason, opportunities for Russian firms from different industries to turn into global players differ. Large Russian MNEs operate in mining, oil and gas, nuclear energy, metallurgy, chemicals and telecoms. It is hardly possible to expect that a Russian MNE may appear in tobacco or brewing as the manufacturing process in these industries in Russia is carried out by subsidiaries of large MNEs from different countries.

Taking into account the nature of the industry and the pressure for national responsiveness, it is perhaps not surprising that there are only a few large Russian MNEs in multidomestic industries. Historically, experience of Russian firms in carrying out operations in other countries is limited, which explains the low level of ability of Russian firms to adapt their strategies and operations to multiple business environments. In global industries, Russian firms have to compete on a truly global basis; in these industries the pressure for national responsiveness is limited. It motivates Russian firms to expand their operations abroad and opens good opportunities to participate in formation of global value chains by applying a wide spectrum of foreign operation modes.

Value-chain configuration in global industries

As a promising framework emerged within SM, a global value-chain approach may help researchers study international inter-firm transactions (Gui, 2010). In this chapter we argue that value-chain configuration and roles of subsidiaries in global industries are probably becoming as important for understanding competitive advantages of Russian MNEs as the support they receive from the Russian government and the positive demand factors in the global markets for natural resources. The value-chain concept extended to cross-border operations of MNEs (*global value-chain* concept) allows managers to formulate clearly a decision as to where to locate separate operations – in other words, to design a configuration of an MNE's activities. Configuration of an MNE's activities may be geographically dispersed or geographically concentrated (Porter, 1986b).

By extending the value-chain analysis to cross-border operations, managers of 'global' (in terms of Prahalad and Doz, 1987) MNEs analyse location-specific advantages which allow the firm to realise *location economy* (like *scale economy* and *scope economy*). The location economy effect is used in 'global factories', allowing MNEs to optimise a configuration of their activities. It is clear that for locating some activities it is not necessary to put an affiliate 'closer to the market'; sometimes, it is more important if a firm is located in a country with cheap raw materials, R&D centres, skilled or inexpensive human resources and access to cheaper financial sources.

Configuration of an MNE's activities predetermines the nature of interactions between its divisions (between the parent and each of its subsidiaries as well as between subsidiaries) and interactions between the MNE's divisions and their external environment (suppliers,

	Cell 1	Cell 3
Large firms	Large MNEs Lukoil, Rosneft, NLMK, Evraz, Rusal, MTS, VimpelCom	Large internationalising firms VSMPO Avisma, Elbrus, Unipro
	Cell 2	Cell 4
Small firms	Mini-MNEs Mai, Dionis Club, Turris	Small internationalising firms
	Value-chain builders	Network joiners

Figure 6.1 The 'value role–company size' matrix

customers, partners, etc.). With the external environment, the MNE's value chain may be transformed into an 'industrial network'. The global firm may be considered today as a set of activities dispersed among the MNE's divisions and its strategic partners located in various geographic points (thus having an appropriate configuration). Such a notion has been reflected in a concept of strategic assembly of global firms, an approach allowed to design an effective strategic organisation of the MNE (Koza *et al.*, 2011).

Because of historical circumstances, Russian firms operating in global industries (as well as firms from some other emerging economies) began their internationalisation rather late. They faced two options: to try to build an integrated value chain themselves, or to join their operations with any existing (or under formation) value chain (in the form of a global production network). We call MNEs selecting the former option 'value-chain builders', while those selecting the latter 'network joiners'. If, in addition to this distinction, we use one more dimension, 'company size', we may construct a typology matrix which can serve for classification of firms from emerging markets. Our 'value role–company size' matrix presented in Figure 6.1 provides a useful framework for analysis of Russian MNEs and their strategies as clustered in four types of firms operating in global industries.

In Cell 1, large MNEs building integrated value chains are located. They may be integrated operators carrying out both vertical and horizontal expansion abroad, for example Russian oil and gas and metal-processing firms such as Lukoil, Rosneft, Novolipetsky metal plant (NLMK) and Evraz. They may also be resource-seekers usually undertaking backward vertical integration, acquiring sources of raw materials and their primary processing facilities as done by metallurgical and chemical firms (Rusal, EuroChem). Finally, they may be market-seekers implementing horizontal foreign expansion, entering markets of other countries, for example Russian mobile operators (VimpelCom, MTS) and some banks and insurance companies.

In Cell 2, mini-MNEs are located, which act as resource-seekers or market-seekers. The growth of small- and medium-sized multinationals (mini-MNEs) has been a recent trend in international business (Hill, 2007). We can name Russian small- and medium-sized enterprises in the food-processing sector which invest abroad in agricultural or industrial assets, used for manufacturing products oriented first at the Russian market (Mai, Dionis Club, Nevskiye Siri). Here, we also mention a small number of Russian mini-MNEs operating in the catering and hospitality sector (GMR Planeta gostepriimstva, Turris).

Cell 3 is for large firms which are not going to form their own value chain, but which can be integrated into existing or newly created production networks. Examples are Russian *suppliers* of certain (often unique) resources to other firms in the value chain (e.g. VSMPO Avisma, the largest world supplier of titanium, which is incorporated in value chains of Boeing and Airbus, as well as in chains of manufacturers of aircraft engines). Another group of firms here are Russian *efficiency providers* (e.g. Severnoye Siyaniye, a Russian cosmetics factory, which was acquired by Unilever in 1994 and later concentrated gradually on manufacturing certain products delivered to the markets across Europe). One more group of firms in Cell 3 are *technology providers* (e.g. Elbrus and Unipro, two prominent Russian research centres with highly skilled computer specialists, which signed an agreement with Intel in 2004 and are part of its value chain). Finally, in the same cell, are Russian firms – marketing satellites which distribute products produced by global MNEs in the Russian market (e.g. dealers of leading global automakers).

In Cell 4, the same types of Russian enterprises may be located as in Cell 3, with the only difference being that they are relatively small internationalising firms.

Strategic motives for foreign expansion of Russian MNEs

MNEs from BRIC countries are often motivated by strategic considerations rather than by short-term financial aims, partly reflecting the
role of state-owned enterprises in foreign expansion of the group.
Ramamurti (2009b) distinguishes five generic strategies, which
EMNEs may follow: natural-resources vertical integrator, local optimiser, low-cost partner, global consolidator and global first-mover.
These generic strategies are based on a mix of different CSAs and FSAs
and result in a distinct internationalisation path.

Among Russian MNEs, a big group may be presented as a natural-
resources vertical integrator; alternatively, Russian firms focused on
operations in the Commonwealth of Independent States (CIS) may
pursue a strategy close to that of a local optimiser. With a rise in factor
costs of manufacture in Russia, Russian firms can hardly play the role
of low-cost partner. Some elements of the global consolidator strategy
can be found in activities of Russian metal-processing firms. As for
global first-movers, only a limited number of Russian firms really own
high technologies and know-how which could find global application,
though in the last decade the idea of technological leadership finds an
active political support in Russia.

The next step of the study aims to understand how to connect such
determinants of internationalisation of Russian firms in a parent
company role, strategic motives for foreign expansion, ways to create
value and design of an effective trajectory of internationalisation. The
same determinants may be matched further with roles of foreign
subsidiaries of Russian MNEs. A consideration of the experiences of
many Russian MNEs leads to the conclusion that in most cases the
parent companies play the roles of integrated operator, resources
seeker, market seeker, technology seeker or, to a lesser extent, technology provider. This conclusion is in line with the observation that
firms from emerging economies internationalise not to transfer their
core competences abroad, but rather to gain access to resources and
capabilities (Mathews, 2006). A generalised list of internationalisation
determinants for some RMNCs is presented in Table 6.1. As seen,
internationalisation of RMNEs may be predetermined by various
strategic motives, connected, in particular, with FSA development.
Among such motives could be access to missing assets and maintenance of effective balance between elements of the value chain, access to

Table 6.1 *Internationalisation determinants for Russian MNCs*

Russian MNCs' parent role	Integrated operator	Resource seeker	Market seeker	Technology seeker	Technology provider
Examples	NLMK, Rosneft, Lukoil, Gazprom	Acron	Norilsk Nickel, VimpelCom, MTS	Lukoil	Atomenergoprom
Industry	Global	Global	Global, mixed (with a multidomestic component)	Global	Global
Strategic goals of internationalisation	Access to assets	Access to resources	Access to markets and end-customers	Access to technology	Technology exploitation
Way to create value	Synergy, location economy	Location economy	Transferring competence, developing marketing competence	Global learning	Transferring competence
Modes of internationalisation	Acquisitions, ISAs	Acquisitions	Acquisitions, greenfields	Acquisitions, ISAs	ISAs
Value-chain direction	Both horizontal and vertical expansion	Vertical backward	Horizontal and vertical forward expansion	Both horizontal and vertical expansion	Vertical forward
Subsidiary role	Rational manufacturer, product specialist	Resource supplier	Rational manufacturer, marketing satellite, autonomous	Technology provider	Receptive subsidiary

resources and markets, access to technologies, brands and management competencies and exploitation of technological potential.

Integrated operators try to gain an access to missing assets in order to balance a product portfolio and to maintain an effective balance between elements of the value chain. These firms look for synergy and location economy as the main way to create value. Thus, NLMK acquired a 50 per cent stake in Luxembourg Steel Invest and Finance, a joint venture with Italian Duferco. Thanks to this transaction, the Russian company could reduce a share of products with low added value with more volatile prices, and increase a share of products with high added cost in its portfolio. Rosneft, a Russian state-owned oil and gas company, declared its goal to acquire 50 per cent of Ruhr Oel, which owns five oil refining plants in Germany, from Venezuelan PDVSA. This would allow Rosneft to increase its processing-to-extraction ratio from 44 to approximately 55 per cent. Managers of Lukoil have set a goal to reach the balance between volumes of processing and extracting oil at the level of 70 per cent (for comparison: ConocoPhillips has almost 100 per cent, ExxonMobil 240 per cent). By 2010, Lukoil capacities in processing were about 70 million tonnes per year, of which 25 million tonnes were abroad (in Bulgaria, Romania, Italy and the Netherlands). At the moment, Lukoil processes about 62 per cent of extracted oil.

Resource seekers create value by realising location economy. Acron, a Russian chemical group, one of the leading world manufacturers of mineral fertilisers, pursues a strategy of vertical integration since the beginning of 2000s. Therefore, plants for raw materials extraction, logistical and marketing companies were added to the group structure in addition to industrial divisions. As part of the strategy, Acron undertakes projects on development of phosphates and potash salt deposits. In particular, the group has licences for geological works at thirty-six sites of a potash salt deposit in Saskatchewan, Canada.

Market seeking RMNEs try to facilitate foreign market entry with their products (for example, in the EU or the US) by acquiring manufacturing capacities in the target countries. In 2003, Norilsk Nickel got the control (51.3 per cent of shares) of Stillwater, the only American company to manufacture palladium and platinum. Managers of Norilsk Nickel recognised that combining mineral stocks of Norilsk Nickel with the client base of Stillwater would provide mutual benefits for both partners. Norilsk Nickel planned to sell palladium to its new affiliate. Since 2004, Norilsk Nickel started to sell its metal products in the US independently. Thanks to Stillwater, Norilsk Nickel received access to large clients in the US. Long-term contracts were signed with Ford Motor Company and Chrysler. For firms operating in multi-domestic industries, the ability to adapt the products and services for local markets effectively is of great importance. Gradually accumulating experience in foreign markets at the initial entry stages, managers of these firms have an opportunity to use new knowledge and skills at the subsequent stages of foreign expansion. VimpelCom, a major Russian telecoms corporation, conducts active operations in several CIS countries (Kazakhstan, Ukraine, Tajikistan, Uzbekistan, Georgia and Armenia). In some of these markets VimpelCom builds new networks as greenfield projects, in others it has acquired already existing assets. Acquisition of Armentel in Armenia has provided it with experience in development of services in fixed-line communication. It was the first experience of telecoms service of the third generation when VimpelCom started this project in Tajikistan. Later, accumulated experience was transferred to other VimpelCom divisions, including Russian ones.

Foreign expansion of *technology seeking* RMNEs may pursue the aim of getting the technologies necessary for effective development of the MNE's business. Since Russian oil and gas MNEs have no competitive technologies of extraction of hydrocarbons from offshore deposits, they are limited in their possibilities to participate in many prospective projects. For example, in the recent years Russian Lukoil has actively developed extraction operations abroad. In 2007, Lukoil Overseas, a Lukoil subsidiary, entered into the agreement with American oil and gas company Vanco Energy to acquire 56.66 per cent of three projects in geological exploration and working out of prospective deep-water sites at an offshore deposit of Ghana in Guinea Gulf. The partnership with Vanco Energy should help Lukoil acquire the experience necessary for participation in prospective offshore projects.

In industries where Russian firms are technological leaders, they may serve as *technology providers*. In such cases, foreign expansion is pursued to increase the return on investment in new technologies due to economies of scale. In 2009, Atomenergoprom, an arm of the state-owned Rosatom corporation, signed an agreement with

Japanese Toshiba Corporation to participate in joint projects on enrichment of uranium for the power energy sector in Japan, and to undertake joint actions on the Asian commodities and services market through the nuclear fuel cycle. Russia is the world leader in technologies of enrichment of uranium, whereas Toshiba is considered as the leading company in nuclear power plant construction. Thanks to cooperation with Toshiba, the Russian firm can access new nuclear fuel cycle markets.

Generalising experiences of Russian MNEs confirms that because of their limited FSAs, parent companies of RMNEs rarely play the role of parental developers and competence transferers. This may also explain why RMNEs almost never undertake greenfields. Operating mainly in global industries, RMNEs usually serve as synergy managers or integrators, trying to develop their value chains by adding either missing assets through horizontal expansion or complementary assets through vertical integration or related diversification. These additional assets are typically added to RMNEs' value chains through acquisitions.

Strategic roles of RMNEs' subsidiaries

The configuration of the MNE's value chain is predetermined by a choice of location of all kinds of operations and also by a choice of strategic role of each foreign subsidiary. A study of MNEs' subsidiary roles and their evolution over time usually sees the subsidiary as a value-adding activity outside the MNE's home country (Birkinshaw, 2001). There are several streams of research on roles of MNEs' subsidiaries; many of them emphasise the growing importance of subsidiaries as sources of competitive advantage for the whole MNE. These sources could be leveraged on a global basis (Bartlett and Ghoshal 1986; Birkinshaw and Hood, 2001).

Combining a dynamic approach to the internationalisation process with analysis of sequences of value-added activities makes it possible to identify several patterns of establishment of foreign subsidiaries by MNEs from emerging economies based on combination of location advantages in the country of origin and the host country (Cuervo-Cazurra, 2007). Though the sequences of internationalising value-added activities by MNEs from emerging countries may differ from those by MNEs from developed economies, the basic decision-making model includes the same set of determinants of strategic roles of subsidiaries as well as of headquarters–subsidiary relations.

The strategic role of each MNE's subsidiary still depends to a great extent on *internal characteristics of the MNE* such as corporate values, its vision, developed competencies and corporate strategy. The corporate strategy describing product, vertical and geographical scope is defined by the multidomestic or global nature of an industry, as well as by the global consolidation rate and degree of competition in the industry. Overall internationalisation goals of the MNE and, in some cases, the MNE's country of origin may also be seen as the MNE's characteristics which influence strategic roles of the subsidiary.

The subsidiary role depends also on *country characteristics*, namely characteristics of particular markets in a host country, access to necessary resources, political and legal conditions of conducting business in the country and on general strategic importance of the country as a destination of MNE's expansion. The combination of MNE's characteristics and characteristics of the target country predetermines *formation of goals* of MNE's business operations in the country. *Resources and capabilities* of the subsidiary may also be seen as a factor affecting its strategic role within an MNE.

In global and transnational MNEs, roles of integrated affiliates in host countries may vary substantially, meeting goals of the selected strategic alternative. Thus, roles of Russian MNEs' subsidiaries are often defined based on strategic motives of the MNEs. Foreign subsidiaries serving as 'resource suppliers', 'technology providers' and 'brand leaders' may be either acquired or established by the RMNEs seeking an access to resources, technologies and brands. A market-seeking RMNE will implement a 'marketing satellite' affiliate into its value chain. To maintain an effective balance between elements of the value chain and have an access to missing assets, RMNEs will appoint 'rational manufacturers of components or finished goods' or 'product specialists'. In the case of exploration of its technological potential, an RMNE may search for a 'receptive subsidiary' abroad.

Roles of subsidiaries in multidomestic and home-replication MNEs are rather clear; they are roles of either an autonomous or a receptive subsidiary, often coordinating its operations with operations of other divisions of the MNE. Thus, in multidomestic industries, RMNEs may own enough autonomous foreign subsidiaries, providing their parents with new local knowledge and experience.

Conclusions

After the recent decade of rapid growth of Russian MNEs, they have become a new and quite visible phenomenon in the contemporary global economy, though still limited in their importance mostly in the natural resources sector. While industry factor is very important for differences in strategic motives for internationalisation intensity and modes undertaken by MNEs, SM concepts provide a useful addition to IB theories in understanding current activities of Russian MNEs. Large Russian MNEs usually pursue either global or trans-national strategies which are characterised by rather ramified value chains where operations conducted in different countries are tightly integrated. Variations in development of separate industries in national economies predetermine to a great extent a balance between inward and outward FDI.

There are only few large Russian MNEs in multidomestic industries. Historically, experience of Russian firms in conducting operations in other countries is limited, which explains the low level of ability of Russian firms to adapt their strategies and operations to multiple business environments. RMNEs operating in multidomestic industries have to apply a different business model in each country, thus grad-ually acquiring the necessary experience of undertaking activities in multiple environments.

In global industries, Russian firms have to compete on a truly global basis. Historically, Russian firms operating in global industries (as well as MNEs from other emerging economies) started their internationali-sation process rather late. They faced a dilemma, either to try to design integrated value chains themselves or to join their operations with any existing (or being under formation) global production network. In the former case, RMNEs are really involved in integrated global value chains; in the latter case, they position themselves as niche players supplementing a value chain of a large MNE with their activities.

Considering the experiences of many Russian MNEs, we can draw the conclusion that in most cases their parent companies play roles of integrated operator, resources seeker, market seeker and technology seeker or, to a lesser extent, technology provider. At the same time, internationalisation of RMNEs may be predetermined by various stra-tegic motives, connected, in particular, with FSA development. Among such motives, one may name not only an access to resources and markets, scale economy and achieving synergies, but also access to new technologies, brands and management competencies.

Russian firms often internationalise their operations not to transfer their competencies abroad but rather to gain access to resources and capabilities of other firms. More and more, internationalisation is pursued to reach competitive advantages for RMNEs by gaining access to missing assets and effective integration (in the form of vertical integration or participation in global production networks). For example, RMNEs in the oil and gas sector try to reach a more effective balance between elements of the value chain, in particular by increasing the role of downstream operations. Among other motives, one may mention exploitation of technological potential and defensive investments to protect competitive positions of the MNE.

In the new decade, Russian MNEs are to find their own solutions to stand and win in the three key battles with companies from developed markets: a battle for emerging customer segments, a battle for industry leadership and a battle for new markets (Boston Consulting Group, 2011). To meet all these challenges, Russian MNEs must develop their own business models – both comparable with best world management practices and powerfully unique to support strong global competitive positions.

7 | Value-chain configurations of Indian EMNEs

SUMA ATHREYE

Approaches to explaining the internationalisation of emerging market MNEs and the relevance of value chains

What motivates emerging market firms to venture abroad? A leading approach, the ownership location internalisation (OLI) theory (Dunning, 1988), explains the internationalisation activity of multinational corporations (MNCs) as their attempts to extend their ownership advantages (e.g. proprietary access to a superior production technology or a valuable brand) to overseas markets by exploiting location advantages (locating abroad to access low cost inputs or better serve local markets) and internalising the efficiency gains from economies of scale and scope by integrating the firm's activities across borders. In short, FDI enables firms to exploit their existing firm-specific assets.

This explanation has limited traction when analysing the internationalisation activity of MNEs from emerging markets (EMs). As latecomers, multinational enterprises from EMs are often more competitive in terms of cost of labour and natural resources compared to mature MNEs from developed markets (Ramamurthi and Singh, 2009a). However, many of these companies lack global experience and so have weak technological and innovation capabilities, have inexperienced managerial and professional expertise and show poor governance and accountability by international standards (Luo and Tung, 2007). Furthermore, to the extent that the cost advantages are generic to all suppliers from other EMs, we can expect such advantages to dissipate over time as the global market shares to EM firms expand and bid up wages in these economies. Thus, Rugman and Li (2007) have questioned the long-term sustainability of such internationalisation based on cost advantages for Chinese firms in the absence of clear ownership advantages.

Other research on MNEs from emerging economies has suggested that ownership advantages may lie in 'capabilities' beyond proprietary assets such as patents, trademarks and brands. Kumar (2007) has argued that the term ownership advantage should be enlarged to include the specific capabilities of developing country firms. Some firms from India and China have acquired a niche in 'frugal engineering' – the ability to manufacture low-cost versions of goods for mass markets. It could even be that forms of corporate governance forged to cope with restrictive regulatory regimes in domestic economies may have created a resilience that provides a comparative advantage in alien markets.

The expansion of the range of 'O' advantages however begs the question, 'What is the nature of competition and rivalry that EM firms face?' The O and I advantages of the OLI model suggest competing with other firms on the basis of non-price advantages (Buckley and Casson, 1976; Rugman, 1981). In an early paper on the OLI model, Caves (1986) argued that the paradigm probably makes sense only in the context of horizontal MNEs as ownership advantages are neither necessary nor sufficient for vertical investments where coordinating the entire value chain may be the essential capability that is commercialised. In fact, revisiting the OLI paradigm, Dunning (1995) also suggests the first version of the OLI assumed complete value chains. Thus we are left with a rather imprecise understanding of the nature of rivalry in the OLI paradigm but it is probably based on control of value chains by firms operating in distinct geographical markets. The OLI paradigm also probably assumes non-cooperative behaviour between firms. As Devinney (2003) recognises the joint creation of proprietary assets such as through strategic alliances poses a problem for OLI.

The 'linkage, leverage, learning' (LLL) pardigm developed by Mathews (2006) aims to fix these deficiencies of the OLI paradigm and keeps the idea of value chains centre stage in the analysis. It captures the idea that 'latecomer' firms will use their overseas investments and global linkages to leverage their existing cost advantage and learn about new sources of competitive advantage. If so, internationalisation may in fact contribute to the building of ownership advantages rather than merely be an outcome of existing advantages. This argument, based mainly on the experience of East Asian multinationals, is not necessarily reversing received wisdom: empirical research has found that the relationship between ownership advantages and outward foreign direct investment (FDI) is weak.

Thus, in contrast with the OLI, the implicit view of the industry in the LLL paradigm is a vertically disintegrated industry or a global value chain. Here, the competition is between producers in a segment of a value chain but there is cooperation across segments of the value chain. Thus, Japanese auto producers benefited from the lowering of costs and improvement in quality of components due to competition among their auto part suppliers from Taiwan and Korea. Rents from growing market share are shared between all those who participate in the value chain. Put differently, strong incumbents benefit from a deepening specialisation within the industry and low-cost producers from emerging markets have a role to play as they can increase the size of overall profit even if they get to keep only small shares of it.

Global suppliers, own value chains and the sources of competitiveness

The foregoing discussion suggests that emerging market multinational enterprises (EMNEs) have only a limited space for internationalisation (a fact also noted by the Brazilian chapters in this book) and this may consign them to acting as global suppliers for Western MNEs – what the chapter on Russia terms as joint value-creating activities. Conditional on this first choice, the ability of EMNEs to grow and become sustainable MNEs in their own right depends crucially on the sources of competitiveness that they can exploit for their future growth. This chapter offers contrasting insights from two sectors in India.

The dominant business model in the Indian software sector is offshore delivery of software development services. By positioning themselves as independent vendors of software services to many MNEs, Indian software firms have chosen to grow internationally through horizontal rather than vertical integration. Correspondingly their own value chains are rather short and their main competitive resource is the endowment of a large trained labour population and the ability to scale up software production through the deployment of firm-specific organisational routines and delivery mechanisms. Most Indian firms have kept the delivery of software production off-shore in India and although they maintain several international subsidiaries they are more like marketing outposts that bring work back to their multiple development centres located in Indian towns.

In contrast to software, some firms in the pharmaceutical industry have tried to actively compete in the generics markets and the discovery of new drugs where the value chain that they must master is much longer. For these firms internationalisation and also international alliances have offered ways by which to fill gaps in their own value-chain configuration and to renew the bases of their competitive strengths. Here we see clearer examples of how firms tried to use internationalisation and subsidiary management to their competitive advantage. Thus, since 1995, Ranbaxy and Doctor Lifeline Remedies (India) Ltd (DRL) used international acquisitions of the US Food and Drug Administration (FDA)-approved plants to both acquire market shares in new geographies and jump nation-specific regulatory hurdles. DRL also drew thirteen patents from its overseas research and development (R&D) laboratory, Reddy US Therapeutics Inc (RUSTI). Both Ranbaxy and DRL have out-licensed new molecules to pharma firms as part of their forays in drug discovery.

Yet by 2010 there were signs that the core 'generics' businesses of both Ranbaxy and DRL were in trouble. Ranbaxy's generic business was bought by Tokyo-based Daichi Sanyo in 2008, with their chief R&D officer having already exited to found his own drug discovery company. In 2010, the family-controlled Dr Reddy's denied that it was in talks to sell its generics business in India to US pharmaceutical giant Pfizer, which had been suing the company for alleged patent infringement. These developments suggest that internationalisation has not delivered enough by way of new competitive advantages for these large firms, and yet they are vulnerable to take over from incumbents with deep pockets. In the remainder of this chapter, we examine the software and pharma experiences in turn.

Labour pools, business model innovation and the internationalisation of Indian software firms

International investment by Indian software firms started in the late 1980s, with subsidiaries of Hindustan Computers Limited (HCL) and Infosys, two of the largest domestic firms (Pradhan, 2007a). By 2007, India's FDI in software represented over $8 billion, with 165 Indian software companies with a total of 645 subsidiaries abroad

(Niosi *et al.*, 2009). The affiliates – most often wholly owned subsidiaries – are located in the US and Canada (37 per cent), Europe (25 per cent), Asia (22 per cent), the Middle East (5 per cent), Oceania (3.5 per cent), Africa (2.6 per cent) and Latin America (2.3 per cent) (Niosi *et al.*, 2009). On a country-by-country basis, the US (221 subsidiaries), the UK (83) and Singapore (60) were the main destinations of Indian FDI in software. Germany (37), China (29) and Malaysia (20) follow. In terms of the number of foreign subsidiaries, the main MNCs from India are Tata Consultancy Services (47 subsidiaries) and HCL Technology (31) – both business group firms.

A noteworthy feature of Indian software firms and their internationalisation was that they developed a new business model to supply software services to their clients worldwide. The so-called global delivery model – which aimed to create software wherever it was cheap to produce and deliver it to customers anywhere in the world – was in essence a business model rooted in the comparative advantage logic.

In the context of the 1980s – when due to technological change, human capital with technical skills became more expensive in the West – Indian firms could have exploited the wage advantage of Indian software programmers in a variety of ways. Each of these ways represents a different business model. First, they could have sold their services in the manner of a labour contractor. The economic output in this model would be the service of matching labour demands with labour supplies. Alternatively, they could have devised a software or technology product utilising this cheap labour (as Israeli software firms did). Here, the economic output would have been the service provided by the software package that was written. Lastly, Indian firms could have used this cheaper labour to deliver an economic output that consisted of some customised software services to other firms. These are all examples of possible business models that could have been explored, given the starting point of an abundance of human capital.

In the three decades of its existence, the Indian software industry has successfully evolved two variants of the customised software services model: the provision of on-site as well as off-shore software services. The latter has a greater value-added component and also requires greater organisational capability on the part of the firm. These humble achievements rested on a decade-long experimentation that saw firms reject the product model in favour of the service model (Athreye, 2005).

Tata Consultancy Services, which pioneered this business proposition in the 1980s, did so because they perceived that they did not have the same opportunities in developing software products and marketing them. In an interview, one of their senior mangers put their choice in the following terms: 'TCS did not create the product market, and that was the subtle difference'. TCS understood well the problems of market creation. It chose outsourcing to large MNEs as a way to avoid addressing the issue of who would buy its products. In choosing this path, the company also recognised the potential that such contracts offered for technology upgrading. In this respect, its strategy was similar to that of firms in the four 'dragon' countries (Taiwan, South Korea, Hong Kong and Singapore). However, the takeover bid for TCS by Burroughs (with whom TCS had a long alliance) also showed the limits of this model. Later firms (such as Infosys) would find contractual ways of avoiding this problem and use client diversification as an important means to obviate such takeover threats.

The large-scale outsourced business model (which would be delivered to multiple clients) was developed in response to booming external demand but required certain complementary organisational capabilities: an ability to scale up quickly in response to the growth in demand, abilities in human resource management, capabilities in software process management (to ensure fewer errors and reliability of the service product) and lastly, given that customers were largely overseas, an ability to manage global operations. Indeed the offshore business model would not have been successful without these parallel organisational capabilities. Athreye (2005) shows that during the 1990s a number of Indian software firms (such as Infosys) developed these process capabilities. The business model innovation that underlies the successful internationalisation by Indian software firms thus forced them to specialise in particular sub-segments of the larger value chain underlying the provision of full software solutions.

Since 2000, there has been an increasing presence of Indian software firms in the business process outsourcing (BPO) segment. The integration of BPO activities with traditional software outsourcing functions allowed large-value contracts to be bagged by Indian software companies who aimed to provide an integrated suite of services to their clients. Large software companies entered this segment either by acquiring equity in an existing third-party facility or by setting up their own unit. Thus, Wipro acquired Spectramind and IBM acquired

Daksh e-Services; while Infosys and Satyam set up their own subsidiaries – Progeon and Nipuna, respectively. Their BPO arms benefited from the brand identity and reputation that they established in providing software services. The downstream integration into lower value BPO activities enabled software firms to grab a larger share of the value chain from their clients.

Value-chain configuration and subsidiary roles in the internationalisation of Indian software firms

The strategic positioning of Indian software firms as independent vendors rather than as part of MNEs' supply chain has had advantages and disadvantages. The advantage has been relative independence and secure growth based upon a large demand. This growth has, however, come at the cost of remaining a generalist producer of software – a service that is fast approaching commodity status – as specialisation in any domain would make the firms highly dependent on a few customers. Second, a unique feature of the offshore model was that the production of software and BPO remained in India (close to the labour stocks). Scaling up production did not mean investing in organising a network of subsidiaries – rather small subsidiaries were set up in overseas locations to scope potential demand and support foreign customers.

Indian software firms could have integrated upstream e.g. through acquisitions of firms with domain expertise or consulting experience. Although a large number of Indian software firms listed on international markets with such intentions (see for example the HBS case study of Infosys) they have been very conservative with regard to actually making international acquisitions. This may be because of worries about organisational fit – for example, interviews with TCS employees at its Brazilian subsidiary revealed they were worried about the lack of capability maturity model (CMM) certification in many Brazilian firms, making them inappropriate targets. There may also be worries about internationalising the management team – Wipro chief Azim Premji declared this as the biggest challenge facing his company in its internationalisation effort.[1]

---

[1] Talk at London Business School, November 2006.

That said, business house subsidiaries like Wipro and TCS have been more ready to make the required investments in expanding their global footprint than their entrepreneurial counterparts such as Infosys or Patni Computers. It is reasonable to conjecture that business house conglomerates make different calculations about the costs and benefits of expanding their international investments than single industry firms.

Patent reform and the strategies of Indian pharmaceutical firms[2]

The market opportunities opened by the Indian Patent Act of 1970, the constraints for expanding the manufacturing base under the 'license raj' and the endogenous evolution of the market together determined the capabilities of Indian firms in the pre-liberalisation period. Market leadership belonged to firms that had competence in chemical process technologies necessary for reengineering targeted drugs and the ability to withstand technology races in process improvements through pursuing a diversified product portfolio. The common features of technological capabilities and strategy among all the leading firms included low R&D intensity, innovation focus on cost-efficient or quality-enhancing processes, direct commercialisation of innovation in countries where the product patent regime was not recognised and technology transactions with Western multinationals in the form of licensing and marketing agreements (which worked both ways).

The knowledge base of Indian pharmaceutical firms was firmly embedded in organic and synthetic chemistry and any R&D investment was specifically targeted to lower the costs of production of selected drugs identified as having good commercial prospects, with the outlays just to the point needed to arrive at the objective (Ramani, 2002). In 1992, only about 47 out of around 23,000 firms in the pharmaceutical sector registered positive R&D expenditures, of which only 7 companies spent more than 1.5 per cent of their sales revenue on R&D. Western multinationals also contributed very little to innovation creation in India. Between 1970 and 1995, only two multinationals in India (Ciba-Geigy and Hoechst) had more than two patents listed in the US Patent and Trademark Office (USPTO).

---

[2] This section draws on joint work with S.V. Ramani and D. Kale (Ramani *et al.*, 2009). I am indebted to these co-authors for sharing their interview transcripts with me.

Trade-Related Aspects of Intellectual Property Rights (TRIPS) introduced three main elements of change in the Indian patent system. It banned production and sales of reengineered pharmaceutical products, it extended product patent protection applied to all branches of manufacturing, including drugs, to twenty years, and it forbade discrimination between imported and domestic products.

Indian pharmaceutical firms adopted one or more of three types of strategic positioning in response to TRIPS (Ramani and Maria, 2005):

(1) Tap into the generics market internationally: target R&D towards the creation of cheaper drugs, vaccines and diagnostics that are off-patent or are soon to be off-patent, especially in regulated Western markets (e.g. Ranbaxy, DRL).
(2) Participate in the international division of labour for the creation of new drugs by Western multinationals: Indian firms vied with each other to offer contract research and custom manufacturing services, bioinformatics services for genomics-based drug research and carrying out clinical trials (DRL and Nicholas Piramal).
(3) Investing in the creation of new drugs for global diseases such as diabetes (Wockhardt and Cipla).

The rationale behind these choices is of course quite clear. The comparative advantage of Indian companies is in reverse engineering and process improvements that lowers the price of generics. The US market is the largest single-nation market for generics in the world and, along with other lucrative European markets, they are even larger. Leveraging the rents to their reverse engineering capabilities by selling to these markets is a prime example of picking the low hanging fruit – and one that totally escaped prediction in the economics literature on the impact of TRIPS in India.

The other two strategic choices involved the development of new technological capabilities in new product and process innovations more linked to the different steps in the sequential process of bringing a new drug to the market. The launch of a new drug typically has to go through the stages of basic research, identifying the appropriate active pharmaceutical ingredients, combining these novel ingredients into a product, performing preclinical and clinical trials to test impact, identifying the right dosage and drug delivery system, seeking regulatory approval through completing a number of procedures and finally marketing the new drug. From start to finish the commercialisation of a new drug can take anything between fifteen and twenty years. With the Patent Law of 1970 Indian firms developed skills in the middle stages and the marketing but not in new drug discovery research techniques or preclinical or clinical trial methods. For Western firms, which are proficient in all the above steps but need to speed up and cheapen the drug discovery process, the presence of Indian firms proficient in reverse engineering offers outsourcing opportunities. For Indian firms aspiring to become new drug manufacturers the task is rather more daunting. They have to develop absorptive capacity and technological capability in creating drugs, performing preclinical and clinical trials and seeking regulatory approval. Finally, they also have to build new capabilities to market new products through doctors in Western hospitals.

Thus, the second choice of strategy, viz. becoming a cog in the wheel of an international division of labour and helping Western multinationals create their innovations, is like the helping hand sought by a poor relative. Indian companies realise that they cannot match the deep pockets of Western multinationals as far as R&D budgets are concerned but want to avoid exclusion. By partnering with Western MNEs in the latter's new drug discovery endeavours, they hope to build new dynamic capabilities.

The third choice for innovation creation through new drug development involves head-on competition with existing pharma majors and is clearly the road least travelled by Indian pharmaceutical firms for two reasons. First, high innovation rents can be reaped in Western markets for generics with more certainty. Another more important reason is the lack of significant complementary competencies required to create a new drug. The drug development process starts with pre-clinical tests on animals on the basis of which a firm applies for an investigational new drug application (INDA). At this stage the drug development process enters into a series of clinical testing phases, at the end of which a new drug application (NDA) is made with the regulatory authority. Then, in order to enter the market, some additional information and technical support may need to be provided to the regulatory authority and such requirements vary from country to country. Under the process patent regime, Indian firms largely skipped the abbreviated new drug application (ANDA), phase I, phase II and phase III of clinical trials, and went straight to the regulatory authorities for an NDA to prove bio-equivalence of the generic form of the drug and to satisfy the additional requirements to market the generic in India. Sometimes, even patents were not necessary. Thus, lack of competencies in the initial and final phases of new drug development are the Achilles heel of Indian firms and leave them vulnerable to costly patent challenges by incumbent firms and the risk of takeover by firms who have capabilities all along the value chain.

Internationalisation, value-chain reconfiguration and subsidiary management in pharmaceuticals[3]

Outward investment from Indian pharmaceutical firms increased dramatically after 1990. Using outward foreign investment approval data, Pradhan and Alakshendra (2006) show that the number of outward investing firms increased from eleven in the pre-1990 period to fifty-five between 1990 and 1999. This increase mirrors the growth in exports of bulk chemicals and active pharmaceuticals ingredients strongly suggesting the outward investment followed the success of Indian generics exports. The firms with the most outward FDI approvals were also the leading generics manufacturers, viz. Ajanta Pharmaceuticals (seventeen projects) followed by Ranbaxy Laboratories (thirteen) and Core Healthcare, Dabur and Sun Pharmaceuticals with seven projects each.

Furthermore, they show that the direction of outward investment changed from being concentrated on Asia and Africa in the period before 1991 to being focused on developed countries of the West, with the US and UK emerging as leading destinations for such investments.[4] Third, the purpose of investment in developed and developing countries differed significantly as Table 7.1 shows. Investments directed towards developed countries are for marketing and trading purposes, while those targeted at developing countries are for establishing manufacturing subsidiaries. This indicates a clear intention of exploiting and leveraging global location advantages. Developing countries are more attractive places to start local production because they can enhance the cost advantages of the Indian firms and the firms also benefit from the soft

---

[3] This section draws on joint work published with Andrew Godley.
[4] Developed countries accounted for 50 of 142 projects (35 per cent) with the most popular destinations being (number of FDI projects in parentheses): US (18), Nepal (13), UK (12), Uzbekistan (9), Mauritius (8), Russia (6) and China, Ireland, Netherlands and Thailand with 5 projects each.

Table 7.1 *Nature of outward greenfield projects over developed and developing countries, 1990–9*

Nature of projects	Developed countries		Developing countries	
	Number	%	Number	%
Manufacturing	16	36.4	35	52.2
Manufacturing and marketing	3	6.8	5	7.5
Marketing and Trading	25	56.8	27	40.3
Total	44	100	67	100

Source: Pradhan and Alakshendra (2006: Table 7).

patent regimes prevalent in these countries. By contrast, their investments in developed countries, as Table 7.1 indicates, are mainly to build their distribution networks in the more regulated Western markets.

Pradhan and Alakshendra (2006) also point to changes in the mode of entry, that has characterised internationalisation of firms from this sector. While joint ventures were the predominant form of outward investment by Indian Pharma firms prior to 1990, between 1990 and 1999 both joint ventures and wholly owned subsidiaries were equally preferred modes of entry.[5] Since 2000, acquisitions have become the most preferred form of entry into foreign markets. The popularity of acquisitions can be overstated. Policy regulations created many restrictions for the free outward flow of foreign exchange prior to full capital market liberalisation of the economy, so the new popularity of acquisitions in international outward investment probably merely reflects the relaxed policy towards outflows of foreign exchange from the Indian economy. Acquisitions have probably also been helped by strong financial positions in international markets enjoyed by the large Indian generics producers noted earlier.

Prominent countries where companies have been acquired are: the US (fourteen), the UK (eight), Germany (five), Brazil and China (three each) and Belgium, France and Italy with two acquisitions each. Only eight firms have accounted for about 70 per cent of all acquisitions, viz.

---

[5] Out of the 127 greenfield projects between 1990 and 1999, for which they have information on the nature of ownership, 64 are jointly owned and 63 are wholly owned subsidiaries. Further, about 58 of these projects were for trading and marketing, while 53 were for manufacturing and 8 for both manufacturing and trading.

Ranbaxy Laboratories (nine), Sun Pharmaceuticals and Glenmark Pharmaceuticals (five acquisitions each), Dr Reddy's and Jubilant Organosys (four acquisitions each), Nicholas Piramal, Wockhardt and Aurobindo Pharma (two acquisitions each).

Analysing the purpose of acquisitions shows three dominant reasons: the need to acquire manufacturing facilities and market share in particular locations and the desire for technological and brand assets. While technological and brand assets clearly reflect a 'buying-in' of firm-specific advantage using relatively strong financial market positions, the acquisition for manufacturing facilities represents better positioning with regard to complementary assets. Not only will the possession of such facilities give Indian firms an advantage in manufacturing generic versions of expired biotechnology and other patents, they are also fungible assets in the sense that any new product developed through a firm's own R&D efforts can also be pushed through these distribution networks.

A closer inspection of the acquisition sequence also reveals that the first international acquisitions made by Indian firms were for laboratories and brand assets. Later investments for each firm were to acquire distribution networks and generics market share. A number of contract manufacturing agreements have also been signed by many of the internationalising firms with Western MNEs with varying degrees of technological collaboration built into the contracts.[6] Nicholas Piramal, for example, has cemented its relationships with many of the former parent companies of Indian subsidiaries, which Nicholas Piramal has acquired in the course of its growth.

A variety of internationalisation strategies were deployed by Indian firms to acquire core assets to enhance their competences in the global generics market. Acquiring the new biotechnology-based NCE Discovery Ltd's capabilities needed systematic investments in R&D, but this had to be complemented with internationalisation strategies of various kinds in the late 1990s and since 2000. In each case, the proximate reasons that dictated the form of internationalisation were a bit different.

Interviews with firms like Ranbaxy, Dr Reddy's Foundation and Wockhardt – all of whom have plans to develop biotechnology capabilities – suggest that their major constraint to doing so is the lack of adequately trained biologists in India. Historically the Indian

---

[6] See Pradhan and Alakshendra (2006, Table 13) for details.

science base has developed good doctors and good chemists but very few dedicated centres of research in biology. Kale and Little (2007) show that several Indian firms tried to attract and employ returning scientists who had worked in US or European MNEs as a way of boosting the firms' skill set and technological competence in these deficient areas. However, this strategy met with only limited success, since many returnees at the senior level had concerns about the working environment in India, while post-doctoral researchers were often too specialised to fit into a firm at an early stage of discovery capability.[7]

The drive to fill skill gaps led to a very early internationalisation of R&D in the case of Dr Reddy's. Kale and Little (2007) note that after establishing discovery research in Hyderabad, Dr Reddy's wanted to introduce modern skills such as drug discovery based on genomics and proteomics and using rational drug design, but struggled. They quote the former R&D president of Dr Reddy's as saying, 'We could not recruit the requisite skills because it's not the one scientist, you need a whole team and we could not do this for the period of three years. We located scientists and one or two might be willing to come out but they had inhibitions and they needed lots of time and they were unable to take decisions. Then we decided there was no point in waiting. We cannot bring people here; we will move our lab there.' Thus in 2000, DRF set up a lab in Atlanta, US dedicated to discovery and design of novel therapeutics using molecular genomics and proteomics approaches. The lab, Reddy US Therapeutics Inc (RUSTI) quickly built a team of twelve scientists, and in seven years the organisation has obtained twelve US patents.[8]

Ranbaxy has also systematically used its internationalisation in the US to build its distribution network and to concentrate on the developmental aspects of R&D. Its internationalisation efforts in the US started with the joint venture with Eli Lilly for the manufacture of Cefaclor in 1992. This joint venture was dissolved in 1995 and in return for an early dissolution, Ranbaxy obtained brand recognition by buying rights to manufacture all the products for which Eli Lilly was sole supplier. In 1995, it made its first acquisition in the US (Ohm Labs) to benefit from its FDA-approved manufacturing facilities. This was followed with the setting up of its own 100 per cent subsidiary

---

[7] For more details based on case study evidence, see Kale and Little (2007).
[8] Numbers from USPTO website updated to 30 October 2007.

in the US for the manufacture of products under the Ranbaxy brand name. However, unlike all the other Indian firms that have used internationalisation to source technology directly from abroad, Ranbaxy has used these investments to gain regulatory and legal expertise for its existing range of products – capabilities recognised as being important to the development stage of a new chemical entity.

Wockhardt placed biotechnology at the heart of its strategy in the early 1990s and spent 20–30 per cent of its total research budget on biotech R&D. In 1993, the company initiated an international joint venture with the International Center for Genetics Engineering and Biotechnology (ICGEB) in Trieste, Italy for research on recombinant products such as a hepatitis B vaccine, serum erythropoietin (EPO) and human insulin. However, the company called the deal off after three to four years because of a lack of output. Subsequently, Wockhardt set up its own R&D centre at Aurangabad in 1994, and in 1995 entered into another international joint venture with Rhein Biotech, a German firm, for the development and manufacture of Recombinant Biopharmaceuticals. The venture was funded by equities on the Wockhardt side and resulted in the successful production of the hepatitis B vaccine, Biovac-B in 2001. However, due to a conflict of interest over the rights to this product, the joint venture was dissolved and Wockhardt bought Rhein's shares and took full ownership of the subsidiary. In 2004, Wockhardt acquired the German pharmaceutical company Esparma GmbH to enter Germany, the largest generic drug market in Europe. Esparma has a portfolio of 135 marketing authorisations, of which 67 are in Germany. The company also has 9 international patents and 94 trademarks to its name.

Patent data help us to establish the success of these strategies in building technological strengths. The patents filed by Indian inventors have been on the rise in the USPTO and one analysis of patents filed in biotechnology and related sectors (in classes 210, 264, 424, 435, 514, 530, 536, 549, 800) at the USPTO reveals that 60 per cent of the total 746 patents filed by Indian resident inventors were assigned to government or research institutions (dominated by the Council of Scientific and Industrial Research [CSIR] with 383 patents).[9] Patents assigned to

---

[9] These estimates are based on research reported by Silico Research, available at http://jungle-research.com/analysis/emerging/briefing/biotechasia (last accessed 29 October 2007).

the generics pharmaceutical company Dr Reddy's constituted the next largest proportion after CSIR (totalling 31 patents, or 4 per cent). Closely following were Dabur Research Foundation, part of the multinational Dabur Group (with 29 patents) and the generics pharmaceutical company Ranbaxy Laboratories (with 28).

Despite these successes there are signs that time is running out for Indian generics producers. Their overall strategy of channelling the profits from generics to investments in new drug discovery was always a risky one because it needed a very rapid ramp up in the capabilities required for the identification of promising molecules and to master the complexities of getting a drug to market. In 2009, Ranbaxy sold off a major stake in its company to Daichi Sanyo, a mid-sized Japanese generics producer. The sale of founder shares raised a few questions about the commitment of the family-owned company towards the long-term growth and strategy initiated in the 1990s. Hot on the heels of the divestment of these shares the US Food and Drug Administration (FDA) announced plans to ban more than thirty generic drugs – including antibiotics and AIDS medications – that were made at two Ranbaxy plants in India. The FDA said Ranbaxy had lied about information on more than two dozen of its generic drugs. Although the agency didn't find any health risks linked to Ranbaxy drugs, the FDA said it would stop reviewing any new drugs made at Ranbaxy's Paonta Sahib plant, although the Dewas plant was found to be alright. Following this, Ranbaxy and Daichi Sanyo have refocused their internationalisation strategy on other emerging markets such as Mexico where cynics may argue regulatory standards are also less stringent.

DRL, too, has found itself in difficulties on two fronts. Its core generics business was shaken when Pfizer sued the company for alleged patent infringement after Dr Reddy's announced that it intended to produce a generic version of Atorvastatin, marketed by Pfizer as Lipitor, an anti-cholesterol medication in 2009. In 2010, DRL denied reports that its generic business was to be sold first to the UK pharmaceuticals multinational Glaxo Smithkline, and later that DRL was in talks to sell the generics business to Pfizer. Its drug discovery programme received severe setbacks due to the withdrawal of venture financing for its subsidiary Perlecan Pharma Private by ICICI Venture Capital and Citigroup Venture International. In 2008, both venture capitalists wanted out because of doubts about the commercial viability of the drugs candidates that were in Perlecan's pipeline.

The disappointing performance of both these pioneering firms suggests that their ability to gain from their international investments was limited ultimately by the lack of capability in key aspects of the pharmaceutical value chain.

Conclusions

Software and pharmaceuticals represent two of India's most internationalised industrial sectors. Using the lens of the dominant strategies in these two sectors, this chapter aimed to shed light on the contribution of value-chain reconfiguration and subsidiary management in enhancing the competitiveness of Indian MNEs from these sectors. Furthermore a large proportion of firms in both sectors have been entrepreneurial firms rather than conglomerates, for which the internationalisation through investment route is quite an expensive way to add to their competitive strengths. This is a somewhat different approach to assessing the issue from that adopted by the other two chapters on India (Chapters 3 and 11) in that it focuses not on particular firms that have led in internationalisation (in the Indian case often business house conglomerates) but on the representative firm in the two sectors.

An important conclusion of our analysis is that the positioning as global suppliers of intermediate products has been a more sustainable strategy for the majority of firms than trying to control the whole product value chain. While Indian software firms have always positioned themselves as global suppliers of software, the recent reverses suffered by the leading Pharma firms like Ranbaxy and DRL have underlined the sustainability of the global supplier strategy in the face of incumbent competition.

However, this renders the value chains that Indian MNEs must master considerably shorter. Since the main advantage of Indian MNEs in these sectors is cheaper domestic costs, their domestic subsidiaries may be much more valuable than their international ones.

8 | Value-chain configurations of Chinese EMNEs

KAIMEI WANG AND YONGJIANG SHI

Introduction

China is widely regarded as a 'world factory' with low manufacturing costs and a huge market. Thus, numerous multinational corporations have rushed to China and set up their manufacturing facilities there in order to achieve cost reduction and market expansion. Although 'made-in-China' products have flooded the world, indigenous Chinese firms contribute less than 50 per cent of the export volume, and they are often confined to the role of contractual manufacturers.

However, there is a group of Chinese manufacturing firms pursuing a reverse process, i.e. they aim to internationalise under their own brands, and even place production activities abroad. As late-movers to enter the global market, especially to enter the most sophisticated and competitive 'Triad' markets of the US, the EU and Japan, Chinese manufacturing firms are facing a number of big challenges. These challenges include the following:

- How can a firm survive, and even succeed, when there are limited competitive advantages to employ and many competitive disadvantages to offset?
- What kind of ownership advantages do Chinese manufacturing firms have? And how can they make the most use of them?
- How can we identify the difference between China and overseas countries in terms of consumer demand, marketing methods, manufacturing concepts and legal issues? And how can they adapt?
- How can they be profitable by operating production facilities in the Triad?
- How do they achieve an integration effect by running a global manufacturing network?

In spite of the challenges that Chinese manufacturing firms confront, an increasing number of firms survive or even succeed in the global market.

149

This chapter is concerned with the mechanism that enables Chinese manufacturing firms to survive or even succeed in global markets by pursuing international production. It aims to address a central question:

How can Chinese manufacturing firms design and implement the manufacturing internationalisation process to survive or even succeed in the global market?

The chapter aims to build on extant theory and good practice from multiple case studies to develop new theoretical insights that may help to provide the necessary understanding to answer that central question. The paper is divided into four parts including an existing literature review to highlight research gaps that exist to reflect the emerging countries' firm internationalisation, especially from the operational perspective. A case study section details two Chinese companies' very different experiences in their foreign direct investments (FDIs). A key learning section summaries the main research findings from the case companies, and the findings' theoretical contributions are discussed in the final implications section.

Literature review

This section provides a focused review of the firm internationalisation process research, especially manufacturing-related theories on internationalisation. Previous manufacturing-related research on internationalisation mainly focused on the drivers to pursue international production and the management of an international manufacturing network. Based on the literature review, the two major gaps are emerging – the lack of research on the identification of forces which drive latecomers to pursue cross-border production, and the formulation of the internationalisation process of the manufacturing function.

The manufacturing system has evolved into various kinds of network-based relationships from the traditional input-output transformation model. During the last twenty years multinational corporations (MNCs) have attempted to globalise their geographically dispersed factories by coordinating them into a synergetic network (Flaherty, 1986; Ferdows, 1997a, 1997b; Shi and Gregory, 1998). This transformation has changed basic manufacturing functions and effectiveness from the orientation of product-based competitive advantages towards the orientation of network strategic capability development, which drives the manufacturing system beyond the factory wall and the strategy beyond product focus.

Besides MNCs' international expansions, it has become more popular for all types of companies to downsize and outsource their non-core business tasks and to set up inter-firm collaborations (Lambert *et al.*, 1998; Lamming *et al.*, 2000; Brewer *et al.*, 2001). This development has pushed the manufacturing system further into a new relationship beyond the traditional concept of the firm that owns and internally operates their factories. Currently, it is no longer a secret that, although a company may only own a very small portion of a supply chain, they are still strategically able to coordinate or integrate the whole supply chain to deliver a competitive product to its targeted market. It is equally interesting to notice that there are increasing observations about geographic clustering emerging worldwide (Piore and Sabel, 1984; Porter, 1998). The clusters actually form different supply networks – some of them are internally self-sufficient in a region and others are virtually integrated with other clusters. The two types of supply networks demonstrate that inter-firm collaborations have emerged as a new type of manufacturing system.

Combining both developments, as Figure 8.1 illustrates, a new type of manufacturing network can be derived with the characteristics of international and inter-firm relationships. The new combination provides a new operational environment for the manufacturing system to access, optimise and operate its strategic resources. The global manufacturing virtual network (GMVN) was suggested to explore the new generation of manufacturing architecture (Li *et al.*, 2000; Shi and Gregory, 2002). Other research on global outsourcing and partnership also seeks to develop the system with similar architecture and strategic capabilities pursuing higher value and innovation (Normann and Ramirez, 1993; Parolini, 1999; Bovel and Martha, 2000).

From Figure 8.1, three trends can be foreseen. (1) The traditional manufacturing strategy focusing on a product and its effective factory might not be enough, especially for creating higher business value. (2) The manufacturing system has been extended into new operational space that includes international locations and inter-firm relationships. (3) Manufacturing system boundary changes imply that manufacturing strategy also needs to be changed in terms of its contents and process.

Based on this literature review, two major research gaps emerged, as illustrated in Table 8.1. First, based on the experience of MNCs

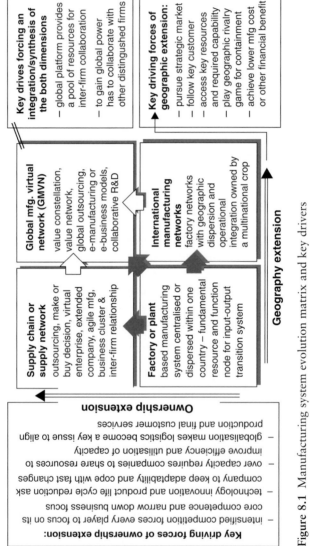

Key drives forcing an integration/synthesis of the both dimensions

– global platform provides a pool of resources for inter-firm collaboration

– to gain global power has to collaborate with other distinguished firms

Key driving forces of geographic extension:

– pursue strategic market
– follow key customer
– access key resources and required capability
– play geographic rivalry game for containment
– achieve lower mfg cost or other financial benefit

Global mfg. virtual network (GMVN)

value constellation, value network, global outsourcing, e-manufacturing or e-business models, collaborative R&D

International manufacturing networks

factory networks with geographic dispersion and operational integration owned by a multinational crop

Supply chain or supply network

outsourcing, make or buy decision, virtual enterprise, extended company, agile mfg, business cluster & inter-firm relationship

Factory or plant

based manufacturing system centralised or dispersed within one country – fundamental resource and function node for input-output transition system

Geography extension

Ownership extension

Key driving forces of ownership extension:

– intensified competition forces every player to focus on its core competence and narrow down business focus

– technology innovation and product life cycle reduction ask company to keep adaptability and cope with fast changes

– over capacity requires companies to share resources to improve efficiency and utilisation of capacity

– globalisation makes logistics become a key issue to align production and final customer services

Figure 8.1 Manufacturing system evolution matrix and key drivers

Table 8.1 *Identification of research gaps*

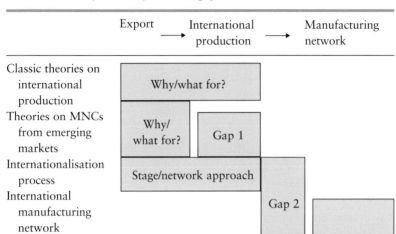

from the Triad, classic theories suggest that the impulse and motives to internationalisation start from the firms' capability to exploit advantages abroad. Theories on MNCs from emerging markets did identify the lack of competitive advantages that could be employed by a latecomer, thus bringing forward the concept of 'pull-oriented' and 'asset-seeking'. However, limited research has focused on the identification of forces that drive latecomers to pursue cross-border production, and even less research is concerned with the mechanism that enables latecomers to survive or succeed by pursuing cross-border production.

Second, an internationalisation process is described, in either incremental or network approaches, as starting from exporting until the establishment of overseas factories. There is limited understanding on the following process – from setting up the first overseas plant until running a global manufacturing network, which also could be regarded as the internationalisation of the manufacturing function.

Case studies

The research gaps indicate that the existing knowledge and solutions have failed to answer the key question – how can Chinese manufacturing companies design and implement their manufacturing internationalisation processes in order to survive or succeed in the very competitive global market?

The research project adopts a theory-building strategy based on multiple case studies. Seven companies were studied, as Table 8.2 illustrates. But this chapter just describes the internationalisation processes of companies A and B, and their international manufacturing reconfigurations from both individual factory and whole network perspectives.

Company A: Chinese white goods champion

Starting with a defunct refrigerator factory in Qingdao, Shandong Province, Company A was founded in 1984 and is now China's largest home appliance maker. In the domestic market, Company A holds more than a 30 per cent share of China's white goods market, and has dominant positions in refrigerator/freezer, washing machine and air conditioner markets. Globally, Company A ranks third in white goods revenues, and is the second largest refrigerator manufacturer with 6 per cent of the global market, behind Whirlpool and ahead of Electrolux, Kenmore and GE (Khanna and Palepu, 2005). In 2006, Company A's annual sales revenue reached $13.1 billion (RMB107.5 billion), 21.4 per cent ($2.8 billion) of which came from overseas markets.

In the past twenty-three years, Company A experienced three development stages:

(1) Branding stage (1984–91): seven years to build a strong brand name in the domestic refrigerator market; quality was emphasised as the essence of brand building and sustainable business. By 1991, Company A became China's leading refrigerator manufacturer.

(2) Diversification stage (1991–7): in 1992, Company A acquired Qingdao Air Conditioner Factory and Qingdao General Freezer Factory. In 1995, Company A took the nearly bankrupt Red Star Washing Machine Company and made it profitable within eighteen months. Then Company A added television and telecoms equipment to its product mix by acquiring Yellow Mountain Electronics in 1997. By 1997 Company A had taken over fifteen companies and thus became a manufacturer of a wide range of household electrical appliances. Its strategy in selecting acquired companies was 'to buy firms with markets and good products but bad management, and then to introduce mature management

Table 8.2 Case companies studied for their manufacturing internationalisation

Case firms	Ownership	Products	Core product in internationalisation	First export Year	First export Region	First FDI Year	First FDI Region	Entry mode	Overseas factory locations (to date)
HISense	SOE	Home appliances	Televisions	1999	Africa	1996	Africa	Greenfield	South Africa (2), Hungary, France
Wanxiang	Private	Conglomerate	Automotive parts	1984	US	2000	US	M&A	US (7)
ZTE	SOE	Telecoms	Telecoms equipment	1998	Asia	1999	Asia	Joint venture	Pakistan, Libya, India, Brazil
Holly	SOE	Medicine, energy meter instruments, real estate	Energy meter instruments	2001	Asia	2001	Asia	Joint venture	Thailand (3), India, Argentina, Uzbekistan
Zhongqiang	Private	Electric tools	Electric tools	1993	Europe	2004	Europe	M&A	Germany
Company A	SOE	White goods	Refrigerators/freezers	1991	Europe	1996	Asia	Joint venture	Indonesia, Philippines, Thailand, Vietnam, Bangladesh, Pakistan, India, Jordan, Nigeria, US, Italy
Company B	Public	Conglomerate	Televisions	1997	US	1999	Asia	M&A	Vietnam, Thailand, Poland, Mexico

systems and quality control systems to turn the firms around', said Mr. Zhang, Company A's chief executive officer (CEO).

(3) Internationalisation stage (1997–now): Company A developed a global expansion strategy – 'three one-third' – in 1997. The goal is to have Company A's revenue derived in equal parts from sales of goods in three categories: one-third from goods produced and sold in China, one-third produced in China and sold overseas and one-third produced and sold overseas. In short, Company A's objective is to produce two-thirds of its total output in China and to sell two-thirds to overseas markets, although in 1997 Company A's overseas sales accounted for less than 15 per cent of its total sales. The Overseas Business Promotion Division was established in 1999 to manage its export business, overseas sales subsidiaries and overseas factories. To date, Company A has established a global business platform with nine overseas main regions – North America, Europe, South-East Asia, East Asia, West Asia, South Asia, the Middle East, Africa and Oceania. It had six overseas R&D centres in Los Angeles, Silicon Valley, Lyons, Amsterdam, Montreal and Tokyo; ten information centres and thirteen overseas factories with a presence in almost every main region.

As illustrated in Figure 8.2, the global market is divided into six regional markets by Company A. In each regional market, Company A experienced a process through export as a contractual manufacturer, export under an 'own brand' and establishment of marketing and sales functions as well as the establishment of its manufacturing function.

The evolution of network dispersion is a structural dimension to identify the internationalisation of a manufacturing function, which does take the competence of factory node into consideration. However, as the development evolution of an overseas individual factory is a key to understanding a firm's manufacturing internationalisation, in this research the overseas individual factory development path is separated from its network dispersion to be a node dimension to identify the internationalisation of the manufacturing function.

Company A's factory in the US experienced an incremental development process from 2000 up to now and to the near future. The factory developed in three main aspects: as an individual plant, in an intra-firm factory network and within a local network.

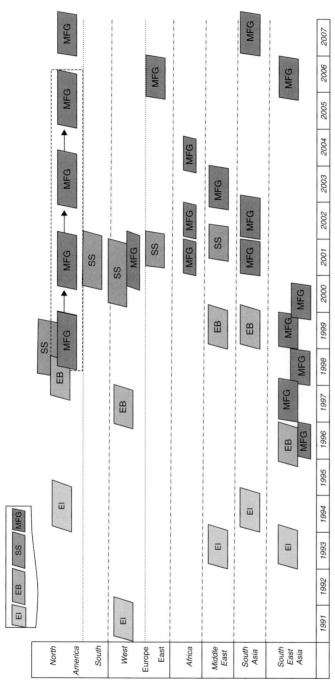

EI = Indirect export (via private label or contract manufacturing)

EB = Export under the company's own brand

SS = Sales subsidiary established

MFG = Manufacturing subsidiary established, acquired or expanded

Figure 8.2 Company A's internationalisation process

Other overseas factories, such as the plants in Italy and Thailand, also experienced development in some aspects. In the Italian factory, some of the new production development processes – pilot production and tooling production – were transferred to China to achieve economies of scale and cost reduction. Some components and raw materials, such as compressors and plastic sheets, are no longer sourced locally but centrally sourced from China; its relationship with factories in China is enhanced in the development process. The development of the Thai factory mainly happens in the aspects of production processes and market supply – from a local plant with final assembly only, to a regional production base with full production processes.

Company A coordinates its international factory network in three main aspects: the production process, new product development and the sourcing process. In each aspect of coordination, factories in China are core players in the factory network.

Production process: some components, such as compressors, defrosters, wires and light fans, are produced in Company A's factories in China and then distributed to overseas factories. The shipping cost of these components is relatively low; the usage volume is stable and can be accurately predicted. Therefore the production of these components can be centralised in China to achieve economies of scale and meanwhile make use of low manufacturing resources in China.

New product development process: capital intensive and low-volume production processes, such as tooling production and pilot production, are completed in China and then distributed to overseas factories. The intention is also to achieve economies of scale and exploit low-cost manufacturing resources in China.

Sourcing process: some components, such as plastic sheets, containers and hook-ups, are centrally sourced from suppliers in China. These components also share similar characteristics: low shipping cost and stable volume. The centralised procurement enables Company A to make use of low-cost sourcing resources in China. In the near future, the procurement of other components, such as foam, metal and plastic, will be integrated. Several overseas factories can share the same supplier by sourcing from the supplier's local subsidiaries. The integration of suppliers enhances Company A's bargaining power at both the group and individual factory levels. Based on a group contract, overseas factories can be supplied at a lower price with better service.

Company B: Chinese colour television champion

Company B is a multi-electronics company. It was founded in 1980 as a cassette manufacturer, and then became the leading telephone producer in China by 1986. In 1992, Company B entered the television industry, first as a distributor, selling colour television sets produced by its Hong Kong-based joint venture partner Changcheng, under Company B's brand 'King'. In 1996, Company B moved into production by forming a joint venture with Luk's Industrial, a Hong Kong manufacturer, to produce television sets in Shenzhen. By 2001, Company B had become the largest television producer in China (Liu, 2007).

Company B has been diversified as it grew its size. It operates six business units: multimedia, telecoms, home appliances, personal computers, consumer electronics and electronics components. However, multimedia is the largest, and its television segment has been Company B's largest business since 1999 and partially depends on its internationalisation strategy.

Company B's international experience began in 1997, when it started to export cathode ray tube (CRT) television sets first to the US and then to South-East Asia. In 1999, Company B took over Luk's factory in Vietnam with the intention of fulfilling local demand and further expanding the South-East Asian market. By 2006, Company B held 22 per cent of Vietnam's CRT television market, ranking second behind Samsung Electronics.

In order to reach global prominence, in January 2004 Company B and Company T signed an agreement to create TTE. This joint venture combined the CRT television assets of each company. Company B dominated the joint venture, with 38 per cent of the shares, while Company T held 30 per cent. Under the joint venture agreement, worldwide TTE owned ten manufacturing plants, including six in China (TTECs), one in Vietnam (TTEV), one in Thailand (TTET), one in Poland (TTEP) and one in Mexico (TTEM). Company T previously owned the latter three factories. With annual capacities of 0.6 million sets of TTEV, 2 million sets of TTET, 2.5 million sets of TTEP and 2.2 million sets of TTEM, TTE was capable of producing 23 million television sets each year, the most in the world. But global competition no longer depended on capacity. The company faced a serious post-mergers and acquisitions (M&A) integration challenge from factory and whole global supply-chain perspectives, plus new technology emerged to replace the classical CRT technology. The company eventually had to give up the joint venture after six years of struggles.

In summary, Company B's internationalisation started in 1997. Up to now, Company B has experienced four internationalisation phases – export, incremental growth, radical expansion via acquisition and post-acquisition integration. The following section details the four phases of its internationalisation.

Phase 1: export (1997–9). As mentioned above, Company B's internationalisation process began in 1997. Since then, it has exported CRT television sets, first to the US, then to South-East Asia. A sales subsidiary in Vietnam was established in October 1998, and then several small sales affiliates were set up throughout Asia. Overseas business at this time came under the control of the import/export division based at the company's headquarters. The import/export division received orders from the overseas subsidiary or sales affiliates, with customer preferences in product appearance and function, sent it to the manufacturing base in Huizhou and waited for the products to be finished. However, as domestic demand during the late 1990s was increasing rapidly and domestic customer preference was quite simple with little variation, overseas orders were given a lower priority by the manufacturing base. The manufacturing base was reluctant to put much effort into changing its product design or production processes to comply with overseas orders. On the other hand, the import/export division and the manufacturing base acted as two independent transaction parties. To be more profitable, the manufacturing base was not willing to provide as competitive a price as the import/export division wanted.

Phase 2: incremental Growth (1999–2004). It is difficult to expand an overseas market with neither differentiated products nor a competitive price. To solve this problem, the overseas business division (originally the import/export division), acquired a CRT television plant in Vietnam from Luk Industrial in 1999. This first overseas plant was located in Vietnam, partly because the television industry in Vietnam was highly protected by the local government – television sets could not be sold without a local production facility.

In September 2002, Company B acquired Company S, Germany's seventh-largest television producer, for €8.2 million, as an attempt to avoid the European Union (EU)'s anti-dumping penalty against

Chinese television makers. After acquisition, Company B obtained three CRT television production lines with a total capacity of one million units, R&D potency, distribution networks and two brand names.

Initially, the Vietnamese plant was positioned, by the overseas business division, as a production hub to supply the Asian market. But soon, Company B found that CRT television sets produced in the Vietnamese plant were even less competitive in the Asian market. Manufacturing costs, manufacturing efficiency and quality control in the Vietnam plant were at a low level and its 200,000-set annual capacity could not satisfy the future annual demand of the Asian market. In 2001, proposed by the overseas business division, the second television manufacturing base was established in Huizhou in China to produce CRT television sets for overseas markets. Subsequently, the Vietnamese plant turned to fulfil local demand only. Although the plant in Vietnam did not accomplish its task to supply the Asian market, Company B's production presence in Vietnam enhanced its brand awareness in South-East Asia. Since 1999, Company B has successfully entered the CRT television markets of Indonesia, the Philippines, Thailand, Malaysia and India, and established sales subsidiaries in all of these countries. In Vietnam, as a 'first-mover', Company B has increased its television market share rapidly. Since 2001, Company B has turned the Vietnamese plant to profitability; by 2005 Company B had 22 per cent of the CRT television market share in Vietnam, behind Samsung Electronics.

The production base in Europe, however, faced serious challenges after acquisition. First, production costs in Germany were too high. Second, the rapid growth of the flatpanel television industry constrained the increase of Company B's sales volume of CRT televisions in Europe. Therefore, in September 2004, Company B did not renew the lease on Company S's production facilities and its television production in Germany was stopped in 2005 (Khanna *et al.*, 2006).

Phase 3: radical expansion via acquisition (2004–7). On 1 August 2004, Company B acquired Company T's CRT television business unit and co-founded the TTE Corporation with Company T. Television sets are the core products of TTE. After acquisition, TTE became the largest CRT television set producer in the world, with an annual production capacity of more than 23 million sets. By taking over Company T's plants in Thailand, Poland and Mexico, TTE rapidly gained production footprints in the three main continents – Asia,

Table 8.3 *CRT TV import duties from China, Vietnam and Thailand to Asian countries (%)*

From / To	China			Vietnam	Thailand
	CBU	SKD	CKD	CBU	CBU
Vietnam	50		6–7	–	5
Thailand	20	15	0	5	–
India	10		6–7	10	0
Indonesia	15		5	5	5
The Philippines	15		1.5	5	5

Europe and America. The four overseas plants were expected to fulfil total overseas markets' demand – the Thai plant (TTET) together with the Vietnamese plant (TTEV) for the Asian market, the Polish plant (TTEP) for the European market and the Mexican plant (TTEM) for the American market. TTET, TTEP and TTEM reported to a global operations centre (GOC), which was based in company B's manufacturing site at Huizhou, while TTEV continued to report to the overseas business unit, which was based in Shenzhen. As two independent systems, TTEV had almost no sharing of product development, technology, managerial capability or supplier information with TTET, TTEP and TTEM.

Originally, TTET was positioned to supply the Asian market (except Vietnam) including Thailand, Indonesia, the Philippines, Malaysia and India. One reason why TTET was considered able to shoulder the task was because the two million set annual capacity in TTET could satisfy the overseas Asian market. Further, as a member of the Association of South-East Asian Nations (ASEAN), CRT television import duty within the Asian Free Trade Area (AFTA) at 5 per cent is much lower than that from China to AFTA; and under the Bangkok Agreement in 2004, made-in-Thailand CRT television sets enjoyed zero import duty to India (see Table 8.3).

However, although enjoying trading benefits it was not an optimum choice to have TTET serve other Asian countries, in terms of manufacturing costs, supply-chain total costs and supply-chain lead time. Manufacturing costs in TTET, including final assembly costs and plastic moulding costs, are twice as high as those in TTEC. Served by TTET, supply-chain total costs in Vietnam, India, Indonesia and the Philippines are all higher than if served by local plant or local contractual manufacturers. TTET is even less competitive than exports from China when serving India, Indonesia and the Philippines. High manufacturing cost is the main reason that makes TTET so uncompetitive in the supply chain's total cost. With reference to supply-chain lead time, TTET cannot compete with China and local contractual manufacturers – it is normally ten to fifteen days longer than if exported from China, and five to ten days longer than when supplied by local contractual manufacturers.

Therefore, TTE adopted 'local serve' mode instead of 'regional serve' mode after the acquisition. India, Indonesia and the Philippines were supplied by local contractual manufacturers, Vietnam by TTEV and Thailand by TTET. Except for the Thai market, TTET exported a third of its production volume to North America to make use of the trading benefits between Thailand and the North American Free Trade Area (NAFTA), and exported another third to branded companies in Europe. All the customers in North America and Europe were Company T's previous customers.

In Europe, TTEP was expected to supply the European market with Company T's brand and meanwhile also to supply branded companies. In October 2006, however, TTE announced that business in Europe entered the stage of reorganisation – production and sales of television sets with Company T brand were suspended; TTEP focused on original equipment manufacturing (OEM) customers only. The reasons are as follows. Although using Company T's brand, it was difficult to increase sales volume in the shrinking CRT television market in Europe. Low sales volume and over-capacity brought huge losses in running the business in Europe; thus ultimately TTE chose to concentrate on contractual manufacturing to serve OEM customers only. TTEV, TTET, TTEP and TTEM's market focus changed a lot after the acquisition. The changing evolution is illustrated in Table 8.4.

Under the 'local serve' mode, however, TTE was experiencing huge losses and facing a lot of problems. First, over-capacity in TTET, TTEV, TTEP and TTEM was increasingly serious. In 2006, production output in TTET was 1.1 million television sets, only 55 per cent of its full annual capacity. Second, manufacturing costs in TTET and TTEM were unbearably high, at 15 per cent and 10.5 per cent of raw material costs, respectively. Manufacturing costs in factories in China, however, were less than 5 per cent of raw material costs. Third, the supply chain for each overseas country was independent, with no supply network integration

Table 8.4 *A changing evolution of overseas factories' market focus after the acquisition*

	August 2004 ——————————→ February 2007		
Factory – market	Reasons to change	Factory – market	Problems facing
TTEC→ China TTEV→ Vietnam TTET→ Thailand Indonesia The Philippines Malaysia India	(1) High cost (2) Long lead time (3) Trading benefits to North America (4) Company T's OEM customers in Europe	TTEV→ Vietnam TTET→ Thailand, Europe, North America, OEMs in Europe Contractual manufacturers (17)→ India Contractual manufacturer → Indonesia Contractual manufacturer → The Philippines TTEC → China, other Asian countries, North America	(1) Over-capacity in TTET and TTEV (2) Cost in TTET is not under control (3) Supply chain is for single country, no integration effect (4) Too many contractual manufacturers in India, supply chain in India is in a mess
TTEP→ Europe with Company T's brand; OEMs in Europe	(1) High cost (2) Low sales volume and big loss	TTEP→ OEMs in Europe	(1) High cost (2) Decreasing OEM orders
TTEM→ Mexico, the US, Canada		TTEM→ Mexico, the US, Canada	(1) High cost

Table 8.5 *Four tasks of TTE post-acquisition integration*

(1) Shut down one overseas plant in Asia (TTET or TTEV) and build up an integrated supply chain in Asian market
(2) Reduce manufacturing costs in TTET, TTEP and TTEM
(3) Reduce number of contractual manufacturers in India; enhance control on contractual manufacturers and supply chain management in India
(4) Change organisation structure to manage overseas business and production

Table 8.6 *TTE sales volume and forecast of CRT televisions in Asia, 2005–10 (units)*

Market	2005	2006	2007	2008	2009	2010 (forecast)
Thailand	112,073	169,389	160,554	185,000	215,000	230,000
Vietnam	294,625	260,994	285,600	316,000	335,000	330,000
Subtotal	**406,698**	**430,382**	**446,154**	**501,000**	**550,000**	**560,000**
The Philippines	148,272	128,044	140,510	157,550	163,550	166,550
Subtotal	**554,970**	**558,426**	**586,664**	**658,550**	**713,550**	**726,550**
India	292,274	422,218	365,600	660,000	1,000,000	1,090,000
Subtotal	**847,244**	**980,644**	**952,264**	**1,318,550**	**1,713,550**	**1,816,550**
Indonesia	282,543	179,500	160,000	312,000	400,000	450,000
Total	1,129,787	1,160,144	1,112,264	1,630,550	2,113,550	2,266,550

effect. Fourth, to avoid the tariff in cross-state transactions, TTE gradually built up relationships with seventeen contractual manufacturers in India. Until early 2007, the TTE supply chain management and control mechanisms on contractual manufacturers in India were in a mess.

Phase 4: post-acquisition integration (2007–9). In February 2007, TTE finally entered its post-acquisition integration period. As exhibited in Table 8.5, TTE's post-acquisition integration mainly occurred in four aspects.

To make full use of production capacity, TTE decided to shut down one overseas production base in Asia. An integrated supply chain to serve the Asian market would be based at the remaining plant.

TTE sales volume and sales forecasts of CRT television sets in Asia from 2005 to 2010 are exhibited in Table 8.6. With two million sets annual production capacity, TTET could easily have satisfied the whole Asian market before 2010. If it remained TTEV, TTE aimed to increase annual production capacity in TTEV to 800,000 sets by 2008 and to one million sets by 2010, which could satisfy the demand from Thailand, Vietnam and the Philippines.

Therefore if TTET remained, an integrated supply chain to serve the Asian market could be built up without further investment to increase its production capacity, and in the next few years, some of its production output could still serve the North American market and (or) OEM customers in Europe. If TTEV remained, two parallel supply chains would be used to supply the Asian markets: with further investment to increase annual production capacity, TTEV would be a production base to supply Vietnam, Thailand and the Philippines; Indian and Indonesian markets would be supplied by local contractual manufacturers.

An in-depth analysis of TTET and TTEV was carried out from February to June 2007 on aspects of local trading policy, local manufacturing, sourcing resources, supply-chain total costs to Asian markets, supply-chain lead time to Asian markets, the trend of exchange rates and the future growth of flat panel television business in Thailand and Vietnam. A comparison of competitive capability in TTET and TTEV was conducted. Based on the comparison, a strategic decision could be made on whether to build up a TTET-based or a TTEV-based supply chain. Considering the supply-chain integration effect and the investment issue, it was decided that keeping TTET was the best choice. Moreover, the Thai flat panel television market was expanding rapidly, with an increasingly rich supply of local resources available.

In summary, Table 8.7 highlights Company B's international manufacturing reconfigurations on factory and network levels. The acquisition of Company T's overseas plants in Thailand, Poland and Mexico, although initially for capability-seeking, is later changed to market-seeking. On the manufacturing internationalisation process, acquisitions make Company B's international factory network dispersion change radically in terms of the number of factories, their dispersion and market supply. The competence of each overseas factory has to be adjusted to match the factory's market strategy, market coverage and the parent company's strategic reason to set up the factory. During the three stages, Company B also changed its coordination mechanism on its global supply chain as well as product design and development processes.

Table 8.7 The development of Company B's several factories before and after the acquisition

Pre acquisition

	Thailand	Poland	Mexico	Vietnam
Factory	Thailand	Poland	Mexico	Vietnam
Market coverage	Local and export	Europe	America	Local
Product segment	Medium-high	High-premium	High-premium	Medium-high
Factory production	High cost high quality	High cost high quality	High cost high quality	Low cost medium quality
Factory competence	Medium	Medium	Medium	Low
Strategic reason	Capability seeking	Access to market	Access to market	Access to market

Post acquisition

(Company T: TTE)

	TTET	TTEP	TTEM	TTEV
Factory	TTET	TTEP	TTEM	TTEV
Market coverage	Local	Europe	America	Local
Product segment	Medium-high	High-premium	Low-medium	Medium-high
Factory production	High cost high quality	High cost high quality	Low cost high quality	Low cost medium quality
Factory competence	Medium	Medium	Medium	Low
Strategic reason	Capability seeking	Capability seeking	Capability seeking	Access to market

Post-acquisition integration

(Company T: TTE)

	TTET or TTEV	TTEP	TTEM	
Factory	TTET or TTEV	TTEP	TTEM	
Market coverage	Asia except for India	Europe	America	
Product segment	Medium-high	Low-medium	Low-medium	
Factory production	Low cost medium quality	Low cost medium quality	Low cost medium quality	
Factory competence	Upper-low	Upper-low	Upper-low	
Strategic reason	Access to market	Access to market	Access to market	

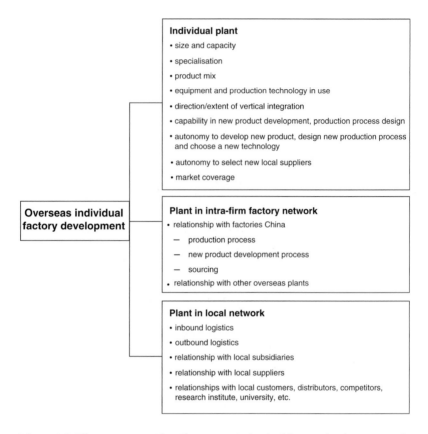

Figure 8.3 Three aspects to identify overseas individual factory development path

Key learning from the Chinese manufacturing pioneers to go to international

Factory level: adaptation

The individual factory (network node dimension) of the manufacturing internationalisation process can be analysed in three constructs: individual plant, plant in an intra-firm factory network and plant in a local network (see Figure 8.3). Based on the three aspects – individual plant, plant in an intra-firm factory network and plant in a local network – the competence of an individual factory can be measured accordingly as low, medium and high. It can be seen that a low-competence factory is largely *dependent* on domestic factories, a medium-competence factory is highly *independent* in each aspect and a high-competence factory is a *network player* to coordinate a factory network to achieve the best in all aspects.

According to the categorisation of factory competence, for example, Company A's factories in China have very high competence. The Italian factory started from a medium competence level, and developed to a more integrated factory network, which means its factory competence grew to be upper-medium level. The factory in the US grew from low competence to upper-medium competence – in the same level as the factory in Italy. The competence of regional plants – the plants in Thailand, Jordan and Pakistan – is in the middle of low and medium, named upper-low; while the competence of other plants is in a very low level, and with very limited development.

Chinese manufacturing firms' domestic factories have very high competence and are 'leaders' in the factory network. Normally, the competence of their overseas individual factories ranges from low, upper-low, medium to upper-medium. Through the experience of the two in-depth company case studies, we can see that the competence of an overseas individual factory must match the factory's market strategy, market coverage and its parent company's strategic reason to set up the factory. Even though a mismatch may occur in the first instance, they will gradually adapt to match each other.

A market-seeking plant, with its focus on local mass markets or the low-to-medium segment, normally has low competence; while market-seeking plants to serve regional markets always have upper-low competence. Capability-seeking plants, focused on specialised or niche markets, or the high to premium segment, with a regional coverage, normally have medium, even upper-medium, competence levels.

Network level: reconfiguration

A Chinese firm's international factory network is coordinated in all the main processes along its value chain, which includes product design and development, procurement and production. In each process, both Chinese and overseas factories play very important roles in achieving integration effects, meanwhile meeting localised demand.

Product design and development: normally, product design and development processes are completed in Chinese factories before they are transferred to an overseas factory with low competence. In some cases, a low-competence overseas factory may be involved in product feature and performance design to meet local demand. An overseas factory with medium or upper-medium competence will be involved more in product design and development processes, such as pilot production, component design, production process design and development. However, most capital-intensive processes, such as tooling production, will still be centrally completed in China to achieve economies of scale. Moreover, a medium-competence overseas factory may provide a platform to transfer advanced product design and development capability back to Chinese factories.

Procurement: in a low-competence overseas factory, most of material components are centrally sourced from China. They are either centrally produced in Chinese factories to achieve economy of production or centrally procured from Chinese suppliers to achieve economy of purchasing. The sourcing processes are much more complicated in an overseas factory with medium competence. Some material or components are centrally sourced from China, being either purchased or produced. They share similar characteristics: low shipping costs, stable volume and ample low-priced resources in China. Some are sourced locally but based upon a group contract to achieve an integration effect. The overseas factory has autonomy to source other material or components from local suppliers.

Production: currently, most low-competence overseas factories can only be called assembly plants. Compete knock down (CKD – a plant assembling complete imported kits into the product) and semi-knocked down (SKD – a plant assembling cars from incomplete kits, supplementing imported parts with local supplies) parts are completed in China and then transported to overseas factories for assembly, testing and packaging. By doing so, Chinese firms can achieve a big reduction of import tariffs and meanwhile make use of low-cost manufacturing resources in China. Medium-competence overseas factories may involve themselves more in production processes, especially the processes for customisation. However, most labour-intensive processes and capital-intensive processes will still be completed in China. Even the acquired overseas factory with full production processes will gradually transfer part of its production processes back to China to reduce manufacturing costs and achieve economies of scale.

Two types of international manufacturing strategy

In each overseas factory, Chinese manufacturing firms clearly select one type of the following two strategies: market seeking or capability seeking. Table 8.8 illustrates two types of basic strategy and their relationship with international manufacturing systems' characteristics.

Implications for international business studies

In existing theories, the internationalisation process is described as starting from export up to the establishment of overseas factories; while international manufacturing network theories mainly focus on how to run an established global manufacturing network. The manufacturing internationalisation process, which begins from the establishment or acquisition of an overseas manufacturing facility to the management of a cross-border factory network, bridges the scope of these two theories. The research reveals that the manufacturing internationalisation process consists of four different but closely linked dimensions, i.e. strategic reasons to pursue cross-border production (motive dimension), international factory network dispersion (structural dimension), operations of overseas individual plant (node dimension) and international factory network coordination (linkage dimension). Therefore, the manufacturing internationalisation process can also be considered as the internationalisation process of a specific function – manufacturing, which strongly enriches the internationalisation process theory.

Prior research assigned strategic roles to plants based upon various dimensions, among which site competence is one of the most important. However, little research has paid attention to how to measure the competence of a plant. This research has significant implications for the understanding of a plant's competence from a supply network perspective. Normally, the competence of a plant can be ranked as high, medium or low depending upon the operations of the individual plant, the plant in the intra-firm manufacturing network and the plant in its local network.

In prior research, a firm's international production is either 'pushed' by ownership advantages or 'pulled' by location advantages and (or) strategic assets in host countries. This research proposes a 'pull + push'

Table 8.8 *Match between international manufacturing strategy and four dimensions*

		Market seeking	Capability seeking
Strategic reasons to pursue cross-border production		Ownership Advantages → Market	Ownership Advantages → Capability
International manufacturing network dispersion	*Location*	Developing countries and developed countries	Mainly in developed countries
	Sequence	Developing countries → developed countries → developing countries	Developed countries → developing countries
	Mode	Incremental	Radical
Operations of overseas individual factory		Low to upper low	Medium to upper medium
International manufacturing network coordination	*NPD*	NPD is completed in China	Overseas plant involves more in NPD process; some processes are still completed in China
	Procurement	Most are sourced from China	Some are sourced from China based on group contract; some are locally sourced according to local plant's selection
	Production	CKD/SKD parts are produced in China; assembly, testing, packaging in overseas plant	Overseas plant involved in production processes for customization; many processes are still completed in China

circular mechanism: a Chinese firm's international production is pushed by China-related advantages; it is also pulled by market seeking and (or) strategic asset seeking; the acquired experiential knowledge and strategic assets advance a parent company's competitive advantages; then the acquired competitive advantages and the China-related advantages push the Chinese firm to further involvement in cross-border production.

It is widely debated whether firms from developing economies could survive or succeed by putting production activities into the Triad. Both researchers and practitioners have shown negative attitudes on this. Here we find that Chinese firms not only possess many China-related competitive advantages, but they could also acquire many firm-related ownership advantages in the manufacturing internationalisation process. The 'pull + push' mechanism enables Chinese firms' survival and success in overseas markets, even in the Triad. This research therefore enhances the confidence of executives and managers in Chinese firms to start or further involve their companies in cross-border production.

COMMENTARIES ON PART II

(II.i) How emerging market multinational enterprises upgrade capabilities using value-chain configuration in advanced economies

ALVARO CUERVO-CAZURRA

Introduction

Global value-chain configuration helps multinational companies improve their competitive advantage due to the integration within the firm of the comparative advantage of other countries and the competitive advantage of firms from other countries. Many studies of global supply chain take the view of developed market multinational enterprises (DMNEs) that tend to off-shore outsource production to developing countries in order to access the comparative advantage of low-cost labour (e.g. Lewin *et al.*, 2009; see articles reviewed by Contractor *et al.*, 2010, in the special issue on off-shore outsourcing). However, the emergence of emerging market multinational enterprises (EMNEs) challenges some of the assumptions of these studies because such firms are already operating in countries with low cost and, in principle, would not benefit from a similar global value-chain configuration. In contrast to DMNEs, EMNEs suffer from comparative disadvantages of operating in home countries with challenging institutions and without sophisticated resource intermediaries (Cuervo-Cazurra and Genc, 2008; Khanna and Palepu, 2010). Thus, the study of EMNEs can provide new insights on global value-chain configuration that previous studies of DMNEs may have overlooked.

In this commentary I analyse global value-chain configuration by EMNEs, specifically describing four strategies that these firms can use in advanced economies to upgrade their capabilities and solve their developing-country comparative disadvantages. I then illustrate the four strategies using the four country studies in this part of the book.

174

How emerging market multinational enterprises upgrade capabilities using value-chain configuration in advanced economies

Insights on global value-chain configuration have been gained mostly by analysing DMNEs. The concept of the value chain is associated with the work of Porter (1985) and his dissection of the creation of value in a firm into separate activities: primary, or those that are directly involved in the creation of products (inbound logistics, production, outbound logistics, sales and marketing and service); and secondary, or those that support the creation of products (firm infrastructure, human resources, technology and procurement). This framework was applied to the study of multinational companies with the argument that parts of the value chain could be relocated to countries that provided a comparative advantage (Kogut, 1985a; Porter, 1986a), thus contributing to the overall advantage of the multinational company by providing arbitrage (Kogut, 1985b; Ghemawat, 2007) and learning opportunities (Prahalad and Doz, 1987; Bartlett and Ghoshal, 1989). Much of the subsequent research focused on studying how DMNEs could relocate parts of their value chain to developing countries in order to benefit from the comparative advantage of those countries in low-cost factors of production, especially labour (e.g. Ferdows, 1989; see recent reviews in Bidgoli, 2010). The relocation to developing countries, first of production and then of higher value-added activities such as research and development (R&D), generated a debate regarding the trend and value to DMNEs of off-shore outsourcing (Mudambi, 2008; Beugelsdijk *et al.*, 2009; Contractor *et al.*, 2010). Studies generally viewed emerging market firms as subcontractors to DMNEs, producing to the specifications of those firms.

Mostly absent in these studies has been the coordination of a global value chain by EMNEs. These MNEs have received limited attention partly because until recently they were not large global players, and despite some studies in the 1980s that identified their emergence (Lall, 1983; Wells, 1983), it was not until the 2000s that these firms started to figure prominently in the popular press (e.g. *The Economist*, 2008) and academic literature (e.g. see articles in the special issues edited by Aulakh, 2007; Luo and Tung, 2007; Cuervo-Cazurra, 2012; and in the books edited by Sauvant, 2008; and Ramamurti and Singh, 2009a).

The coordination of global value chain by EMNEs challenges some of the assumptions of previous studies analysing DMNEs, particularly the relocation of activities to benefit from low-cost labour, because EMNEs are already operating in low-cost countries.

I argue that EMNEs configure their global value chains, in part, to upgrade their capabilities and solve the comparative disadvantages of their countries of origin. EMNEs suffer a comparative disadvantage of operating in home countries that lack advanced institutional and technological infrastructures (Cuervo-Cazurra and Genc, 2011). EMNEs can solve some of these comparative disadvantages by reorganising their value chains in advanced economies. Thus, I propose four strategies, based on a two-by-two matrix illustrated in Table II.1. One axis represents the type of advantage the EMNE is accessing, either the comparative advantage of advanced countries or the competitive advantage of advanced country firms. The other axis represents the location within the value chain of the advantage that is being upgraded, either upstream in the value chain or downstream.

The first strategy improves the financial possibilities of the EMNE by accessing the comparative advantage in low-cost, abundant and reliable capital markets in advanced economies. In contrast to other factors of production such as labour or land, finance tends to have lower costs and be more accessible in advanced economies than in developing countries because the more stable macro-economic policies and better investor protection both support deeper capital markets. The EMNE can relocate some of its financing activities to advanced economies, obtaining loans or quoting shares in capital markets in advanced economies, to reduce its cost of capital at home. Relocating financial

Table II.1 *EMNE strategies for global reconfiguration of the value chain in advanced economies*

		Type of advantage accessed	
		Comparative advantage	Competitive advantage
Location in value chain of the advantage accessed	Upstream (inputs)	Low-cost and reliable finance	Technology
	Downstream (outputs)	Customer intelligence and innovation	Brands and marketing

activities to advanced economies can also help it exit some of the problematic governance conditions of the home country (Stulz, 1999; Coffee, 2002).

The second strategy enhances the EMNE's customer responsiveness and innovation by accessing the comparative advantage in sophisticated consumer knowledge present in advanced economies. In advanced economies there are large pools of sophisticated and demanding consumers. These consumers can be a market for products, but more importantly they can also provide a source of demand for advanced products and a sounding board for innovations (Vernon, 1966). The EMNE can relocate part of its marketing and sales function to an advanced country to directly learn the intricacies of the demands of sophisticated consumers and improve its products and customer responsiveness at home.

The third strategy upgrades the technological base of the EMNE via access to the competitive advantage of advanced country firms. The EMNE can establish alliances or purchase advanced economy firms to obtain their sophisticated technologies; it can then relocate part of its technological development to the advanced country and transfer knowledge about advanced technologies to the home country operations to compensate for the deficiencies in technological development at home. Alliances and acquisitions of advanced economy firms facilitate the transfer and understanding of complex technology in a manner that is not possible by licensing technology from an advanced economy supplier (Kogut and Zander, 1993).

The fourth strategy improves the brands and distribution of the EMNEs by accessing the competitive advantage of firms in advanced economies. The EMNE can purchase firms in advanced economies that have well-established brands and extensive distribution systems there. By acquiring the advanced economy firm, the EMNE obtains the reputation and brand name that it lacked in an advanced economy, linking this to its existing competitive and comparative advantage of producing in the emerging market.

Insights from Brazil, Russia, India and China

The preceding four chapters that analyse firms in Brazil, Russia, India and China provide deeper insights on the four strategies discussed. The chapters present examples of firms from very different countries, illustrating the variety of operational environments. In terms of sources of comparative advantage, two countries have large consumer markets (China and India) and two have large sources of natural resources (Russia and Brazil). In terms of economic systems, two countries used to be communist and have transitioned to capitalism (Russia and China) and two had a long capitalist tradition and liberalised their economies (Brazil and India). Hence, instead of being exemplars of what an average developing country is, they are exceptional countries that can help build theory by analysing extreme cases (Yin, 2003). Rather than summarise the four chapters, I review how some of the examples discussed in the articles illustrate the strategies introduced in this chapter.

Fleury, Fleury and Borini (Chapter 5) analyse the internationalisation of leading Brazilian MNCs. They discuss how the meat-packer JBS-Friboi acquired the US firm Swift to access established brands and distribution systems in the US. The autoparts firm Sabo's acquisition of the German firm Kako illustrates the use of acquisitions to access superior technology and R&D that helps improve the firm's operations. Similarly, the apparel maker Coteminas purchased the US firm Spring-Wells to access established brands and market distribution in the US, linking this with its production facilities in low-cost Mexico.

Katkalo and Medvedev (Chapter 6) review value-chain configuration by Russian firms. They mention how the mining firm Norilsk Nickel purchased the US firm Stillwater to access its client base and facilitate the sale of Norilsk Nickel products in the US. The oil firm Lukoil expanded in the US using acquisitions to access off-shore exploration technology it lacked at home.

Athreye (Chapter 7) analyses Indian MNCs in the software and pharmaceutical industries. Whereas software firms invested in advanced countries mostly to gain customer intelligence on the products needed, relying on the comparative advantage of India in product development, pharmaceutical firms invested in advanced economies to obtain the advanced R&D and regulatory and legal expertise they lacked.

Finally, Wang and Shi (Chapter 8) analyse the experience of two Chinese MNEs. One of the firms, a white goods manufacturer, located its overseas R&D centres in advanced countries (Canada, France, Japan, the Netherlands and the US). The other firm, a television producer, purchased a European firm to improve distribution and upgrade its capabilities.

Conclusions

The conditions of the country of origin induce EMNEs to manage their value chains somewhat differently from how DMNEs do. EMNEs reconfigure their value chains in advanced economies in search of low-cost factors of production, but not the usual ones such as labour; instead they access the comparative advantage of advanced country firms in low-cost and reliable finance. EMNEs also reconfigure their global value chains in advanced economies in search of sophisticated resources to solve the comparative disadvantage of their home countries. These sophisticated resources take the form of knowledge about demanding consumers prevalent in advanced economies, frontier technology or well-known brands and distribution systems that advanced economy firms have at home. Other reconfigurations of the value chain in developing countries by EMNEs, such as the search for natural resources or the search for markets for existing products, are similar to what DMNEs can do in other advanced economies and were not discussed here.

Thus, this chapter and the accompanying ones contribute to a better understanding of not only EMNEs and how they differ from DMNEs (Cuervo-Cazurra, 2007, 2012; Guillén and Garcia-Canal, 2009; Ramamurti, 2009b), but also how the conditions of the home country of the firm influence its global strategy (Cuervo-Cazurra, 2006; Cuervo-Cazurra and Genc, 2008, 2011; Peng *et al.*, 2009; see Cuervo-Cazurra, 2011, for a review). EMNEs not only benefit from comparative advantages in low-cost labour, but also suffer from comparative disadvantages in under-developed institutions and technological infrastructure that drive their internationalisation and the reconfiguration of their global value chains.

(II.ii) Value-chain configurations of emerging country multinationals

J A G J I T   S I N G H   S R A I

Introduction

The papers by Fleury *et al.* (Chapter 5), Katkalo and Medvedev (Chapter 6), Athreye (Chapter 7) and Wang and Shi (Chapter 8) consider aspects of value-chain configuration and subsidiary management of emerging market multinational enterprises (EMNEs), each building on studies from one of the four major 'BRIC' countries (Brazil, Russia, India and China).

In this cross-case review, the collective commentaries suggest that, in addition to dimensions widely discussed in the international business (IB) domain, integrating the analysis of industry context and partner network tier-structure and dynamics can provide new insights to the configuration of these value chains, and how these impact their internationalisation evolution paths. The chapters under review consider how the internationalisation of both developed market multinational enterprises (DMNEs) and emerging market multinational enterprises (EMNEs), and the role of their subsidiaries, is impacted by value-chain configuration considerations. It is useful to synthesise these perspectives and suggest whether analysis of value-chain configuration across these studies can suggest more generalisable patterns.

The ownership location internalisation (OLI) eclectic model, for example, suggests exploitation of firm advantages (Dunning, 1988), but is perhaps most relevant in horizontal MNEs (Caves, 1986), and where internationalisation takes place within complete chains. As Dunning notes in later revisions, the model does not extend to the reconfiguration of MNE assets and the development of industrial networks. More recent work, as in the 'linkage, leverage, learning' (LLL) model developed by Mathews (2006), builds on observations from the latecomer 'dragon' multinationals from the Far East, and suggest a more fragmented value-chain perspective involving cooperative upstream supply networks that support downstream competitive

180

advantages. The Uppsala model also suggests a more network perspective involving incremental internationalisation paths by exploring and exploiting (Johansson and Vahlne, 1977) network opportunities and knowledge acquisitions.

The routes followed by EMNEs in their international strategies typically involve a mix of mergers and acquisitions (M&A), strategic alliances and/or greenfield investments, depending on the phase of development. Combinations of country-specific advantages and firm-specific advantages (CSA–FSA) are key contextual factors that might influence the value-chain configurations adopted. Srai and Fleet (2010) extend configuration research in international operations management (Srai and Gregory, 2008) and value-chain configuration analysis (Srai and Shi, 2008) to review M&A behaviours of EMNEs and how they might differ from traditional MNC behaviours. While the value-chain concept is not new, the analysis framework is used to capture the alternative configurations EMNEs adopt during their investment and internationalisation strategies, with the aim to identify the main drivers and trends at each 'stage' of the value chain, the key linkages between these stages, and the importance or otherwise of their international location. This is particularly relevant for EMNEs whose manufacturing value chains are increasingly fragmented and globally distributed; Table II.2 summarises results observed in their review of EMNEs and their M&A activity in both developed and emerging country contexts.

Srai and Fleet's (2010) reviews show how EMNE investment patterns differ from the traditional MNEs, and that their investments in emerging markets are largely supply-side *resource* and demand-side *market seeking*, and those in developed markets reflect objectives linked to *network access* (technology and markets). In contrast, traditional MNEs' international investments are driven by the need for *network efficiency* (particularly in the case of emerging markets) *and market access* driven arrangements that integrate low labour cost country (LCC) resources and emerging market potential.

The contributions of the BRIC cases

The four chapters, in terms of their analytic approaches, consider the role of subsidiaries from a number of research perspectives; the dynamic capabilities of the firm (Brazil), the changing role of the subsidiary (all),

Table II.2 Description of internationalisation investment motives (adapted from Srai and Fleet, 2010)

EMNEs invest to secure

	R&D/design and technology	Input materials and supply management	Production/core company operations	Customers and distribution routes to market	Service provision and after sales service
E to E	Unlikely (except where local solutions are required)	To secure sources of cheap or scarce materials	To acquire production capacity close to target markets	Not a major motive (except in distribution channel development)	Unlikely (other than in home markets or where product–service offering are coupled)
E to D	To acquire advanced R&D/design capability	Only likely in resource-rich countries and for scarce resources	To acquire production know-how or reputation	To acquire customers or developed routes to market	Unlikely (except in product–service solutions)
	Vertical upstream		Horizontal	Vertical downstream	

evolving competencies in both parent and subsidiary (Brazil, China) and coordination patterns (all). The studies consider strategic motives and influence of CSA/FSA, capability seeking, capability and competency development and coordination patterns. From a value-chain perspective, particular insights emerge on applying the value-chain configuration analysis approach. The approach is amenable to both intra-firm network analysis as well as inter-firm studies where significant network relationships between third parties are present.

The chapters *collectively* confirm the significant influence of industry structures on value-chain activity and internationalisation patterns. Wang and Shi consider the white/brown goods sector, a highly modular product category that permits dispersion of activities and significant decoupling of R&D from the assembly process, and equally distributed and decoupled sales models. They describe how Chinese white goods firms show a product technology, market and brand focus in their internationalisation rather than a production network-based efficiency agenda which the home country already possesses.

Fleury *et al.* discuss Brazilian firm internationalisation in the context of late-movers, following previous waves of internationalisation by Western firms seeking low-cost labour and developing market access, Japanese waves of internationalisation preferring greenfield operations that exploit home-country competencies while seeking local production in developed and developing markets, and the exploration of the new frontier markets of Latin America and Africa in more recent times.

Katkalo and Medvedev comment on the limitations of largely descriptive accounts of EMNE development. They convincingly argue that traditional perspectives of CSA and FSA analyses do not explain the rise of EMNEs, and that foreign direct investment (FDI) analysis cannot capture easily non-equity-based arrangements that MNEs increasingly favour, a trend identified in recent world investment trends (UNCTAD, 2011). They suggest a focus on production value chains and the assessment of business models may provide insights on EMNE development. Also they recognise that the industry sector (or in this author's view industry context, tier-structure and dynamics) in which EMNEs sit will determine many aspects of their international development. In their review of Russian MNEs they note that size can support more vertically integrated models (largely natural resource firms), whereas smaller firms will globalise through more partnered approaches, and that these descriptions often characterise particular industry sectors. A key exception in the data is where a natural resource firm in the production of titanium, due to its position in the value chain, requires a partnered model as the resource is used in many industries and forward vertically integrated models are not viable options.

The home-country context across the four BRIC host economies also reflect a rather divergent mix; from more market-based environments (Brazil, India) to those that operate in more centralised economies (China, Russia), strongly impacted by the role of governments. From a value-chain perspective, centralised economies appear to enable more vertically integrated arrangements as internationalising firms represent regional and national flagships supported by strong institutional bodies, and CSAs that often enable dominant home-market positions, often institutionally insulated from direct internal/external competition. In more market-based economies, more disaggregated value-chain models are observed, perhaps more able to accommodate outsourcing arrangements and partnerships. Access to finance can also vary significantly at national levels, where availability of capital for foreign acquisition may lie within the purview of institutional bodies.

Empirical data from Brazilian studies suggest that firms are cautious in their internationalisation, incrementally developing a multidomestic footprint, with subsidiaries with production facilities particularly contributing to advancing corporate knowledge. Fleury *et al.* comment on how configuration perspectives described by Srai and Gregory (2008) might provide potential explanations on the internationalisation development of firms. The data suggest value-chain activities that are internationalised are driven by efficiency with economies of scale in some industries not warranting overseas subsidiaries in Latin America, but off-shoring/outsourcing is often the case in more remote locations where demand justified local production. They also note that the reverse smile curve is evident where the 'space' left by traditional MNEs provides entry points for Brazilian subsidiaries to operate. Beyond production, other upstream and downstream functional investments result in more multidomestic footprints emerging as firms move up the maturity phase of international development.

Wang and Shi explore the development of two Chinese MNEs, both in disaggregated value-chain sectors of white/brown goods, and identify their motivations as being essentially market- and/or capability-seeking. This perhaps confirms that network design takes place at the function level, each function optimising based on CSA/FSA considerations, rapidly resulting in idiosyncratic multidomestic footprints. In the case of Chinese firms in mature technology sectors, the CSA/FSA advantages of home country production drive more market- and capability-seeking investments rather than in overseas production.

Athreye examines Indian MNEs in knowledge-intensive industries of software and pharmaceuticals, suggesting that their strengths lie in suppliers of intermediate products, operating positions in a narrow segment of the value chain, where the home country context provides competitive advantages. Attempts at a broader role within the value chain, attempting to emulate traditional MNEs, have been problematic, suggesting that 'value' lies at home and less so in their overseas subsidiaries. This concept of chain length and position in the chain, widely discussed in the operations management community, is perhaps less considered in IB circles and may be considered as a form of boundary condition in which EMNEs can operate during their early stages of development.

Ownership structures and CSA also appear to influence value-chain configuration where figurehead leadership patterns (such as family-owned firms (India), regional leaders (China) or monopolistic positions (Russia) can enable greater risk-taking extending the value-chain footprint of the firm in areas not previously within firm remits. However, these may not necessarily be acquisition-based but involve more partnership-based models, which require understanding of how supply-chain configurations are evolving.

Conclusions

Several themes emerge from the studies of value-chain internationalisation patterns of firms from the BRIC countries. Industry context, tier structure and dynamics can be seen to play a vital role in the internationalisation paths of EMNEs at both firm and subsidiary level. Furthermore, firm position in short/long value chains within a particular industry structure can essentially determine possible evolution paths.

In the case of platform technologies that support multi-tiered supply-chain industry structures, a specialist supplier or coordination role within a highly dispersed and partnered model emerges. Where industry structure is highly integrated, with close coupling of value-chain activities, these tend to support more vertically integrated solutions with part/full co-location of value-chain activities. In these two extreme cases we can see that:

- in highly fragmented industrial systems, fine slicing of the value chain (Rugman *et al.*, 2011) allows 'network design' at the functional level across each element of the disaggregated value chain; and
- that where industry structures require close-coupling of value-chain activities or short assembly-based supply chains, more integrated value-chain models emerge that conform more closely to the archetypal models first introduced by Bartlett and Ghoshal.

Porter's (1986b) multidomestic and global organisation concepts remain relevant but are nuanced by more complex subsidiary-specific arrangements, with different drivers for EMNEs linked to location-specific resource-filling entry strategies, often determined by spaces released by established MNEs and where CSA/FSA make these attractive options.

In summary, we can observe that in largely decoupled value chains, where cross-functional integrations are less significant, value-chain network design largely takes place at the functional level, by:

- internationalisation of product development and marketing largely driven by knowledge acquisition motives in developed markets;
- upstream supply integration in distant markets where sizeable volume/demand supports investments in component manufacture;
- production internationalisation generally complies with 'standard' manufacturing and supply-chain footprint analysis, with overseas production units driven by economies of scale and value-density considerations requiring near-to/local market sourcing for distant markets;
- downstream investments in routes-to-market that support sales and product servicing channel developments.

However, in product categories where particular functional integrations are critical to effective industrial systems, or where disaggregation is not practical or advantageous, then partly or fully vertically integrated value-chain configuration patterns are observed, in:

- largely vertically integrated models where backward integration is driven by extraction-based industries that represent 'closed' networks;

- part upstream integration where R&D and production are necessarily closely coupled activities (e.g. in bio-pharma due to close interactions between process, product and regulatory approval as found by Srai and Alinaghian, 2013), or where supply-side integration supported by access to local supplier base supports efficient supply (e.g. automotive);
- part downstream integration where market exploitation requires near-to-market production and integrated product-service business models (e.g. aerospace).

The cases suggest that industry dynamics associated with the structure and aggregation (or disaggregation) of value-chain activities support more centralised (or dispersed) business models. Disaggregation involves more complex footprint options, with the design of networks involving value-chain functional level optimisation, resulting in global networks with high variety idiosyncratic subsidiaries, often with specialised roles emergent in long multi-tier supply chains. The network design and coordination challenges that these more complex value-chains options present, with alternative arrangements in different international subsidiaries, imply that network design and effective coordination implementation are critical yet elusive competencies EMNEs will increasingly need to develop.

PART III

Mergers and acquisitions and competitive advantage

9 Cross-border M&A and competitive advantage of Brazilian EMNEs

ALVARO B. CYRINO AND ERIKA P. BARCELLOS

Introduction

Cross-border mergers and acquisitions (M&A) are becoming increasingly important as a source of financing for foreign direct investment (FDI; Dunning and Lundan, 2008; Hitt *et al.*, 2001). According to UNCTAD's *World Investment Report* (2010), from 2000 to 2009 the total value of M&A transactions peaked in 2007 at around $1,023 trillion and, due to the world financial crisis, fell to $707 billion in 2008 and $250 billion in 2009. Foreign M&A have been reported to be the preferred vehicle of FDI during the last twenty years.

Lately, the importance of emerging countries as sources and recipients of FDI flows has been increasing. Thus, from 2000 to 2009, participation of emerging countries in the world's total outward FDI flows has grown from 11 per cent to 27 per cent of the total world's outward FDI (UNCTAD, 2010). Since the nineties, the world has witnessed the growth of multinationals from emerging economies, notably from the so-called BRIC countries (Brazil, Russia, India and China). For instance, the number of companies from these countries reported in the *Fortune Global 500* study has grown from twenty-four in 2005 to sixty-seven in 2010. The Boston Consulting Group study on global challengers (Verma *et al.*, 2011) in its 2011 edition on the 100 most successful companies from emerging markets, reports seventy-two companies from the BRIC countries (thirty-three from China, twenty from India, thirteen from Brazil and six from Russia).

Brazil is a player in this global trend. Trade and investment liberalisation policies introduced by the federal government in the late eighties, including the privatisation of several state-owned enterprises (SOEs), led first to an increase in inward foreign investments, by foreign multinational corporations (MNCs) in Brazil. A great part of this inward FDI came from developed countries and was achieved through M&A deals, mostly directed to the recent privatised utilities.

These new international players contributed to increase the level of rivalry in Brazilian markets, forcing many large domestic companies to upgrade product, process and management capabilities in order to remain competitive. The new competitive landscape also induced many large Brazilian firms to search for new sources of growth beyond those provided by their previously protected domestic markets. In this process, cross-border M&A became one of the preferred vehicles of international expansion for Brazilian MNCs, in relation to other forms of investments.

This chapter is structured as follows. The next section briefly characterises the internationalisation process of Brazilian companies and their underlying firm-specific advantages (FSAs).

There follows a description of the evolution of M&A as a preferred mode of international expansion by Brazilian multinationals. In particular, the authors focus on the drivers and motives of cross-border M&A for Brazilian companies trying to relate them to their specific strategic considerations. The final section is dedicated to the conclusions.

M&A entry and expansion mode in the internationalisation process of Brazilian companies

As a general reminder, research on M&A could be characterised as prolific, yet profoundly contradictory and inconclusive in its results, especially when it focuses on performance issues. One of the recent reviews on the acquisition performance has described the current situation in the following terms:

> Unfortunately, research does not uniformly support managers' alleged enthusiasm for the practice, with the impact of acquisitions on acquiring firms' performance remaining 'inconclusive' … Further, [existing research] has not consistently identified antecedents that can be used to predict post-acquisition performance. (King et al., 2004)

Compared to domestic M&A, research on cross-border M&A poses considerably more challenges to researchers, since it involves companies from different nationalities adding another layer of complexity, including the risks linked to the 'liability of foreignness' (Zaheer, 1995) and 'double-layered acculturation' (Barkema *et al.*, 1996).

Therefore, it is no surprise that research on cross-border M&A has also produced deceiving evaluations by leading researchers on the subject. In a review paper on the state of extant research, Shimizu *et al.*, (2004) characterise it as 'unfortunately fragmented, leaving gaps that need to be addressed'.

Indifferent to the shortcomings pointed out in the literature, cross-border M&A continue to be one of the preferred means for international expansion, at least for Brazilian companies expanding abroad.

As usual, most of the Brazilian MNCs began their internationalisation efforts through exports. After accumulating the required knowledge to deal with international customers, they began to internationalise through more committed forms of internationalisation, usually involving outward FDI. The first movement was the establishment of sales, marketing and after-marketing services subsidiaries or offices in the host countries. After these initial forays, the escalation of international commitments usually included the acquisition of a local company, in the same line of business or in related ones, involving production assets and marketing and sales capabilities (Cyrino and Barcellos, 2007; Dunning and Lundan 2008).

As a whole, Brazilian multinationals seem to form a very diversified group. The number of companies reported as Brazilian multinationals in several studies on the subject has varied from forty-six (Fundação Dom Cabral, 2011) to eighty-one (Fleury and Fleury, 2011). Contrary to common thinking, only a few can be said to draw their competitive advantages on Brazilian natural resource endowments. From the forty-six most internationalised non-financial companies (using UNCTAD's transnationalisation index), only six of them rely heavily on natural resource endowments (meat and poultry processing, oil and minerals) for their internationalisation. Actually, Vale (mining) and Petrobras (oil and energy), due to their size, dwarf many other Brazilian multinationals on the list. However, among these forty-six companies, there are four companies from basic industrial products (steel, pulp and paper, cement); four utilities; eight manufacturers of intermediate industrial products; five information technology (IT) companies (hardware, software and services); three heavy construction companies; four services companies (transportation and logistics); one aircraft and two bus manufacturers; and five consumer good companies (Fundação Dom Cabral, 2011).

In spite of their differences, there appears to be some underlying similarities regarding the internationalisation process of Brazilian multinationals.

The great majority of them have developed well-honed capabilities to operate successfully in the relatively large and complex Brazilian

market. Most of them have been market leaders and have also accumulated experience as exporters before investing abroad. As such, they
were able to develop economies of scale and scope, and also marketing,
distribution and management capabilities, which could later be used as
a springboard to expand internationally.

This background seems important for the discussion of the evolution
and importance of cross-border M&A for the international expansion
of Brazilian multinationals, which are examined in the next section.

Outward M&A of Brazilian companies

To analyse the evolution of cross-border M&A, the authors relied on
data of individual transactions extracted from the ThomsonONE.com
Investment Banking database.[1] 1990 was chosen as the starting point
of the series because it marks the beginning of the economic liberalisation process, which strongly affected FDI flows to and from Brazil.
The specific data considered were the identification of the acquiring
Brazilian firm (name, Standard Industrial Classification [SIC] code),
the target firm nationality and business line (SIC code), the date of the
announced or realised acquisition or merger, the reported value of
the transaction, the current status of the deal and the percentage of
control of the acquiring firm in the acquired. Only transactions that
were formally announced or realised were considered. Rumoured
transactions were excluded, as were withdrawn deals.

During the last twenty-one years, Brazilian companies were involved
in 433 foreign transactions of M&A. The total value of the reported
transactions during the 1990–2010 period amounts to $65 billion.
Since the reported values represent only 51 per cent of the total number
of transactions, the actual value of transactions could be significantly
higher (Table 9.1).

While the data present some fluctuations from year to year, the
trend points clearly towards a marked increase in the number of
transactions and in the total value of the deals during the period.
The median value shows a more erratic evolution due, in particular,

---

[1] In the text, the authors use the term mergers and acquisitions (M&A) to express
their affiliation to the subject as it is referred in the literature. Strictly speaking,
there was only one merger reported in our study: all the other transactions were
acquisitions.

Table 9.1 *Number and value of transactions ($m): outbound cross-border M&A from Brazilian companies*

	Announced and completed transactions	Unreported values	Reported values	Total value of reported transaction	Median
1990	1	1	0	–	–
1991	2	0	2	44.98	22.49
1992	5	3	2	55.57	27.79
1993	8	2	6	272.17	26.49
1994	8	4	4	54.01	14.85
1995	16	9	7	260.12	30.00
1996	9	5	4	66.44	16.51
1997	8	2	6	494.30	48.24
1998	16	6	10	634.04	44.86
1999	14	9	5	485.85	102.00
2000	27	17	10	909.25	36.30
2001	12	5	7	1,662.95	69.00
2002	13	8	5	2,058.24	346.38
2003	10	5	5	83.98	11.80
2004	19	10	9	8,924.22	100.45
2005	23	12	11	3,313.50	240.00
2006	31	18	13	22,161.79	155.00
2007	54	23	31	7,492.22	92.50
2008	62	34	28	3,900.79	36.18
2009	37	21	16	2,491.02	33.25
2010	58	28	30	9,609.02	131.87
Total	433	222	211	64,974.46	

to the high value of some of the individual acquisitions. Figure 9.1 depicts the data in a graphic form.

The number of transactions also confirms the importance of international M&A. From only a few in the early 1990s, transactions peaked in 2008, with a total of sixty-two for this year alone. While in 2009, during the peak of the world financial crisis, foreign M&A have declined in number and value, they rapidly rebounded in 2010 to their previous 2007 levels.

An indicator of the importance of cross-border M&A as a vehicle of FDI can be obtained by the comparison of the outward flows of investments with the announced and completed acquisitions values over the period. Outward FDI flows from Brazil have been increasing, except

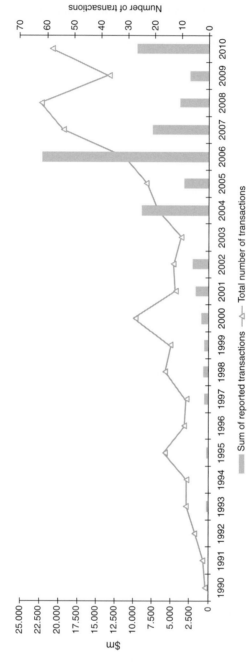

Figure 9.1 Number of transactions and total reported values. Outbound M&A from Brazilian companies

Source: ThomsonONE.com Investment Banking; UNCTAD, 2010

Table 9.2 *Outward FDI and foreign acquisitions of Brazilian companies*

	1990–2	1993–4	1995–6	1997–8	1999–2000	2001–2	2003–4	2005–6	2007–8	2009–10
Outward FDI from Brazil ($bn)	1.776	1.182	0.627	3.97	3.972	0.225	10.056	30.719	27.524	1.416
Reported value of outbound M&A from Brazilian companies ($bn)	0.101	0.326	0.327	1.128	1.395	3.721	9.008	25.475	11.393	12.100

Source: ThomsonONE.com Investment Banking

for during the 2001–2 and the 2009–10 periods. The same growth trend is verified by the total value of the reported acquisitions during the period. The comparison of the two sets of data reveal that outbound M&A have been an increasingly important mode of expansion utilised by the Brazilian MNCs in their internationalisation trajectories.[2] Table 9.2 presents the evolution of the two series of data.

Analysis of individual transactions also shows an extreme level of concentration of acquiring Brazilian MNCs. Table 9.3 shows the value and the number of transactions by individual companies during the period covered by this study.

According to Table 9.3, the twenty largest acquirers by value were responsible for 94.1 per cent of the total reported value of all transactions during the period. The first five main acquirers represent more than 73 per cent of the value of total acquisitions announced and completed during the period, but only 26.1 per cent of the number of acquisitions. The highest individual deal – Vale's acquisition of Canadian Inco – represented 26.3 per cent of the total value of all reported transactions during the whole period.

[2] Data on outward FDI and total reported transaction values are not directly comparable. The main difference among the two series of data is that FDI flows depict the real flows of capital from Brazil to other countries in a specific period, while many of the outbound M&A figures are total values of announced deals, which can take time to be approved. Even when they are completed, the capital flows can be spread over several years, depending on how the deal is structured.

Table 9.3 *The twenty main Brazilian cross-border acquirers*

Company	Announced transactions	Unreported values	Reported values	Total value of reported transaction ($m)	% total value of transactions from 1990–2010	Cumulative % total value	% of total number of acquisitions from 1990–2010	% of value reported
Vale SA	20	7	13	25,098.86	38.6	38.6	4.6	41.0
Ambev	14	4	12	10,391.60	16.0	54.6	4.2	17.0
Grupo Votorantim	23	8	15	5,230.00	8.0	62.7	6.2	8.5
Gerdau SA	22	4	18	3,486.77	5.4	68.0	5.1	5.7
Petrobras	26	9	17	3,473.87	5.3	73.4	6.0	5.7
JBS SA	8	2	6	2,653.14	4.1	77.5	1.8	4.3
Banco Itau Holding Financeira	10	4	6	1,720.00	2.6	80.1	2.5	2.8
Martrig Frigorificos e Alimentos SA	8	3	5	1,601.00	2.5	82.6	2.3	2.6
Grupo Camargo Correa	3	1	2	1,205.17	1.9	84.4	0.7	2.0
Telemar Norte Leste SA	1	0	1	961.32	1.5	85.9	0.2	1.6

Magnesita SA	1	0	1	943.69	1.5	87.4	0.2	1.5
Banco do Brasil SA	6	3	3	814.43	1.3	88.6	1.4	1.3
BM&F Bovespa SA	1	0	1	620.00	1.0	89.6	0.2	1.0
CSN	6	2	4	578.33	0.9	90.5	1.4	0.9
Banco Bradesco SA	5	0	5	573.52	0.9	91.3	1.2	0.9
DH&C Outsourcing SA	1	0	1	421.79	0.6	91.9	0.2	0.7
Suzano Holding SA	3	0	3	380.00	0.6	92.5	0.9	0.6
Ocean Air	1	0	1	364.00	0.6	93.1	0.2	0.6
Centennial Asset Ltd	1	0	1	350.47	0.5	93.6	0.2	0.6
Braskem SA	1	0	1	350.00	0.5	94.1	0.2	0.6
Total	**161**	**47**	**116**	**61,217.96**	**94.1**			**100.0**

Source: ThomsonONE.com Investment Banking

Table 9.4 *Percentage of controlling power targeted by the acquiring company*

	100%	Between 51% and 99.99%	Below 50%	Not informed
Number of transactions	185	67	75	106
Total transaction (%)	43	15	17	24

Source: ThomsonONE.com Investment Banking

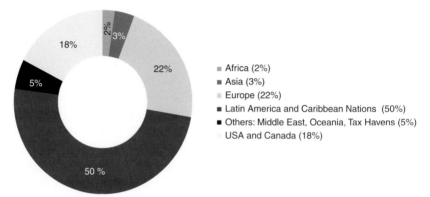

Figure 9.2 Geographic location of the foreign acquisition targets, 1990–2010 (% of total transactions)
Source: ThomsonONE.com Investment Banking

Only one of the reported deals was a hostile takeover. Of the informed deals, 77 per cent were targeted to total control or the majority of the voting shares (Table 9.4).

The acquisition targets were concentrated in Latin American and Caribbean countries (50 per cent), Europe (22 per cent) and US/ Canada (18 per cent). Other regions represented only 10 per cent of the total transactions during the period, as shown in Figure 9.2.

Factors driving cross-border M&A and its effects on competitive advantage of Brazilian multinationals

Regarding the Brazilian multinationals, the authors search for a better understanding of (1) the drivers that are associated to the M&A mode of international expansion, and (2) the kind of FSAs that companies engaged in foreign acquisitions consider important for gaining and sustaining competitive advantage.

Looking for a plausible explanation of the underlying motives of cross-border M&A of the Brazilian multinationals, the authors used primary data from a previous survey (Cyrino *et al.*, 2007) with a sample of 161 companies from Argentina, Brazil and Chile about their internationalisation practices and intents. In order to control for the expansion strategy, a sample of the fifty-four Brazilian companies participating in the survey were divided in two groups: (1) companies that have made one or more foreign acquisitions; and (2) companies that have not internationalised through M&A. The authors tested for differences in the means of the motives of international expansion and in the competitive advantages between the two groups, using the independent sample t-test for comparison of means. Table 9.A1 in the appendix to this chapter shows the results of the t-tests for the motives of the groups, and Table 9.A2 the results of the t-tests for the competitive advantages of the groups.

Analysis of Table 9.1 indicates that the Brazilian companies that have internationalised through mergers and acquisitions are more motivated than those that have not used this mode by: (1) overcoming tariff and non-tariff barriers in international markets; (2) acquiring a better understanding of the international consumers; (3) exploiting their existing technological, product differentiation, brands, patents managerial capabilities of the company in international ventures; (4) acquiring international assets for low prices; and (5) taking advantage of the positive effect for the company's image in the home country.[3]

The analysis of the companies' perceived competitive advantages (Table 9.A2) indicates that the ones that have internationalised through M&A differentiate themselves from the others in terms of the following FSAs: (1) the ability to develop relationships with international government and regulatory bodies; (2) privileged access to a pool of talented managerial, technical or scientific people at competitive costs; (3) higher scale in relation to international competitors; (4) capabilities to operate in the conditions of other emergent markets; (5) relatively more efficient and modern equipments and plants; (6) better technical support services in the markets where the company is present; and (7) headquarters support in terms of corporate services and resources.[4]

---

[3] At 5 per cent or 10 per cent confidence intervals.
[4] At 5 per cent or 10 per cent confidence intervals.

These data suggest that Brazilian multinationals use foreign acquisition in order to exploit the FSAs already accumulated through previous experience. The set of FSAs perceived to be exploited are linked to economies of scale, product and process technological assets, support services and other intangible capabilities and resources, like brands, patents and managerial knowledge, particularly when these competences are deployed in other emergent markets.

Companies that use M&A as their international expansion strategy also search to acquire new capabilities, to overcome the liability of foreignness, in particular, their marketing capabilities and managerial competences to operate in different business environments. The acquisition of these 'local' competences may be an important complement to the firm-specific home advantages, especially in relation to market and institutional knowledge.

The results also indicate the perception by Brazilian multinationals using foreign acquisition that international asset prices are under-valued in relation to domestic asset prices. This may be explained by the favourable exchange rates experienced in the Brazilian economy, a point that will be elaborated further. Another significant motive that is associated with the preference of cross-border acquisitions is the positive reputational effects of the acquisition at the home market, not only for investors, but also for customers and the general public – a point frequently neglected in the literature on internationalisation of companies from emerging economies.

Some of the competitive advantages of the Brazilian multinationals seem to support their ability to perform foreign acquisitions, such as the ability to develop relationships with international government and regulatory bodies.

Although important to a general picture of the importance of M&A in the internationalisation process, these general drives and motives do not explain the centrality and purpose of M&A at the firm strategy level. For this to happen, it is necessary to perform a more fine-grained analysis that fits specific strategies of different groups.

The role and importance of foreign M&A at the firm level

While it is useful to understand the general motives that may drive foreign acquisition, it is important to try to link them to the dominant strategies that they employ in their internationalisation paths. For this purpose, the authors use as reference the typology developed by Ramamurti (2009b). He classified companies for emerging markets according to their international strategies in five groups: natural-resource vertical integrator, local optimiser, low-cost partner, global/regional consolidators and global first-mover. The similarities of their international strategies enables a more precise level of analysis regarding the use of foreign acquisition strategies and their effect on the competitive advantages of the companies belonging to the group.

Natural-resource vertical integrator

A significant volume (in terms of transaction value) of the cross-border M&A from Brazilian companies was originated in the mineral, agricultural and industrial commodity sectors (mining, oil and gas, processed meat and steel). These industries are characterised by mature markets, with low levels of product innovation and high price pressure on the profit margins. As a country, Brazil has developed exceptional comparative advantages in this area, creating great companies in order to exploit and leverage its abundant natural resource endowments. At their origin, Vale and Petrobras were SOEs. Vale was completely privatised in the early nineties and Petrobras was partially privatised, with the Brazilian government holding the golden share.

In these markets, global economic drivers predominate. Economies of scale and market power are vital in order to thrive in a very competitive environment. With increasing globalisation pressures, concentration in these industries is reaching new levels. In the race towards the first position, companies need to increase their global footprint in order to remain competitive in the global arena.

Cross-border acquisitions play an important role in this strategic group. In industries characterised by high levels of global competition over scarce resources, foreign acquisition may increase the speed of international market entries when compared to other modes of expansion. Cross-border M&A also help companies to overcome the host country barriers and minimise the risk of retaliations on the part of established local competitors.

Most of the large acquirers from our sample were companies that followed a natural resource internationalisation path. Vale is one of the key players in the global mining industry. As a late-mover in the global arena, the company has been growing aggressively through horizontal acquisitions in the iron-mining segment. Among the company's twenty international acquisitions there are some in related business lines, like zinc and coal mining, and more recently, phosphate mining. Vale also has invested strongly in logistic services, a critical factor in many emerging countries, where access to ports is frequently difficult due to poor public infrastructure and services.

The energy sector giant Petrobras has also grown through acquisitions. Among the twenty-six reported acquisitions, several of them were in upstream operations, several of them in the refining business and petrochemicals, and some in the downstream activities. One of the most important was the acquisition of Perez Companc, a leading energy group from Argentina, caught in the midst of the early 2000 economic currency crisis of the country.

Local optimisers

The companies in this group focus on leveraging their specific technological and managerial home advantages in other emergent markets. Leveraging their FSA, they are very efficient in adapting their products to local conditions, and use acquisitions as a mode of entry to access international markets in order to overcome the liabilities of foreignness. Brazilian companies like Marcopolo, one important world player in the bus body assembler industry; Eurofarma, a pharmaceutical company; and Tigre, in the construction material segment, follow this path. Usually the company acquires an important part of the controlling share of a local company, and then exploits established home advantages in product, process and managerial capabilities, combining them with the complementary market assets of their local business associates.

Low-cost partners

The internationalisation paths these companies usually rely on are based on strong ownership advantages in product and process technologies in intermediary segments of industrial or service markets. They used to follow their customers – generally the leaders of the global value system – in their internationalisation path. Acquisitions play an important role in their strategy, since they usually target companies in developed markets and use their established capabilities to restructure them. Examples of Brazilian acquirers that belong to this group are WEG and Lupatech in the industrial equipment sector; Sabo, an automotive parts supplier; Stefanini Solutions; and Totvs, in the IT services and software sectors. Through their previous relations with their clients, they are able to extend their markets in foreign countries as a part of a global supply chain led by an important client.

Global/regional consolidators

For these companies, global acquisitions constitute the central piece of their strategies. Although latecomers in the global markets, their leading positions in their huge domestic markets has enabled these companies to develop strong capabilities in process, industrial, logistic, distribution and project management activities that they are eager to exploit in international markets. Their strong cash positions help them to accelerate their internationalisation paths. Ambev, the Brazilian beer and beverages company, has successfully used this strategy, by first acquiring companies in Latin America to exploit their marketing, distribution and industrial capabilities to build a strong regional position. Later, Ambev merged with Interbrew, a Belgian brewery holding an important share in the newly created company, InBev, which recently acquired American Anheuser Bush. Other main acquirers also fit in this strategy such as Gerdau, in the steel industry, an American leader in the segment that is recently tapping the European and Asian markets. Votorantim Cimentos and Camargo Correa, following the steps of the Mexican Cemex, are regional leaders in the cement industry. Recently, JBS-Friboi, strongly backed by government financial assistance through the National Development Bank (BNDES), made a series of bold acquisitions, among them the American Pilgrim's Pride and Swift operations. Through these acquisitions, it became the world leader in the processed meat industry. As in the case of natural-resource vertical integrators, economic drivers like economies of scale and scope, market power and global footprint are central to the success of their operations.

Global first-movers

These companies excel in engineering, production and business innovation capabilities. Companies in this group are usually global leaders in important growing technology segments. In these cases, other entry modes, like greenfield investments, strategic alliances or joint ventures could be more interesting, and acquisitions usually are used for strategic purposes. One Brazilian MNC comes to mind: Embraer, the third largest aircraft producer. Nevertheless, acquisitions have not played an important role in Embraer's international expansion: the company

made one minor registered acquisition of a small aircraft parts company in the US. Embraer's internationalisation is being pursued
through the establishment of commercial and after-market services
subsidiaries in the most sensible markets, or by engaging in joint-
ventures with local partners, for technology development or other
strategic reasons. Table 9.5 below summarises the main drivers for
international acquisitions and their relative importance for each of
these groups.

Other driving factors

There are two other important driving forces in the Brazilian case
that seem to play an important role towards the use of international
acquisitions as a means for international expansion. Although not
considered as primary economic drivers, they seem to have an important ancillary role, which helps to explain the increase of foreign M&A
by Brazilian companies.

The first is related to the Brazilian currency valuation in relation to
the US dollar. In fact, as shown in Figure 9.A1, the value of the US
currency has shown a continuous devaluation during the last decade.
From January 2005 to December 2010, the value of the dollar
decreased from R:$2.69 to R:$1.71, or by 36 per cent. While the
reasons for this phenomenon can be traced back to Brazilian macro-
economic policy and other institutional factors, it has influenced the
strategic behaviour of Brazilian companies, particularly in regard to
the choice of international modes of expansion, in at least two ways.
On the one hand, the strong Real has impacted exports from Brazil
negatively, by increasing the relative cost of goods in other currencies.
For the Brazilian MNCs, most of which still rely heavily on exports, the
valuation of the Real has been problematic, obliging them to rethink
their international strategies. On the other hand, the valuation of the
Real has been an incentive to acquire 'cheaper' assets abroad, denomin-
ated in other currencies. Those factors, in combination, could have
influenced the increase of foreign acquisition activity during the period.

The second driver relates to government policy and incentive programmes to support the internationalisation of 'national champions'.
In particular, BNDES has created special credit lines for international
investments, including the financing of M&A. For instance, JBS-Friboi
has been granted financing of around $7 billion to support the acquisition

Table 9.5 *Generic strategic groups and drivers of foreign acquisition*

Generic strategies	Importance cross-border M&A	Drivers of foreign acquisitions	Examples of Brazilian companies
Natural-resource vertical integrator	Central	Economic and industry drivers of scale, scope and market power Access to natural resources and to markets Geographical diversification and the increasing global footprint	Vale, Petrobras
Local optimiser	Important	Multi-domestic expansion using product, process and management FSCs Use of market and supply chain capabilities of the acquired firms to adapt their main home-built advantages to local conditions	Marcopolo, Eurofarma and Tigre
Low-cost partners	Very important	Global expansion using low-cost process capabilities to increase local response to global clients Restructuring of local operations to reduce costs and increase local market responsiveness to important global clients	Weg, Lupatech, Stefanini, Totvs, Sabo
Global/regional consolidators	Central	Economic and industry drivers predominate Rapid catch-up for late-movers FSCs developed in process technology, management, combined with strong cash resources	JBS-Friboi, Votorantim Cimentos, Camargo Correa, Gerdau
Global first-movers	Important for certain reasons e.g. strategic assets acquisitions	Fast and sometimes disruptive technological changes drive the industry Access to technological capabilities plays a key role	Embraer

Source: Elaborated by the authors, based on Ramamurti (2009b)

of the Swift and Pilgrim's Pride operations. The financing is also extended to other Brazilian companies in the heavy construction and other sectors that the government considers eligible for international support.

Cross-border M&A and psychic distance

It has been argued in the literature that distance is an influential factor regarding the decisions of international expansion.

In the case of the Brazilian companies, past studies have suggested a sequence of entries in international markets that followed an incremental route, by entering first the less distant markets (usually Latin American), and only after them the more distant European and North American markets.

The results of the geographic evolution of international acquisition seem less clear. While Latin America still concentrates most of the transactions value, Brazilian companies looked for European and North American targets, since the beginning of the 1990s. Asian, African and Australian transactions became more frequent only after 2000.

Conclusions

This chapter tries to contribute to the understanding of the role of outbound cross-border M&A of Brazilian companies and, in this way, helps to fill the gaps in the current literature on cross-border acquisitions from emerging economies.

Analysis of individual transactions of the last two decades points to the increasing importance of foreign acquisitions as a vehicle of FDI. They also indicate the strong concentration of the deals on a small number of large Brazilian companies. The largest six acquirers, with one exception, are companies from the natural resources and agricultural commodities sector. Manufacturing and services (including banking) companies were also important foreign acquirers during the period analysed.

Other modes of international expansion are also present in Brazilian companies. Although absence of systematic data on these other modes of entry renders direct comparison problematic, there are some indications that other leading Brazilian multinationals follow different expansion strategies. For instance, among the forty-six most internationalised companies, there are several companies and sectors that do not rely on cross-border acquisitions as their primary mode of expansion

(Embraer, Natura, heavy construction companies, franchise operations and other service companies). Also, Brazilian companies that access foreign markets through M&A may use other forms of direct investments for post-entry expansion in these locations.

Factors driving international expansion through M&A of Brazilian MNCs can be divided into different levels. On the macro-environment level, the opening of the economy in the early 1990s had played an important role. The valuation of the Real could also be considered an important factor for the increase of the foreign acquisition activity among Brazilian companies. The support of the Brazilian government, mainly through financial and credit support of BNDES, was also instrumental in the increase of foreign investments through M&A.

At the firm level, motives for foreign acquisitions may be attributed to the catch-up efforts of Brazilian late entrants in the search to improve their global positions in mature and oligopolistic industries. But motives also seem to vary according to the specific strategy of the company involved. M&A have been preferred as a rapid and efficient way to leverage and exploit pre-existent FSAs, but also to acquire market, managerial and institutional knowledge assets in order to circumvent the liability of foreignness, in different business and cultural environments.

Finally, the pattern of geographical evolution of international acquisition does not indicate an incremental path from less to more psychically distant countries, as the Uppsala theorist predicted. Since the early nineties, several international acquisitions by Brazilian firms were located in Europe and North America, along with other Latin American countries. The acquisitions in Asia, Africa and Australia only began to appear after 2000.

As an exploratory study, this chapter had no intention to provide definitive explanations to the foreign M&A activity of Brazilian companies. The purpose was to shed light on a relatively new area of enquiry. In this sense, the authors hope to have contributed to spot and to inspire more rigorous and robust analysis in the future.

Appendices

Table 9.A1 Mode of entry versus motivations to internationalise

Motivation	Entry mode (*)	N	Mean (**)	Std. deviation	Std. error mean	Significance (t-test for equality of means)
Access to raw materials and natural resources	No acquisition	29	2.48	1.66	0.31	0.9718
	Acquisition	22	2.50	1.79	0.38	
Access to specialised human resources	No acquisition	29	2.07	1.28	0.24	0.1237
	Acquisition	23	2.70	1.61	0.34	
Access to new markets	No acquisition	32	5.66	0.55	0.10	0.3573
	Acquisition	23	5.78	0.42	0.09	
Access to low-cost labour force	No acquisition	29	2.31	1.71	0.32	0.5548
	Acquisition	23	2.57	1.27	0.27	
Access to strategic resources that are rare in home country (R&D, technological know-how, infrastructure, institutions, etc.)	No acquisition	31	2.77	1.65	0.30	0.7607
	Acquisition	23	2.91	1.65	0.34	
Search for more knowledge about international consumer needs	No acquisition	31	4.00	1.67	0.30	0.0132
	Acquisition	22	4.91	0.87	0.19	
Positive effect for the company's image in home country	No acquisition	30	3.93	1.74	0.32	0.0788
	Acquisition	22	4.73	1.32	0.28	

Table 9.A1 (*cont.*)

Motivation	Entry mode (*)	N	Mean (**)	Std. deviation	Std. error mean	Significance (t-test for equality of means)
Incentives from other countries' government	No acquisition	31	2.10	1.54	0.28	0.4752
	Acquisition	21	2.38	1.16	0.25	
Overcome tariff and non-tariff barriers in international markets	No acquisition	30	2.13	1.53	0.28	0.0241
	Acquisition	22	3.14	1.55	0.33	
Pressure from global competition	No acquisition	30	3.77	1.55	0.28	0.2461
	Acquisition	23	4.26	1.48	0.31	
Get closer to main clients in the regions where they are present (client-following)	No acquisition	31	3.90	1.56	0.28	0.0739
	Acquisition	23	4.70	1.61	0.34	
Reduce logistical costs	No acquisition	31	2.97	1.68	0.30	0.1852
	Acquisition	23	3.61	1.80	0.38	
Reduction of business risk through geographical diversification and lower dependence on domestic market	No acquisition	31	4.55	1.41	0.25	0.6195
	Acquisition	23	4.74	1.36	0.28	

		N	Mean	SD		p-value
Vision or desire from shareholders/owners/directors	No acquisition	31	4.77	1.28	0.23	0.8831
Learning and development of new competences	Acquisition	23	4.83	1.27	0.26	
	No acquisition	31	4.42	1.41	0.25	0.4688
Search for economies of scale	Acquisition	23	4.70	1.33	0.28	
	No acquisition	31	4.29	1.55	0.28	0.7914
	Acquisition	23	4.17	1.64	0.34	
Saturation and/or low growth rates in Brazilian market	No acquisition	30	3.23	1.52	0.28	0.2580
	Acquisition	23	3.74	1.68	0.35	
Support of government programmes for internationalisation	No acquisition	31	1.87	1.26	0.23	0.2429
	Acquisition	23	2.39	1.80	0.38	
Opportunity to explore internationally the technological and managerial competence of the company	No acquisition	30	4.07	1.64	0.30	0.0046
	Acquisition	23	5.09	0.79	0.17	
Opportunity to explore internationally the cost competitiveness of the company	No acquisition	31	4.00	1.69	0.30	0.3142
	Acquisition	23	4.43	1.34	0.28	

Table 9.A1 (*cont.*)

Motivation	Entry mode (*)	N	Mean (**)	Std. deviation	Std. error mean	Significance (t-test for equality of means)
Opportunity to explore internationally the competitiveness of the company in terms of product differentiation	No acquisition	31	3.87	1.61	0.29	0.0345
	Acquisition	23	4.70	1.18	0.25	
Opportunity to explore internationally the company's patents and brands	No acquisition	32	3.09	1.89	0.33	0.0769
	Acquisition	23	3.91	1.47	0.31	
Access financial resources at lower costs	No acquisition	30	3.10	1.60	0.29	0.3307
	Acquisition	23	3.52	1.47	0.31	
Acquisition of international assets at lower prices	No acquisition	30	2.03	1.35	0.25	0.0001
	Acquisition	23	3.65	1.40	0.29	

* Companies that have made acquisitions/companies that have not made any acquisition abroad
** On a 6-point Likert scale, ranging from 1 = not important to 6 = very important

Table 9.A2 Mode of entry versus competitive advantages

Competitive advantage	Entry mode (*)	N	Mean (**)	Std. deviation	Std. error mean	Significance (t-test for equality of means)
Access to natural resources and/or raw materials at lower costs or favourable conditions	Acquisition	21	3.857	1.459	0.318	0.3335
	No acquisition	30	3.433	1.569	0.286	
Ability to develop relationships with international government and regulatory bodies	Acquisition	22	3.500	1.406	0.300	0.0692
	No acquisition	31	2.742	1.505	0.270	
Qualified labour force at competitive costs	Acquisition	23	4.304	0.822	0.171	0.2100
	No acquisition	30	3.867	1.634	0.298	
Access to pool of talented managerial, technical or scientific people at competitive costs	Acquisition	23	4.043	1.186	0.247	0.0507
	No acquisition	30	3.333	1.348	0.246	
Access to capital at lower costs	Acquisition	23	3.652	1.465	0.305	0.2215
	No acquisition	30	3.133	1.548	0.283	
Higher scale in relation to international competitors	Acquisition	23	4.043	1.461	0.305	0.0217
	No acquisition	31	2.968	1.779	0.320	

Table 9.A2 (cont.)

Competitive advantage	Entry mode (*)	N	Mean (**)	Std. deviation	Std. error mean	Significance (t-test for equality of means)
Favourable access to distribution channels abroad	Acquisition	23	3.217	1.594	0.332	0.6680
	No acquisition	30	3.033	1.497	0.273	
International brand/reputation	Acquisition	23	4.043	1.186	0.247	0.7180
	No acquisition	30	3.900	1.583	0.289	
Innovation capacity (introduction of new technologies and/or fast development of new products/processes)	Acquisition	22	4.318	1.211	0.258	0.2915
	No acquisition	31	3.903	1.513	0.272	
Competence to operate at the conditions of other emergent markets	Acquisition	23	4.348	1.335	0.278	0.0772
	No acquisition	31	3.645	1.473	0.265	
Ability to understand and serve global riches	Acquisition	23	4.261	1.251	0.261	0.3566
	No acquisition	30	3.933	1.285	0.235	
Relatively efficient and modern equipments and plants	Acquisition	22	4.682	1.249	0.266	0.0475
	No acquisition	30	3.800	1.730	0.316	

Control of supply-chain stages (degree of verticalisation)	Acquisition	22	4.409	1.532	0.327	0.1846
Competence in international supply-chain management (logistics and access to qualified suppliers)	No acquisition	30	3.800	1.669	0.305	
	Acquisition	22	3.636	1.465	0.312	0.6772
Larger and more diversified international presence	No acquisition	32	3.813	1.554	0.275	
	Acquisition	23	4.043	1.331	0.277	0.3084
Operational efficiency/low production costs	No acquisition	31	3.613	1.647	0.296	
	Acquisition	23	4.217	1.242	0.259	0.2308
Better technical support services in the markets where the company is present	No acquisition	30	3.733	1.574	0.287	
	Acquisition	23	4.043	1.147	0.239	0.0386
Holding support in terms of corporate services and resources	No acquisition	30	3.267	1.437	0.262	
	Acquisition	23	3.739	1.251	0.261	0.0503
Synergy among businesses within a company or business group	No acquisition	29	2.966	1.476	0.274	
	Acquisition	21	3.952	1.396	0.305	0.1307
	No acquisition	29	3.276	1.709	0.317	

Table 9.A2 (*cont.*)

Competitive advantage	Entry mode (*)	N	Mean (**)	Std. deviation	Std. error mean	Significance (t-test for equality of means)
Ability to attend international clients' expectations	Acquisition	23	4.826	1.072	0.224	0.2526
	No acquisition	31	4.419	1.409	0.253	
Competence to manage international portfolios	Acquisition	23	4.217	0.998	0.208	0.3851
	No acquisition	31	3.871	1.688	0.303	

* Companies that have made acquisitions/companies that have not made any acquisition abroad

** On a 6-point Likert scale, ranging from 1 = not important competitive advantage to 6 = very important competitive advantage

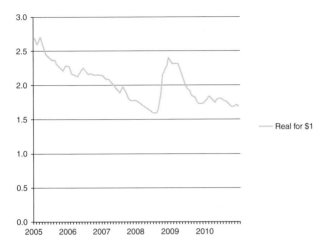

Figure 9.A1 Exchange rates (monthly average)
Source: Ipeadata

10 | Cross-border M&A and competitive advantage of Russian EMNEs

KALMAN KALOTAY AND ANDREI
PANIBRATOV

Analysis in this chapter revolves around two main questions: (1) Why do Russian multinational enterprises (MNEs) choose acquisitions as an entry mode? and (2) Which competitive advantages do they gain via acquisitions abroad? Both foreign market entry strategies and operation methods of Russian companies are discussed.

The chapter begins with a brief overview of relevant literature, followed by an overall picture of foreign acquisitions carried out by Russian firms. Next, selected cases of foreign acquisitions are analysed, aiming at finding out the main motivations and main competitive advantages of the firms involved in those transactions. The subsequent section consists of snapshots of MNEs in Russian oil and gas and metallurgy industries, and in non-resource-based industries. It is followed by a short survey of failures and half-failures in the foreign acquisitions of Russian firms. At the end of the chapter we conclude by discussing how our findings can advance new research on Russian MNEs and predict the future of developing their competitive advantages through mergers and acquisitions (M&A).

Extant literature on the rise of Russian multinationals

The process of internationalisation of MNEs from developing and transition economies – popularly referred to as emerging markets – has become a widely studied topic in the last decade, with few important publications giving special emphasis on this phenomenon. The focus of most of the studies on emerging market multinational enterprises (EMNEs) so far has been on Asian and Latin American firms. This focus was understandable given the fact that firms from those regions started to expand abroad much earlier (in the 1960s) than from Russia.[1]

---

[1] The country has two constitutional names: the Russian Federation and Russia. The United Nations uses the first version. This chapter, for the sake of brevity, calls the country Russia.

Nevertheless some important studies on Russian MNEs have been published since the end of the 1990s (Bulatov, 1998, 2001; Crane *et al.*, 2005; Filatotchev *et al.*, 2007a, 2007b; Filippov, 2008; Heinrich, 2003, 2006; Kalotay, 2005, 2008; Kets de Vries *et al.*, 2004; Kuznetsov, 2010; Liuhto and Jumpponen, 2003; Liuhto and Vahtra, 2007; Panibratov, 2009, 2012; Panibratov and Verba, 2011), providing insights into the strategies of Russian MNEs.

With transition to market economy accelerating in the 2000s, foreign direct investment (FDI) from Russia got a new impetus. In their international expansion, Russian MNEs often opted for acquisitions abroad, reflecting their preference for quick returns and their lack of the from-the-bottom experience. From the point of view of the topic of this chapter – FDI through foreign acquisitions – it has to be noted, however, that the majority of studies on Russian MNEs, similar to the literature on emerging MNEs in general, paid limited attention to the question of the mode of entry, except for remarks on the leapfrogging of Russian MNEs to the global scene (e.g. Panibratov and Kalotay, 2009) which could not be possible without massive acquisitions abroad.

The question of leapfrogging leads us back to the basic question of motivation of investors. Before the 2000s in particular, some of the FDI from Russia was seen as system escape, as firms were investing abroad driven by an unfavourable domestic business environment (Kalotay, 2002). This phenomenon was discussed related to MNEs based in developed economies, too, where institutional barriers in the home country may result in avoidance of political constraints through investment abroad (Boddewyn and Brewer, 1994; Witt and Lewin, 2007). Nevertheless, recently there may be a shift towards motivations of controlling foreign markets (Panibratov and Kalotay, 2009). More-over, in the current setting, the motives of Russian firms' outward FDI (OFDI) vary significantly. The most typical motive is search for markets and resources. Besides, OFDI from Russia is sometimes driven by image-building motives or domestic political risk prevention con-siderations rather than by seeking of efficiency or strategic asset (IMEMO and VCC, 2009).

The effects of the historical and cultural ties as well as physical proximity are evident in the geographical distribution of Russian OFDI. This may serve as another explanation of Russian OFDI in the Commonwealth of Independent States (CIS). This destination has

Table 10.1 *Russian OFDI to 'Western' and 'Eastern' economies, 2007–9 ($ million and %)*

Destination	2007	%	2008	%	2009	%
All the world	45,211	100.00	54,202	100.00	44,868	100.00
Non-CIS countries	41,967	92.82	51,789	95.55	41,760	93.07
CIS countries	3,244	7.18	2,413	4.45	3,109	6.93

Source: Bank of Russia, 2010.

not been dominant in terms of the value invested (Table 10.1); however it has often served as a stepping stone for firms aiming to become bi-regional multinationals (the CIS plus the European Union) or global multinationals (Kuznetsov, 2010).

The importance of acquisitions abroad

Our approach to foreign acquisitions in this chapter follows the findings of the general literature on the topic, based on the experience of all firms (including developed market firms, for which the literature is broader). We acknowledge that foreign acquisitions, together with greenfield investment, constitute one of the main forms of expansion abroad (UNCTAD, 2000). There are also auxiliary modes that play a role in special circumstances, for example, expansion investment in mature projects, equity-based alliances or, in the case of economies in transition, brownfield investment (Meyer and Estrin, 2001). There are differences between the two main modes of entry, although they tend to diminish over time. Acquisitions in principle mean only a change of ownership (although in practice it is difficult to differentiate from brownfield projects, where capacities are immediately overhauled and expanded). They usually result in an instant access to resources abroad. They also tend to result in deeper linkages in the host economy, as business relationships are inherited from previous owners. At the same time, foreign investors have greater and fuller control over their technology in greenfield projects, and they are less bound by the heritage of technologies taken over from previous owners.

The strategies of Russian MNEs to acquire assets abroad are intricately interlinked with other transactions carried out in the overall Russian M&A market, viz. Russian investors in Russia (domestic deals) and acquisitions by foreign investors of Russia. This is so because deals aimed at increasing the international competitiveness of Russia are taking place in all three segments of that market. The overall M&A market is not the main focus of this study. It is worth mentioning, however, that it is dominated by domestic deals (KPMG, 2009) and that it moves in tandem with international acquisitions by Russian firms. The dynamics of the domestic and international M&A markets are driven by the same two inter-related processes: industry consolidation and redistribution of oil and gas assets between leading groups, on the one hand, and joint ventures between state-controlled companies and foreign players for development of large and technologically challenging deposits in Russia and abroad, on the other.

Within that general context, one of the main features of the foreign acquisitions by Russian firms (and in general) is that they confer various advantages on the acquirers, including enhanced competitiveness, synergies between assets, growth, cost reduction and improved reputation; access to new product lines, technologies, capacities, markets and industries; and reduction of the number of competitors (Croyle and Johnsey, 2007). Nevertheless, despite the potential benefits, foreign acquisitions are risky and complicated, creating more complex structures. Indeed, they are riskier than either greenfield investment or acquisitions at home. Statistics on acquisitions including foreign acquisitions (Burksaitiene, 2010) show that real results are often different from expected; and even some M&A activities resulted in complete failures instead of new successful companies. The success of foreign acquisitions depends on the ability to create added value after it has taken place (Quah and Young, 2005). Despite all of the effort put into the process, foreign acquisitions might fail due to a variety of reasons: financial, managerial, strategic and people-related problems of M&A (Mercer, 2011).

Overall patterns of foreign acquisition by Russian firms

According to internationally available data from 1992 until May 2010, the net foreign acquisitions (after allowing for divestments) by Russian firms exceeded $67 billion (Figure 10.1 shows the pattern to the end of 2009). In databases on foreign takeovers these transactions are classified as cross-border mergers and acquisitions although practically all of

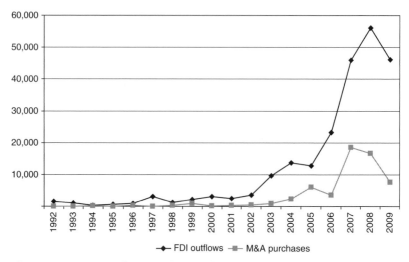

Figure 10.1 FDI outflows and cross-border M&A purchases of Russia, 1992–2009 ($ million)[a]
Source: UNCTAD cross-border M&A database
[a]Cross-border M&A are calculated on a net basis. Sales are the 'equivalent' of FDI inflows, purchases correspond to FDI outflows.

these deals are acquisitions (even when they are formally registered as mergers). In the statistical part of this study we follow nevertheless the international statistical terminology. It has to be noted that acquisitions carried out by Russian firms are indicated as cross-border M&A purchases, while the acquisitions carried out by foreign firms are registered as cross-border M&A sales.

At first sight, statistics would indicate that cross-border M&A purchases by Russia accounted only for one-quarter of the cumulative outward FDI flows of the country over 1992–2009. However, the two data series are not strictly comparable, and the statistics on FDI include a large component of round-tripping (which involves the investment of funds in an off-shore company that, in turn, reinvests most of its capital back in Russia), inflating those numbers. In reality, the share of cross-border M&A in FDI outflows is much higher, although it is difficult to estimate with precision. As expected, cross-border M&A and OFDI follow a similar trend, confirming that indeed the former are often the engines of the latter. Until the onset of the crisis they both increased significantly (Figure 10.1). In 2008, cross-border M&A purchases started to decline, bringing down outward FDI flows in the subsequent year.

The data available on the number of transactions by type (M&A, greenfield projects and strategic alliances) confirms the close relationship between the different forms of FDI. In these data sets, the number of greenfield projects exceeds the number of M&A deals. However, given the fact that acquisitions tend to be larger than greenfield projects, it is not too far-fetched to deduct that foreign acquisitions are still the engines of outward FDI from Russia. Moreover, strategic alliances are becoming popular among Russian companies; their number has fluctuated since 2000, but it has been steadily growing since 2004 (after a temporary decrease). It has to be noted that equity-based strategic alliances are counted among FDI statistics, while the non-equity-based ones are counted separately. Overall, all three modes of internationalisation (M&A deals, greenfield projects and strategic alliances) were on the rise until 2008 (see Table 10.2). In 2009, due to the crisis, the number of both greenfield projects and M&A declined.

In terms of shares in global cross-border M&A purchases and global FDI, the performance of Russia continued to be strong even in the crisis years of 2008 and 2009 (Figure 10.2). By 2009, the country's share in global FDI flows exceeded 4 per cent, and its share in global cross-border purchases exceeded 3 per cent. At first sight, these may seem to be marginal figures, but in these areas long dominated by developed country firms, these shares are quite respectable. Compared to other BRIC countries (Brazil, India and China), Russia is behind China, but ahead of Brazil and India. And in contrast to other BRIC countries, which are still net capital importers, Russia breaks even in its capital exports and imports registered in its cross-border M&A purchases and sales.

The industry and host country composition of cross-border M&A purchases of Russia shows a high level of concentration (Figure 10.3). Metals and metal products alone represent almost half (44 per cent) of all transactions, and mining, quarrying and petroleum more than a quarter (29 per cent). These two resource-based industries account for almost three-quarters of the total, and will be the special focus of the subsequent analysis. Finance, transport, storage and communications and trade account for more modest values, and the role of other industries remains marginal. Of the top ten target countries (Figure 10.4), seven were developed countries (following the UN classification which considers new EU members as developed

Table 10.2 *Number of foreign acquisitions, greenfield projects and strategic alliances initiated by Russian companies, 2000–10*

Type	2000	2001	2002	2003	2004	2005	2006	2007	2008	2009	2010[a]
Foreign acquisitions	7	21	20	19	27	45	54	70	108	65	19
Greenfield projects	–	–	51	120	109	139	155	134	194	150	47
Strategic alliances	29	21	51	28	15	37	52	89	–	–	–

Source: Based on Filippov (2010) and UNCTAD (2010).

[a] January–May for M&A; January–June for greenfield projects.

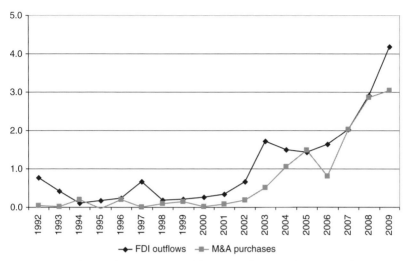

Figure 10.2 Share of Russia in world FDI outflows and cross-border M&A purchases, 1992–2009 (%)[a]
Source: UNCTAD cross-border M&A database.
[a]Cross-border M&A are calculated on a net basis. Sales are the 'equivalent' of FDI inflows, purchases correspond to FDI outflows

countries). Natural-resource-rich Canada and US occupy the first two positions, followed by three EU members (the UK, the Netherlands and Italy, in that order). There are also two CIS countries (Ukraine and Belarus) among the top ten.

Within the cross-border M&A universe, mega deals (transactions over the value of $1 billion) indicate the existence of firms with global ambitions and global strategies. In this area, the leapfrogging of Russian firms to the global scene is remarkable: all the twenty mega deals it is possible to identify (Table 10.3) are very recent: the oldest one (Norilsk Nickel's acquisition of Gold Fields in South Africa) is dated 2004. Since then, the number of these deals has exploded: two in 2005, a peak of six in 2007 (the last pre-crisis year), then a moderate slowdown in 2008 and 2009 (five and four deals, respectively). Their aggregate value over 2004–10 attained the impressive sum of $44 billion.

These transactions clearly reflect the strategic ambitions of Russian firms. When they acquire mining assets, they do not do it with the aim of ensuring resources for Russia but with the aim of controlling the value chain globally. When they acquire companies

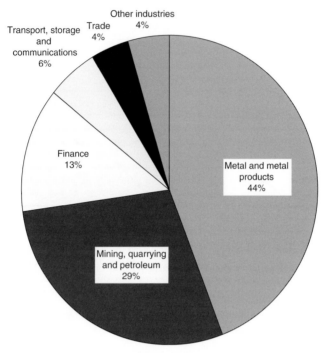

Figure 10.3 Cross-border M&A purchases of Russia by industry, 1992–2009 (%)[a]
Source: UNCTAD cross-border M&A database.
[a]Cross-border M&A are calculated on a net basis. Sales are the 'equivalent' of FDI inflows, purchases correspond to FDI outflows

in their own industry, their main aim is horizontal control (market power). This horizontal control is important not only in the resource-based industries which constitute the bulk of these transactions, but also in telecoms, in which Russian firms are equally active. There are also important technology-seeking motivations behind these transactions (especially present in the acquisition of Magna in the automotive industry).

Beside the global deals, one can also take stock of more than seventy medium-sized deals (between $50 million and $1 billion) in 1998–2010, for a total value of more than $20 billion. These deals either confer the acquirers specific assets (mostly in developed markets), or regional market power. Some of these medium-sized transactions will be referred to in detail in the subsequent section.

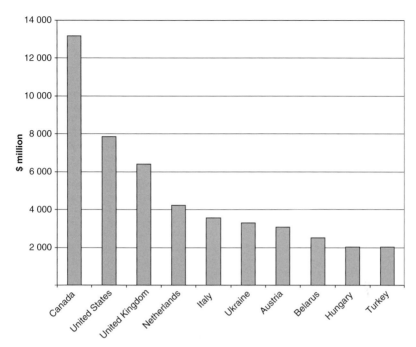

Figure 10.4 Cross-border M&A purchases of Russia, top ten target countries, 1992–2009 ($ million)[a]
Source: UNCTAD cross-border M&A database.
[a]Cross-border M&A are calculated on a net basis. Sales are the 'equivalent' of FDI inflows, purchases correspond to FDI outflows

Snapshot of selected Russian acquirers abroad

Snapshots of selected acquirers in resource-based industries

As the list of mega-deals indicates, the foreign acquisitions of Russia are dominated by some firms, especially from natural-resource-based industries. State-owned Gazprom – which is the largest Russian company by total assets and the second largest outward investor by foreign assets (IMEMO and VCC, 2009) – is one of them. Beside foreign acquisitions, Gazprom's collaboration with Italy's Eni is another proof of the company's strategic motivation to control the value chain of natural gas. They have agreed to develop the South Stream gas pipeline linking Russia to Bulgaria through the Black Sea. Gazprom is also active in the Nord Stream AG joint venture created

Table 10.3 Cross-border M&A mega-deals (over $1 billion) by Russian MNEs, 2004–10

Year	Target company	Target industry	Target nation	Acquiring company	Acquiring industry	Transaction value ($ million)	Shares acquired (%)
2004	Gold Fields Ltd	Mining	South Africa	Norilsk Nickel	Mining	1,205	20.0
2005	Nelson Resources Ltd	Gold ores	UK	Lukoil	Oil and gas	2,000	100.0
2005	Turkcell	Telecoms	Turkey	Alfa Group Consortium	Conglomerate	1,602	13.0
2007	LionOre Mining International	Mining	Canada	Norilsk Nickel	Mining	6,287	100.0
2007	Beltransgaz	Oil and gas	Belarus	Gazprom	Oil and gas	2,500	50.0
2007	Oregon Steel Mills Inc	Iron and steel	US	Evraz Group	Iron and steel	2,088	90.0
2007	Strabag	Construction	Austria	Rasperia Trading	Construction	1,637	30.0
2007	Magna International Inc	Automotive	Canada	Basic Element	Conglomerate	1,537	18.0
2007	Strabag	Construction	Austria	Basic Element	Conglomerate	1,427	30.0
2008	IPSCO Inc – Canadian Tubular Operations	Iron and steel	Canada	Evraz Group	Iron and steel	4,025	100.0
2008	Sukhaya Balka	Iron ores	Ukraine	Evraz Group	Iron and steel	2,189	99.0
2008	ERG Raffinerie Mediterranee – ISAB Refinery	Oil and gas	Italy	Lukoil	Oil and gas	2,098	100.0

Year	Acquirer	Industry	Home country	Target	Target industry	Value	%
2008	Oriel Resources plc	Iron and steel	UK	Mechel	Iron and steel	1,524	100.0
2008	Penfold Capital Acquisition Corp	Iron and steel	Canada	Severstal	Iron and steel	1,115	95.0
2009	MOL Group	Oil and gas	Hungary	Surgutneftegaz	Oil and gas	1,852	21.0
2009	Lukarco BV	Pipelines	Netherlands	Lukoil	Oil and gas	1,599	46.0
2009	Donbass Industrial Union	Iron and steel	Ukraine	A. Katunin and partners	Investors	1,250	50.1
2009	Donetskiy Electro-metallurgical Plant	Metals	Ukraine	Alfa Group Consortium/A1 Group Holding	Conglomerate	1,000	–
2010	Kyivstar GSM	Telecoms	Ukraine	VimpelCom	Telecoms	5,516	100.0
2010	Uranium One Inc	Mining	Canada	Atomenergoprom	Electric services	1,055	37.0

Source: Authors' collection based on data from the UNCTAD cross-border M&A database.

in December 2005 (Gazprom 51 per cent, BASF and E.ON 24.5 per cent each) in order to build a pipeline and to transport gas from Russia to Germany through the Baltic Sea. Coupled with this deal, Gazprom and E.ON-Ruhrgas entered into cross shareholdings, an additional gas supply contract to E.ON (until 2036) was signed, access to the gas retail market in Germany was agreed upon and recently a joint venture between Gazprom and E.ON was concluded for the exploitation of Gazprom's Siberian Yuzhno Russkoye gas field.

Examples of Gazprom's acquisitions abroad illustrate again a company strategy based on control over the whole value chain to reap the associated margins (especially in the Baltic region and several CIS countries, where Gazprom is the sole provider of natural gas). In one of the largest deals of the company so far, in 2007 Gazprom acquired 50 per cent of Beltransgas, a major gas transportation company in Belarus. In the UK, Gazprom's affiliate acquired two distribution companies: PNG in 2006 and Natural Gas Shipping Services in 2007. In 2008, Gazprom bought a 50 per cent stake in Central European Gas Hub (CEGH) at Baumgarten in Austria from Austria's OMV. According to the purchase agreement, these companies would jointly develop new underground gas storage facilities in Austria and neighbouring countries. Another example of foreign acquisitions is Gazprom Neft's purchase of a 51 per cent share in Serbia's NIS (at a price of €400 million) in 2009, increasing Gazprom Neft's global refining capacity by about 20 per cent. In 2010 Gazprom acquired a controlling stake in Automated Meter Reading (AMR, UK), following an earlier acquisition of a 30 per cent stake in March 2008. This acquisition would enhance Gazprom's capacity for smart energy management towards both suppliers and end customers worldwide, and its capacity to offer integrated energy solutions to its clients.

The main purpose of Gazprom's foreign acquisition strategy was building a sustainable competitive advantage vis-à-vis other firms. With the help of the strategy of joint ventures and shares acquisition, Gazprom is strengthening its market position in its traditional export markets, tapping new market opportunities and internalising its value-chain business activities. Being a company with a strong international presence, in the EU Gazprom pursues two objectives: to increase its control over gas transportation pipelines, and to enter the European retail gas markets. In the oil segment, Gazprom Neft's strategic focus is to improve the quality of its refineries in

Russia and other transition countries with the aim of bringing the output of a number of new Russian fields to market.

Lukoil, Russia's largest oil producer and largest outward investor by foreign assets (IMEMO and VCC, 2009), has made around fifty acquisitions abroad, and over the past six to seven years the company has spent about $5.6 billion on new acquisitions in exploration and production alone. The most recent large acquisition has been the purchase of a 46 per cent stake in LukArco BV, a subsidiary of the Russian oil company Lukoil, from an affiliate of British Petroleum (BP), making Lukoil the sole owner of the company. Lukoil has acquired extensive petroleum retail chains, especially in the US. In addition, the company has acquired modern oil refineries in Eastern Europe (e.g. Neftochim in Bulgaria) and in the Netherlands and in Italy that supply key export markets in Europe. In upstream activities, Lukoil's foreign acquisitions serve to extend the company's hydrocarbon resource base and to cover for an eventual depletion of its domestic resources.

For Lukoil, acquisition of new assets is not merely a way to increase oil and gas reserves and production, but also a way to strengthen competitive positions in key regions and to obtain significant synergy effects. Gazprom's presence is strong in several Central and Eastern European countries, and more recently in the US.

Severstal, the third largest outward investor of the country by foreign assets (IMEMO and VCC, 2009), has so far made about thirty acquisitions abroad since 1993. Severstal has been an active acquirer in the CIS, Europe and North America. In 2003, Severstal purchased the US steel producer, Rouge Steel Industries, for $360 million. This integrated steel-making facility based in Michigan was later renamed Severstal Dearborn. The acquisition provided Severstal with a means to circumvent the US steel import restrictions and to strengthen considerably the company's position in the world steel market. In 2005, Severstal acquired a 62 per cent share in a major Italian steel producer, the Lucchini Group, with its integrated steel-making facility based in Italy and France. This $574 million acquisition has given the Russian company a stronger foothold in the European market, allowing it to bypass the EU import quotas and to increase its output and sales of high value-added products. In 2010 Severstal acquired Sparrows Point (Maryland, US) steel mill.

In upstream activities, in 2007 Severstal acquired Celtic Resources, a gold mining company with a number of assets in Kazakhstan. In 2008 Severstal acquired African Iron Ore Group Ltd (AIOG), which is active in West Africa, and in the same year a 53.8 per cent stake in High River Gold, the owner of a number of plants in the Buryatia and Amur regions of Russia and a gold mine in Burkina Faso. In 2010 Severstal further expanded its gold mining business through the acquisition of a stake in Crew Gold.

Severstal is the classical case of a company aiming at full control of its value chain (mining and coke assets through steel mills), while conglomerating them with auxiliary activities such as gold mining. Severstal is also a company that has acquired assets on practically all continents of the globe.

Snapshots of selected acquirers in non-resource-based industries

Despite the dominance of natural-resource-based companies, there are Russian firms from other industries which are engaged in foreign acquisitions. For instance, the state-owned **Bank VTB** has acquired assets in several foreign banks, benefiting from a capital infusion of $2 billion from the Bank of Russia (the Central Bank of the Russian Federation) and the Russian Government. With that help, VTB has bought the assets of seven Western European banks from the Bank of Russia for the value of $9 billion. In telecoms, **Mobile TeleSystems** and **VimpelCom** are the most active foreign acquirers, focusing on the CIS. Mobile TeleSystems has entered the Armenian, Kyrgyz, Ukrainian and Uzbek markets, while VimpelCom targeted Armenia, Kazakhstan, Ukraine and Uzbekistan. Outside the CIS, AFK Sistema seemed to be in the lead, by acquiring assets in Greece (2006), the UK (2006) and India (2007). More recently VimpelCom has caught up through the acquisition in 2010 of a 20 per cent stake in Egypt's Weather Investments (Harper, 2011), which is the majority shareholder (51.7 per cent) of Orascom Telecom Holding operating in Algeria, Bangladesh, Burundi, the Central African Republic, Namibia, Pakistan, Tunisia and Zimbabwe, and sole owner of Italy's Wind Telecomunicazioni. In exchange, Weather Investments gained a 19 per cent interest in VimpelCom.

When success is not fully achieved

As highlighted by the literature on M&A in general and cross-border deals in particular (UNCTAD, 2000), a part of the deals are to fail, mostly because of excessive expectations at the outset, or because of unforeseen or discounted difficulties. The discounting of unforeseen difficulties is particularly patent in the soft areas of social and political considerations. However, the definition of failure is not straightforward. In some cases, it means a complete reversal of the deal; in other cases, it means worse than expected results. In Russia, the onset of the financial crisis in 2008 increased the scope for failures. Some of the examples are:

- In 2008, Russia's fourth largest MNE, Evraz Group, agreed to buy 51 per cent of Delong Holdings in China. However, the Chinese government blocked the deal.
- In 2008, Natsionalnaya Reservnaya Korporaciya (NRK) decided to purchase a 76 per cent stake in Oeger Tours Gmbh (Germany) for €120 million. However, NRK did not transfer the cash value of the deal in due time, allegedly because Oeger Tours had failed to provide the financial reports required by the deal, and the deal was cancelled.
- In August 2008, NLMK Steel (Russia's seventh largest MNE) agreed to buy the JMC Steel Group (US) for $3.5 billion, excluding debts and cash assets. NLMK revoked this agreement in November 2008, due to changing market conditions. DBO, the parent company of JMC, sued NLMK for breach of contract.
- In August 2008, GAZ Group agreed to buy from Penske Automotive Group (US) a 50 per cent stake in VM Motori owned by the latter for $100 million. According to contract GAZ had to pay by the end of October 2008, which it failed to do due lack of cash in the midst of the financial crisis.
- In December 2009, Sberbank agreed to buy 100 per cent of the shares of Belpromstroibank (Belarus). However, due to lack of cash, it paid only $280 million, purchasing 'only' 93 per cent of the bank.
- In March 2009, Surgutneftegas bought 21.2 per cent of Hungary's MOL from Austria's OMV for $1.9 billion. The effective take over of these shares was blocked by both the target company and the target country (Kalotay, 2010). Hungarian resistance to Surgutneftegas was prompted by local sensitivities: it targeted the energy sector in a net energy importing country and it affected the largest and most successful MNE of the country. In the end, Surgutneftegas accepted in 2011 to resell its stake to the Hungarian government for about €1.9 billion, making the attempt at least financially viable.

- In 2009, Polyus Gold, Russia's leading gold producer, agreed to buy a controlling stake in KazakhGold for $11 billion. Instead of completion, the two parties filed lawsuits against each other, alleging breaches of contract. In December 2010, a new agreement was signed between AltynGroup Kazakhstan, controlled by the (former) owners KazakhGold, and the Polyus Group. Under the deal, completed in July 2011, KazakhGold became the parent company of Polyus Gold in a reverse takeover and the new group was then renamed Polyus International.
- In 2009, intense negotiations were taking place between GM and a consortium of the Canadian car maker Magna and the Russian state-owned bank Sberbank for a purchase of a 55 per cent stake in Opel AG Germany, an affiliate of GM. GM at the last minute decided to keep Opel AG in its portfolio, probably because the deal would have hurt various sensitivities. It would have provided a Russian state-owned entity with a direct stake in the industrial heartland of Europe. Moreover, Sberbank is the largest creditor of the Russian car maker GAZ, and may have represented the commercial interests of the latter in the deal. The deal may therefore have also been a way for the Russian car maker to gain access to advanced technology.

Summing up the motivations of Russian MNEs

This study has analysed the competitive advantages that Russian MNEs derive from acquiring assets abroad. It seems that Russian firms have for a long time left behind the phase when these acquisitions were motivated by defensive, 'system-escape' motives, and that the majority follow genuinely offensive strategies on the global scene ('expansion'). The global crisis of 2008–10 created turbulences on that foreign expansion (e.g. the financing of international projects became more difficult); however they have not stopped the expansion drive of Russian MNEs. After the depth of the crisis, it seems that foreign acquisitions by Russian MNEs are on their way to revival.

This study has also found that although most of the Russian MNEs are based in natural-resource-based industries, their motivations are far from being purely resource-seeking, even when they aim at upstream markets such as exploration and extraction. The explanation lies in the fact that, unlike their Chinese or Indian counterparts, the motivation of Russian firms is not to ensure supply of resources to their home market (Russia possesses the majority of the materials it needs for its development), but to control the global markets of their resources, especially in developed countries. On the basis of available information it is difficult to judge the success versus failure rates of Russian acquisitions abroad. It is also the time frame that is missing for such a definitive judgment (most acquisitions are fairly recent). At the time of writing, it seems that Russian firms have a surprisingly good success rate, perhaps related to their capacity of turning acquired assets to technological and business success even under difficult circumstances, under which traditional MNEs would fail. However this optimism has to be tempered by the fact that during the crisis the state needed to help out firms that expanded too fast in the previous period. Moreover, the fact that most of the Russian MNEs leapfrogged to global status carries in itself the inherent risk of medium- to long-term failure (if the lessons of economic history prove to be right). This chapter has highlighted some cases of failures and semi-failures. It is notable that some of them are due to commercial reasons (e.g. lack of cash); however, others are related to strategic factors (resistance in the target companies/markets).

Another major finding of this study is the importance of the role of the state. Here we do not limit it to its influence on the strategies of firms in which it is the majority shareholder (such as Gazprom). We can talk about state-influenced firms even if the state does not own any share at all. It is evident in the case of the firms that were bailed out during the crisis. The government's aim was to ensure that the momentum of foreign expansion is maintained, or even accelerated, despite commercial logic that would have dictated a rollback. It is also evident in the case of the transactions where the acquisition of assets confers important strategic advantages on the Russian government. The existence of state ownership and state influence is not unique to Russia, though. In the BRIC universe, that influence is quite palpable in the foreign expansion of Chinese firms; but it is present, and sometimes even more dominant, in the explanation of outward FDI from certain CIS countries such as Kazakhstan (Amagoh and Markus, 2010), the Czech Republic (where state-owned CEZ energy company dominates foreign acquisitions) and, in the case of OFDI from Venezuela, singularly dominated by state-owned PDVSA.

Conclusions

Most of the studies analysing international acquisitions have aimed at finding answers to three central questions: why do companies decide to invest abroad (i.e. why do foreign acquisitions occur)? If they do, why do they opt for foreign acquisitions, instead of other forms of investment such as greenfield projects? What kind of factors make certain locations attractive to acquirers (i.e. why are certain countries attractive targets for acquisitions) (cf. Neto *et al.*, 2010)? If the acquirers are located in an emerging economy, such as Russia, the answer is relatively complex to find out as those firms are less transparent than firms located in developed countries, and their motivations and arguments can be hidden. Nevertheless it seems that firms from developing and transition economies, including Russia, often follow strategic motivations, and whether they opt for acquisitions or for greenfield projects, they target locations where strategic assets are available.

Although the traditional focus of the literature on the success and failure of M&A has been on financial and strategic factors, interest in the organisational and human resources implications of M&A has increased in prominence over recent years. An emerging and growing field of inquiry has been the cross-cultural aspects of M&A, and the implications of cultural differences for acquirer–target relationships, for the degree of relatedness of partners, and for post-M&A integration (cf. Stahl and Voigt, 2008). The decisions of Russian MNEs to acquire assets in CIS and other transition countries can be reassessed through the lens of cross-cultural advantages of operating there, differentiated from acquisitions in developed markets such as Europe.

11 | Cross-border M&A and competitive advantage of Indian EMNEs

RAVI RAMAMURTI

Introduction

Why did Indian firms make foreign acquisitions and how has that affected their competitive advantage at home and abroad? By way of answer, this chapter offers two propositions.

The first is that Indian firms, compared to Brazilian, Chinese, or Russian firms (which make up the BRIC countries), seem to have relied more heavily on firm-specific advantages (FSAs) than country-specific advantages (CSAs) for their international competitive advantage. In terms of CSAs, India is not richly endowed with natural resources like Brazil or Russia, nor blessed with a competent government that creates a business environment in which firms can thrive internationally, as in China.[1] It is sometimes said that Chinese firms have thrived *because* of the state while Indian firms have thrived *in spite of* the state (Das, 2006). In Rugman's CSA–FSA framework (Rugman, 2009), CSAs include natural endowments such as land, natural resources, labour, location, climate and so on, and FSAs consist of firm-level assets and capabilities that contribute to competitive advantage. To this scheme, one might add a third category of advantages labelled 'government-specific advantages' (GSAs) to capture the quality of government-created assets, such as a country's physical infrastructure, human capital and the quality of governance, reflected in the competency of policy makers to fashion and implement effective policies, including industrial targeting. Although Rugman would probably regard GSAs as a subset of CSAs, it is helpful and meaningful to distinguish natural endowments from volitional acts of government that contribute to the international competitiveness of firms.

Indian firms enjoy some important CSAs, such as a big internal market and a large labour pool, but they do not enjoy GSAs such as good infrastructure, good educational systems, business-friendly policy

[1] I am referring here to the Indian central government in New Delhi. The quality of governance is also bad in most states, with a few exceptions, e.g. Gujarat.

Figure 11.1 Determinants of international competitiveness of emerging market firms: CSA–GSA–FSA framework
CSAs: country-specific advantages
FSAs: firm-specific advantages
GSAs: government-specific advantages

makers or effective industrial policies (as in China). Nor do they enjoy exportable surpluses of natural resources that can be the foundation of internationalisation, as in Brazil or Russia. In China's case, GSAs have reinforced CSAs, making the country a very attractive location from which to compete globally. The Chinese market is also three or four times as large for most products as the Indian market, and has been growing faster, making the home market that much more important for Chinese firms. In the case of Brazil and Russia, the abundance of natural resources and the compelling need for cross-border vertical integration in these businesses have provided the impetus for several firms in both countries to internationalise. Thus, compared to the other BRIC countries, the strongest leg of the Indian multinational enteprise (MNE)'s stool may be its FSAs, not CSAs or GSAs (see Figure 11.1). More broadly, the point is that when the BRIC countries are compared in terms of CSAs, GSAs and FSAs, some interesting differences emerge that have a bearing on why or how their firms internationalise.

The second proposition is that the motivations and consequences of international mergers and acquisitions (M&A) are not similar across all Indian firms; instead, they depend on the internationalisation strategy of those firms. For some firms, international M&A is largely a means of exploiting existing FSAs, for others it is primarily a means of acquiring new FSAs, and for still others it is a bit of both, depending on which generic strategy for internationalisation they are pursuing (Ramamurti and Singh, 2009a).

There is a tendency in the literature to assert that most EMNEs internationalise to acquire new capabilities (Mathews, 2006). Luo and Tung (2007) speak of the 'springboard' theory, wherein EMNEs make overseas acquisitions to strengthen their international competitiveness. The more one believes that emerging market multinational enterprises (EMNEs) lack valuable FSAs to begin with (Madhok, 2012), the more one is likely to believe that EMNEs internationalise mainly to acquire FSAs. EMNEs' extensive reliance on international acquisitions (Pradhan and Alekshendra, 2006; Conselho Empresarial Brasil-China, 2011), lends credence to the view that EMNEs are looking for quick and easy ways to gain intangible assets, such as brands, technologies and customer relationships. An alternative view is that EMNEs do have FSAs, but that these are different from the familiar FSAs of developed-country MNEs (Ramamurti 2009b: 405). When those traditional FSAs are absent in EMNEs we mistakenly conclude that they do not have any FSAs. Building on this false premise, Rugman (2009) concludes that EMNEs rely largely on home country CSAs for their international competitiveness, which he argues is unsustainable because CSAs are not inimitable advantages – they can be matched easily by local and foreign rivals. Lessard and Lucea (2009: 404) echo the same view when they define CSAs as 'advantages that are common to all firms located in a country'. But the argument advanced here is that Indian firms do have important FSAs which, when combined with the country's weak GSAs, motivate them to look for better locations from which to leverage those FSAs. Indian firms are internationalising not only to acquire new FSAs for use in the home market; but also in search of better locations than India from which to leverage their existing FSAs. In this regard, Indian firms may be different from Chinese firms and similar to non-resource-based Brazilian MNEs.

International acquisitions by Indian firms

The basic facts about the international acquisitions of Indian firms have been studied thoroughly by Pradhan (2007b, 2008, 2011) and others.[2] These show that starting around 2005, Indian firms ratcheted up their foreign direct investments (FDI), taking a break in 2008

---

[2] This section draws on Ramamurti (2008) and Ramamurti (2011).

and 2009 as financial markets tightened, but bouncing back in 2010 (see Table 11.A1). The internationalisation of Indian firms may seem like the logical consequence of the country embracing globalisation in the 1990s, but the fact is that in 2009, just fifteen emerging economies accounted for 88 per cent of the total overseas FDI stock of all emerging economies, and twelve of these were countries like Brazil, Korea, Singapore, Hong Kong and Taiwan that had per-capita incomes in the range of $6,000 to $30,000.[3] India, China and Indonesia were the only countries in that elite group with per-capita incomes below $3,000 (at official exchange rates). Dunning's Investment Development Path model predicted that poor countries would be net recipients of FDI for many years, until their per-capita income rose to middle-income levels (Dunning and Narula, 1996). In 2009, India's per-capita income was only $1,200, yet its OFDI flow reached $14.9 billion (vs. $6 million in 1990) and the value of its cross-border M&A purchases soared to $29 billion in 2007 (vs. $630 million in 1990), before collapsing in 2008 and 2009 and rebounding to new records in 2010 and 2011 (UNCTAD, 2010, Annex Table 2; Bloomberg, 2010).What explains the premature growth of outward FDI from India?

Part of the answer is that as a large and diverse country, India has regions and industries in which its firms are quite advanced, in terms of technology, operations and management. In these areas, Indian firms are able to compete globally, be it software services or engineered goods. The contrast in economic development between parts of Bihar or Uttar Pradesh, on the one hand, and parts of Gujarat, Maharashtra or Tamil Nadu, on the other hand, is striking. If Mumbai or Bengaluru were city-states like Singapore, their per-capita incomes would be three or four times India's average. In other words, India is a collection of highly developed and highly under-developed parts, and it is understandable that the more developed parts would spawn internationally competitive firms.

But there is a deeper puzzle in the Indian case, which is that in recent years total outward FDI by India has been almost as large as total inward

---

[3] The top fifteen OFDI countries (or entities) in 2009 in descending order of importance were: Hong Kong, Russia, China, Singapore, Taiwan, Brazil, Korea, India, Malaysia, United Arab Emirates, Mexico, Saudi Arabia, Chile, Indonesia and Argentina. Their total stock of OFDI was $2,381 billion, out of the total stock of all developing countries of $2,691 billion (UNCTAD, 2010, Annex Table 2, pp. 174–6).

FDI into India. It is not just that some firms are net overseas investors, but that India as a whole is close to being a net outward investor. In this regard, India is significantly different even from China, which received about $500 billion in inward FDI before its firms began to make outward investments. Even as late as 2007, China's inward FDI was five times its outward FDI, whereas in India's case both inward FDI and outward FDI began to surge at about the same time – around 2005; in 2007, the two flows may have been nearly equal, if measured by deal value.[4]

In the last few years, China too has recorded outward FDI flows that are comparable to inward flows, but part of the explanation is the state's encouragement for Chinese firms to 'go global', supported by the government's $2.8 trillion foreign exchange reserves. Many of the largest Chinese firms are partly or wholly state-owned and they have been at the forefront of internationalisation, although private firms are gaining in importance (*The Economist*, 2011). China's huge appetite for resources has also resulted in big investments in natural resources in Australia, Africa and South America. In the last few years, both Brazil and Russia have also recorded outward FDI flows comparable to inward FDI flows. Several of Brazil's home-grown multinationals tend to be in primary sectors, such as agro-based products or minerals, with notable exceptions such as Embraer, Gerdau or Odebrecht. In 2008 in Russia, thirteen of the country's top twenty MNEs were in energy and other resource-based industries, and they accounted for 80 per cent of the foreign assets of those firms.[5] Indian outward FDI is neither state-led nor predominantly in natural resource sectors but rather in knowledge or skill-intensive industries (Kapur and Ramamurti, 2001; Sauvant and Pradhan, 2010). What explains the volume and industry composition of Indian outward FDI?

I suspect the answer has two parts, one of which has to do with the capabilities of India's private sector, and the other stems from weaknesses

---

[4] Official statistics define FDI inflows and outflows somewhat narrowly, but total deal value looks at the size of cross-border investments, regardless of how they are financed.

[5] The leading Russian MNEs, in terms of foreign assets, included Lukoil, Gazprom, Severstal, Evraz, Basic Element and Norilsk Nickel. Thirteen Russian MNEs in natural resource-based industries had $93.7 billion in foreign assets, out of the total foreign assets of the top twenty firms of $117.8 billion. Oil/gas and steel/non-ferrous companies accounted for 72 per cent of the foreign assets (compiled from Vale Columbia Center, 2009).

in the Indian business environment. On the positive side, India's outward FDI is led by highly entrepreneurial private firms that have capabilities in design, production, branding and distribution, and are innovative at providing products and services of 'good enough' quality at ultra-low prices (Ramamurti and Singh, 2009b; Govindarajan and Ramamurti, 2011). These capabilities transfer well to foreign markets, especially other emerging markets. The growth of Indian multinationals is founded largely on the entrepreneurial talent of its private firms. The entrepreneurs behind successful firms include many old names, such as Tata, Birla or the Essar groups, but also a host of new names, such as Sunil Mittal, Tulsi Tanti, Anil Agarwal and Naresh Goyal. When India opened up in 1991, rather than getting wiped out by foreign competitors with state-of-the-art technology and well-known brands, Indian firms held their own in the home market, because they upgraded their products, plants, marketing and distribution networks faster than foreign MNCs could figure out how to win in the complex Indian market. The home-field advantage of Indian firms turned out to be quite substantial. Then, in the late 1990s, Indian firms turned from defending the home market to attacking foreign markets, partly to counter the Indian economic downturn of 2002–3. With the rupee falling, and with such events as Y2K and the post-Y2K boom in offshoring, Indian exports increased. Then, starting in 2006, several Indian firms began to make multi-million dollar, followed by multi-*billion* dollar, acquisitions, not just in other developing countries but also in developed countries, a case in point being the Tata Group's takeover of Corus Steel for $12 billion and Jaguar-Land Rover for $2.3 billion.

The focus of Indian MNEs in skill-intensive businesses, such as IT services, pharmaceuticals and engineering, rather than labour-intensive businesses, may be explained by India's technical skills, which are more advanced than its per-capita income would suggest, and its under-developed physical infrastructure, which has forced private Indian firms to compete in the middle of the skill spectrum rather than at the bottom, where costs are paramount and China has a big edge. The Indian private sector has found ways to compensate for the country's underwhelming public services, that is, to make up for the country's weak GSAs.

While it is true that China's reforms preceded India's by at least a decade, observers overlook the fact that China's indigenous private sector lags India's by a decade or two. This is not because the Chinese are less entrepreneurial than Indians – witness the Chinese community's dynamism outside China – but because the Chinese state suppressed them until only a few years back.[6] In the long run, China's private firms, such as Wanxiang or Cherry, may turn out to be more successful MNCs than behemoths owned by the Chinese government, such as Shanghai Automotive Industries Corporation or the Baosteel Group.[7]

Huang (2003) expresses the view that China's large inward FDI flows in the 1990s and early 2000s reflected the weaknesses of its private sector, while India's low inward FDI flows in those years reflected the strengths of its private sector. As for the higher skill- or knowledge-intensity of India's OFDI, I think it merely reflects the high cost of doing business in India, notably the infrastructure and logistical penalty of getting goods in and out of the country. As a result, the internal efficiency of Indian firms is offset by external inefficiencies, making them unable to compete in foreign markets in businesses where cost is paramount. This not only skews Indian exports in the direction of skill-intensity (where margins are high enough to overcome the India penalties), but also makes the FDI option more attractive relative to exports than would otherwise be the case. In contrast, efficient Chinese firms can compete globally with production inside China.

A final puzzle in the Indian case is why so much of the outward FDI is directed at the rich countries. During 1961–89, 82 per cent of Indian OFDI went to other developing countries; but in 1990–2007, almost 62 per cent went to developed countries (Pradhan and Sauvant, 2011: 5–6). Several answers have been provided for this puzzle, including the view that Indian firms are seeking Western technology and brands in

---

[6] The Boston Consulting Group's 2011 list of the top-100 'global contenders' from emerging markets includes thirty-three Chinese firms, three-quarters of which appear to have some state ownership, and twenty Indian firms, none of which are state-owned (BCG, 2011: 13). By 2010, the Chinese government was well on its way to realising the goal of having thirty to fifty Chinese firms in *Fortune*'s Global 500 list. In contrast, the Indian government had no strategy for turning state-owned enterprises (SOEs) into global champions, although a few among them ventured overseas on their own, e.g. ONGC and IOC.

[7] *The Economist* (2011: 13) reports the share of gross domestic product (GDP) produced by enterprises that are not majority-owned by the state to be 70 per cent, and that, according to one source in the Communist Party, 90 per cent of China's 43 million companies were private.

which they are weak. I think this reflects again the greater willingness of Indian private firms to venture into the advanced countries not only in search of ideas, technologies and brands, but also markets. Not being state-owned may provide a double advantage to Indian MNEs compared to Chinese MNEs, because it allows them to move more boldly and swiftly (Vernon, 1979) and it generates fewer red flags in industrialised countries.

Revisiting the CSA–FSA framework

The above discussion can be summed up using the expanded CSA–FSA framework shown in Figure 11.1, which includes the GSA variable as well. The international competitiveness of firms in a country can be regarded as shaped by God-given factors (CSAs), government decisions and actions (GSAs) and firm-level strategic choices (FSAs). In such a schema, I would assert that Indian firms enjoy valuable CSAs, although a surplus of natural resources is not among them, but they suffer from weak GSAs, and FSAs may well be their strongest suit, at least compared to firms the other BRIC countries.

Exploitation versus exploration in international M&A

I turn next to the question of whether international M&A by Indian firms is undertaken to exploit existing FSAs or to acquire new FSAs. The exploitation–exploration dichotomy (March, 1991) is a simple concept but difficult to apply in practice, because firms may attempt a bit of both in the same international acquisition and their intent can be hard to discern. If you start with the premise that Indian MNEs lack valuable FSAs, then presumably the only reason for international M&A is acquiring new FSAs that could be exploited at home, abroad or both. But if one accepts the premise that at least some Indian firms may have significant FSAs to begin with, then internationalisation to exploit those FSAs in other emerging economies or developed countries is also a plausible scenario. Based on Lessard and Lucea's (2009) analysis of the CEMEX experience, one could add feedback arrows from international operations to domestic operations, to show that exploration and exploitation occur iteratively at home and abroad. But in this discussion I will speculate on the first stage of this process, i.e. when Indian firms make overseas acquisitions. The argument I will make is that the mix of exploitation and exploration varies predictably, according to a firm's internationalisation strategy, using the typology proposed in Ramamurti and Singh (2009b).

The local optimiser: Bharti Airtel

The *local optimiser* strategy involves a firm that develops products and processes optimised for the Indian market (Ramamurti, 2009b). This often involves making products and services a lot cheaper, a lot easier to use and maintain, and otherwise tailored to the needs of local customers (Govindarajan and Ramamurti, 2011). Relative to foreign MNEs, Indian firms have the advantage of not being constrained by prior investments in high-cost products or products optimised for other markets. Having thus developed products optimised for India, the Indian firm is likely to find that there is a ready demand for the same products in other emerging markets, providing a basis for internationalisation. The logic here resembles that of the product cycle hypothesis (Vernon, 1979), but with products and ideas flowing from one emerging economy to even less-developed emerging economies. In this case, there is ample opportunity for the firm to leverage its home-based FSAs in its foreign operations.

Bharti Airtel, an Indian wireless telephone service provider, illustrates the point. Its approach to wireless service involved many innovative elements: the heavy reliance on prepaid service, rather than postpaid service, which took away the risk of customer defaults; the use of third parties to recharge cell phone balances, which reduced the need for sales offices and costly paperwork; and very low prices for service and very low minimum recharge amounts, which made wireless service extremely affordable for India's low-income consumers. In addition, Bharti Airtel used a business model based on the outsourcing of all IT-related services, such as customer servicing, billing, promotion and so on, to IBM, and the outsourcing of telecoms equipment supply, installation, maintenance and operation to firms like Ericsson and Nokia-Siemens (Martinez-Jerez *et al.*, 2006). As a result, Bharti Airtel's investments and headcount were minimised, even as speed and flexibility were increased. Bharti Airtel's suppliers became risk-sharing partners.

The result of this strategy was that Bharti Airtel became the top wireless service provider in India, with over 175 million customers, and along with other firms brought wireless telephony to over 700 million

Indian consumers. Bharti Airtel's average revenue per user (ARPU) per month was less than $5, compared to $51 for Verizon Wireless in the US. Even China Telecom had an ARPU of $15 per month. Despite such low rates, in 2009 Bharti Airtel had a 25 per cent net margin on sales and had a market capitalisation of $27 billion. How could anyone argue that such a firm did not possess FSAs?

As expected of a local optimiser, Bharti Airtel embarked on international expansion when domestic opportunities approached saturation, and then it did so by entering other emerging markets (see Table 11.A1 in the appendix for a list of major cross-border M&A deals by Indian firms in 2008–10). The company tried unsuccessfully to merge with MTN, the South Africa-based wireless telephone provider with 95 million customers in nineteen African countries. When that deal fell through, despite two attempts, Bharti Airtel acquired 70 per cent of Warid Telecom of Bangladesh for $300 million from an Abu Dhabi group. Then, in June 2010, it acquired 100 per cent of Zain Africa for $10.7 billion, in what was the largest overseas M&A deal by an Indian company in 2008–10. The acquisition gave Bharti Airtel access to 42 million African consumers with average ARPUs of $9–13 per month, which was significantly higher than its Indian ARPUs. The expectation was that Bharti Airtel would apply its Indian business model (FSAs) to dramatically lower the cost of wireless telephony in Africa. Thus, this major international M&A deal was based to a large extent on exploiting pre-existing FSAs in countries that shared common features with India.

There are many more examples of local optimisers leveraging their FSAs in other emerging markets, but they do not appear in Table 11. A1, which only lists deals over $100 million; entry into most emerging markets required outlays lower than $100 million, whether done through greenfield investment or M&A. In such cases, internationalisation was likely based on the exploitation of FSAs developed in the home market.

The low-cost partner: Indian IT firms

The low-cost partner strategy (Ramamurti, 2009b) is pursued by firms whose international competitiveness arises primarily from labour cost arbitrage, i.e. the substitution of high-cost Western labour by low-cost Indian labour. The customers of such firms will be largely in advanced economies although most of their own headcount will likely be in low-cost India. The firm focuses on a few stages of the value chain in which India has comparative advantage or CSAs, freeing up its developed-country customers to focus on their own core competencies. The low-cost partner's internationalisation involves creating centres for service delivery in other low-cost countries and in creating subsidiaries in developed countries to tap higher-end skills, move up the value curve and strengthen relationships with customers.

On the surface it would appear that low-cost partners such as Indian information technology (IT) firms Infosys, TCS or Wipro, are merely leveraging India's low-cost talent, i.e. its CSAs. But in fact these firms possess important FSAs. First, raw Indian talent is mostly unfit for employment in IT services without a great deal of careful selection and training. Large Indian IT firms have spent a fortune on improving the educational institutions that feed them talent and then on training and retaining that talent. At the same time, they have had to invest in telecoms links, backup power supply, water supply and housing and transportation for employees. These firm-level investments compensate for weak GSAs, i.e. the state's failure to provide good physical infrastructure and develop human capital. Thus, private firms have taken on public functions, but in so doing appropriate these advantages as FSAs. India's infrastructure may be awful for most Indian firms – that is, the country's GSAs are weak – but for the leading IT firms they were quite good within their posh campuses. Foreign firms could not leverage India's talent unless they could replicate the private 'infrastructure' or master the human resources (HR) skills for screening, selecting, training and retaining talent on a large scale.[8] In IBM's case, the acquisition of a local company, Daksh, served as the nucleus of the company's growing footprint in India.

Second, Indian IT firms embarked on the labour cost-arbitrage strategy in the 1970s and 1980s, long before Western MNEs recognised India's potential as a centre for off-shoring services. The leading Indian IT companies were pioneers who created and perfected the 'global delivery model' through which the services value-chain could be geographically dispersed across thousands of miles (initially between the US and India) and then integrated seamlessly. This

---

[8] TCS, for instance, expected to hire 80,000 employees in 2011, and Infosys had a 10,000-person training centre in Mysore, Karnataka.

required project management skills, which the best Indian IT firms have mastered, in addition to technical skills. Firms in other emerging economies looking to replicate India's success in IT services are stymied by the lack of project management skills and tools, without which the global delivery model cannot be scaled up. If IBM, Accenture and other Western firms have adopted the global delivery model themselves, it is because they have now acquired FSAs in these areas to match those of Indian counterparts.

Against this background, one can see how Indian IT firms may in fact be *exploiting* home-based FSAs when they internationalise. Their capabilities in overcoming weak GSAs in human capital development or physical infrastructure could help them set up and operate centres in other low-cost countries where GSAs may be similarly weak (most emerging economies have weak GSAs like India, rather than strong GSAs like China). And Indian firms' expertise in project management could help them implement the global delivery model in locations outside India. Consistent with the view that FSA exploitation may be central to the internationalisation of Indian IT firms, most of their international expansion came through greenfield investments rather than acquisitions, despite hoards of cash and high market capitalisations (see Table 11.A1). However, when acquisitions were made, part of the motivation was obtaining new FSAs, such as building capability in specialised areas that provided a toehold in a new line of business, such as consulting, or provided access to high-end clients. Examples include TCS' acquisition of Unisys Insurance (UK) and Wipro's acquisition of Infocrossing for $600 million. But even in such cases, a key part of the integration strategy was to move work from the target firm's high-cost country to low-cost India at a faster rate than might have happened; in other words, exploiting existing FSAs was very much a part of the logic of even these acquisitions.

The global consolidator: Indian steel and aluminum firms

The *global consolidator* strategy typically arises in industries that have matured in developed countries but are booming in emerging markets – industries like cement, steel, chemicals, white goods, automobiles, beverages and processed foods. Two key success factors in such industries are process efficiency and scale. Before an Indian firm internationalises in one of these industries, it must build FSAs in process efficiency to lower costs and operational excellence to reach international quality standards. It must also build scale in the home market, as demand grows, through state-of-the-art plants and domestic consolidation of the industry. Firms from the large emerging economies, such as the BRICs, are more likely than firms from smaller emerging economies to become global players in such industries. After becoming leaders at home, some of these firms are likely to consolidate the industry globally by acquiring firms in the same industry in developed countries. Targets in developed countries are likely to be in financial difficulty, because of high legacy costs, vintage plants and declining volumes, and this may explain why developed-country firms are less likely to be the ones to try global consolidation.

Indian examples of global consolidators include the Tata group in steel, chemicals, autos and beverages; the Aditya Birla group in copper and aluminum; Mahindra's in tractors; Videocon in consumer electronics; and so on. These firms account for some of the largest foreign acquisitions made by Indian companies (see Table 11.A1), and many of their deals involved buying firms in developed countries that were already multinational in scope, e.g. Tata Steel's purchase of Corus, or Hindalco's purchase of Novelis.

What mix of exploiting pre-existing FSAs versus acquiring new FSAs does one find in these cases? Here, both motivations seem to be in play; on the one hand, the prospect of improving the performance of acquired firms by leveraging FSAs such as operational excellence is cited as a justification for overseas acquisitions.[9] Such improvement is also posited to come from the longer time horizon of Indian buyers compared to Western owners (e.g. Tata's taking a longer term view of Jaguar's prospects than Ford), or by their willingness to invest in industries that Western investors have given up on. At the same time, an equally important motivation for M&A seems to be the desire to learn from acquired firms about technologies and high-value-added products that could be exploited in India. A case in point is Hindalco's intent to bring aluminum can-making technology from Novelis (Canada) for use in India. However, in 2011, the jury was still out on whether the anticipated improvements in acquired firms would actually materialise. The early evidence in the Tata Steel acquisition of

[9] The Tata Steel acquisition of Corus Steel, for instance, was based on a synergy target of $450 million (Tata Steel Annual Report, 2007–8).

Corus, and Tata Motors' acquisition of Jaguar-Land Rover, seems to be that their performance was significantly stronger in 2010. Acquired organisations were being integrated successfully with Indian operations and best practices were being transferred in both directions. For instance, Tata Steel achieved £866 million in cost savings in 2010, with improvements in Corus' hot strip mills in the Netherlands, based on practices transferred from Tata's Indian plant (Jamshedpur), while its Indian cold rolling mills benefited from practices transferred from Corus' plants (Tata Steel Group, 2010: 16, 25).

The global first-mover: Suzlon Energy

The last type of EMNE is the *global first-mover*, which is not merely catching up with competitors from developed countries but is a prominent player in an emerging industry. An example in the Indian context is wind energy firm Suzlon. In this case, international M&A has a large element of FSA acquisition rather than FSA exploitation, and the process is akin to the 'double handspring' strategy described in Williamson and Raman (Chapter 12), wherein international M&As are used to acquire FSAs that are integrated with domestic capabilities for use initially in the home market, followed by exploitation of the combined capabilities in foreign markets. Suzlon's evolution followed a similar path, starting in 1996 (see Vietor and Seminerio, 2008; Awate and Mudambi, 2010).

When Tulsi Tanti started Suzlon he had no background in the industry (his original business was textiles). His great insight was recognising the promise of wind energy in India, and his strategy was to provide one-stop service, from prospecting, design, installation and commissioning of the full facility, to operation and maintenance for ten or twenty years.[10] The other distinctive element of his strategy was vertical integration, so that Suzlon would not be at the mercy of critical component suppliers. But Suzlon lacked the technology for making the most of a wind energy system, including blades, gearbox, generator, controls and so on, and it obtained these, one by one, through international deals, such as licensing or outright purchase of know-how, and the acquisition of technical talent rather than whole companies.

---

[10] This section draws on interviews with Suzlon founder and CEO, Tulsi Tanti, on 25 January 2011 in Paris, and via telephone on 17 March 2011.

Doing it this way on the cheap was characteristic of many Indian companies. Tanti also bought European companies in bankruptcy, keeping key technical talent while selling off the assets to companies like GE. After a very successful initial public offering (IPO) in India in 2005, he made two large acquisitions, namely, Belgian gearbox maker Hansen (2006) for $565 million and German wind turbine maker REpower (2007 onwards) for a total outlay of over $2 billion (see Table 11.A1). Initially, Suzlon also adapted European technology to suit Indian conditions, such as unstable electricity grids and high humidity and temperatures.

In the context of this chapter, what is interesting is that Suzlon's initial forays abroad were to acquire technologies as cheaply as possible for absorption and exploitation in India. In this it was wildly successful, gaining 50 per cent or more of the Indian market, despite being a late entrant behind firms like NEPC. After the IPO, Suzlon raised its sights to include gaining market share in the US, Europe and then China. At this point, it sought to combine its large footprint in low-cost India and China with access to key global markets. The jury is still out on whether it will succeed in this more ambitious goal, including winning in China, where it has invested more than $400 million to become a 'local' company that sources parts mostly from China. But it has been struggling to gain business there, faced with state-owned buyers and state-supported local competitors. The economic slowdown after 2008 and the slump in demand in the US have also hurt Suzlon badly. Regardless of whether this strategy works, it is probably fair to say that Suzlon used international M&A (and other) non-equity arrangements to *acquire* new FSAs (technology initially, and then market access in Europe) for use in India rather than to *exploit* pre-existing FSAs. What is often asserted as a generally valid hypothesis about all international M&A deals by EMNEs – that they are mainly intended to acquire FSAs – may be largely true only in this case, at least in the Indian context.

Conclusions

This chapter makes two main points. The first is that in considering the international competitiveness of firms in emerging markets, it is necessary to consider not just comparative advantage (CSAs) and competitive advantage (FSAs) but also advantages created through government

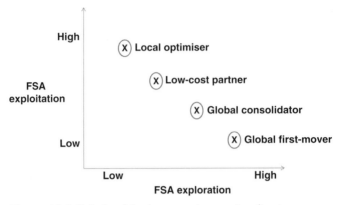

Figure 11.2 Relationship between internationalisation strategy and FSA exploitation or exploration

actions and investments (GSAs). When this three-legged stool of inter-national competitive advantage is applied across the BRIC countries, some interesting differences appear, at least to this observer: The strongest leg of the competitive advantage stool in the Indian case appears to be FSAs, while CSAs are quite important and GSAs are particularly weak. In contrast, China has stronger CSAs (because of its bigger market size and faster growth) and much stronger GSAs, such as infrastructure, human capital development, business-friendly policies and industrial targeting. FSAs may not be the strongest leg of Chinese MNEs, and the 'double handspring' dynamics presented in Williamson and Raman (Chapter 12) may indeed be an effective approach to building their global competitiveness. If my assertion about Indian MNEs is correct – that FSAs are their strongest suit – then internation-alisation may also be a way for them to exploit those capabilities from locations more attractive than India, not just a way to obtain new FSAs, although surely that too was happening.

The second point of the chapter is that the balance of exploitation and exploration in international M&A deals varies according to a firm's internationalisation strategy. I have tried to illustrate each gen-eric internationalisation strategy with an example, asking whether the firm brings value to the cross-border M&A or seeks to take value from it for use at home. Based on that analysis, in the Indian context, the mix of exploitation and exploration seems to be different across the four inter-nationalisation strategies considered in this chapter (see Figure 11.2).

The internationalisation strategy of local optimisers and low-cost partners seems to involve a fair amount of FSA exploitation, while FSA acquisition seems to be more important in the case of global consolidators, and the dominant motivation in the case of global first-movers. It is a mistake, at least in the Indian case, to assume that international M&A is always motivated by the search for new FSAs.

Appendix

Table 11.A1 International acquisitions over $100m by Indian firms, 2008–2010 (in descending order of value)

No.	Acquirer name	Target name	Target nation	Year	% shares acquired	Transaction value ($m)[11]	Target firm's industry and other comments
1	Bharti Airtel Ltd	Zain Africa BV	Nigeria	2010	100.00	10,700	Wireless service
2	Tata Motors Ltd	Jaguar Cars Ltd and Land Rover Ltd	UK	2008	100.00	2,300	Automotive. From Ford Motor Co
3	GMR Infrastructure Ltd	InterGen NV	Netherlands	2008	50.00	1,107	Electric utility. From a unit of AIG
4	Tata Chemicals Ltd	General Chemical Industrial	US	2008	100.00	1,005	Chemicals (soda ash). From Harbinger Capital Partners, etc.
5	Aamby Valley Ltd (a unit of Sahara India Parivar)	Grosvenor House Hotel	UK	2010	100.00	725	Hotel. From Royal Bank of Scotland
6	Hindustan Zinc Ltd (unit of Vedanta Resources)	Anglo American PLC-Skorpion	Namibia	2010	100.00	698	Mining. Acquired from Anglo American plc
7	Fortis Healthcare Ltd	Parkway Holdings Ltd	Singapore	2010	23.90	685	Hospitals. From TPG Capital LP, private transaction
8	Suzlon Energy Ltd	REpower Systems	Germany	2008	30.00	546	Wind energy. From AREVA (a unit of French state-owned atomic energy co.)

#	Company	Target	Country	Year	%	Value	Notes
9	Suzlon Energy Ltd	REpower Systems	Germany	2009	22.48	394	Wind energy. From Martifer Construcoes Metalomecanicas LDA. Total ownership rises to 88.48%
10	Reliance Industries Ltd	Marcellus Shale Natural Gas	US	2010	60.00	392	Natural gas
11	Reliance Industries Ltd	Atlas Energy Inc, Marcellus	US	2010	40.00	339	Oil and gas exploration and production
12	Shree Renuka Sugars Ltd	Equipav SA Acucar e Alcool	Brazil	2010	50.79	331	Sugar and ethanol. From Equipav Group
13	Hindustan Zinc Ltd	Lisheen Minig, Killoran Lishee	Ireland	2010	100.00	308	Zinc. From Anglo American plc
14	Siva Ventures Ltd	JB Ugland Shipping AS	Norway	2008	100.00	302	Shipping. From Norwegian group
15	Bharti Airtel Ltd	Warid Telecom	Bangladesh	2010	70.00	300	Wireless service. From Abu Dhabi group
16	Indiabulls Real Estate Ltd	Dev Property Development plc	UK	2008	100.00	276	Real estate
17	Aegis BPO Services Ltd	PeopleSupport Inc	US	2008	100.00	264	Business process outsourcing

Table 11.A1 (*cont.*)

No.	Acquirer name	Target name	Target nation	Year	% shares acquired	Transaction value ($m)[11]	Target firm's industry and other comments
18	Jubilant Organosys Ltd	DRAXIS Health Inc	Canada	2008	100.00	255	Specialty pharmaceuticals
19	Mapletree India China Fund Ltd	Beijing Gateway Plaza (BVI) Ltd	Hong Kong	2010	100.00	245	Office building owner/operator
20	Shree Renuka Sugars Ltd	Vale Do Ivai SA	Brazil	2010	100.00	240	Sugar and ethanol
21	Religare Enterprises Ltd	Northgate Capital Group LLC	US	2010	65.00	200	Private equity firm
22	Investor Group	APC-Rovuma Offshore Area	Mozambique	2008	20.00	150	Oil and gas. Acquired by unit of Videocon Industries (India) and state-owned Bharat Petroleum
23	Essar Global Ltd	Aries Coal Mines	Indonesia	2010	100.00	148	Coal mining
24	Sona Koyo Steering Systems	Thyssenkrupp GmbH	Germany	2008	100.00	146	Steel and automotive parts
25	Asian Hotels (North) Ltd	Darius Holdings Ltd	Mauritius	2010	53.00	136	Hotels
26	Cals Refineries Ltd	Petro Canada – distillation	Canada	2008	100.00	110	Petroleum refining

27	MW Unitexx SA	Klopman International SpA	Italy	2008	100.00	108	Polyester and cotton fabrics
28	JBF Industries Ltd	JBR Global Pte Ltd	Singapore	2010	10.62	104	Polyester chips and yarns
29	Glodyne Technoserve Ltd	DecisionOne Inc	US	2010	100.00	104	IT services
30	3i Infotech	Regulus Group PLC	US	2008	100.00	100	Remittance processing services
31	JSW Steel Ltd	Undisclosed coking coal mine	US	2010	100.00	100	Coking coal

Source: Compiled from SDC M&A Database
[1]Rounded to nearest million.

12 | Cross-border M&A and competitive advantage of Chinese EMNEs

PETER J. WILLIAMSON AND ANAND P. RAMAN

Introduction

In 2000, shortly before acceding to the World Trade Organization (WTO), the Chinese government came to the view that local companies would need to be globally competitive if they were to match growing rivalry from established multinationals in the home market as well as contributing to China's broader integration into the world economy. It announced a *zou chuqu* policy (which loosely translates as 'go global') that encouraged local companies to make acquisitions abroad. Numerous state-owned enterprises (SOEs) as well as private corporations took up the opportunity, investing in companies large and small on five continents. According to statistics from Thomson-Reuters, from $1.6 billion in 2000, the value of Chinese mergers and acquisitions (M&A) rose to $70.3 billion by 2008, falling back to $40.6 billion in 2009 in the aftermath of the global financial crisis, but then recovering in 2010 to reach $55.4 billion (see Figure 12.1).

Behind the aggregate statistics, however, the type of cross-border M&A activity undertaken by Chinese companies has varied considerably

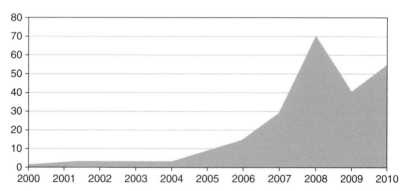

Figure 12.1 The evolution of Chinese EMNEs' M&A activity in aggregate (value of foreign acquisitions, $ billion)
Source: Thomson Reuters

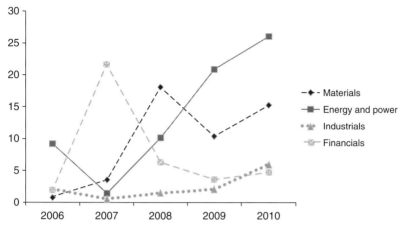

Figure 12.2 Chinese EMNEs' M&A activity by sector (value of foreign acquisitions, top four sectors, $ billion)
Source: Thomson Reuters

over time. The first wave of overseas M&A deals, up until 2006, were aimed at accessing products' designs, brands, distribution and sometimes production capacity, overseas, with the aim of growing sales in foreign markets – what has been termed in the literature 'springboard' acquisitions (Luo and Tung, 2007). A second wave of acquisitions began in 2006 when the focus of acquisitions shifted to hard assets like mineral deposits and oil and gas reserves – 'resource seeking' acquisitions (Bresman *et al.*, 1999; Forsgren, 2002) in the narrowest sense of the term. There was also a boom in acquisitions of stakes in financial services companies abroad in 2007 as Chinese financial institutions, with large cash reserves, sought to expand their operations abroad. The timing, with hindsight, was catastrophic – although Chinese financial institutions were hardly alone among their global peers in having their fingers burnt in this arena.

Since 2008, deals aimed at securing the supply of raw materials and energy resources into China have continued to grow apace. But a third wave of acquisitions has also commenced with the steady growth in acquisitions of 'industrial' companies abroad (see Figure 12.2). As we will see, these acquisitions are primarily aimed at capturing technology, know-how and sometimes brands – but this time with a difference: the acquirers are using these intangible assets in the first instance to improve their businesses in China, before trying to win share abroad.

This chapter analyses the impact of this Chinese cross-border M&A activity on the evolution of Chinese emerging market multinational enterprises' (EMNEs) competitive advantage. Drawing on a series of case examples, particular attention is given to the changing ways in which Chinese firms have attempted to combine their own, indigenous resource and competence bases with those accessed through off-shore acquisitions to strengthen and extend their competitiveness. In the initial deals, these attempts were largely unsuccessful. The subsequent wave of pure resource-seeking acquisitions has had limited impact on Chinese EMNEs' competitive advantage. In the new phase of acquisition activity that began in 2008, however, we will argue that cross-border M&A is now providing Chinese EMNEs with access to resources and capabilities that can be combined with their existing capabilities and advantages to create *new* and unique sources of competitive advantage which can ultimately be exploited in global markets (as postulated by Teece *et al.*, 1997; Morck *et al.*, 2008; and Williamson and Zeng, 2009a).

The sources and limitations of Chinese EMNEs' existing competitive advantages

Their home base provides Chinese EMNEs with the potential to access a number of country-specific advantages (CSAs). Perhaps most important among these is the benefit of a large pool of low-cost, low-skilled labour that can be parlayed into low manufacturing cost. Many observers argue that EMNEs have no firm-specific assets (FSAs) and rely mainly on CSAs to compete globally (e.g. Rugman, 2009). But CSAs alone are insufficient to act as such a source of competitive advantage, either against other Chinese competitors with access to similar CSAs or in the global market, because foreign companies are also readily able to exploit this low-cost labour advantage, by either setting up manufacturing in China or outsourcing manufacturing and other basic operations to domestic companies in China.

Nor do potential CSAs deriving from widespread state ownership provide a sustainable source of competitive advantage capable of underpinning Chinese EMNEs' successful global expansion. State interests have provided many of the leading Chinese companies with initial advantages in the form of hard assets, capital and intellectual property made available to them more cheaply than the prevailing value of these assets on world markets. But beyond this initial endowment, significant ongoing subsidies or special support from the state cannot be relied upon for most companies. Rather, once restructured and partially privatised, they are generally forced to stand on their own feet and often compete against other firms with hybrid ownership in the market (Zeng and Williamson, 2003).

Chinese companies wishing to succeed both domestically and globally, therefore, have been forced to find radical new ways of using Chinese cost advantages so as to parlay their country-specific advantage into firm-specific advantages which would be difficult for rivals, both foreign and domestic, to replicate. They first achieved this through what has been termed *cost innovation* (Zeng and Williamson, 2007). Within the broad strategy for creating FSAs and competitive advantages, leading Chinese companies have undertaken cost innovation along some combination of three dimensions:

- First, they have developed strategies and organisational routines (Nelson and Winter, 2002) that have allowed them to offer customers high technology at low cost. This has the potential to create competitive advantage because established global competitors have a disincentive to imitate this strategy for fear of interrupting the cycle whereby they maximise their profits along the product life cycle by only slowly migrating new technology from high-priced segments towards the mass market; they also face considerable organisational and cultural rigidities in replicating these routines (Williamson and Zeng, 2009b).
- Second, Chinese EMNEs are finding processes that enable them to offer customers a wide choice of product varieties or customisation at prices that are competitive against incumbents' standardised, mass-market offerings. These processes involve many detailed process innovations that are difficult for competitors both to recognise and then to replicate (Zeng and Williamson, 2007).
- Third, Chinese companies have developed strategies and processes that enable them to use their low costs to reduce the break-even of producing specialty products. This enables them to reduce the risk of trying to 'explode' hitherto niche markets into volume businesses by dramatically lower prices. This creates a competitive advantage because foreign multinationals have often found it difficult to match this FSA because it would require them not only to access CSAs in China, but also to completely reengineer their existing business models that are based

around the assumption that specialty products must forever remain low-volume and high-priced (Zeng and Williamson, 2008).

Similarly, Chinese EMNEs have also been able to develop other types of FSAs based on their home-base experience including the ability to unlock latent demand in low-end segments (Prahalad, 2005) or capabilities in dealing with weak institutions and infrastructure (Morck *et al.*, 2008) that can complement the existing advantages of firms acquired in developed markets. It is not the purpose here to present a full analysis of the development of FSAs by Chinese EMNEs, rather to establish that they have gone beyond their initial endowment provided by access to Chinese CSAs to create a number of proprietary advantages.

Many of these FSAs are particularly useful in competing in the Chinese market and in other emerging markets. At the same time, the types of FSAs amassed by most Chinese EMNEs have significant limitations as a basis for effective competition in the global market, especially compared with the requirements to build successful businesses in developed economies (Nolan and Hasecic, 2000; Nolan, 2005; Hutton, 2007). Examples include: weak brands, lack of proprietary technology, inexperience in adapting their offerings to the myriad of local consumer tastes and market environments around the world, a limited number of managers with international experience and the fact that they generally lack well-honed organisations with global reach that their multinational competitors have built up over decades.

Cross-border M&A has provided Chinese EMNEs with opportunities to try and fill these gaps in the capability portfolios they need to be globally competitive. This can be done in a number of possible ways, outlined below. Depending on the chosen strategy the result may go beyond pure 'catch up' and allow the Chinese EMNE to use off-shore acquisitions to build new types of competitive advantage not available to incumbent multinational enterprises (MNEs). To understand these possibilities it is useful to briefly review the alternative explanations for cross-border acquisitions advanced in the international business (IB) literature.

Possible explanations for Chinese EMNEs' cross-border M&A

Traditional theories of cross-border acquisitions have tended to focus on the potential for acquirers to add value to their targets by transferring know-how, systems and capabilities honed in advanced economies to less developed ones in line with long-established models of international expansion (Johanson and Vahlne, 1977). The fact that a number of Chinese EMNEs' cross-border acquisitions have involved targets based in developed markets (such as Lenovo's takeover of IBM's personal computer business), however, might be seen as counter to these explanations, especially if the FSAs Chinese EMNEs bring are primarily applicable to competing successfully in emerging markets (Gubbi *et al.*, 2009; Guillén and Garcia-Canal, 2009).

An alternative explanation for Chinese cross-border acquisitions is that they represent pure resource-seeking moves (Bresman *et al.*, 1999; Forsgren, 2002). But this leaves unanswered the question of how Chinese acquirers can out-bid their rivals in the market for corporate control and still make such acquisitions profitable. If Chinese EMNEs were playing a pure catch-up game against established MNEs, then their post-acquisition performance would be unlikely to deliver returns in the global market that would put them in a position to economically out-bid global rivals.

Various purely financial explanations could explain this behaviour. Information asymmetries may mean that Chinese acquirers are winning acquisition battles by paying excessive premiums. Case study evidence, however, suggests that Chinese companies seldom bid well above alternative acquirers and often lose out against MNEs from developed markets in bidding wars. Nor is it clear that the high price–earnings ratios often enjoyed by many Chinese EMNEs or the proceeds of large initial public offerings (IPOs) or other financial factors give them a decisive advantage in the international market for corporate control.

A third possible explanation is that, in the case of acquisitions by Chinese EMNEs, the generally accepted idea of adding value to an acquisition by adding new capabilities may need to be extended to give more emphasis to the dynamics of creating new types of competitive advantage (Teece *et al.*, 1997) through the interaction between diverse and previously dispersed capabilities (Doz *et al.*, 2001) being brought together through cross-border M&A activity by Chinese EMNEs. This would lead to the possibility of extending the idea of resource-seeking as an explanation for Chinese EMNEs' cross-border acquisitions to include the possibility that, rather than simply allowing them to catch up with more established rivals, these acquisitions are allowing Chinese EMNEs to differentiate themselves in the global market by opening the way to the creation of unique FSAs and hence sources of competitive advantage.

In what follows we analyse the three waves of Chinese EMNEs' M&A activity described above using a set of detailed case studies. While not a formal test of these alternative explanations of Chinese EMNEs' M&A activity, the aim is to shed light on which of these theoretical possibilities (or mix thereof) provides the most plausible fit with observed behaviour.

The first wave of Chinese cross-border M&A: failed springboards

In the 1990s, the government allowed mostly SOEs to buy small stakes in energy and other natural resource producers abroad in order to secure the supplies to meet domestic demand. This approach changed in October 2000, in the run-up to China signing the WTO agreement in December 2001. The Ministry of Foreign Trade and Economic Cooperation (MOFTEC) announced that: 'By "going global", enterprises can invest and set up factories overseas, better utilise the domestic and foreign markets and resources, further expand the export of equipment, materials and labour services, and create new export growth points. Thus we can enhance the level of China's opening to the outside world.' The Chinese government dismantled a host of bureaucratic hurdles and barriers in the path of foreign investments erected during the 1990s. This was given further impetus in late 2004 when Premier Wen Jiabao formally announced that the 'Chinese government encourages more domestic enterprises to go global'.

An analysis of three case studies, detailed below, helps understand the strategy Chinese EMNEs followed during this first phase of the go-global policy and why it failed to create sustainable competitive advantage.

SAIC–SsangYong Motors

Shanghai Automotive Industrial Corporation (SAIC) – one of China's largest and oldest automobile manufacturers – acquired a 49 per cent equity stake in South Korea's SsangYong Motors for $500 million in October 2004. Its aim was to gain access to the capabilities to help it design a state-of-the-art sports utility vehicle (SUV) to which

SAIC had not gained access, despite operating joint ventures with Volkswagen and GM since the 1980s.

SsangYong Motors was struggling under the weight of a heavy debt burden, but it had developed a reputation for coming up with smart SUVs and recreational automobiles. As South Korea's fourth-largest automaker, it controlled 10 per cent of that market and had a growing export business. By buying SsangYong Motors, SAIC expected to improve its development capabilities and gain a platform to build its sales in foreign markets such as the US. The SAIC–SsangYong Motors management team quickly planned the expansion of manufacturing capacity in South Korea and the launch of five new models worldwide, starting with a four-door sedan, the SsangYong World Zenith.

However, things did not go as planned. Rising oil prices in 2006 and the introduction of stringent emission standards in Europe and North America sent sales of SUVs tumbling. During the time, SAIC's relations with the powerful trade unions at SsangYong Motors became strained while cultural differences between the Chinese and Korean executives prevented them from arriving at a consensus about how to improve performance. These post-merger integration problems were aggravated when the global recession began in December 2007, causing global demand to collapse. Sales of SUVs were particularly hard hit and by December 2008, SsangYong Motors' sales had fallen by 53 per cent compared to the previous year. SAIC initially supported its subsidiary, buying $4.5 million of SsangYong Motors' vehicles in December 2008 for the China market.

When the situation worsened SAIC's management team unveiled a tough restructuring plan which entailed the shake-up of work practices to improve productivity as well as a 36 per cent cut in the workforce as a condition for pumping in $200 million more into the Korean company. SsangYong Motors' trade unions refused to endorse the turnaround plan and went on strike.

SsangYong Motors filed for bankruptcy protection in January 2009. SAIC wrote off most of its original investment; blamed the losses for a 26 per cent drop in its first-half profits for 2009; and in mid-July 2010, diluted its holdings in the subsidiary to 3.79 per cent. In the six years that SAIC controlled SsangYong Motors, it invested $618 million to acquire the company – and made little progress in using it to expand its sales abroad.

D'Long Group–Murray

One of the first Chinese EMNEs to push into the North American market was the D'Long Group. Started by the Tang brothers in Xinjiang as a small company to develop and print photographs, it had grown into a large conglomerate by acquiring companies involved in businesses ranging from tomato paste to automobile parts. In 2000, D'Long entered the global lawnmower and garden-equipment business by acquiring Murray Inc with $400 million in financing provided by GE Capital. Murray, based in Brentwood, Tennessee, traced its roots back to 1919 and was one of America's leading brands of outdoor power equipment products. The company employed approximately 1,700 people in the US, its subsidiary Murray Canada and a British sister company, Hayter. Its profitability had been falling because it faced aggressive cost-based competition from overseas, especially from China.

Following the acquisition, D'Long integrated its production facilities in China with those of Murray; restructured the organisation to reduce overhead costs; and identified lower-cost sources of components. Having linked the American brand, distribution and design skills with a cost-competitive supply chain, D'Long believed it had created formidable competitive advantages over both its Chinese and Western rivals and projected that Murray's sales would rise to $700 million by 2005. However, Murray suffered from a series of quality problems and product recalls that dented the brand and led to declining sales. In 2004, for instance, D'Long had to recall 100,000 Murray lawn tractors in the US because some fuel tanks developed cracks that allowed fuel to leak. Costs in the US organisation also proved stubbornly high.

Murray Inc eventually filed for bankruptcy in February 2005. Its operations were shut down, and Briggs and Stratton Power Products of the UK bought its brands on the condition that they would not have to support any Murray-branded products sold earlier.

TCL–Thomson Electronics

As China's largest colour television set maker and second-largest mobile telephone maker, TCL started promoting its brand internationally in 2000. In January 2004, it struck a $560 million deal to merge its TV and DVD operations with those of French consumer electronics company, Thomson. It became TCL-Thomson Electronics Co Ltd (TTE), in which TCL held a 67 per cent equity stake before acquiring the rest in 2006.

The strategy was to complement TCL's manufacturing cost advantages with Thomson's strengths in brands and research capabilities as a way to build competitive advantage in global markets. But, even by 2006, it became clear that TCL was struggling to make the acquisition a success.

TCL did not realise that the Thomson brand in Europe and its RCA brand in America, rather than providing clear differentiation, were both old and tired and needed a great deal of investment if there was to be any hope of them being revived. Thomson's TV and DVD operations had lost more than $100 million in 2003, which is why it needed to sell. Moreover, TCL lacked the combinative capabilities to integrate and assimilate Thomson. The shortage of TCL managers with international experience and expertise in global marketing was a major constraint. There was also a clash of different cultures and routines; when TCL imposed structures on the venture that were suitable for China, many of the French staff quit.

By 2007, TCL had become infamous as a Chinese company that had failed in overseas M&A. Due to the problematic European operations, it suffered a combined loss of $680 million in 2005 and 2006. In November 2007, TCL declared its European operation insolvent, and overhauled its TV operations, doing away with Thomson's business model, distribution channels and even the brand. It closed five of its seven European operational centres and executed massive layoffs.

As these cases (and others the authors have analysed) show, the first wave of Chinese acquisitions was aimed at providing a springboard to grow global sales (Luo and Tung, 2007). The logic for these acquisitions creating competitive advantage seemed impeccable: take low-cost Chinese manufacturing capacity and connect it to the latest technology, brand equity and distribution relationships by buying a Western company endowed with all those ingredients, but hampered by high costs. Competitive advantage would result from a dream marriage of Chinese manufacturing with American or European technology and marketing. However, the theoretical benefits were not realised in practice, in part because the Chinese EMNEs involved turned out to lack the capabilities for due diligence on, and subsequent integration of, complex organisations in a foreign context.

This lack of capabilities was aggravated by the fact that many Chinese EMNE acquirers at the time focused on cheap deals, which proved to be costly turnarounds. These acquisitions were also a bet on building competitive advantage through complex synergies that required the management of intangible assets such as brands, systems, people, culture and know-how – all fragile and difficult to integrate across borders. In many cases, the Chinese companies also responded to the realities of the foreign environment or changing market conditions poorly, with top-down thinking from headquarters, reflecting a lack of depth in international management capability and the fact that the Chinese EMNEs' international organisational structures, systems and processes were relatively underdeveloped.

The second wave of Chinese cross-border M&A: a 'retreat' to hard assets

By 2007, there were signs that the Chinese government was concerned about the difficulties Chinese EMNEs were having with their acquisitions overseas. As a result the government signalled that, as far as possible, Chinese companies should target only profitable or viable companies. At the same time, with China's foreign exchange reserves crossing the $2 trillion mark in 2008, diversification from US Treasury bonds into physical assets that offered a hedge against inflation and did not run the risk of defaults looked increasingly attractive. Moreover, the stock market crash had reduced company valuations. So instead of trying to create competitive advantage by acquiring and integrating intangible assets such as brands and distribution relationships, the focus of foreign acquisitions shifted to tangible assets such as mineral deposits and oil reserves. Due diligence on these assets is relatively straightforward: they can be objectively assessed by China's army of engineers and do not require subtle assessments of corporate culture or brand essence. Integration is also simpler because these acquisitions are focused on extending proven supply chains for resources where there is a ready market in China.

Unsurprisingly, by 2009, over 75 per cent of Chinese M&A deals involved either energy or natural resources. Among these was Yanzhou Coal's $2.8 billion takeover of Australia's Felix Resources and Sinopec's $7.2 billion acquisition of the Swiss-registered oil and gas company Addax.

The retreat to cross-border acquisitions based on accessing hard assets and natural resources limited the ability of Chinese EMNEs to use their acquisitions to create competitive advantage in the global market. However, they did enable Chinese EMNEs to build more reliable and stable supply chains and to lock in their raw materials costs (often at low levels by buying assets in the wake of the financial crisis). But because of the nature of the assets acquired, these acquisitions were necessarily limited in the breadth of competitive advantages they could help Chinese EMNEs to build. Resource acquisitions, for example, offered little potential to create new sources of value added, for product differentiation or to increase the conversion efficiency of the firms' operations. While these narrow, resource-seeking deals continued (and often captured publicity due to their large size), it was therefore not surprising that Chinese EMNEs also began to take a new look at potential cross-border acquisitions that could potentially make a contribution to helping them create broader and more significant sources of competitive advantage.

The third wave of Chinese EMNEs' cross-border M&A: the 'double handspring'

Since 2008, Chinese EMNEs have placed increased emphasis on acquisitions that could deliver new technologies and off-shore R&D facilities. Cross-border acquisitions that involve technology and R&D facilities are somewhat more difficult to integrate; their value lies in their intellectual property, knowledge, reasearch and development (R&D) and design processes. However, integrating them is less complicated and risky than integrating entire organisations. Patents and blueprints can be beamed back to China, where a Chinese engineer can easily understand them. R&D centres involve relatively small numbers of staff. These highly skilled individuals do need very careful management and motivation. But Chinese acquirers' willingness to invest in R&D as part of a strategy to improve their competitive advantage, added to the new prospect of exploiting their innovations in the Chinese market, excites most of the R&D staff in these acquisitions.

Interfaces with the Chinese organisation, meanwhile, can be kept simple: foreign engineers produce innovative ideas for products and processes, and the Chinese EMNEs use their complementary capabilities to scale up the inventions and drive down their costs.

X'ian Aircraft International (XAC), the Shenzhen-listed subsidiary of the state-owned China Aviation Industries Corporation (AVIC), is a good example of the strategy of using off-shore acquisitions to access technology and R&D capabilities. Surprising industry experts, in October 2009, XAC announced that it had reached an agreement to buy 91.25 per cent of Austria's Fischer Advanced Composite Components (FACC) – a tier 1 supplier of advanced materials to aircraft manufacturers like Airbus and Boeing.

FACC is one of the leading suppliers of the composites used in everything from an aircraft's wings to engine nacelles and interior cabins. By 2008, FAAC's turnover had reached $393 million and it had 1,580 employees. However, it had invested $230 million to support the new generation Boeing Dreamliner and the Airbus 350 XWB, 50 per cent of which was to be made of composites, as well as the Airbus A380, 20 per cent of which consisted of composites. When these programmes were delayed, FACC started making losses, which grew because of a slowdown in deliveries due to the worldwide recession. It had accumulated $28.9 million in losses by the beginning of 2009, and cash reserves were running low when XAC appeared on the horizon. The Chinese company agreed to invest $60 million in new capital as part of an undisclosed purchase price estimated be around $135 million. FACC's management thus secured the company's financial future, received an injection of capital for expansion and improved its access to China's aircraft market through AVIC, as well as the new plants Airbus and Boeing were building in China.

Because of the acquisition, XAC (and parent AVIC) gained access to leading-edge composite materials technology and a large pool of engineers that could be used to support its aircraft programmes back in China, including the development of the ARJ21 regional jet and the C919 that would compete with the Airbus 320 and Boeing 737. XAC also started working indirectly with the major international aircraft-makers because of FACC's tier 1 supplier status.

Meng Xiangkai, XAC's president, explained that he did not wish to change FACC into a Chinese company in Europe, but wanted to form an international executive team and keep the original management style that underpinned FACC's success in high-technology R&D.

A string of other companies have embarked on this strategy of using overseas acquisitions to access high technology or gain a ready-made network of R&D centres in leading-edge technology clusters abroad.

The auto industry is a prime example. The automotive components supplier, Beijing West Industries, gained state-of-the-art MagneRide technology, R&D centres in North America, China, Japan, France and Poland and applications support centres in Australia, Germany, India, Taiwan and the UK, when it acquired Delphi's brake and suspension systems business for $100 million in November 2009. Beijing Automotive Industry Holdings Co. Ltd (BAIC) acquired the rights and tools for the Saab 9–3 and 9–5 models, two engine technologies and two transmission systems for $200 million in December 2009. The deal also provided BAIC with access to engineers and designers under an agreement where Saab will provide assistance to help integrate these technologies into upcoming BAIC vehicles for the China market. Just four months later, BAIC launched the C-71 based on Saab technology at The Beijing Auto Show.

The other difference notable as this third wave of Chinese acquisitions gathers pace is that instead of using takeovers to gain market share abroad, acquirers are using them to strengthen their positions inside China. This reverse from the original springboard strategy has distinct advantages. First, the China market provides a much more conducive environment in which Chinese EMNEs can learn to integrate the acquired company's assets and capabilities. The task of integrating new technology, products and know-how is easier to accomplish in the home market where the parent's executives know the terrain. Second, instead of wresting market share from entrenched rivals in mature developed markets, the acquirer can reap the takeover's benefits quickly in the fast-growing Chinese market.

Third, since the acquisition provides the managers and employees of the acquired company with an opportunity to apply their skills in arguably the world's fastest growing market, it helps them to see the takeover as beneficial. For example, after its $1.5 billion acquisition of Volvo in August 2010, Geely announced that its first goal would be to integrate Volvo's technology and design know-how into three new manufacturing facilities in Shanghai, Chengdu and Daqing to serve the local market. The plan is to ramp up sales in China from 24,000 units to 300,000 cars a year – almost as much as Volvo's worldwide sales of 335,000 cars in 2009.

Having successfully integrated the technology and flow of R&D from the acquisition into their China operations, some Chinese EMNEs then plan to use their improved capability base and scale as a platform for a second 'handspring' into the global market. One company that has deployed this approach successfully is National Chemical Corporation (ChemChina) after its $480 million takeover of the French manufacturer of animal nutrition additives, Adisseo Group, in December 2006. Adisseo is the world's second-largest producer of methionine, a key additive used in the poultry industry, and had a global market share of 29 per cent, but had failed to make any headway in China's rapidly growing poultry sector and could not expand on its own because of a weak balance sheet that bore the scars of the Severe Acute Respiratory Syndrome (SARS) outbreak in 2003.

By buying the French company, ChemChina obtained methionine production technologies that were non-existent in China. As one of the country's largest chemicals producers – which had acquired 107 SOEs and with $20 billion of sales – it already had the distribution channels and ground organisation to rapidly ramp up sales. ChemChina's chairman, Ren Jianxin, calls the strategy 'going out and bringing in'. He sold the idea assiduously to Adisseo's management, which recommended the ChemChina bid to shareholders because it would open the door to China and thereby lead the company to a brighter future.

So far, this strategy for managing the overseas acquisition to create competitive advantage appears to have worked well. After ChemChina acquired Adisseo it made the acquired company's management team responsible in the methionine business in China as well as globally. Given the responsibility of helping ChemChina grow the business in China, Adessio's managers and engineers have contributed to it becoming the country's largest supplier in just four years. Subsequently, ChemChina announced that it would make major, new investments to expand and upgrade its European plants and expand global capacity.

What ChemChina has done, therefore, is to acquire foreign technology and know-how and combine it with its own Chinese capabilities in cost innovation and rapid scale-up for the mass market in China, along with its know-how and processes for developing cost-efficient production and distribution processes to create competitive advantage capable of winning market share in China. Once this had been successfully achieved, it has then begun to move on to a second stage in which it takes this newly created competitive advantage and learns to apply and adapt it, backed by its capability for large-scale capital investment, to win in markets outside China. This two-stage strategy is illustrated in Figure 12.3.

Figure 12.3 The 'double handspring' strategy of EMNEs' M&A

Having proven the two-stage strategy: first, acquire foreign technology, know-how and talent, deploy it to build a winning position in the Chinese market, and second, use this as a newly powerful platform to capture the global market, ChemChina has set out down the road of repeating it.

In 2006 ChemChina acquired Qenos, Australia's leading producer of polyethylene products used in packaging, homewares, construction wiring and many other industries. In 2007 it also acquired the organic silicones business of France's Rhodia for $500m, capturing technology for the manufacture of silicon rubber, silicon oil, silicone adhesives and coatings. On 29 December 2010, it paid $1.44 billion for a 60 per cent share of Israel's Makhteshim-Agan Industries, the world leader in branded off-patent crop protection solutions including fungicides, pesticides and herbicides.

Conclusions

This chapter began by briefly restating some of the FSAs developed by budding Chinese EMNEs along with the limitations and capability gaps that have constrained the extent of their competitive advantage in global markets. It then examined a number of ways in which foreign M&A might be used by Chinese EMNEs to improve their global competitiveness: by attempting to use foreign acquisitions as springboards for international expansion; through resource-seeking foreign acquisitions; and to use overseas acquisitions as a way of accessing capabilities that could be combined with their existing FSAs to create new types of competitive advantage.

While there were inevitable differences in the strategies of individual firms, an analysis of aggregate data and a significant number of case studies of specific acquisitions identified three waves in the role of cross-border M&A in contributing to the creation of Chinese EMNEs' competitive advantage in the global market. The first wave, in which Chinese EMNEs attempted to use foreign acquisitions as a springboard for global expansion, mostly ended in failure. The second phase of Chinese EMNEs saw a retreat to acquiring companies most of whose value was in hard assets and natural resources. In these cases the acquired resources were much easier to integrate because they involved little more than 'plug and play' connections to the Chinese companies' existing supply chains and the core operations of the acquired firm could be left to run relatively independently by existing management. On the other hand, the nature of the resources and capabilities required, and the fact that integration potential was limited, meant that the potential to use these acquisitions to create broad and significant sources of competitive advantages was limited.

Recognising these inherent limitations, Chinese EMNEs began to take a new look at potential cross-border acquisitions. Their focus shifted towards acquiring companies with proprietary technology, know-how and international networks of R&D centres (and sometimes, but rarely, brands as well). The strategy was to combine the acquired capabilities with the Chinese EMNEs' own FSAs to create new types of competitive advantage. The types of resources and capabilities being acquired in this phase were inherently easier to integrate with the Chinese EMNEs' existing FSAs because hard technology and intellectual property is generally less tacit and context-dependent than broader operating know-how, culture, values and capabilities such as brand building. R&D centres, meanwhile, involve relatively small numbers of staff who could be motivated by Chinese EMNEs' willingness to invest in R&D and the prospect of exploiting their innovations in larger and faster-growing markets than they had access to at home. Interfaces with the Chinese organisation were also kept simpler so that foreign engineers produced innovative ideas for products and processes, and the Chinese EMNEs then used their complementary skills to scale up the inventions and drive down costs.

Equally importantly, the Chinese EMNEs decided that in this new phase they would focus on integrating the acquired capabilities inside the Chinese market – allowing the integration to be effected in a home environment that the Chinese EMNEs already knew intimately and where they could bring to bear the depth, scale and scope of resources which they had amassed in China.

Once they had succeeded in creating new sources of competitive advantage by undertaking integration inside China of the resources and capabilities they had accessed through foreign acquisitions, the Chinese EMNEs then began to look for ways to leverage these new competitive advantages in global markets.

Overall, therefore, the conclusion is that through an iterative process of experimentation, failure and learning, Chinese EMNEs are converging on strategies that open the potential for the successful use of cross-border acquisitions to strengthen and broaden their sources of competitive advantage in a way that can underpin their further expansion into the global market.

COMMENTARIES ON PART III

(III.i) Cross-border M&A by the new multinationals: different reasons to 'go global'

SIMON COLLINSON

The past decade has seen a rise in the importance of emerging economies as sources and recipients of foreign direct investment (FDI) and a rise in cross-border mergers and acquisitions (M&A) as a preferred vehicle for FDI. Both trends are linked to the rising prominence of emerging market multinational enterprises (EMNEs) from these economies. The preceding chapters provide new insights into these trends from leading country-specialists: Cyrino and Barcellos on Brazil (Chapter 9), Kalotay and Panibratov on Russia (Chapter 10), Ramamurti on India (Chapter 11) and Williamson and Raman on China (Chapter 12). Their studies give us a better understanding of the different ways in which cross-border M&A have contributed to the evolving competitive advantages of EMNEs across these four BRIC countries. In the following commentary we will examine, compare and contrast the country-specific patterns of the outward M&A they present and discuss their explanations for these trends.

The preceding country chapters focus on the question: why have we seen an increase in cross-border M&A activity from these emerging economies? What has been the dominant motivation for EMNEs to engage in international acquisitions in recent years? One important conclusion is that differences in motivation, in the drivers of internationalisation via M&A, are more apparent than similarities across these four countries. While EMNEs all face the same evolving global economic environment, including a recent rise in opportunities to acquire Western-based assets at relatively low prices, they are based, born and bred in very different home environments. Local context, including industry specialisation; gaps in resources, assets and capabilities; the structures and strategies of local flagship firms; and the role of government, all vary significantly. This in turn creates variety in the internationalisation strategies of these new multinationals.

278

Table III.1 *Dominant patterns in cross-border M&A across the BRIC economies*

	Brazil	Russia	India	China
CSA exploitation? (leveraging existing CSAs)	Partly	Yes	No	Yes
FSA exploitation? (leveraging existing FSAs)	Yes	No	Yes	No
For home (H) or international (I) market advantage?	Mainly I	–	H & I	–
FSA exploration? (seeking new FSAs)	Yes	Yes	Yes	Yes
For home (H) or international (I) market advantage?	Mainly I	Mainly H	H & I	H
Role of the state? Strong (S), strong in selected industries (Ss), weak (W)	Ss	Ss	W	S

Rugman's country-specific advantages–firm-specific advantages (CSA–FSA) internationalisation matrix, used in the analyses put forward in Chapters 11 and 12, provides one useful conceptual framework for understanding these differences (Rugman, 1981; Rugman and Collinson, 2009). Another conceptual lens is the 'exploitation vs. exploration' dichotomy coined by March (1991) in connection with organisation learning and applied by Ramamurti in his analysis (Chapter 11). This has been applied in innovation studies in relation to the dilemma faced by firms in deciding whether to develop new knowledge internally or source (including acquire) knowledge externally. But it also has parallels with the 'make or buy' dilemma explored in the resource-based view of the firm. We combine these frameworks to create a simplified comparison of the conclusions of the above authors in their analysis of outward M&A from these four emerging economies (Table III.1).

Table III.1 provides an overview of the similarities and differences across the four countries in terms of the motivations for EMNEs to engage in cross-border M&A. Are they exploiting existing CSAs or FSAs, and/or seeking new FSAs? Are they trying to gain home and/or international competitive advantage? Finally, what is the role of the state in guiding and financially supporting EMNEs? We will explore the issues raised in Table III.1 in the sections below.

M&A for FSA exploration or exploitation?

A common perception actively supported by Rugman (Rugman, 2008, 2009; Rugman and Doh, 2008) is that EMNEs are primarily involved in FSA exploration. They seek to acquire new FSAs to complement strong CSAs and compensate for weak or non-existent FSAs. The 'springboard' theory (Luo and Tung, 2007), further developed by Williamson and Raman here (with the 'double handspring'), also proposes that EMNEs engage in overseas acquisitions to strengthen their international competitiveness.

The evidence here only partly confirms the above findings. As Rugman and Luo and Tung propose, the EMNEs described in the previous chapters are all actively seeking new FSAs, although FSA acquisition is driven by very different motivations across the four BRIC countries. However, in contrast to the common perception described above, Brazilian and Indian EMNEs are said to have strong existing FSAs and engage in cross-border M&A in order to exploit these to strengthen their competitive advantages in both the domestic market and abroad. Moreover, as shown in Table III.1, CSA exploitation is not seen to be a uniform motivation for international M&A across our country studies. Ramamurti's finding for Indian EMNEs in particular suggests that they suffer from relatively weak CSAs. Variations in the role of the state, among a range of other differences in the home context, partly explain these patterns.

According to Cyrino and Barcellos, Brazilian multinationals are 'exploiting their existing technological, product differentiation, brands, patents and managerial capabilities' in international ventures. Brazilian EMNEs that are engaging in international M&A possess superior capabilities for operating in other emerging economies, relative to those that are not. Existing FSAs enable such firms to develop relationships with international government and regulatory bodies and gain access to a pool of talented managerial, technical or scientific people at competitive costs, among other advantages.

Indian EMNEs, according to Ramamurti, have had to compensate for relatively weak CSAs and more particularly weak government-specific advantages (GSAs) which firms must overcome through the development of strong FSAs. M&A motivations for Indian EMNEs therefore vary depending on the internationalisation strategy of the individual firms. For some FSA exploitation dominates, for others FSA exploration dominates. A typology, introduced by Ramamurti and Singh (2009a) is applied to help differentiate between these drivers and explain the varying motivations.

In contrast to this, Chinese and Russian EMNEs are seen to have weaker FSAs and are driven more by FSA exploration than exploitation. Strong CSAs and CSA-exploitation are emphasised more in relation to these countries. Natural resources in the Russian case and a large domestic market plus cheap labour and other manufacturing endowments in the Chinese case are obvious examples.

M&A to gain home-market or international advantage?

The country studies featured in the previous chapters also examined the question: what kinds of competitive advantage are EMNEs looking to gain through international M&A? Again we have mixed findings. Indian and Brazilian firms are both exploring new FSAs and exploiting existing ones, aiming to enhance their position in both home and international markets. There is, however, a stronger emphasis on market-seeking internationalisation in the Brazil study where advanced manufacturers, information technology (IT) firms, consumer goods and services firms are more prevalent among the largest MNEs than is commonly perceived. These firms are leveraging existing FSAs and acquiring new ones to gain increased access to advanced markets and to other emerging markets. They are also seeking assets and capabilities to enhance their position in the growing Brazilian market. This is similar for the Indian firms, although a stronger focus on home-market advantage is proposed by Ramamurti.

Williamson and Raman's findings on Chinese EMNEs, relating to the latest phase of outward M&A, firmly supports the view that they are seeking home-market advantages which will in turn and in time translate into stronger international advantages.

The role of government

Emerging economies in general are characterised by strong governments which have led the liberalisation process to open up access to local resources and markets to foreign firms, target certain kinds of trade of FDI and shape local industry development. The role of government varies considerably across our four countries as an influence on the internationalisation of EMNEs.

China's 'go global' (*zou chuqu*) policy symbolises the strong intent of the Chinese government to drive local firms to internationalise. Williamson and Raman's example of X'ian Aircraft International (XAC), the Shenzhen-listed subsidiary of the state-owned China Aviation Industries Corporation (AVIC), illustrates some of the mechanics of this as government funding supports the FSA acquisition strategies of EMNEs.

Again by way of contrast, the Indian government is weak, according to Ramamurti, not just in terms of a lack of direct funding and a lack of coherent policy guidance, but actually because government-specific 'disadvantages' create a form of liability which local firms have to overcome, by developing strong FSAs to succeed at home and abroad.

We find yet another pattern in Russia and Brazil, where governments are very active in selected industries and sometimes in openly supporting particular state champions. Kalotay and Panibratov discuss differences between Russian EMNEs that are directly government-supported and others that are 'government-influenced'. Direct involvement is evident when we examine state-owned giants in natural-resource-based industries, such as Gazprom. Gazprom, Lukoil and Severstal are strongly driven not just to engage in M&A for resource-seeking purposes, but to gain further control up and down their respective global value chains.

Cyrino and Barcellos' excellent dataset on Brazilian EMNEs suggests that support from the Brazilian government is less open and obvious than the support given to Chinese and Russian EMNEs by their respective governments. But there is a proactive policy in relation to national champions, including special credit lines from the Brazilian National Development Bank (BNDES) for firms like JBS-Friboi.

Conclusions

To summarise, then, the country-level studies in the preceding chapters provide excellent insights into why EMNEs from these four BRIC economies are increasingly engaging in international M&A. They provide new data and case studies on the target locations and the types of resources, assets and capability sought by these new multinationals. They find that while firms from these countries face the same global acquisition opportunities and constraints they display different strategic motives, encompassing various combinations of CSA and FSA exploration and exploitation, home and international market-seeking and resource-seeking. These country-level variations are partly the result of differences in local industry strengths and weaknesses and government policy which together influence patterns of outward FDI.

The studies also note considerable heterogeneity across EMNEs from each of the BRICs, particularly in the India case (Ramamurti) and in the Brazil case (Cyrino and Barcellos). Both employ the strategic groups typology developed by Ramamurti and Singh (2009a) to differentiate local optimisers, low-cost partners, global consolidators and global first-movers. The simple lesson for policy and practice is not to treat these EMNEs, even those from the same emerging economy, as the same.

Despite the progress made by these studies into patterns of outward FDI from emerging economies and M&A as a favoured route to internationalisation for EMNEs, there is more to do. Given the high failure rates of M&A in general, future research could usefully focus on the post-M&A integration process which we know is critical to leveraging the potential synergies of a merger. Some of the analysis presented here suggests that EMNEs are less experienced at managing the integration process so the failure rate may be higher. Previous studies show that the degree of intervention by a new parent is a critical factor (Collinson, 2007) as is a strategic and organisational focus on key complementarities at the post-integration stage. Further in-depth, longitudinal and qualitative research would help provide insights into the different approaches that EMNEs adopt to combine CSAs, existing FSAs and new FSAs to improve competitive advantage. Such empirical research would also help us understand whether existing theory provides adequate explanations of EMNE behaviour or whether we now need to revise or even replace our existing theories to account for these new multinationals.

(III.ii) Cross-border acquisitions by EMNEs

RAVI SARATHY

The chapters by Cyrino and Barcellos (Chapter 9), Kalotay and Panibratov (Chapter 10), Ramamurti (Chapter 11) and Williamson and Raman (Chapter 12) review cross-border mergers and acquisitions (M&A) activity by multinationals from Brazil, Russia, India and China (the BRICs), attempting to understand the motivations underlying such M&A activity, and then assessing whether such M&A helps these BRIC multinationals create and enhance sustainable competitive advantage in global markets. The chapters note that cross-border M&A activity by BRIC firms has been growing in importance over the past decade or more, accounting for an increasing portion of overseas foreign direct investment (OFDI) from BRIC nations, as well as accounting for an increasing portion of global M&A activity, reaching a peak in 2008, with larger deals becoming more prevalent and extending to a variety of industries, including natural-resource and mature commodity-type industries, as well as more technology intensive industries, business-to-business as well as consumer industries, and financial services.

An important precursor to M&A activity is national government policy, with government policies and support of cross-border acquisitions playing a strong catalyst role. Williamson and Raman, for example, note the important of Chinese Government initiatives, such as *zou chuqu*, the 'going global' slogan from 2000, as well as a later emphasis on 'going-out and bringing-in'. Given the Chinese government's significant control of the Chinese economy, and its influence through state-owned and state-controlled enterprises, such a strong role is to be expected. Beyond macro-economic growth goals, government industrial policy initiatives for specific industries, such as to support natural resources-based growth in Russia, solar and alternative energy industries in China and aerospace in Brazil, all encourage the use of cross-border M&A as one of many modes of internationalisation in supporting such industry-specific goals. Further, given the growing size

284

of M&A transactions, government financial support, through subsidised interest loans, and earmarked funds to promote international M&A are further catalysts for the growing number and amount of total international M&A from BRICs.

Governments can sometimes be a negative influence, paradoxically stimulating M&A activity, as Ramamurti notes in discussing government-specific advantages (GSAs), comparing China's positive fillip to its firms from investments in infrastructure and growth-oriented regulations, to India's weak government acting as a hindrance to industry growth, suggesting that such home market negative conditions motivate Indian firms to actively seek cross-border M&A as a means of escape from the negative drag on growth of home market conditions, a point echoed by Kalotay when he refers to 'system escape' in the Russian context.

The four chapters also stress the importance of domestic economy conditions, giving rise to country-specific advantages (CSAs), in influencing cross-border M&A, particularly when CSAs such as low labour cost advantage or natural resource access advantage allow firms to draw on these CSAs in opting for cross-border M&A and in identifying specific M&A candidates. Since CSAs are also open to foreign entrants, later sections analyse how CSAs may be combined with firm-specific advantages to stimulate and motivate M&A activity. Interesting aspects of such CSAs include the accumulation of foreign-exchange reserves, as in the case of China, stimulating national policies to employ such reserves effectively while quarantining the domestic economy from imported inflation, and using a portion of such reserves as a commodity hedge, exchanging specie for hard assets, obtained through the process of acquiring foreign firms. Cyrino and Barcellos refer to another related aspect of trade surpluses and accumulated reserves, in suggesting that an appreciating Brazilian Real enhanced Brazilian firms' interest in making foreign acquisitions, enhancing their capacity to make financial acquisitions, as well as making them more affordable.

An example of firm-specific advantages (FSAs) unique to emerging market firms is the role of scale economies arising from access to and dominance of large domestic markets, giving rise to cost advantages, a facet which Williamson and Raman refer to in the Chinese context as cost innovation. Cost innovation arises from combining a low cost advantage with additional capabilities and organisational routines, consisting of offering high technology at low cost, process innovation allowing for customisation at low prices, and lowering costs to reduce the break-even point of producing specialty products (in low volumes). Such FSAs form a baseline to which cross-border M&A can provide accretive advantages.

The heart of these four chapters lies in examining how M&A can contribute to this accretive process of combination with existing FSAs. Williamson and Raman find three waves of motivation underlying Chinese M&A, with a wave seeking to strengthen home market competitive position, with several costly acquisitions in this period proving unsuccessful – examples such as SAIC's acquisition of SsangYong Motors (South Korea), D'Long's acquisition of Murray and TCL's marred acquisition of Thomson in consumer electronics. As a corrective reaction, a second wave focused on horizontal acquisitions in natural resource industries, a motivation also dominant in Kalotay and Panibratov's examination of Russian natural resource and commodity industry acquisitions. A third (and ongoing) wave is described by Williamson and Raman as the 'double handspring', referring to an initial step in which foreign capabilities, obtained through the cross-border merger, are first used and integrated with existing domestic FSAs to further enhance domestic advantage; then, these refined and combined FSAs are deployed in international expansion, seeking to obtain global competitive advantage. Ramamurti's research in Indian firm M&A offers a more nuanced version of this double handspring, suggesting that not all acquisitions follow such a path, and that it might depend on the basic strategy developed and implemented by the various Indian firms. While some Indian firms may use cross-border M&A primarily to leverage home market FSAs in foreign operations (a group that Ramamurti delineates as 'local optimisers'), others may seek to add on capabilities acquired through cross-border M&A to their existing FSAs to further enhance competitive advantage, in the cost arena; in the technology capabilities area; in the range of products offered; and in penetrating new foreign markets – a group following different strategy types, classified as 'global consolidators', 'low-cost partners', and 'global first-movers'. Cyrino and Barcellos find similar differential motivations to underlie Brazilian acquisitions, though they note that relatively few firms account for the vast majority of M&A transactions by value, suggesting that access to financial resources and existing size may further moderate the strategic motivations of emerging market firms. In summarising these various motivations, Williamson and Raman, and Ramamurti, suggest that both exploitation and exploration motives shape emerging market cross-border M&A, with firms relying on existing FSAs primarily looking towards exploitation, while firms in strategy types such as the double handspring or the global first-movers balance exploitation with exploration motivations.

The research findings reported in Part III are primarily case-based, drawing inferences from a variety of cases and industries, in the four BRIC nations, over several years. The results are suggestive and raise interesting propositions which can serve as a basis for more empirical and detailed investigation with larger and multi-country samples, and greater statistical depth.

Given that M&A often destroy rather than create value, and that some of the examples cited summarise resounding failure to create value (e.g. Williamson and Raman's brief summaries of the SsangYong, Murray and Thomson acquisitions), it is useful to ask whether cross-border M&A represent an optimal strategy for BRIC and other emerging market firms, and if so, under what conditions? As the examples of ChemChina/Adisseo and XAC/Fischer suggest, post-merger integration may be a critical step in avoiding dramatic value destruction. Such an intangible capability is difficult to acquire, even through acquisition, and may be a discriminator that merits further exploration. Moreover, the ability of the acquiring firm to become more of a learning organisation, and achieve internal knowledge transfer, may be critical to M&A success. Williamson and Raman note the motivating effect of offering acquired-firm technologists and managers the opportunity to develop products for a rapidly growing and large internal market, in the ChemChina and Fischer acquisitions, as an important factor in helping retain key talent. Additionally, timing may be an important variable affecting value creation, with firms caught in later stages of merger waves likely to overpay, amidst a diminishing pool of worthy candidates. Moreover, firms seeking to obtain value, and hence attempting to ferret out 'cheaper' firms, may in fact find themselves buying weaker firms that can add little to the process of strengthening already existing home market capabilities.

Another interesting area for research would be the role of government barriers to M&A, e.g. the US government's opposition to

Huawei's attempt to acquire US telecoms firm 3Com (Reuters 2008), or the role of trade barriers stimulating M&A in an attempt to get under such tariff walls, a factor alluded to by Cyrino and Barcellos. Tax and fiscal policies can also support or deter M&A, such as the Indian government's attempt to tax capital gains made by Verizon in its sale of Indian telecoms assets, and more broadly, accounting and tax regulations concerning book value recognition upon acquisition, and goodwill recognition and amortisation policies.

At the firm level, factors such as slack resources and unutilised borrowing capacity, the risk-taking propensity of the chief executive officer and his top management team, as well as governance quality (e.g. the existence of an independent board offering an additional level of oversight of proposed M&A transactions) and the accumulated learning and hubris consequences of past (successful) M&A transactions, may all be influential in affecting the level of cross-border M&A activity. Cultural differences can affect such learning, and Cyrino and Barcellos note the possible role of cultural distance in affecting the choice of M&A candidates, with regional and colonial history, as well as diaspora managers possibly having an important role in this process. In discussing firm-level strategies as they affect M&A propensity, Ramamurti notes the role of M&A in affecting value-chain choices, and in shaping value-chain configuration and reconfiguration across international borders. This could be related to broader M&A studies on the relative role of unrelated and related diversification as a factor in determining and influencing M&A success, and whether similar schema could be useful in evaluating M&A candidates being considered by BRIC firms. Reference is also made to the image building and positive reputational consequences of cross-border M&A, and it would be useful to understand the path by which such image enhancement happens: is it primarily in the home market, or in the market where the acquisition takes place, or is global image enhanced? Further, is there a cumulative reputational effect of a strategy of planned and implemented acquisitions? And, how should such image enhancement be included in calculating value enhancement through the acquisition?

The chapters also suggest that industry plays a significant role in influencing the direction and level of M&A activity, with natural resource industry acquisitions dominant in China, Russia and Brazil. Principal motivations here are scale economies through horizontal and vertical (downstream and upstream) integration, and gaining control of scarce global resources. It would be interesting to explore whether factors such as rising commodity prices, rising global demand and perceived levels of scarcity of new resource discovery affect the relative balance between acquisitions emphasising reserve replacement – upstream deals and downstream deals, focusing on supply and distribution chains and market power. A related question would be: Which kind of natural resource deals are less risky? Are upstream natural resource deals more likely to be successful, create value, than downstream deals?

The chapters focus solely on M&A transactions, noting that M&A assumes an increasingly important share of total OFDI. It would be useful to compare M&A activity with other modes of OFDI and entry, essentially considering the possibility and relative efficacy of using alliances, and greenfield investments as alternatives to M&A, in achieving strategic goals such as the 'double handspring' and the integration of new FSAs from the foreign firm with existing FSAs. Moreover, many of the examples analyse and draw inferences from relatively large M&A transactions – Kalotay and Panibratov note that in Russia a few firms account for a large number of acquisitions – Lukoil, Severstal, Vimpel, Norilsk Nickel; Ramamurti lists acquisitions of over $100 million; and, in Brazil, the top five acquirers account for nearly 75 per cent of all acquisitions. It would be useful to specifically examine whether the same strategic drivers underlying large firm and large transaction M&A also apply to smaller firms and small transactions. For example, are smaller firms likely to face greater liability of foreignness in developing and executing a cross-border M&A strategy?

Finally, given that these chapters focus on BRIC cross-border acquisitions, it is important to ask, is BRIC cross-border M&A activity different from cross-border M&A by developed market firms? Are the findings and propositions about BRIC M&A different from the research findings and theory surrounding cross-border acquisitions in general? If so, how can a theory of BRIC M&A behaviour inform a general theory of M&A (Barkema and Schijven, 2008; Haleblian *et al.*, 2009), and of M&A as effective internationalisation strategy? This might be the greatest benefit of BRIC-focused M&A research, in that it helps revise and elevate our general understanding of global M&A.

Conclusion: rethinking the implications of EMNEs' rise

PETER J. WILLIAMSON, RAVI
RAMAMURTI, AFONSO FLEURY AND MARIA
TEREZA LEME FLEURY

The aim of this book has been to better understand the extent, nature and roots of the competitive advantage of emerging market multinational enterprises (EMNEs) and, in particular, the ways in which their internationalisation is contributing to the enhancement of that competitive advantage. To do so we examined three, inter-related factors that might potentially help EMNEs build competitive advantage: innovation, value-chain configuration and cross-border mergers and acquisitions (M&A); we compared and contrasted the experience of firms from each of the BRIC countries (Brazil, Russia, India and China). We now step back to draw some conclusions from this analysis.

We begin with some general observations about the way innovation, value-chain configuration and cross-border M&A appear to interact to create competitive advantage for EMNEs. Our aim is to provide a framework that will help to bring together the various strands of our analysis and provide an appropriate context for the interpretation of our findings. With this integrated framework in mind, we offer generalisations about the competitive advantages of EMNEs observed from the evidence in the earlier chapters. In doing so, we show how some of the puzzles that the behaviour of EMNEs has posed for international business theorists might be resolved. We also discuss whether findings from our BRIC sample might apply to the next rung of emerging economies. Finally, we look at the implications for managers of the appearance of EMNEs as global competitors (both for managers within incumbent competitors and the EMNEs themselves) and for policy makers in governments.

Towards an integrated view of EMNEs' competitive advantage

The behaviours and experiences of EMNEs drawn from the BRIC countries with diverse factor endowments, institutional contexts and histories will inevitably be heterogeneous. None the less, one over-arching

290

pattern stands out amid all the variation: for the majority of EMNEs we studied, internationalisation is as much about accessing new resources and knowledge to enable them to extend their competitive advantages, as it is a route to exploiting existing advantages over a larger set of markets. In other words, for most EMNEs, learning is an equally important goal of internationalisation as market exploitation. In many cases the learning potential of internationalisation is, at least initially, the more important goal. This is in sharp contrast to the development path of traditional developed market multinational enterprises (DMNEs) who went abroad primarily with the aim of exploiting homespun competitive advantage (Doz *et al.*, 2001). As we will see, this significant difference between EMNEs and DMNEs in their internationalisation goals has important implications for both theory and practice.

Viewed in this context, the three potential sources of EMNEs' competitive advantage we have studied in the book – innovation, value-chain configuration and cross-border M&A – closely interact to facilitate the process of learning and to transform that learning into new capabilities that can then be exploited for competitive advantage both in their home market and in foreign markets. The capacity for innovation embodies a whole set of competences (or capabilities).[1] It is much more than the capability for research and development (R&D). The capacity for profitable innovation in an international context involves not only the development of novel and valuable products, processes and technologies, but also the operational capability to deliver that improved value in practice and to align the innovation and the value chain underpinning it to foreign market environments. To gain competitive advantage, meanwhile, some of these aspects of innovation must be achieved more effectively or efficiently than rival incumbents. Broadly defined in this way, the capacity for profitable innovation may require improvements in both operational competences (those associated with managing any given set of assets and resources; Teece, 2009: 55) and dynamic capabilities (the capacity to renew an organisation's competences so as to maintain an appropriate fit with a changing business environment; Teece *et al.*, 1997).

By expanding its international reach a firm has the opportunity to access new knowledge that can be used as a raw material for profitable

---

[1] For our purposes here we use the terms 'competences' and 'capabilities' as synonymous and interchangeable, following Helfat *et al.* (2007: 121).

innovation (Santos *et al.*, 2004). Many examples of EMNEs improving the competitive advantage through this process of knowledge acquisition have been documented in Part I of this book that focused on innovation within EMNEs headquartered in the BRIC countries.

At the same time, the second potential driver of EMNEs' competitive advantage we studied, value-chain configuration, can also contribute to the capacity for profitable innovation as defined above. By internationalising its activities, a firm has the opportunity to configure and coordinate its value chain to improve its operational competences and to deliver more value (e.g. through higher quality or more responsive service) at equal or lower cost. New value-chain configurations can also provide new opportunities for learning at the operational level (Johanson and Vahlne, 1977; Nelson and Winter, 1982). Thus value-chain configuration can be an important contributor to profitable innovation; it is not only a way of relocating activities so as to reduce costs by tapping into cheaper factors of production, such as low-cost labour. Again as we explore in more detail below, one of the interesting aspects of EMNEs' internationalisation is that many of the EMNEs we studied have arguably placed greater emphasis on configuring the value chains so as to accelerate learning and improve their capacity for innovation, broadly defined, than many of their DMNE cousins. One reason may be that because many DMNEs are headquartered in high-cost countries and have well developed innovation capabilities at home, their value-chain configurations tend to be more focused on achieving cost reductions than on harnessing the potential for learning and innovation.

The third driver of EMNEs' competitive advantage examined in this book, cross-border M&A, also has the potential to enhance a firm's capacity for profitable innovation. The acquisition of a firm in a foreign market can be a way of accessing new knowledge and capabilities that can fuel innovation. It can also enable a firm to rapidly reconfigure its value chain in ways that improves its operational capabilities so as to deliver more value to its customers. Overseas M&A can also allow a firm to directly reconfigure its value chain by providing, for example, 'ready-made' R&D facilities or marketing units in new locations – operations that can be used to assist it in delivering innovation to the market. To achieve the benefits, of course, it will need to be integrated into the firm's global operations in an appropriate way. And in order to make an ongoing contribution to sustaining

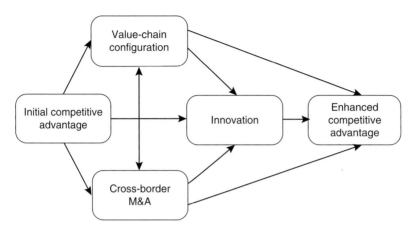

Figure C.1 Competitive advantage through internationalisation

competitive advantage in the longer run, the acquired competences will need to be managed so as to maintain their vitality.

The enhancement of a firm's competitive advantage through these interactions is summarised and illustrated in Figure C.1. A firm's initial competitive advantage can be enhanced through innovation based on its competences. Internationalisation, meanwhile, can involve the reconfiguration of a firm's value chain. By providing access to new competences, this may lead either directly to enhanced competitive advantage or enhance it indirectly, by fuelling innovation. The goal of reconfiguring a firm's international value chain can also lead it to undertake cross-border M&A activity. Likewise cross-border M&A can improve a firm's competitive advantage both by directly contributing new competences and by stimulating profitable innovation through new learning. Cross-border M&A may itself also create new opportunities for reconfiguring the firm's value chain.

Of course a firm may also internationalise in order to exploit its competitive advantage. This may involve entering new markets (in turn stimulating innovation), re-configuring its value chain and undertaking cross-border M&A. The process of exploitation, therefore, may itself contribute to the enhancement of competitive advantage through the cycle depicted in Figure C.1.

Using this framework we can look to synthesise the findings presented in earlier chapters of this book to provide a more integrated perspective on the role internationalisation has played in allowing EMNEs to develop new sources of their competitive advantage. In particular it allows us to focus on how the internationalisation of EMNEs is providing them with access to new *learning* opportunities and expanded capability sets, as well as access to new environments that enable them to better *exploit* their existing capabilities (many of which have been developed by leveraging country-specific advantages in their home markets).

EMNEs' internationalisation and competitive advantage

EMNEs typically gain competitive advantage in two ways: the first is by doing the things necessary to build a strong business in the home market, which often involves innovations in processes, products and business models to better serve local customers; the other is by enhancing those competitive advantages through the learning and knowledge transfer that occurs when they internationalise their value chain or make foreign acquisitions. In other words, internationalisation itself can enhance their competitive advantage at home and abroad. We begin with the first half of this process, looking at how innovation contributes to the competitive advantage of EMNEs, and then turn to the question of how those advantages are enhanced by internationalisation.

Innovation and competitive advantage

Break-through innovation, often based on cutting-edge technology, is at the heart of the competitive advantage of many DMNEs (Bartlett and Ghoshal, 1986). Existing evidence suggests this is not the case for most EMNEs, because typically they are late-movers in their industries and technologically backward (Keyhani and Madhok, 2012). The evidence in the book broadly confirms this finding. However, innovation of other kinds, consistent with their late-mover status and home-market conditions, is still at the heart of the competitive advantage of EMNEs.

Product innovation, to the extent EMNEs do it, largely consists of adapting existing products and know-how to the special needs of their home markets or to novel uses. Their distinctive capability, compared to developed-country firms, is a superior insight into customer needs, which allows them to optimise product features and price to fit the purchasing power of customers and the harsh conditions under which products are sold and used in emerging economies.

As the preceding chapters show, a few EMNEs have managed over time to reach the technological frontiers of their industry. In these cases – such as Huawei of China in telecoms, Embraer of Brazil in regional jets and Dr Reddy's of India in pharmaceuticals – EMNEs are introducing new products in direct competition with the new products of DMNEs. In other cases – such as Suzlon of India in wind energy or Tencent of China in instant messaging platforms – the firms are first-movers in emerging industries, even if their technical capabilities have sometimes been built through the acquisition of developed-country firms, not through in-house R&D.

Closely related to product innovation is the capability of EMNEs in *process innovation*, which allows them to lower costs dramatically to meet the low price points necessary to serve mass markets at home or to operate in the price-conscious, turbulent business environment found in many developing countries. And while they may not possess cutting-edge technology, EMNEs have adequate absorptive capacity to modify existing technologies to lower costs dramatically or to add and subtract product features (Wells, 1983). As Tidd *et al.* (2001: 5) have noted, 'being able to make something no one else can, or to do so in ways which are better than anyone else, is a powerful source of advantage'.

A third kind of innovation prevalent among EMNEs is *business model innovation*, in which an existing product or service is produced, sold, financed and serviced in wholly new ways, with costs, risks and profits generated in ways that may not have been seen in developed countries. This may sound like an extreme case of process innovation, which it is, if 'process' is taken very broadly to mean every aspect of how something is made, sold, financed, delivered or maintained. Chinese firms, such as Tencent, Brazilian firms such as Gerdau and AmBev and Indian firms such as Bharti Airtel and SKS Microfinance, have revolutionised their respective industries through new business models.

Our studies uncovered several examples of all three types of innovation by EMNEs, but process innovations seem to be the most common source of competitive advantage for EMNEs. This sets them apart from other local competitors that lack the absorptive capacity, capital, scale, brands and local distribution to invest in extensive process innovations. It also sets them apart from DMNEs, which often have considerable difficulty modifying products developed for the 'Triad' markets of the US, the EU and Japan to suit the peculiar needs of emerging economies.

The key point is that the competitive advantage of EMNEs is not just based on low costs, nor is their low cost based solely on the home country's low factor costs, particularly labour costs. Rather their competitive advantage comes from using cost and other locational advantages in innovative ways to create better value-for-money offerings (dubbed 'cost innovation' by Zeng and Williamson, 2007), higher efficiencies and, sometimes, new sources of value. Leveraging this experience, the EMNEs in the vanguard of internationalisation are also beginning to undertake more traditional technological innovation as well – a process that has begun to narrow the technological gap between EMNEs and DMNEs.

Certainly, the scope of innovation by EMNEs varied across the BRICs. China and India appeared to be bubbling with entrepreneurship and, in China's case, this seemed to be somewhat true even in state-owned enterprises (SOEs). Much of the innovation in these countries was targeted at consumers at the middle or the base of the economic pyramid, because of the large size of their poor populations, compared to middle-income Brazil or Russia.

In Brazil, process innovations occurred mainly in manufacturing and natural resource industries, e.g. in deep-sea oil exploration or gasohol (low ethanol blends) production. Companies such as Vale and Petrobras not only developed new techniques for resource extraction, their technical knowledge allowed them to pursue opportunities for exploring new mineral or oil and gas fields abroad. Similar achievements were recorded by Brazilian agribusiness firms working in concert with national research institutes

In Russia, the competitive advantage of local firms relied more heavily on close ties to politicians and privileged access to natural resources or finance than on innovation. The giant oil and gas firms were either SOEs, such as Gazprom and Rosneft, or privatized entities bought by investors with close ties to government (e.g. Lukoil). Likewise, giant MNEs in steel (Severstal, Evraz) and non-ferrous metals (Norilsk Nickel, Basic Elements) resulted from the privatisation of SOEs and their subsequent expansion. Together, these resource-based MNEs accounted for 72 per cent of the foreign assets of the top twenty Russian MNEs in 2008 (IMEMO-VCC, 2009: 15). Innovation seemed to suffer in Russia from institutional weaknesses, despite state subsidies and repeated calls by the country's leaders for more innovation.

DMNEs appear to face significant barriers to engaging in the kinds of innovation that are the forte of many EMNEs, because DMNEs are geared to develop new products based on cutting-edge technology, at high price points and with high margins. They have difficulty deviating from that business model, which has served them well in the past (Govindarajan, 2012). Their organisational culture, standard operating procedures, incentives and mind-set are at odds with the needs of frugal innovation or business model innovation. Power in these firms also lies in the hands of managers based in developed countries, making it difficult for emerging-market subsidiaries to change the organisation's strategy or culture.

Innovations of all three types – product, process and business model – had value beyond an EMNE's home country. Products that fit the needs of one emerging market also appealed to customers in other emerging markets. In addition, lowering costs drastically through process innovation had value even in developed countries, where it could be applied to low-income consumers or the growing number of financially strapped middle-class consumers. Occasionally, an innovation developed for emerging markets could appeal to more than a narrow sliver of the market in developed countries, resulting in 'reverse innovation' (Govindarajan and Ramamurti, 2011).

These innovations provided the impetus for many EMNEs to internationalise. That impulse was sometimes reinforced by government policy and strategy (China), by the desire of top management to spur the organisation to new heights (Brazil) or by the sheen that internationalisation added to an organisation's reputation and image (Brazil, India). Regardless of the motivation, however, internationalisation itself enhanced the competitive advantages of EMNEs, including their innovation capability, and it is to this feedback process that we turn next.

Enhancing competitive advantage through value-chain reconfiguration

The idea of value-chain configuration (VCC) as a competitive advantage probably originated in studies of the Japanese keiretsu (the Japanese term for a set of companies with interlocking business relationships) and was later formalised by Porter (1985). That approach led eventually to the view that VCC creates competitive advantage through the spatial disaggregation of value creation by placing each activity of the value chain at the place where it can be performed best.

DMNEs have taken significant advantage of these opportunities for reconfiguring their value chains. In many cases this involved moving lower-value operations (such as simple assembly) to lower cost countries and sales and distribution activities into locations with large and growing local markets. Over time DMNEs refined their value-chain configurations to take advantage of differences in resource and knowledge endowments, dispersing many parts of the value chain from procurement through to design, marketing and support services. Key innovation activities were perhaps the one exception; many companies still kept these firmly located in the home country even after other activities had become widely dispersed around the globe.

There are a number of reasons to expect the VCCs chosen by EMNEs to differ significantly from these common patterns adopted by DMNEs. The first, and perhaps the most obvious, reason is that it will generally not be economic for EMNEs to move the bulk of their labour-intensive operations (such as processing and assembly) away from an already-rich natural-resource or low-cost home country.

Second, EMNEs typically lack the well-developed managerial processes and experience to enable them to efficiently manage a value chain where activities are highly dispersed. DMNEs equipped with these management and coordination capabilities are likely to opt to disperse their value chains even where the gains in terms of lower costs or improved access to local resources are relatively small. But EMNEs facing their paucity of these capabilities will only incur the extra strains of coordination that would be incurred by dispersing their value chains where the potential pay-offs are relatively high. This could be the case where EMNEs were able to obtain resources and capabilities critical to underpinning their international competitiveness that would otherwise not be available to them. In fact, early studies of the VCCs of EMNEs (e.g. Mathews, 2006) suggested that this is the case: EMNEs tended to locate activities abroad mainly in order to access resources and capabilities that were scarce or unavailable in their home countries. This observation was confirmed by the studies of the BRIC multinationals in this book: their VCCs tended to be driven by the need to fill critical resource gaps or access knowledge or learning opportunities overseas. Their preference is to retain the bulk of the operations they have already mastered (often manufacturing, for example) in their home countries so as to maintain the cost and scale advantages they enjoy there.

Third, because the EMNEs are mostly late-movers to internationalisation, the current snapshots of the VCCs we observe may reflect an immature stage on the path to a different future VCC. For many DMNEs, by contrast, we may be observing a mature VCC developed over decades. To the extent that we are observing different stages in the cycle of development of different firms' VCCs, therefore, any variations (such as maintaining core operations at home) may reflect timing rather than differences in their choices about what VCC is optimal in the long run.

Fourth, the VCC chosen by a firm will depend on the length of the value chain it chooses to operate. As Katkalo and Medvedev pointed out in Chapter 6, some EMNEs seek to be 'value-chain builders' of fairly complete chains, while others choose to focus on a few activities that can slot into the value chains controlled by others ('value-chain joiners').

The evidence in Part II of this book, summarised and structured in the commentaries by Cuervo-Cazurra and Srai, suggests that many of these different influences on EMNEs' VCCs are at work. In some cases the resulting VCCs do make a significant contribution to the competitive advantage of EMNEs. In the case of Brazilian firms, the role of overseas activities in the VCC included obtaining access to foreign technology and customer knowledge and using overseas distribution subsidiaries to improve the route to market for Brazilian products. Brazilian firms also used their VCC to implement a strategy of backward vertical integration with the aim of controlling inputs of natural resources. Presumably this was aimed at increasing competitive advantage by reducing transactions costs and improving the stability of the supply chain. In a few cases Brazilian firms sought to use their overseas subsidiaries to help them build their brands overseas or to improve their access to international finance.

In the case of Russian high technology firms, the VCC involving overseas subsidiaries was primarily aimed at accessing customer intelligence. In the case of Russian firms that sought to be value-chain builders, including important firms in the energy sector, the main role of overseas subsidiaries was to improve the distribution of products and energy overseas. In the case of Russian value-chain joiners the main role of overseas subsidiaries was to cement partnerships with others involved in the international value chain of which they were a part.

The impact of Indian EMNEs' VCCs on their competitive advantage varied by industry. In the case of information technology (IT) firms, mainly those providing IT services to overseas customers, the main purposes of their overseas subsidiaries were to capture information about customer requirements and to provide local service capability to complement their global delivery model where the bulk of activities were undertaken in India. In the case of the pharmaceutical sector, overseas subsidiaries provided capacity for innovation as well as a way of sidestepping regulatory restrictions by manufacturing locally in the customers' countries. In developing markets local manufacturing subsidiaries could also provide some cost advantages. In developed markets the other major role of local subsidiaries was to provide local marketing and distribution support.

Chinese EMNEs most commonly established overseas subsidiaries in order to access new technology and design capabilities that were absent or in short supply in China and could be linked to highly efficient manufacturing operations in China to improve the level of quality and value added of products supplied both to the domestic and international markets. In some cases Chinese MNEs also used their overseas subsidiaries to assist in gathering customer intelligence and brand building. Other evidence (Williamson and Raman, 2011) suggests that in industries such as steel and aluminium, Chinese firms established overseas subsidiaries to perform extraction and transport of raw materials in order to gain the benefits of vertical integration, including lower transactions costs and security of supply.

In summary, the evidence assembled in this book suggests that:

- the role of subsidiaries in developed markets is primarily to access new capabilities, including technology and design skills that can be used to strengthen the international competitiveness of EMNEs;
- in the natural resource industries, EMNEs have tended to try to increase their competitive advantage through vertical integration, expanding abroad both downstream and upstream, creating long value chains;
- in the services industries EMNEs tend to expand horizontally across different geographic markets to exploit their home-based advantages, maintaining short value chains; with limited additional roles of foreign subsidiaries in accessing customer intelligence and providing local service support;

- in other industries where the primary goal of international expansion is 'market seeking', the emphasis is mostly on winning business in other emerging markets and the role of overseas subsidiaries is to support local marketing and distribution.

Our overall conclusion, therefore, is that EMNEs configure their global value chains first and foremost as a way of using their international subsidiaries to improve their access to new capabilities, knowledge and customers rather than to optimise efficiency and improve the cost competitiveness of their value chains. In fact, rather than disaggregating the value chain and relocating activities within low-cost countries (as is the dominant pattern for DMNEs), the overseas subsidiaries of EMNEs often duplicate activities already undertaken at home with the aim of accessing new additional capabilities and knowledge to strengthen their overall competitiveness. In natural resources industries, meanwhile, the configuration of EMNEs' value chains tends to be driven by the objectives of security of supply, potentially increased market power and growth aspirations, rather than efficiency per se.

Enhancing competitive advantage through cross-border M&A

Cross-border acquisitions are playing an increasingly important role in the international development of many EMNEs. Consistent with the integrative framework presented earlier, a primary role of cross-border M&A by EMNEs revealed by the evidence in this book is to provide access to new capabilities, resources and knowledge that will assist in accelerating and improving innovation and adjusting the firms' VCCs in ways that will enhance their competitiveness in both the domestic and international markets. In fact, cross-border M&A deals involving pure technology or R&D outfits seem to be particularly attractive to many EMNEs (especially those from China). This is because they provide access to existing intellectual property or R&D capacity without the burden of large and uncompetitive manufacturing or service capacity that is likely to lead to complex restructuring and associated shutdowns and redundancies that EMNEs are generally ill-equipped to undertake, especially in unfamiliar developed economies. Relatively unencumbered technology and R&D acquisitions mean that the people, knowledge and capabilities acquired can be nurtured through additional investment, and their day-to-day activities left to operate relatively independently, with only broad direction and the establishment of sufficient links back to the parent company necessary to ensure that the knowledge and capabilities they generate are transferred back home. In fewer cases, the assets and capabilities acquired and repatriated also include under-utilised brand assets and marketing capabilities. This strategy has been pursued most strongly by Chinese MNEs, but has also been adopted by Indian, Brazilian and Russian MNEs and predominantly involves acquisitions of companies based in developed economies.

In industries where the technology is relatively mature and customer needs tend to be well defined (sometimes referred to as 'sunset industries') such as steel, petrochemicals and even business process outsourcing, EMNEs tend to use cross-border M&A to promote global industry consolidation. This helps them to reap greater economies of scale and scope, gives them the opportunity to transfer and leverage FSAs developed in their home markets where these industries enjoy a favourable environment and remain dynamic and potentially to increase their market power. Interestingly, cross-border M&A in these industries also allows EMNEs to acquire capabilities and knowledge that have been 'orphaned' by the decline of volume product in these industries in developed markets and to redeploy these assets (be they physical plants that are dismantled and relocated or technicians or intellectual property that can be transferred) in their vibrant home-market operations or in other emerging markets. Brazilian, Chinese and Indian MNEs most commonly adopt this strategy.

In other cases the role of cross-border M&A is primarily to allow the EMNEs to enhance their competitive advantage by pursuing a strategy of vertical integration. In resource-based industries this type of M&A tends to be used as a tool to create long value chains designed to achieve increased market power, control of distribution and access to customer intelligence as well as to reduce transactions costs and promote security of the supply chain. In industries where EMNEs' goal is to participate in a more limited range of activities (short value chains) the primary roles of acquisitions are to secure access to customer intelligence or accelerate the building of capacity to provide local distribution or service.

The primary attraction of M&A as a tool for achieving any of these goals appears to be speed. As latecomers, many EMNEs see themselves in 'catch-up mode' with a limited window of opportunity to close the gap with global incumbents. The opportunity to use M&A as a route to accessing assets (especially intangibles) that are slow and costly to build or are in scarce supply is therefore alluring. If successfully integrated, they allow the acquirer to gain speedy access to people, knowledge and capabilities that would otherwise be slow and difficult to assemble, and/or a way to rapidly reconfigure the firm's value chain. Speed is particularly attractive to EMNEs who generally operate in fast-changing markets both at home and in other developing markets that are often their key targets in which to win market share.

The extent to which EMNEs are using cross-border M&A as a tool to achieve improved competitive advantage in these ways varies by country of origin. As the commentaries by Collinson and Sarathy in Part III of this book demonstrated, the factors behind these differences include stimuli and support from some governments, the lack of support from other governments, the strong cash position of some late-movers, the evolution of exchange rates, the role of diasporas and the political and regulatory barriers EMNE acquirers from some countries face in foreign markets. At the same time, EMNEs seem to show preference for cross-border acquisitions where cultural distance is low or, if the capabilities they require are only available in unfamiliar or culturally dissimilar environments, where they can use ethnic diasporas to help bridge the gap.

Generalisations and theoretical implications

We turn next to some generalisations about the competitive advantages of EMNEs, including how those are shaped by the home country context, how they are different from the competitive advantages of DMNEs and the managerial challenges of enhancing advantages through internationalisation. Throughout, we keep an eye out for areas in which EMNEs appear to differ from DMNEs, because such dissimilarities can point us to the limitations of existing theory, which is based largely on studies of DMNEs.

Country-level variables

We begin by considering country-level factors that affect the competitive advantage of EMNEs.

Country of origin and competitive advantage: differences among the BRICs

A recurring question in the literature is whether the nationality of MNEs matters. Some have argued that the behaviour of multinationals transcends their national origin (Wilkins, 1986: 202, quoting Vernon; Rugman, 2009), while others have argued the opposite (e.g. Mathews, 2002; Luo and Tung 2007). Indeed, the booming literature on EMNEs rests on the premise that these firms are different because they hail from emerging economies. Our view is closer to the latter position, but with an important caveat: country of origin is only one contextual factor shaping the internationalisation of EMNEs and, analytically, its effect must be disentangled from that of other contextual variables that also matter (Ramamurti, 2012). With this caveat in mind, we consider the evidence in this volume about how the home country affects the competitive advantage of EMNEs, looking for commonalities as well as differences across the BRICs.

The most obvious commonality among the BRICs is economic size; after all, these are the four largest emerging economies. But even on this variable, it should be noted that China's gross domestic product (GDP) is greater than that of the other three combined; by 2011 China was the only one to have reached the upper ranks of the G6 economies. A second commonality among the BRICs is their technological and industrial heritage. All four countries have a long history of technical capabilities. Before the industrial revolution, China and India were the world's top two industrial economies, and over the decades Brazil gained substantial technical capabilities through catch-up efforts, especially in the natural resources and basic inputs industries (Fleury and Fleury, 2011). Russia was a military superpower, and two of the other three BRIC countries were also nuclear powers. Today, all four also have educational institutions that produce first-rate technical and scientific talent.

On several other variables, however, the BRICs are a heterogeneous group (a diversity mirrored in the different research designs adopted by the chapters in these book). Brazil and Russia, for instance, have large endowments of natural resources, with huge exportable surpluses, unlike China and India, which are huge net importers of natural resources. China and India have populations six to eight times those of Brazil or Russia. A similar disparity exists in the size of their labour forces and wages, although the disparity in wages has been narrowing, because of wage escalation in the last few years in China and India. Finally, the BRICs differ significantly in the ability of their governments to lead and manage economic development, with the Chinese government being head and shoulders above the rest on this dimension.

All this is simply another way of saying that the country-specific advantages (CSAs) of the BRICs have both similarities and differences, which in turn influences the competitive advantage of their EMNEs and the generic internationalisation strategies they follow (Ramamurti and Singh, 2009a: 410–16).

In all four countries, the large and fast-growing home market has helped local firms develop products optimised for the local market, which provided the basis for international expansion into other emerging economies, particularly within the region (e.g. Chinese firms in white goods, Brazilian firms in processed food, meat, steel and metal-mechanical engineering, Russian firms in telecoms and Indian firms in transportation equipment and pharmaceuticals). The countries' technical and industrial heritage has meant there were local firms with the absorptive capacity to master, adapt and integrate imported technologies. Coupled with a large home market, EMNEs from the BRICs have also produced many 'global consolidators' in mature industries, such as steel, cement, autos, chemicals, white goods, beverages and processed foods.

Differences among the BRICs, meanwhile, account for differences in the industries in which EMNEs operate in each country and their motivations for internationalisation. Thus, for example, the Russian economy is dominated by the natural resource sector, which has not only meant that the largest Russian MNEs belong to this sector but that the emergence of MNEs in other sectors has probably been stifled, for instance, by the impact of resource-based exports on the strength of the rouble (Panibratov, 2012). China and India, with their voracious appetite for resources, have seen some of their largest EMNEs go abroad in search of natural resources, rather than downstream in search of markets. In all four countries, however, 'natural resource vertical integrators' are among the largest EMNEs.

On the other hand, low-income China and India have been more attractive locations than middle-income Brazil or Russia for labour-intensive, low-skill activities. China and India have therefore spawned 'low-cost partners' that have internationalised over time to become MNEs in their own right. Much of the initial investment in low-end assembly work in China was made by Hong Kong and Taiwanese firms rather than local firms, as a result of which those firms seized a big part of the opportunity for labour-cost arbitrage (e.g. Foxconn and Acer from Taiwan, or Early Light from Hong Kong). To be sure, Chinese firms do so as well, for example Galanz in microwaves and Lenovo in PCs. But because such labour arbitrage can be replicated by competing firms, it offers limited scope for underpinning sustainable profits. This fact has led Chinese and Indian firms both to innovate and to search for new competences and knowledge abroad in an attempt to counter downward pressure in their margins. Labour-cost arbitrage in low-skilled work, by contrast, had less scope in middle-income Brazil and Russia. But there was some potential for labour arbitrage in higher skill work, such as engineering, design or software development. This led to a different industry focus and possibly more emphasis on the potential of internationalisation as a way to exploit these advantages, so that the chapters in this volume identified a number of EMNEs in such medium-skilled activities in both countries.

Country of origin and competitive advantage: similarities among the BRICs

Even though the BRICs are different from one another, as a group they are all still quite different from developed countries. This means that EMNEs from the BRICs are likely to share some common differences with DMNEs, notwithstanding their internal differences.

One such common difference is that, compared to incumbent DMNEs, EMNEs are in the early stages of evolution as multinational enterprises (Ramamurti, 2009a: 419–22). Therefore, their competitive advantages are likely to be more heavily influenced by their home-country CSAs, such as the endowment of natural resources, low-cost labour or sizeable home markets. Other home-market characteristics, such as the need to offer potential customers exceptional value-for-money to unlock mainstream demand, or the need to cope with dispersed potential customers, undeveloped hard and soft infrastructure, archaic distribution networks or volatile government policy, encourage EMNEs to find innovative solutions for these challenges. In the process, they create distinctive competitive advantages, or firm-specific advantages (FSAs), that can underpin internationalisation.

Second, because EMNEs from the BRICs share the common feature of being latecomers to globalisation and internationalisation, they are faced with entrenched multinational incumbents in many global markets that have accumulated large stocks of knowledge and other intangible assets. In order to compete, therefore, we can expect them to view internationalisation more as a means of accessing new competences and learning opportunities than was the case for DMNEs, which generally ventured abroad in search of new markets or low-cost production sites.

Third, given that the BRICs are lower cost locations than most developed countries (especially in the case of China and India), EMNEs from these countries have less incentive than DMNEs to relocate core production or service operations to other countries. Of course as wages and salaries rise in the BRICs because of rapid economic growth, they too will look for alternative locations at which to perform some core activities – witness the movement of call centre work by Indian IT-service firms from India to the Philippines.

Role of government

Government played an important but variable role across the BRICs in enhancing the competitiveness of local firms. In China, the government is generally competent and helped modernise the country's infrastructure, strengthen educational facilities, create special economic zones and pursue industrial policies effectively. In none of the other countries was the government nearly as capable. In Brazil, the initial reluctance to support internationalisation shifted, after 2005, to an ambiguous and controversial programme to pick national champions (Fleury and Fleury, 2011). In Russia, the government was powerful and arbitrary, and quite capable of expropriating private firms or their profits at will. In India, the government was widely seen as inept. In both India and Russia, part of the motivation for internationalisation by local firms was 'system escape', that is, the desire to flee the country's unattractive business environment.

The role of the government also varied in terms of the extent of state ownership of key firms. China is probably at the high end of the spectrum, with SOEs controlled by the central government being among the largest firms in the country. In Russia, some of the large firms in the oil and gas sector were SOEs, while in Brazil and India the largest MNEs were mostly privately owned (although in Brazil, some of the largest are privatised SOEs).

Figure C.2 Determinants of international competitiveness of emerging market firms: CSA–GSA–FSA framework

In Rugman's CSA–FSA framework (Rugman, 2009), CSAs include natural endowments such as land, natural resources, labour, location, climate and so on, and FSAs consist of firm-level assets and capabilities that contribute to competitive advantage. To this scheme, it is helpful to add a third category of advantages that might be labelled 'government-specific advantages' (GSAs), which captures the quality of government-created assets and the quality of governance, reflected in the competency of policy makers to fashion and implement effective policies, including industrial targeting (see Figure C.2).

Firm-level variables

We turn next to firm-level factors that appear to affect the competitive advantage of EMNEs.

Intangible assets of EMNEs

Among the puzzles EMNEs pose to international business theorists is the notion that they appear to be multinationals without 'ownership advantages', but this view is based on the flawed assumption that their ownership advantages must be the same as those of DMNEs, e.g. the possession of proprietary technology or global brands (Ramamurti, 2012). The theoretical argument about when MNEs will exist does not require firms to possess these specific FSAs; it only requires them to possess intangible assets whose exploitation in other countries is best done through hierarchy (that is, through internalisation by the firm) rather than arm's-length market transaction (Buckley and Casson, 1976;

Dunning, 1988). Therefore, the question is, do EMNEs possess any valuable intangible assets that might form the basis for internationalisation? Framed this way, our studies show that EMNEs do indeed possess many valuable intangible assets, and their internationalisation does not depend only on country-specific advantages (as asserted by Rugman, 2009).

We have discussed two examples of such intangible assets – the capacity to innovate and the capacity to configure and manage the value chain across multiple countries, including the home country. Innovation by EMNEs involves reinventing existing products, processes and business models, though not necessarily the development of entirely new products based on cutting-edge technologies (as with DMNEs). This innovation capability is based on deep insights into emerging-market customers, and how best to satisfy those needs at the right price points. Gathering, analysing and making sense of all the underlying information requires intangible assets, such as the capability to hire the right people, gain the right intelligence and develop the right products for emerging markets. Similarly, process innovation requires capabilities in technology absorption, process optimisation to suit local factor costs and so on. The mainstream literature takes an overly narrow view of innovation, measuring it only in terms of a firm's R&D-intensity or the size of its patent portfolio.

The same is true of value-chain optimisation, which requires, first and foremost, knowing how to leverage the low-cost talent and resources of emerging economies, where EMNEs usually have the largest share of their workforce and assets. Developed country firms often struggle to operate effectively in the unpredictable, unstable environment of emerging economies, whereas EMNEs, having grown up in that environment, are adept at doing so; this is a non-trivial capability. In addition, EMNEs have had to learn how to leverage suppliers and knowledge abroad, including in advanced countries.

The thirst for learning
Our studies offer several interesting findings about the role of knowledge and learning in EMNEs. The earlier discussion about FSAs made one such point, namely, that one must not underestimate the tacit knowledge and know-how required to execute the unglamorous aspects of the value chain, such as manufacturing or assembling products. Stan Shih's famous 'smiling curve' (Bartlett and Ghoshal, 2000)

may give the wrong impression that manufacturing, which is viewed as a low value-adding stage, does not require tacit knowledge or intangible assets. We believe that intangible assets and tacit knowledge exist in all stages of the value chain.

Moreover, we believe that EMNEs can and do move up the smiling curve to higher value-added activities over time, even if they began as 'low-cost partners' of DMNEs (Ramamurti, 2009a), e.g. Indian software companies. EMNEs aspire to control more stages of the value chain, including upstream research/innovation and downstream branding/marketing, although their ability to do so may depend on their relative position in the governance of the value chain. In the natural resources sector, Brazilian and Russian firms have integrated backwards to find additional supplies, or forwards to control downstream stages of the value chain. As already discussed, a popular method for EMNEs to get into other stages of the value chain has been cross-border mergers and acquisitions.

A second point is that EMNEs are not content to sit still with their existing stock of knowledge and capabilities, but are looking to build on it. The simple low-cost assembler becomes also a low-cost designer and perhaps later a low-cost innovator. In earlier research, there is reference to the original equipment manufacturer (OEM) growing into the original design manufacturer (ODM), and eventually becoming a full-fledged original brand manufacturer (OBM) (Amsden and Chu, 2003). In other words, EMNEs may start with low-end manufacturing but over time acquire capabilities in design and innovation. There appear to be compelling advantages in co-locating manufacturing, design and innovation, not just with one another but also in the most dynamic markets. EMNEs are obvious actors for bringing the manufacturing–design–innovation nexus to emerging markets, which were the hottest markets in the 2000s for many products. As EMNEs migrate up in the value curve, developed countries are apt to find that their own economies are being 'hollowed out'.

A third point about knowledge and learning highlighted by our studies is that EMNEs may be *better* learners than DMNEs. One reason for this is that EMNEs are painfully aware that they are late-movers in their industries and cannot live off their technological lead and cutting-edge products. Ever since their home countries embarked on economic reforms in the 1990s, EMNEs have lived with the fear of being overrun by DMNEs with strong brands and superior products in their home markets. As a result, unlike DMNEs, EMNEs have felt weak and vulnerable, with strong incentives to reduce the technology and knowledge gap with DMNEs.

A fourth point gleaned from our studies is that EMNEs know quite well the gaps in knowledge and intangible assets that they need to plug through learning, imitation or M&A in advanced countries. In terms of the exploitation–exploration framework proposed by March (1991), it has been suggested that EMNEs often internationalise with the intent of exploring for new knowledge and acquiring new capabilities rather than exploiting existing capabilities. We agree with this general characterisation, with some caveats to follow, but we believe that 'exploration' is too open-ended a term to capture what EMNEs do when they venture abroad, because in fact they go in search of very specific capabilities that are missing in their capability portfolios. Late-movers have the advantage of being able to learn from the experience of first-movers, whereas first-movers must live with greater uncertainties about new and untested technologies or new and unproven customer needs.

A new dispersion of knowledge, capabilities and markets
Another important difference between DMNEs and EMNEs is the geographical distribution of their core capabilities and their principal markets. DMNEs typically began with a technological lead of some sort in the home market, which was exploited later in foreign markets. Core technological competencies continued to be based at home (or in the home region), which was often also the single most important market (or region) for the DMNE. As foreign markets grew in importance, the DMNE had to learn about those markets and integrate that market knowledge with technical knowledge residing at home. Over time, mature DMNEs even began to do some of their R&D in other countries (Kuemmerle, 1997; Cantwell and Mudambi, 2005). On the other hand, EMNEs tried to reduce their technological gap with DMNEs by acquiring companies in developed countries. The result is that the most advanced knowledge resources of EMNEs (people, labs, relations with the technical community) are in far-away developed countries, while their most important markets are closer to home. This spatial distribution of resources and functional capabilities is not only different from that of most DMNEs, but we suspect it may also be harder to integrate far-flung R&D with home markets than it is to exploit home-based

R&D in far-flung markets. Further research is needed to understand more deeply the managerial implications of this hypothesised difference and how EMNEs are coping with the resulting challenges.

Replacement of incumbents in mature industries

The 'global consolidator' strategy is pursued by EMNEs in industries that have matured in developed countries but are booming in emerging economies, e.g. cement, steel, chemicals, paper, processed food, beverages and so on (Ramamurti and Singh, 2009a: 140–6). In these cases, assets and capabilities are often atrophying in the developed world, because firms are in a downward spiral with declining local demand, legacy liabilities and uncompetitive cost structures, while the capabilities potentially have great value in emerging markets, where demand is expanding and moving upscale. EMNEs seem to play an important role in leveraging capabilities that have been 'orphaned' in developed countries by applying them in emerging markets, through the acquisition of firms, people or assets in developed countries. EMNEs are likely to find that their main rivals for these assets are EMNEs from other emerging economies. The reason for this, presumably, is that EMNEs can generate more value with those capabilities than developed-country firms, because of their ability to apply the capability to high-growth emerging markets. Firms in these industries in developed countries are often not well placed to seize these opportunities in emerging markets, because local firms enjoy first-mover advantages in the emerging market and can be hard to acquire because of impediments that range from regulatory restrictions through to lack of transparency and the desire of family owners to maintain control.

In fact, it may prove easier for EMNEs to transfer codifiable technological capabilities and process know-how acquired abroad back to their home countries than it is for DMNEs to acquire and internalise the more tacit and messy knowledge they would require to successfully expand in emerging and developing country markets. This raises the possibility that EMNEs could pursue a two-stage strategy (termed the 'double handspring' by Williamson and Raman in Chapter 12). First, EMNEs acquire foreign technology, know-how and the services of experienced staff and deploy these in their home market to strengthen their competitive advantage and build a strong position at home. In a second stage, they could then use this home-base position as a newly powerful platform to capture share in the global market.

Beyond the BRICs

As the largest of the emerging economies, the BRICs understandably have been singled out for study by us and others, but a broader group of countries has also attracted attention in recent years. This includes the 'CIVETS', which stands for Colombia, Indonesia, Vietnam, Egypt, Turkey and South Africa (Economic Intelligence Unit, 2009; HSBC, 2010), or the 'N-11', which consists of all of the CIVETS except Colombia and South Africa, plus Bangladesh, Iran, Mexico, Nigeria, Pakistan, Philippines and South Korea (Goldman Sachs Asset Management, 2005).[2] To what extent would findings from our BRIC sample apply to these or other emerging economies?

The answer follows from our earlier discussion of the effect of home country on the competitive advantage and internationalisation strategy of EMNEs. Despite the heterogeneity among emerging economies, some features are likely to be common to all EMNEs. Drawing on the earlier discussion, it can be hypothesised that EMNEs from the CIVETS or N-11 will share the following features with their BRIC cousins but *not* with their DMNE predecessors:

- the competitive advantages (FSAs) of EMNEs will be shaped by home-country CSAs, which will cast a longer shadow on their competitive advantage than is the case with mature DMNEs, which already tap into the locational advantages of many countries;
- those competitive advantages will rarely be based on cutting-edge technology or global brands but rather on innovation that involves product adaptation, process improvisation and novel business models. To the extent that the CIVETS or N-11 offer substantive CSAs, we would predict that EMNEs will start to emerge from those countries in increasing numbers and significance. The idiosyncratic advantages of these EMNEs will almost certainly differ from those of multinationals from developed countries. For example, several 'multilatinas' from Spanish-speaking Latin America have developed distinctive advantages in environmentally sustainable processes, including Costa Rica in coffee, Colombia in coffee and flowers, and Chile in fruit, salmon and wine;

---

[2] It is curious that Goldman Sachs included South Korea in this set, given that it was one of the earliest to embrace globalisation and whose largest MNEs could be regarded as mature MNEs.

- EMNEs from the CIVETS, N-11 or other emerging economies will internationalise at a faster pace than DMNEs did at the same stage of evolution but not unlike today's early-stage multinationals in developed countries, which are also internationalising in a world that is flatter and more integrated;
- as latecomers, learning and the acquisition of intangible assets, such as technology and brands, will be a more important motivation behind their internationalisation than is the case with established DMNEs;
- the evolution of their VCCs will likewise resemble that of the BRIC MNEs, with core production operations remaining at home, and technology or R&D activities undertaken abroad, often in developed countries;
- given their motivation to catch up with DMNEs, and their propensity to be strong in mature (or sunset) industries, EMNEs are likely to resort extensively to cross-border M&A, often in developed countries.

At the same time, MNEs based in the CIVETS or N-11 will differ from one another based on their home-country context, just as EMNEs from the BRICs differ from one another. For instance:

- those from countries with exportable surpluses of natural resources (e.g. South Africa, Nigeria, Indonesia), will find themselves integrating forwards to secure downstream markets, and those from countries with resource deficits (e.g. Egypt, South Korea) will integrate backwards to secure resources abroad;
- those from countries with large home markets (e.g. Mexico, Turkey) will use that to gain scale in mature industries, first at home and then globally (e.g. Cemex in cement, SABMiller in beverages, or Koç in Turkey);
- those from countries with large pools of low-cost labour (e.g. Philippines, Vietnam and Indonesia) will begin as low-cost partners of Western firms, and then become multinational themselves, as firms from China or India have done. However, if for any reason local firms are slow to seize these opportunities, the vacuum may be filled by EMNEs from other emerging economies (such as Taiwan, South Korea, China or India).

One dimension on which the BRIC sample is clearly unrepresentative of all emerging markets is the size of the home economy, because even the smallest of the BRICs would be a giant compared to most emerging economies. Therefore, our study cannot shed light on the kinds of MNEs that small and medium emerging economies will spawn. We would only add that small economies in the developed world, such as Canada, Israel, Netherlands and Switzerland, have produced several important MNEs, as have South Korea and Taiwan, among the 'newly industrialised countries' (NICs). It is therefore entirely likely that some small emerging economies, including those smaller than the CIVETS or N-11, will also produce home-grown MNEs. No evidence from our project supports or contradicts this prediction, but it is a promising topic for further research.

Managerial and policy implications

Our findings in this book concerning the competitive advantages of EMNEs and their evolution have a number of more general implications for managers and policy makers. Perhaps the most over-arching message is that EMNEs and their likely impacts on global competition and the geographic configuration of activities should not be underestimated. EMNEs are rapidly becoming an important force in shaping the global economic landscape. Yet the power of their competitive advantages is easily overlooked. One reason is that their advantages tend to be different from those of established DMNEs. Rather than strong brands or technologically leading edge products, EMNEs' competitive advantages tend to lie in process capabilities, unconventional types of innovation and new business models (particularly those that help EMNEs deliver unmatched value for money to mass-market customers). Another reason why EMNEs are sometimes underestimated is that many of their relative strengths lie in dealing with volatile environments, limited infrastructure and 'institutional voids' (Khanna and Palepu, 2005) that characterise many of the world's high-growth, emerging and developing markets rather than the environments of mature economies that are widely viewed as more sophisticated. As we look to the future, however, the capabilities to win the competitive battles in emerging markets may be precisely those that are required to succeed in the next round of global competition. This suggests that to succeed in the future incumbent multinationals may need to focus more attention on building some of the skills and capabilities enjoyed by EMNEs to complement their own portfolios of advantages. Rather than simply a question of EMNEs playing a game of 'catch-up', maybe a race between EMNEs and DMNEs to equip themselves to thrive in new global competitive landscape of tomorrow has begun.

Another implication from the analysis in this book is that the emphasis we observed EMNEs place on using internationalisation as a way to access new, complementary capabilities and as a route to learning relative to incumbent DMNEs suggests that the current gaps between the technologies and capabilities available to EMNEs and DMNEs may well close more quickly than many observers assume. Moreover, many of the leading EMNEs we examined in this study are extending their VCCs abroad and using cross-border M&A not only to catch up with DMNEs, but also to access complementary capabilities, knowledge and resources to fuel their innovation engines. While there is still a wide gulf in experience and organisational maturity between most EMNEs and DMNEs, therefore, managers of DMNEs need to be alert to the growing possibility of innovative and potentially disruptive competition from EMNEs in global markets. As EMNEs gain experience and expand their capability bases this new, disruptive competition will not be confined to low-end segments and low value-added activities; EMNEs will increasingly compete by adding value to their offerings.

In parallel, our findings suggest that as EMNEs develop their capabilities, they are increasingly competing for greater control of the global value chains. Historically many EMNEs focused on particular stages of the global value chain (such as low-cost assembly operations). Some EMNEs will continue to concentrate in a limited number of value-generating steps, operating as 'value-chain joiners' and seeking to compete by achieving greater scale and efficiency. But a significant number of the EMNEs from the BRIC countries we studied are moving to become 'value-chain creators', seeking to control the global value chain for their products and services. In some cases this shift is achieved by integrating forward from a strong resource base to gain control of value-added activities in processing, distribution and marketing. In other cases, EMNEs are using strong positions in their large domestic markets, and their associated economies of scale, as a base for which to extend their own value chains overseas. For managers of DMNEs this means that competition from EMNEs will not simply be for particular activities; increasingly DMNEs will need to compete with alternative global value chains constructed by EMNEs and designed to leverage their own innovations and capabilities.

Likewise our findings suggest that some EMNEs have distinctive advantages and managerial mind-sets that help them drive consolidation of existing value chains in industries that are considered 'mature' in developed economies (such as steel making and bulk chemicals). While these industries are seen as being in decline in developed markets they remain growth industries in emerging economies. Our findings suggest that this encourages the management of EMNEs to see greater potential in these industries, including opportunities to deploy the process capabilities developed at home to drive up productivity and share economies of scale, as well as a greater willingness to invest in restructuring and renewal. EMNEs are also acquiring and accessing pockets of capabilities and technology 'orphaned' by the decline of production capacity in these industries that they can use to complement and extend the capabilities they have built in their operations at home and in other emerging markets. Managers in developed economies should therefore expect increasing competition from EMNEs in these industries as they deploy these 'contrarian' approaches and gain the scale and scope benefits by driving further global industry consolidation.

Our findings also suggest a number of implications for policy makers. There is a clear trend towards increased foreign direct investment (FDI) by EMNEs. Although this varies by country of origin, EMNEs from the BRICs together are investing right along the value chain from natural resources, through production, technology and R&D, distribution and brand building. This FDI spans different modes from greenfield establishment of subsidiaries through joint ventures and partnerships to cross-border M&A. As FDI by EMNEs continues to rise in importance, regulatory and political issues will inevitably arise by virtue of the fact that EMNEs are headquartered in countries with different institutional contexts from those of many of the recipient countries. Among these differences are the degree of state ownership (China and Russia being particular examples), levels of transparency and disclosure requirements, and the degree of development and effectiveness of 'soft infrastructure', such as legal and regulatory systems. Such differences arise most starkly when EMNEs invest in developed economies – a trend that we can expect to continue in view of the important role these investments play in EMNEs' strategies to build competitive advantage. Policy makers will need to develop ways of resolving these tensions if they are to avoid costly frictions and lost opportunities as EMNEs continue to globalise.

More generally, as EMNEs become a more powerful force in the global economy, policy makers will need to decide how and where EMNEs fit into their national economic strategies. In some emerging and developing economies this raises issues of perceived over-dependence and potentially excessive market power of EMNEs in national economies – especially in the case of EMNEs from large economies with access to deep pockets and considerable resources. Policy makers in developed economies, meanwhile, will need to adapt to the on-going shift of EMNEs to higher value-added activities, greater control of global value chains, and an increasing role as potential investors and acquirers of existing businesses. Some national governments will see these developments as an opportunity and welcome EMNEs as potential job creators. Singapore, for example, is actively promoting itself as an attractive location from which Asian EMNEs can run their international networks, and London is seeking to position itself as a key node for Chinese banks in the growing market in off-shore renminbi transactions. Other countries, meanwhile, have welcomed EMNEs, especially global consolidators from Brazil and India, to assist in restructuring industries that have faced excess capacity and declining fortunes.

Elsewhere, politicians and policy makers may perceive the continued rise of EMNEs as a threat both to established competitors headquartered in their countries and to employment and wage levels of the local citizens. They may attack what they regard as unfair competition and artificial subsidies provided by governments in EMNEs' home countries. As we have seen in this book, governments do adopt policies that directly and indirectly support the expansion of their home-grown EMNEs (as well as sometimes hindering them). But it is also clear from our findings that successful EMNEs have built real and distinctive competitive advantages and seem set to continue to strengthen these advantages in the future. Policy makers in host and home countries, as well as in organisations concerned with international governance, need to recognise and adjust to these new realities. Host country policies and international governance will need to adapt to the rising importance of EMNEs alongside DMNEs in the global economic system. Meanwhile, governments in emerging economies will need to consider policies that promote the role of EMNEs in national development and enhance their international competitive advantage.

References

Amagoh, F. and Markus, U. 2010. Kazakhstan's outward foreign investments: issues and perspectives. *Central Asia Business Journal* 3 (Nov): 12–25.

Amsden, A. H. 1989. *Asia's Next Giant: South Korea and Late Industrialization*. Oxford University Press.

Amsden, A. H. and Chu, W. 2003. *Beyond Late Development: Taiwan's Upgrading Policies*. Cambridge, MA: MIT Press.

Aoki, M. 1990. Toward an economic model of the Japanese firm. *Journal of Economics Literature* 28: 1–27.

Athreye, S. 2005. The Indian software industry. In A. Arora and A. Gambardella (eds.), *From Underdogs to Tigers: the Rise of the Software Industry in Brazil, China, India, Ireland, and Israel*. Oxford University Press, 740.

Aulakh, P. S. 2007. Emerging multinationals from developing economies: motivations, paths and performance. *Journal of International Management* 13: 338–55.

Awate, S. and Mudambi, R. 2010. *Blowin' in the Wind: Suzlon as an Emerging Economy Multinational Enterprise*. Fox School of Business, Temple University (mimeo).

Awate, S., Larsen, M.M. and Mudambi, R. 2012. EMNE catchup strategies in the wind turbine industry: is there a trade-off between output and innovation capabilities? *Global Strategy Journal* 2(3): 205–23.

Baldwin, C. and Clark, K. 2000. *Design Rules: the Power of Modularity*. Cambridge, MA: MIT Press.

Barkema, H. G. and Schijven, M. 2008. How do firms learn to make acquisitions? A review of past research and an agenda for the future. *Journal of Management* 34: 594–634.

Barkema, H. G., Bell, J. H. J. and Pennings, J. 1996. Foreign entry, cultural barriers and learning. *Strategic Management Journal* 17: 151–66.

Barney, J. and Clark, D. N. 2007. *Resource-based Theory: Creating and Sustaining Competitive Advantage*. New York: Oxford University Press.

Bartlett, C. A. and Ghoshal, S. 1986. Tap your subsidiaries for global reach. *Harvard Business Review* (Nov–Dec): 87–94.

1989. *Managing Across Borders: the Transnational Solution*. Boston, MA: Harvard Business School Press.

319

2000. Going global: lessons from late movers. *Harvard Business Review* 78: 133–42.

Baskaran, A. and Muchie, M. 2011. Can the relative strength of the national systems of innovation mitigate the severity of the global recession on national economies? The case of selected developed economies. Dynamics of Institutions and Markets in Europe (DIME) Final Conference, Maastricht, 6–8 April: 1–31.

Bell, D. E. and Ross, C. 2008. JBS Swift & Co. *Harvard Business School N9–509–021*, 12 December: 21.

Bell, M. and Pavitt, K. 1993. Technological accumulation and industrial growth: contrasts between developed and developing countries. *Industrial and Corporate Change* 2(2): 157–210.

Berliner, J. S. 1988. *Soviet Industry from Stalin to Gorbachev: Studies in Management and Technological Progress*. Ithaca, NY: Cornell University Press.

Beugelsdijk, S., Pedersen, T. and Petersen, B. 2009. Is there a trend towards global value chain specialization? An examination of cross border sales of US foreign affiliates. *Journal of International Management* 15: 126–41.

Bidgoli, H. (ed.) 2010. *The Handbook of Technology Management*. Hoboken, NJ: John Wiley and Sons.

Birkinshaw, J. 2001. Strategy and management in MNE subsidiaries. In A. M. Rugman and T. L. Brewer (eds.), *The Oxford Handbook of International Business*. Oxford University Press, 380–401.

Birkinshaw, J. and Hood, N. 2001. Unleash innovation in foreign subsidiaries. *Harvard Business Review* 79(3): 131–8.

Birkinshaw, J. M. and Morrison, A. 1995. Configurations of strategy and structure in subsidiaries of multinational corporations. *Journal of International Business Studies* 26: 729–54.

Bloomberg 2010. *Bankers see India's M&A Deals Passing 2010 Record of $71bn* (Mumbai, 30 December). Available at www.business-standard. com/india/news/bankers-see-india%5Cs-ma-deals-passing-2010-record71-bn/420042.

Boddewyn, J. J. and Brewer, T. 1994. International business political behavior: new theoretical directions. *Academy of Management Review* 19(1): 119–43.

Borini, F., Fleury, M. T. and Fleury, A. 2009. Corporate competences in subsidiaries of Brazilian multinationals. *Latin American Business Review* 10(3): 161–85.

Boston Consulting Group (BCG) 2010. *Innovation 2010. A Return to Prominence – and the Emergence of a New World Order*. Boston, MA: BCG.

2011. *Companies on the Move: Rising Stars from Rapidly Developing Economies are Reshaping Global Industries.* Boston, MA: BCG.

Bovel, D. and Martha, J. 2000. From supply chain to value net. *Journal of Business Strategy* (Jul/Aug): 24–8.

Bresman, H., Birkinshaw, J. and Nobel, R. 1999. Knowledge transfer in international acquisitions. *Journal of International Business Studies* 30(3): 439–60.

Brewer, A. M., Button, K. and Hensher, D. (eds.) 2001. *Handbook of Logistics and Supply Chain Management.* Amsterdam: Pergamon.

Breznitz, D. and Murphree, M. 2011. *Run of the Red Queen: Government, Innovation, Globalisation, and Economic Growth in China.* New Haven, CT: Yale University Press.

Brock, D. M. and Jaffe, T. 2008. International diversification and performance: the mediating role of implementation. *International Business Review* 17(5): 600–15.

Brown, J. S. and Hagel, J. 2005. Innovation blowback: disruptive management practices from Asia. *McKinsey Quarterly* 1: 35–45.

Buckley, P. J. 1990. Problems and developments in the core theory of international business. *Journal of International Business Studies* 31(4): 657–65.

Buckley, P. J. and Casson, M. C. 1976. *The Future of the Multinational Enterprise.* London: Macmillan.

Bulatov, A. 1998. Russian direct investment abroad: main motivations in the post-Soviet period. *Transnational Corporations* 7(1): 69–82.

2001. Russian direct investment abroad: history, motives, finance, control and planning. *Economics of Planning* 34(3): 179–94.

Burksaitiene, D. 2010. Cross border M&A in developed countries: a study in 2008–2009. *Economics and Management* 15: 32–8.

Cantwell, J. and Mudambi, R. 2005. MNE competence-creating subsidiary mandates. *Strategic Management Journal* 26(12): 1,109–28.

2011. Physical attraction and the geography of knowledge sourcing in multinational enterprises. *Global Strategy Journal* 1(3–4): 317–23.

Casanova, L. 2009. *Global Latinas: Latin America's Emerging Multinationals.* Basingstoke/New York: Palgrave Macmillan.

Caves, R. E. 1982. *Multinational Enterprise and Economic Analysis.* Cambridge University Press.

1986. *The Economic Analysis of the Multinational Firm* (2nd edn.). Cambridge University Press.

Chandler, A. D. Jr. 1980. *Managerial Hierarchies.* Cambridge, MA: Harvard University Press.

Chandy, R. and Tellis, G. 1998. Organizing for radical innovation: the overlooked role of willingness to cannibalize. *Journal of Marketing Research* 35: 474–87.

Chiesa, V. 1995. Globalizing R&D around centers of excellence. *Long Range Planning* 28(6): 19–28.

Child, J. and Rodrigues, S. 2005. The internationalization of Chinese firms: a case for theoretical extension? *Management and Organization Review* 1(3): 381–410.

Coffee, J. C. Jr. 2002. Racing towards the top? The impact of cross-listings and stock market competition on international corporate governance. *Columbia Law Review* 102: 1,757–831.

Cohen, W. M. and Levinthal, D. A. 1990. Absorptive capacity: a new perspective on learning and innovation. *Administrative Science Quarterly* 1(35): 128–52.

Collinson, S. C. 2007. M&A as imperialism? In D. Angwin (ed.), *Images of M&A*. Oxford: Blackwell Publications.

Conselho Empresarial Brasil–China 2011. *Chinese investments in Brazil: a new phase in the China–Brazil relationship*. New York: Vale Columbia Center.

Contractor, F. J., Kumar, V., Kundu, S. K. and Pedersen, T. 2010. Reconceptualizing the firm in a world of outsourcing and offshoring: the organizational and geographical relocation of high-value company functions. *Journal of Management Studies* 47: 1,417–33.

2011. *Global Outsourcing and Offshoring*. Cambridge University Press.

Crane, K., Peterson, D. J. and Oliker, O. 2005. Russian investment in the commonwealth of independent states. *Eurasian Geography and Economics* 46(6): 405–44.

Croyle, R. M. and Johnsey, A. L. 2007. Dow's novel approach to managing the human element of mergers and acquisitions. *Global Business and Organizational Excellence* 26(4): 18–26.

Cuervo-Cazurra, A. 2006. Who cares about corruption? *Journal of International Business Studies* 37: 803–22.

2007. Sequence of value-added activities in the internationalization of developing country MNEs. *Journal of International Management* 13(3): 258–77.

2008. The multinationalization of developing country MNEs: the case of multilatinas. *Journal of International Management* 14: 138–54.

2011. Global strategy and global business environment: the direct and indirect influences of the home country on a firm's global strategy. *Global Strategy Journal* 1: 382–6.

2012. How the analysis of developing country multinationals helps advance theory: solving the Goldilocks debate. *Global Strategy Journal* 2(3): 153–67.

Cuervo-Cazurra, A. and Dau, L. A. 2009. Pro-market reforms and firm profitability in developing countries. *Academy of Management Journal* **52**(6): 1,348–68.

Cuervo-Cazurra, A. and Genc, M. 2008. Transforming disadvantages into advantages: developing country MNEs in the least developed countries. *Journal of International Business Studies* **39**: 957–79.

2011. Obligating, pressuring, and supporting dimensions of the environment and the non-market advantages of developing-country multinational companies. *Journal of Management Studies* **48**(2): 441–5.

Cuervo-Cazurra, A., Meyer. K. and Ramamurti, R. 2011. *Country of Origin and Firm Specialization in Resource Development: the Case of Emerging Country Multinational Companies*. Paper presented at the Academy of International Business Conference, Nagoya, Japan.

Cullen, J. B. and Parboteeah, K. P. 2005. *Multinational Management. A Strategic Approach* (3rd edn.). Mason, OH: Thomson South-Western.

Cyrino, A. and Barcellos, E. 2007. Benefícios, riscos e resultados do processo de internacionalização das empresas brasileiras. In Almeida, A. (ed.), *Internacionalização de Empresas Brasileiras: Perspectivas e Riscos*. Rio de Janeiro: Elsevier.

Cyrino, A., Barcellos, E. and Oliveira, M. M. Jr. 2007. *Global Player II: Internacionalização de Empresas da América Latina: Desafios, Obstáculos e Perspectivas das Multinacionais Emergentes*. Sao Paulo: Relatório de Pesquisa, available at www.fdc.org.br.

Das, G. 2002. *India Unbound: from Independence to the Global Information Age*. London: Profile Books Ltd.

2006. The India model. *Foreign Affairs* (Jul–Aug): 2–16.

Dertouzos, M. L., Lester, R. K. and Solow, R. 1989. *Made in America: Regaining the Productive Edge*. New Baskerville: The MIT Press.

Devinney, T. M. 2003. The eclectic paradigm: the developmental years as a mirror on the evolution of the field of international business. In J. L. C. Cheng and M. A. Hitt (eds.), *Managing Multinationals in a Knowledge Economy: Economics, Culture (Advances in International Management, Vol. 15)*. Bingley, UK: Emerald Group Publishing, 29–42.

Doz, Y. L., Santos, J. and Williamson, P. 2001. *From Global to Metanational: How Companies Win in the Knowledge Economy*. Boston, MA: Harvard University Press.

Dunning, J. H. 1988. The eclectic paradigm of international production: a restatement and some possible extensions. *Journal of International Business Studies* **19**: 1–31.

1995. Reappraising the eclectic paradigm in an age of alliance capitalism. *Journal of International Business Studies* **26**(3): 461–91.

2000. The eclectic paradigm of international production. A personal perspective. In C. N. Pitelis and R. Sugden (eds.), *The Nature of Transnational Firm* (2nd edn.). New York: Routledge, 119–39.

2001. The eclectic (OLI) paradigm of international production: past, present and future. *International Journal of the Economics of Business* 8(2): 173–90.

Dunning, J. H. and Lundan, S. 2008. *Multinational Enterprises and the Global Economy* (2nd edn.). Cheltenham: Edward Elgar.

Dunning, J. H. and Narula, R. 1996. The investment development path revisited: some emerging issues. In J. H. Dunning and R. Narula (eds.), *FDI and Governments: Catalysts for Economic Restructuring*. London: Routledge, 1–33.

Economist, The 2008. *Emerging-market Multinationals: the Challengers.* 10 January, 3–4. Available at www.economist.com/node/10496684, accessed 13 September 2011.

2010. *Networked networks.* 17 April, *Asian* Print Edition, 67.

2011. *Let a Million Flowers Bloom.* 12 March, 79–82.

Economist Intelligence Unit 2009. *BRICS and the BICIS.* Available at ,www. economist.com/blogs/theworldin2010/2009/11/acronyms_4, accessed 20 May 2012.

Enright, M. and Subramanian, V. 2008. *Biocon: from Generics Manufacturing to Biopharmaceutical Innovation.* Hong Kong: ACRC Case.

Erber, F. 2004. Innovation and the development convention in Brazil. *Revista Brasileira de Inovacao* 3(1): 35–54.

Ernst, H. and Dubiel, A. 2009. *How to Build and Manage a Global R&D Center: the Case of GE in India.* European Case Clearing House (ECCH) 309–039–1.

Ferdows, K. 1989. Mapping international factory networks. In K. Ferdows (ed.), *Managing International Manufacturing.* Amsterdam: Elsevier Science Publishers, 3–21.

1997a. 'Made in the world': the global spread of production. *Production and Operations Management* 6(2): 102–9.

1997b. Making the most of foreign factories. *Harvard Business Review* Mar–Apr: 73–88.

Figueiredo, P. 2007. What recent research does and doesn't tell us about rates of latecomer firms' capability accumulation. *Asian Journal of Technology Innovation* 15(2): 161–94.

Filatotchev, I., Buck, T. and Wright, M. 2007a. Soviet all-union enterprises as new multinationals of the CIS. *The International Executive* 35(6): 525–38.

Filatotchev, I., Strange, R., Piesse, J. and Lien, Y. C. 2007b. FDI by firms from newly industrialized economies in emerging markets: corporate governance, entry mode and location strategies. *Journal of International Business Studies* 38(4): 556–72.

Filippov, S. 2008. *Russia's Emerging Multinationals: Trends and Issues.* UNU-MERIT Working Paper Series 2008–062, Maastricht.

2010. Russian companies: the rise of new multinationals. *International Journal of Emerging Markets* 5(3–4): 307–32.

Flaherty, M. T. 1986. Coordinating international manufacturing and technology. In M. E. Porter (eds.), *Competition in Global Industries.* Boston, MA: Harvard Business Press.

Fleury, A. and Fleury, M. T. 2011. *Brazilian Multinationals: Competences for Internationalization.* Cambridge University Press.

Forsgren, M. 2002. The concept of learning in the Uppsala internationalization process model: critical review. *International Business Review* 11(3): 257–77.

Fundação Dom Cabral 2011. Ranking das transnacionais Brasileiras 2011: crescimento e gestão sustentável no exterior. *Relatório de pesquisa*, available at www.fdc.org.br.

Garabato, N. 2009. *BRIC and MENA Countries: the Emergence of M&A Opportunities. Insight: February.* London: WatsonWyatt.

Gereffi, G., Humphrey, J. and Sturgeon, T. 2005. The governance of global value chains. *Review of International Political Economy* 12(1): 78–104.

Ghemawat, P. 2001. Distance still matters: the hard reality of global expansion. *Harvard Business Review* (Sep): 137–47.

2007. Managing differences. *Harvard Business Review* 85(3): 58–68.

Girod, S. G. J. and Bellin, J. B. 2011. Revisiting the 'modern' multinational enterprise theory: an emerging-market multinational perspective. In R. Ramamurti and N. Hashai (eds.), *The Future of Foreign Direct Investment and the Multinational Enterprise, Research in Global Strategic Management, 15.* Bingley, UK: Emerald, 167–210.

Goldman, M. 2003. *The Piratization of Russia: Russian Reform Goes Awry.* London/New York: Routledge.

Goldman Sachs Asset Management 2005. *Investing in Growth Markets.* Available at www.goldmansachs.com/gsam/individuals/products/growth_markets/n11/index.html, accessed 30 June 2012.

Goldstein, A. 2007. *Multinational Companies from Emerging Economies: Composition, Conceptualization and Direction in the Global Economy.* Basingstoke: Palgrave Macmillan.

Govindarajan, V. 2012. The reverse innovation playbook. *Harvard Business Review* (Apr): 120–3.

Govindarajan, V. and Ramamurti, R. 2011. Reverse innovation, emerging markets, and global strategy. *Global Strategy Journal* 1(3–4): 191–205.

Grant, R. M. 2008. *Contemporary Strategy Analysis* (6th edn.). Malden, MA: Blackwell.

Gubbi, S. R., Aulakh, P. S., Ray, S., Sarkar, M. B. and Chittoor, R. 2009. Do international acquisitions by emerging economy firms create shareholder value? The case of Indian firms. *Journal of International Business Studies* **40**: 1–22.

Gui, L. 2010. Reshaping the boundaries of the firm: global value chains and lead firm strategies. In J. Pla-Barber and J. Alegre (eds.), *Reshaping the Boundaries of the Firm in the Era of Global Interdependence, Progress in International Business Research (Vol. 5)*. Bingley, UK: Emerald, 29–55.

Guillén, M. F. and Garcia-Canal, E. 2009. The American model of the multinational firm and the 'new' multinationals from emerging economies. *Academy of Management Perspectives* **23**(2): 23–35.

Haleblian, J., Devers, C. E., McNamara, G., Carpenter, M. A. and Davison, R. B. 2009. Taking stock of what we know about mergers and acquisitions: a review and research agenda. *Journal of Management* **35**: 469–502.

Hall, P. A. and Soskice, D. 2001. An introduction to varieties of capitalism. In P. A. Hall and D. Soskice (eds.), *Varieties of Capitalism: the Institutional Foundations of Comparative Advantage*. Oxford University Press, 1–68.

Hamel, G. 1994. The concept of core competence. In G. Hamel and A. Heene (eds.), *Competence-based Competition*. Chichester: John Wiley & Sons, 11–34.

Hamel, G. and Heene, A. 1994. *Competence-based Competition*. Chichester: John Wiley & Sons.

Harper, N. 2011. Wind Telecom optimistic about Vimpelcom merger. *Middle East Economic Digest* **55**(3): 17.

Haspeslagh, P. and Jemison, D. 1990. *Managing Acquisitions: Creating Value through Corporate Renewal*. New York: Free Press.

Hayes, R. H. and Wheelwright, S. C. 1984. *Restoring Our Competitive Edge: Competing Through Manufacturing*. New York: Wiley.

Hedlund, G. 1986. The hypermodern MNC: a hetararchy? *Human Resource Management* **25**(1): 9–35.

Heinrich, A. 2003. Internationalisation of Russia's Gazprom. *Journal of East European Management Studies* **8**(1): 46–66.

2006. Russian companies in old EU member states: the case of Germany. *Journal of East–West Business* **11**(3–4): 41–59.

Helfat, C., Finkelstein, S., Mitchell, W., Peteraf, M., Singh, H., Teece, D. and Winter, S. 2007. *Dynamic Capabilities: Understanding Strategic Change in Organisations*. Malden, UK: Blackwell Publishing.

Hill, C. W. L. 2007. *International Business: Competing in the Global Marketplace* (6th edn.). Boston: McGraw-Hill/Irwin.

Hill, C. W. L., Hwang, P. and Kim, W. C. 1990. An eclectic theory of the choice of international entry mode. *Strategic Management Journal* 11: 117–28.

Hill, T. 1989. *Manufacturing Strategy: Text and Cases*. Homewood, IL: Irwin.

Hill, T. L. and Mudambi, R. 2010. Far from Silicon Valley: how emerging economies are re-shaping our understanding of global entrepreneurship. *Journal of International Management* 16(4): 321–7.

Hitt, M. A., Harrison, J. S. and Ireland, R. D. 2001. *Mergers and Acquisitions: a Guide to Creating Value for Shareholders*. New York: Oxford University Press.

HSBC 2010. *After BRICs, Look to CIVETS for Growth*. Available at: www.reuters.com/article/2010/04/27/hsbc-emergingmarkets-idUSL-DE63Q26Q20100427, accessed 15 May 2012.

Huang, Y. 2003. *Selling China: Foreign Investment During the Reform Era*. Cambridge University Press.

Hutton, W. 2007. *The Writing on the Wall: China and the West in the 21st Century*. London: Little Brown.

Hymer, S. H. 1976. *The International Operations of National Firms: a Study of Direct Foreign Investment*. (PhD dissertation 1960, published posthumously). Cambridge, MA: The MIT Press.

InnovaLatino 2011. *Fostering Innovation in Latin America*. Available at www.innovalatino.com.

Institute of World Economy and International Relations (IMEMO) and Vale Columbia Center (VCC) 2009. *Russian Multinationals Continue their Outward Expansion in Spite of the Global Crisis*. Report prepared by IMEMO of the Russian Academy of Sciences and the VCC of Columbia University as part of the Emerging Market Global Players (EMGP) project, 2 December. Available at www.vcc.columbia.edu/files/vale/documents/Russia_2009.pdf.

Johanson, J. and Vahlne, J. E. 1977. The internationalization process of the firm: a model of knowledge development and increasing foreign market commitments. *Journal of International Business Studies* 8(1): 23–32.

Johnson, M. W., Christensen, C. M. and Kagermann, H. 2008. Reinventing your business model. *Harvard Business Review* (Dec): 1–12.

Jones, G. 2005. *Multinationals and Global Capitalism: from the Nineteenth Century to the Twenty First Century*. Oxford University Press.

Kafouros, M., Buckley, P. J., Sharp, J. A. and Wang, C. 2008. The role of internationalisation in explaining innovation performance. *Technovation* 28(1–2): 63–74.

Kale, D. and Little, J. 2007. From imitation to innovation: the evolution of innovative R&D capabilities in the Indian pharmaceutical industry. *Technology Analysis and Strategic Management* 19(5): 589–609.

Kalotay, K. 2002. Outward foreign direct investment and governments in central and eastern Europe: the cases of the Russian federation, Hungary and Slovenia. *The Journal of World Investment* 3(2): 267–87.

2005. Outward foreign direct investment from Russia in a global context. *Journal of East–West Business* 11(3–4): 9–22.

2008. Russian transnationals and international investment paradigms. *Research in International Business and Finance* 22(2): 85–107.

2010. The political aspect of foreign direct investment: the case of the Hungarian oil firm MOL. *Journal of World Investment and Trade* 11(1): 79–90.

Kao, J. 2009. Tapping the world's innovation hot spots. *Harvard Business Review* (Mar): 109–14.

Kappen, P. 2011. Competence-creating overlaps and subsidiary technological evolution in the multinational corporation. *Research Policy* 40(5): 673–86.

Kapur, D. and Ramamurti, R. 2001. India's emerging completive advantage in services. *Academy of Management Executive* 15(2), 20–33.

Kets de Vries, M., Shekshnia, S., Korotov, K. and Florent-Treacy, E. 2004. The new global Russian business leaders: lessons from a decade of transition. *European Management Journal* 22(6): 637–48.

Keyhani, M. and Madhok, A. 2012. Acquisitions as entrepreneurship: asymmetries, opportunities, and the internationalization of multi-nationals from emerging economies. *Global Strategy Journal* 2(1): 26–40.

Khanna, T. and Palepu, K. 1997. Why focused strategies may be wrong for emerging markets. *Harvard Business Review* 75(7): 3–10.

1999a. Emerging giants. *Harvard Business Review* 84(10): 60–9.

1999b. The right way to restructure conglomerates in emerging markets. *Harvard Business Review* (Jul/Aug): 125–34.

2005. Strategies that fit emerging markets. *Harvard Business Review* 83(6): 63–76.

2006. Emerging giants. Building world class companies in developing countries. *Harvard Business Review* (Oct): 60–9.

2010. *Winning in Emerging Markets: a Road Map for Strategy and Execution.* Boston, MA: Harvard Business Press.

2012. Winning in emerging markets: spotting and responding to institutional voids. *The World Financial Review.* Available at www.worldfinancialreview.com/?p=483.

Khanna, T., Oberholzer-Gee, F. and Lane, D. 2006. *TCL Multimedia.* Boston, MA: Harvard Business School Press.

Khanna, T., Palepu, K. and Bullock, R. 2010. Winning in emerging markets. *Harvard Business Review* 88(6): 80–5.

King, D., Dalton, D., Daily, C. and Covin, J. 2004. Meta-analyses of post-acquisition performance: indications of unidentified moderators. *Strategic Management Journal* 25: 187–200.

Knight, G. and Kim, D. 2009. International business competence and the contemporary firm. *Journal of International Business Studies* 40(2): 255–73.

Kodama, F. 1985. *Alternative Innovation: Innovation Through Technological Fusion*. Saitama University, mimeo.

Kogut, B. 1985a. Designing global strategies: comparative and competitive value-added chains. *Sloan Management Review* 26(4): 15–28.

    1985b. Designing global strategies: profiting from operational flexibility. *Sloan Management Review* 27(1): 27–38.

    1991. Country capabilities and the permeability of borders. *Strategic Management Journal* 12: 33–47.

Kogut, B. and Zander, U. 1993. Knowledge of the firm and the evolutionary theory of the multinational corporation. *Journal of International Business Studies* 24: 625–45.

Kostova, T. 1996. *Success of the Transnational Transfer of Organizational Practices within Multinational Companies*. Unpublished doctoral dissertation, University of Minnesota, Minneapolis.

Koza, M. P., Tallman, S. and Ataay, A. 2011. The strategic assembly of global firms: a microstructural analysis of local learning and global adaptation. *Global Strategy Journal* 1(1–2): 27–46.

KPMG 2009. *Russian M&A Market in 2009*. London: KPMG.

Krugman, P. R. and Obstfeld, M. 2006. *International Economics: Theory and Policy* (7th edn.). Boston, MA: Pearson/Addison-Wesley.

Kuemmerle W. 1997. Building effective R&D capabilities abroad. *Harvard Business Review* (Mar–Apr): 61–70.

Kumar, A. 2010. The India imperative for the global corporation. *The Financial Executive* 26(3): 48–50.

Kumar, N. 2007. Emerging multinationals: trends, patterns and determinants of outward investment by Indian enterprises. *Transnational Corporations* 16(1): 1–26.

Kumar, N. and Fodea, A. 2009. *Perspective on Economic Growth of BRIC Countries: a Case of Brazil and India*. India: National Institute of Science, Technology and Development Studies (NISTADS), 13 February, 1–13.

Kuznetsov, A. V. 2010. *Industrial and Geographical Diversification of Russian Foreign Direct Investments*. Electronic Publications of Pan-European Institute, Turku School of Economics, Finland.

Kyläheiko, K., Jantunena, A., Puumalainena, K., Saarenketo, S. and Tuppura, A. 2010. Innovation and internationalization as growth strategies: the role of technological capabilities and appropriability. *International Business Review* **19**(2): 119–25.

Lall, S. 1983. *The New Multinationals: the Spread of Third World Enterprises.* New York: Wiley.

Lambert, D. M., Cooper, M. C. and Pagh, J. D. 1998. Supply chain management: implementation issues and research opportunities. *International Journal of Logistics Management* **9**(2): 1–19.

Lamming, R., Johnsen, T., Zheng, J. and Harland, C. 2000. An initial classification of supply networks. *International Journal of Operations and Production Management* **20**(6): 675–91.

Larçon, J.-P. (ed.) 2009. *Chinese Multinationals.* New Jersey: World Scientific/EFMD.

Lasserre, P. 2007. *Global Strategic Management* (2nd edn.). Basingstoke/ New York: Palgrave Macmillan.

Lee, K. and Lim, C. 2000. Technological regimes, catching-up and leapfrogging: findings from the Korean industries. *Research Policy* **30**: 459–83.

Leo, F. D e 1994. Understanding the roots of your competitive advantage. In G. Hamel and A. Heene (eds.), *Competence-based Competition.* Chichester: John Wiley.

Lessard, D. and Lucea, R. 2009. Mexican multinationals: insights from CEMEX. In R. Ramamurti and J. Singh (eds.), *Emerging Multinationals in Emerging Markets.* Cambridge University Press, 280–311.

Lewin, A. Y., Massini, S. and Peeters, C. 2009. Why are companies offshoring innovation? The emerging global race for talent. *Journal of International Business Studies* **40**: 901–25.

Li, X., Shi, Y. and Gregory, M. J. 2000. Global manufacturing virtual network (GMVN) and its position in the spectrum of strategic alliance. In R. V. Dierdonck and A. Vereecke (eds.), *Operations Management: Crossing Borders and Boundaries: the Changing Role of Operations.* Belgium: EurOMA 7th International Annual Conference, Ghent, 4–7 June, 330–7.

Liu, C. Z. 2007. Lenovo: an example of globalization of Chinese enterprises. *Journal of International Business Studies* **38**(4): 573–7.

Liu J. and Tylecote, A. 2009. Corporate governance and technological capability development: three case studies in the Chinese auto industry. *Industry and Innovation* **16**(4–5): 525–44.

Liuhto, K. and Jumpponen, J. 2003. *The Russian Eagle has Landed Abroad: Evidence Concerning the Foreign Operations of Russia's 100 Largest Exporters and Banks.* Research Report 141, Department of Industrial Engineering and Management, Lappeenranta University of Technology.

Liuhto, K. and Vahtra, P. 2007. Foreign operations of Russia's largest industrial corporations – building a typology. *Transnational Corporations* **16**(1): 117–44.

London, T. and Hart, S. 2004. Reinventing strategies for emerging markets: beyond the transnational model. *Journal of International Business Studies* 35: 350–70.

Luce, E. 2008. *In Spite of the Gods: the Rise of Modern India*. New York: Doubleday.

Luo, Y. D. and Tung, R. L. 2007. International expansion of emerging market enterprises: a springboard perspective. *Journal of International Business Studies* 38(4): 481–98.

Madhok, A. 2012. Acquisitions as entrepreneurship: internationalization, acquisition and multinationals from emerging economies. *Global Strategy Journal* 1(2): 24–54.

March, J. G. 1991. Exploration and exploitation in organizational learning. *Organization Science* 2(1): 71–87.

Martinez-Jerez, F. A., Narayanan, V. G. and Jurgens, M. 2006. *Strategic Outsourcing at Bharti Airtel (Case no. 107003-PDF-ENG)*. Boston, MA: Harvard Business School.

Mathews, J. A. 2002. *Dragon Multinational: a New Model for Global Growth*. Oxford and New York: Oxford University Press.

2006. Dragon multinationals: new players in 21st century globalization. *Asia Pacific Journal of Management* 23(1): 5–27.

McCann, P. and Mudambi, R. 2005. Analytical differences in the economics of geography: the case of the multinational firm. *Environment and Planning Analysis* 37(10): 1,857–76.

Medvedev, D. 2011. Opening remarks at meeting of the Commission for Modernisation and Technological Development of Russia's Economy, 31 January. Available at http://eng.kremlin.ru/transcripts/1702.

Mercer 2011. *Corporate Acquisitions – What the Numbers Don't Tell You*. Available at www.mercer.com/articles/1408640.

Meyer, K. and Estrin, S. 2001. Brownfield entry in emerging markets. *Journal of International Business Studies* 31(3): 575–84.

Meyer, K., Mudambi, R. and Narula, R. 2011. Multinational enterprises and local contexts: the opportunities and challenges of multiple embeddedness. *Journal of Management Studies* 48(2): 235–52.

Morck, R., Yueng, B. and Zhao, M. 2008. Perspectives on China's outward foreign direct investment. *Journal of International Business Studies* 39: 337–50.

Moura, P. G. 2007. *O Processo de Internacionalização do Desenvolvimento de Produtos em Empresas Multinacionais Brasileiras*. MSc thesis, Universidade de Sao Paulo.

Mudambi, R. 2008. Location, control and innovation in knowledge-intensive industries. *Journal of Economic Geography* 8(5): 699–725.

2011. Hierarchy, coordination and innovation in the multinational enterprise. *Global Strategy Journal* 1(3–4): 317–23.

Mudambi, R. and Venzin, M. 2010. The strategic nexus of offshoring and outsourcing decisions.*Journal of Management Studies* **48**(2): 1,510–33.

Nascimento, B. J. 2009. Redes em subsidiarias de multinacionais: um estudo de caso com analise de redes sociais de inventores e patentes. *Revista de Administracao Publica* **43**: 1,037–66.

Nelson, R. R. and Winter, S. G. 1982. *An Evolutionary Theory of Economic Change*. Cambridge, MA: Harvard University Press.

  2002. Evolutionary theorizing in economics. *Journal of Economic Perspectives* **16**(2): 23–46.

Neto, P., Brandão, A. and Cerqueira, A. 2010. The macroeconomic determinants of cross-border mergers and acquisitions and greenfield investments. *IUP Journal of Business Strategy* **7**(1–2): 21–57.

Niosi, J. and Tschang, T. 2009. The strategies of Chinese and Indian software multinationals, implications for internationalisation theory. *Industrial and Corporate Change* **18**(2): 269–94.

Nolan, P. 2005. China at the crossroads. *Journal of Chinese Economic and Business Studies* **3**(1): 1–22.

Nolan, P. and Hasecic, M. 2000. China, the WTO and the third industrial revolution. *Cambridge Review of International Affairs* **13**(2): 164–80.

Normann, R. and Ramirez, R. 1993. From value chain to value constellation: designing interactive strategy. *Harvard Business Review* (Aug–Sep): 75–6.

OECD 2011. *OECD Reviews of Innovation Policy: Russian Federation 2011*. Moscow: OECD Publishing.

Panibratov, A. 2009. Internationalization process of Russian construction industry: inward investments perspective. *Journal for East European Management Studies* **14**(2): 210–28.

  2012. *Russian Multinationals: From Regional Supremacy to Global Lead*. Abingdon, UK: Routledge.

Panibratov, A. and Kalotay, K. 2009. *Russian Outward FDI and its Policy Context*. New York: Columbia FDI Profiles, No. 1, Vale Columbia Center on Sustainable International Investment, 13 October.

Panibratov, A. and Verba, C. 2011. Russian banking sector: key points of international expansion. *Organizations and Markets in Emerging Economies* **2**(1–3): 63–74.

Parolini, C. 1999. *The Value Net: a Tool for Competitive Strategy*. Chichester, UK: John Wiley.

Patibandla, M. and Petersen, B. 2002. The role of transnational corporations in the evolution of a high tech industry: the case of India's software industry. *World Development* **30**(9): 1,561–77.

Peng, M. W., Wang, D. L. Y. and Jiang, Y. 2009. An institution-based view of international strategy: a focus on emerging economies. *Journal of International Business Studies* **39**: 920–36.

Piore, M. J. and Sabel C. F. 1984. *The Second Industrial Divide: Possibilities for Prosperity*. New York: Basic Books.

Pitelis, C. N. and Sugden, R. (eds.). 2000. *The Nature of the Transnational Firm* (2nd edn.). London/New York: Routledge.

Podmetina, D., Smirnova, M., Vaatanen, J. and Turkkeli, M. 2009. Innovativeness and international operations: case of Russian companies. *International Journal of Innovation Management* 13(2): 1–23.

Porter, M. E. 1985. *Competitive Advantage*. New York: Free Press.

    1986a. Changing patterns of international competition. *California Management Review* 28(2): 9–40.

    1986b. Competition in global industries: a conceptual framework. In M. E. Porter (ed.), *Competition in Global Industries*. Boston, MA: Harvard Business School Press.

    1990. *The Competitive Advantage of Nations*. New York: Free Press.

    1998. Clusters and the new economics of competitiveness. *Harvard Business Review* (Dec): 77–90.

Pradhan, J. P. 2007a. *New Policy Regime and Small Pharmaceutical Firms in India*. Working Paper No. 2007/02, Institute for Studies in Industrial Development, New Delhi.

    2007b. *Trends and Patterns of Overseas Acquisitions by Indian Multinationals*. Working Paper No. 2007/10, Institute for Studies in Industrial Development, New Delhi (Oct).

    2008. *Indian Direct Investment in Developed Regions*. Paper presented at the Copenhagen Business School (CBS) Conference on 'Emerging Multinationals: Outward Foreign Direct Investment from Emerging and Developing Economies'. 9–10 October, CBS.

    2011. Emerging multinationals: a comparison of Chinese and Indian outward foreign direct investment. *International Journal of Institutions and Economics* 3(1; Apr): 113–48.

Pradhan, J. P. and Alekshendra, A. 2006. *Overseas Acquisition versus Greenfield Foreign Investment: Which Internationalization Strategy is Better for Indian Pharmaceutical Enterprises?* Working Paper No. 2006/07, Institute for Studies on Indian Development (ISID), Delhi (Aug).

Pradhan, J. P. and Sauvant, K. P. 2011. Introduction: the rise of Indian multinational enterprises: revisiting key issues. In K. P. Sauvant and J. P. Pradhan (eds.), *The Rise of Indian Multinationals*. New York: Palgrave Macmillan.

Prahalad, C. K. 2005. *The Fortune at the Bottom of the Pyramid*. Philadelphia, PA: Wharton School Publishing.

Prahalad, C. K. and Bhattacharyya, H. 2008. Twenty hubs and no HQ. *Strategy and Business* 50 (May): 24–9.

Prahalad, C. K. and Doz, Y. L. 1987. *The Multinational Mission: Balancing Local Demands and Global Vision*. NY: The Free Press.

Prahalad, C. K. and Hamel, G. 1990. The core competence of the corporation. *Harvard Business Review* **68**(3): 79–91.

Prahalad, C. K. and Mashelkar, R. A. 2010. Innovation's Holy Grail. *Harvard Business Review* (Jul–Aug): 116–26.

Prencipe, A., Davies, A. and Hobday, M. 2003. *The Business of Systems Integration*. Oxford University Press.

Quah, P. and Young, S. 2005. Post-acquisition management: a phases approach to cross-border M&As. *European Management Journal* **23**(1): 65–75.

Ramamurti, R. 2008. *Made-in-India Multinationals. India in Transition Series (Oct)*. Philadephia, PA: Center for Advanced Study of India, University of Pennsylvania.

    2009a. Why study emerging-market multinationals? In R. Ramamurti and J. V. Singh (eds.), *Emerging Multinationals in Emerging Markets*. Cambridge University Press, 3–22.

    2009b. What have we learned about emerging-market MNEs? In R. Ramamurti and J. V. Singh (eds.), *Emerging Multinationals in Emerging Markets*. Cambridge University Press, 399–426.

    2011. Foreword. In K. P. Sauvant and J. P. Pradhan (eds.), *The Rise of Indian Multinationals*. New York: Palgrave Macmillan, xvii–xix.

    2012. What is really different about emerging market multinationals? *Global Strategy Journal* **2**(1): 41–7.

Ramamurti, R. and Singh, J. V. 2008. *Indian MNEs: Generic Internationalization Strategies*. Cambridge University Press.

    (eds.) 2009a. *Emerging Multinationals in Emerging Markets*. Cambridge University Press.

    2009b. Indian multinationals: generic internationalisation strategies. In R. Ramamurti and J. V. Singh (eds.), *Emerging Multinationals in Emerging Markets*. Cambridge University Press, 110–66.

Ramani, S. V. 2002. Who's interested in biotechnology: R&D strategies, knowledge base and market sales of Indian biopharmaceutical firms, *Research Policy* **31**, 381–98.

Ramani, S. V. and Maria, A. 2005. TRIPS and its possible impact on the biotech based segment of the Indian pharmaceutical industry. *Economic and Political Weekly* (12–18 Feb): 675–83.

Ramani, S. V., Athreye, S. and Kale, D. 2009. Experimentation with strategy and evolution of dynamic capability in the Indian Pharmaceutical sector. *Industrial and Corporate Change* **18**(4): 729–59.

Reuters 2008. *3Com Rebuff due to 'Complexities' and Costs – Huawei* (23 Feb). Available at www.reuters.com/article/2008/02/23/us-huawei-3com-idUSHKG5460020080223.

Rugman, A. M. 1981. *Inside the Multinationals: the Economics of Internal Markets*. New York: Columbia University Press.

2005. *The Regional Multinationals: MNEs and 'Global' Strategic Management*. Cambridge University Press.

2008. How global are TNCs from emerging markets? In K. Sauvant (ed.), *The Rise of Transnational Corporations from Emerging Markets: Threat or Opportunity?* Cheltenham: Elgar, 86–106.

2009. Theoretical aspects of MNEs from emerging markets. In R. Ramamurti and J. V. Singh (eds.), *Emerging Multinationals in Emerging Markets*. Cambridge University Press, 42–63.

Rugman, A. M. and Brain, C. 2003. Multinationals are regional, not global. *Multinational Business Review* **11**(1): 3–12.

Rugman, A. M. and Collinson, S. C. 2009. *International Business* (5th edn.). London: FT Pearson.

Rugman, A. M. and Doh, J. 2008. *Multinationals and Development*. New Haven, CT: Yale University Press.

Rugman, A. M. and Li, J. 2007. Will China's multinationals succeed globally or regionally? *European Management Journal* **25**(5): 333–43.

Rugman, A. M. and Verbeke, A. 2001. Subsidiary-specific advantages in multinational enterprises. *Strategic Management Journal* **22**: 237–50.

2008. A regional solution to the strategy and structure of multinationals. *European Management Journal* **26**: 305–13.

Rugman, A. M., Verbeke, A. and Wenlong, Y. 2011. Re-conceptualizing Bartlett and Ghoshal's classification of national subsidiary roles in the multinational enterprise. *Journal of Management Studies* **48**(2): 253–77.

Saarenketo, S., Puumalainen, K., Kuivalainen, O. and Kylaheiko, K. 2004. Dynamic knowledge-related learning processes in internationalising high-tech SMEs. *International Journal of Production Economics* **89**(3): 363–78.

Santos, J., Doz, Y. and Williamson, P. 2004. Is your innovation process global? *MIT Sloan Management Review* **45**(4, summer): 31–7.

Santos, J., Spector, B., and Van der Heyden, L. 2009. Defining the business model. *INSEAD Working Papers Collection* **16**: 5–14.

Saranga, H. and Banker, R. 2009. Productivity and technical changes in the Indian pharmaceutical industry. *Journal of Operational Research Society* **12**: 305–21.

Sauvant, K. P. (ed.). 2008. *The Rise of Transnational Corporations from Emerging Markets: Threat or Opportunity?* Northampton, MA: Edward Elgar.

Sauvant, K. P. and Pradhan, J. P. (with A. Chatterjee and B. Harley) 2010. *The Rise of Indian Multinationals*. New York: Palgrave Macmillan.

Schonberger, R. 1982. *Japanese Manufacturing Techniques*. New York: The Free Press.

Shi, Y. and Gregory, M. J. 1998. International manufacturing networks – to develop global competitive capabilities. *Journal of Operations Management* **16**: 195–214.

   2002. Global manufacturing virtual network (GMVN): its dynamic position in the spectrum of manufacturing collaborations. In U. J. Franke (ed.), *Managing Virtual Web Organisations in the 21st Century: Issues and Challenges*. New York: Idea Group Publishing.

Shimizu, K., Hitt, M. A., Vaidyanath, D. and Pisano, V. 2004. Theoretical foundations of crossborder mergers and acquisitions: a review of current research and recommendations for the future. *Journal of International Management* **10**: 307–53.

Silveira, F. F. 2008. *As Práticas de Comunicação em Projetos Globais de Desenvolvimento de Produtos em Empresas Multinacionais Brasileiras*. MSc Thesis, Universidade de Sao Paulo.

Sistema 2010. *Annual Report and Accounts*. Available at: http://sistema-annual-report-2010.production.investis.com/en.aspx.

Skolkovo Research 2008. *Emerging Russian Multinationals: Achievements and Challenges* (Nov). Moscow: Skolkovo Research.

   2009. *Operational Challenges Facing Emerging Multinationals from Russia and China. SIEMS Monthly Briefing*, Skolkovo Institute for Emerging Market Studies (Jun).

Srai, J. S. and Alinaghian, L. S. 2013. Value chain reconfigurations in highly disaggregated industrial systems: examining the emergence of healthcare diagnostics. *Global Strategy Journal* **3**: 88–108.

Srai, J. S. and Fleet, D. E. 2010. Exploring the configuration of emerging country multinationals. In E. L. Brennan (ed.), *The Emergence of Southern Multinationals and their Impact on Europe*. New York: Palgrave Macmillan, 261–80.

Srai, J. S. and Gregory, M. 2008. A supply network configuration perspective on international supply chain development. *International Journal of Operations and Production Management* **28**(5): 386–411.

Srai J. S. and Shi, Y. J. 2008. *Understanding China's Manufacturing Value Chain*. Cambridge University Press.

Stahl, G. K. and Voigt, A. 2008. Do cultural differences matter in mergers and acquisitions? A tentative model and examination. *Organization Science* **19**: 160–76.

Stefanovitz, J. and Nagano, M. 2006. Aquisição e criação de conhecimento na indústria de Alta Tecnologia. *Revista Producao Online* **6**(6): 1–15.

Stulz, R. 1999. Globalization, corporate finance, and the cost of capital. *Journal of Applied Corporate Finance* **12**: 8–25.

Sull, D. 2005. Strategy as active waiting. *Harvard Business Review* (Sep):120–9.

Sull, D. and Escobari, M. 2004. *Made in Brazil*. Rio de Janeiro: Editora Campus.

Tata Steel Group 2010. *Annual Report 2010*. Mumbai: Tata Steel Group.

Täube, F., Wadhwa, A., Frenzel, A. and Karna, A. 2011. *Low Cost Pills or High End Innovation? Strategic Growth Options for Emerging Economy Firms*. DRUID Conference, Copenhagen Business School, Denmark, 15–17 June.

Teece, D. J. 2009. *Dynamic Capabilities and Strategic Management: Organizing for Innovation and Growth*. Oxford University Press.

Teece, D. J., Pisano, G. and Shuen, A. 1997. Dynamic capabilities and strategic management. *Strategic Management Journal* 18(7): 509–33.

Tidd, J., Bessant, J. and Pavitt, K. 2001. *Managing Innovation: Integrating Technological, Market and Organisational Change*. Chichester, UK: John Wiley and Sons Ltd.

United Nations Conference on Trade and Development (UNCTAD) 2000. *World Investment Report 2000: Cross-border Mergers and Acquisitions and Development*. New York/Geneva: United Nations.

  2010. *World Investment Report 2010: Investing in a Low-Carbon Economy*. New York/Geneva: United Nations.

  2011. *World Investment Report 2011: Non-equity Modes of International Production and Development*. New York/Geneva: United Nations, 163. Available at www.unctad-docs.org/files/UNCTAD-WIR2011-Full-en.pdf.

Vahlne, J.-E. and Wiedersheim-Paul, F. 1973. Economic distance: model and empirical investigation. In Hornell, E., Vahlne, J.-E. and Wiedersheim-Paul, F. (eds.), *Export and Foreign Establishments*. Uppsala: University of Uppsala, 81–159.

Vahtra, P. 2010. *A Dawn for Outward R&D Investments from Russia?* Electronic Publications of Pan-European Institute 5/2010, Turku School of Economics.

Vale Columbia Center 2009. *Russian Multinationals Continue their Outward Expansion in Spite of the Global Crisis*. Moscow and New York: Institute of World Economy and International Relations (IMEMO) of the Russian Academy of Sciences, Vale Columbia Center, Columbia University. Available at www.vcc.columbia.edu/files/vale/documents/Russia_2009.pdf.

Verbeke, A. 2009. *International Business Strategy*. Cambridge University Press.

Verma, S., Sanghi, K., Michaelis, H., Dupoux, P., Khanna, D. and Peters, P. 2011. *Companies on the move: rising stars from rapidly developing economies are reshaping global industries*. In Boston Consulting Group

(BCG), *Global Challengers*. Boston, MA: BCG. Available at www. bcg.com.

Vernon, R. 1966. International investment and international trade in the product cycle. *Quarterly Journal of Economics* **80**(2): 190–207.

   1979. The product cycle hypothesis in a new international environment. *Oxford Bulletin of Economics and Statistics* **41**(4): 255–67.

Vietor, R. H. K. and Seminerio, J. 2008. *The Suzlon Edge*. HBS Case Services N9–708–051.

Wells, L. T. Jr. 1983. *Third World Multinationals: the Rise of Foreign Investment from Developing Countries*. Cambridge, MA: MIT Press.

Wilkins, M. 1970. *The Emergence of Multinational Enterprise: American Business Abroad from the Colonial Era to 1914*. Cambridge, MA: Harvard University Press.

   1974. *The Maturing of Multinational Enterprise: American Business Abroad from 1914 to 1970*. Cambridge, MA: Harvard University Press.

   1986. Japanese multinational enterprises before 1914. *Business History Review* **60**(2): 199–232.

Williamson, P. J. and Raman, A. P. 2011. How China reset its acquisition agenda. *Harvard Business Review* **89**: 109–14.

Williamson, P. J. and Yin, E. 2009. Racing with the Chinese dragons. In I. Alon, J. Chang, M. Fetscherin, C. Lattemann and J. R. McIntyre (eds.), *China Rules: Globalization and Political Transformation*. New York: Palgrave Macmillan, 69–100.

Williamson, P. J. and Zeng, M. 2009a. Chinese multinationals: emerging through new gateways. In R. Ramamurti and J. V. Singh (eds.), *Emerging Multinationals in Emerging Markets*. Cambridge University Press, 81–109.

   2009b. Value-for-money strategies in recessionary times: lessons Western businesses must learn from emerging-market companies to succeed – at home and abroad. *Harvard Business Review* (Mar): 66–74.

Witt, M. A. and Lewin, A. Y. 2007. Outward foreign direct investment as escape response to home country institutional constraints. *Journal of International Business Studies* **38**(4): 579–94.

Womack, J., Jones, D. and Roos, D. 1990. *The Machine that Changed the World*. New York: Harper Perennial.

World Economic Forum (WEF) 2010. *The Global Competitiveness Report 2010–2011*. Geneva: WEF.

Xu, D. and Shenkar, O. 2002. Institutional distance and the multinational enterprise. *Academy of Management Review* **27**(4): 608–18.

Yang, Q., Mudambi, R. and Meyer, K. 2008. Conventional and reverse knowledge flows in multinational corporations. *Journal of Management* **34**(5): 882–902.

Yin, R. K. 2003. *Case Study Research. Design and Methods* (3rd edn.). Thousand Oaks, CA: Sage.

Yu, A. and Tromboni, P. 2002. *The Management of Product Development Projects: the Cases of Embraer and Natura.* Paper presented at the IAMOT Conference, Vienna.

Zaheer, S. 1995. Overcoming the liability of foreignness. *Academy of Management Journal* 38(2): 925–50.

Zeng, M. and Williamson, P. J. 2003. The hidden dragons. *Harvard Business Review* 81(10; Oct): 92–9.

　2007. *Dragons at your Door: How Chinese Cost Innovation is Disrupting Global Competition.* Boston, MA: Harvard Business School Press.

　2008. How to meet China's cost innovation challenge. *Ivey Business Journal* (May/Jun): 37–43.

Index

ABBYY 41
absorptive capacity 6
Acron 126
Aditya Birla 251
AFK Sistema 234
airline business models 70–1
Ajanta Pharmaceuticals 142
Alpargatas 18–19
Amanco 18
AmBev 17, 23, 205, 295
Anil Agarwal 244
Antas Chemical Company 69–70, 72
arbitrage-based internationalism
    47–53, 82, 90
arbitragers 3
asset-seeking concept 153
Atomenergoprom 127–8
Aurobindo 63, 143–4
AVIC *see* China Aviation Industries
    Corporation
AvtoVAZ 35

backward integration 186
Banco Postal 15, 24
Bank of Russia 234
Bank VTB 234
Baosteel Group 245
Basic Elements 296
Beijing Automotive Industry Holdings
    Co. Ltd (BAIC) 273
Beijing West Industries 273
Bharat Forge 55
Bharti Airtel 54–5, 57, 63, 247–8, 295
Biocon 53–4
Birla 53, 244
BNDES (Brazilian National
    Development Bank) 205–8,
    282
BOP (bottom-of-the-pyramid)
    innovation 15, 23–4, 85

Borini, F. M. 81–2, 90, 178
BPO (business process outsourcing)
    137–8
branding 6
Braskem 15, 19–20, 104
Brazil
    aerospace policy 284
    African market 106–7, 112
    biofuel 17, 37
    BOP (bottom-of-the-pyramid)
        innovation 15, 23–4, 83
    business models innovation 15, 21–3
    commodity innovations 14–17
    company strategy groups
        global first-movers 205–6
        global/regional consolidators 205
        local optimisers 204
        low-cost partners 204–5
        natural-resource vertical integrator
            203–4
    competitive advantages 215–18
    competitiveness 13, 81–2, 112–14
    cross-border M&A patterns 279, 285
    currency valuation 206
    educational institutes 304
    FDI (foreign direct investment) flows
        243
    five-year plans 12
    and foreign multinationals 12
    free market economy 12–13
    future research 86
    government policy 206–8
    import substitution industrialisation
        policy 11–12
    incentive programmes 206–8
    inflation 12
    innovation and competitive
        advantages 16–26
    innovation by multinationals
        11–28

innovation as priority 35
innovation rankings 14
innovation types 14–16
international value-chain
    configurations 97–111
internationalisation 115, 178, 183–4,
    192, 209, 211–14
investment levels 81–2
and JPM (Japanese Production
    Model) 13–14, 22
labour force 304–5
local market development 12
main cross-border acquirers 198–9
management impetus 297
mergers and acquisitions (M&A)
    191–209
  cross-border 192
    factors driving 200–2
    and psychic distance 208
    role/importance at firm level
        202–6
  double-layer acculturation 192
  and internationalisation process
      192
  liability of foreignness 192
  and liberalisation policies 191
  outward 194–208
  strategic groups and drivers 207
military regime 12
multinationals
  in Africa 106–7, 112
  characteristics of 101–2
  competitive advantage and cross-
      border M&A 200–2
  competitive strategies 113–14
  competitiveness 107–8
  conflict between 97
  distribution by industry 102
  diversification 193
  key competencies 113
  regional locations 101
  similarities in 193–4
  subsidiaries 110–12, 114, 181–3
    activity structures 111
  TNI (transnationality indices) of
      101–2
national development plans 12
national innovation system 11
natural resources 304
off-shoring 112

oil exploration 16–17
operational excellence 13–14
organisational capability 83
organisational competencies 113–14
patents 11
performance indicators 90
petrochemicals 12
population 304–5
process innovation 296
product innovation 17–19
product and services development
    113
R&D investment 11, 14–15, 44–5
reverse innovations 15–16, 24–6
S&T (science and technology) 44–5
scientific and technological
    development plans 12
sources of comparative advantage
    178, *see also* CSA
sustainable innovation 15, 19–20, 28
technological progress 81–2, 280
transfer of competencies 6, 113–14
value-chain location 109–12
VCC (value chains), set up
                preferences structure 111
VCC (value-chain configurations)
    107–14, 299
wages 304–5
Brazilian Agricultural Research
    Corporation *see* Embrapa
BRICs *see* Brazil; China; India; Russia
Brin, Sergey 45
Broad 70
brownfield investment 222
business model innovation 15, 21–3,
    51–2, 54–5, 57, 63, 66, 70–3,
    76–9, 84, 295
BYD 64–5, 68

Caboclo sandals 15, 23–4
CAGE distances 106–7
Camargo Correa 205
Casas Bahia 5, 15, 24
case study companies *see* China
Cemex 104, 246
CENPES 16
centralised economies 184
Chaparral Steel 103
ChemChina *see* National Chemical
    Corporation

Cherry 245
China
    acquisitions and new technology 6
    application innovation 66, 69–70,
        76–9, 84
    automobile sector 92
    business model innovation 66, 70–3,
        76–9, 84
    case study A (white goods
        manufacturing) 154–8, 178
        branding stage 154
        diversification stage 154–6
        incremental development process
            156–8
        internationalisation stage 156
        new product development process
            158
        product technology 183
        production process 158
        sourcing process 158
    case study B (colour television
        manufacturing) 155, 159–66,
        178
        diversification 159
        export phase 160
        incremental growth phase 160–1
        internationalisation process
            159–66
        overseas factory development 167
        post-acquisition integration phase
            165–7
        radical expansion/acquisition
            phase 161–5
    competitive advantages 260–77
    cost innovation 66–8, 76–9, 263–4,
        285–6
    counterfeit products 73
    cross-border M&A patterns 279
    CSA (country-specific advantages)
        262–3, 281, 285
    educational institutes 304
    emerging challenges 149
    energy policy 284
    entrepreneurship 296
    factor-cost advantage 82–3
    FDI (foreign direct investment) flows
        243, 245
    foreign exchange reserves 270
    FSA (firm-specific assets) 262–4,
        275–6, 281

    future research 86
    GDP (gross domestic product) size
        304
    global competitiveness 78–9, 275
    global product leaders 64–5
    global value-chain reconfiguration
        149–72
    government policy 297
    import duties 162
    innovation
        and commercialisation 30
        and competitive advantage 64–77
        as priority 35
    innovation models 78–9
    innovation rankings 14, 82–3
    innovation sustainability 75–8
    integration tasks 165
    internationalisation 149–72, 183
    labour force 304–5
    labour-intensive skills 305–6
    manufacturing
        factory competence levels 168–9
        factory networks 169–70
            procurement 170
            product design 169–70
            product development 169–70
            production 170
        international strategies 171–2, 300
        trends in 151
    market dominance 90
    market focus 164
    mergers and acquisitions 260–77,
        281, 286
        cross-border 264–6, 276
        excessive premiums payments 265
        first wave (failed springboards)
            266, 276
        resource-seeking motives 265, 271
        second wave (retreat to hard
            assets) 270–1, 276
        TCL failure 269
        third wave (double handspring)
            271–5
    natural resources 304–5
    organisational capability 84
    patent activity 65, 83
    PC sector 64
    population 304–5
    private sector success 245
    process innovation 74, 82–3

product innovation 74
R&D 14, 35–7, 44–5, 66–8, 75, 82,
    84, 271–4, 276
resource-seeking acquisitions 261–2
S&T (science and technology) 44–5
scientific innovation 66–7
second-generation innovation 82–3
shanzhai innovation 66, 73–4,
    76, 84
sources of comparative advantage
    178, *see also* CSA
springboard acquisitions 261
supply chains 271, 276
technological innovation 66, 74–6,
    78–9, 300
TV sales volumes 165
wages 304–5
zou chuqu policy 260, 282, 284
China Aviation Industries Corporation
    (AVIC) 272, 282
China Mobile 64–5, 71
Cipla 140
Cisco 2, 41
CIVETS (Columbia, Indonesia,
    Vietnam, Egypt, Turkey and
    South Africa) 313–15
Coca-Cola 48
Commission for Modernisation of and
    Technological Development
    of Russian Economy 32
commodity innovations 14–17
company size dimension 122
competence formations and
    environment 98
competence networks 98
competence transfers 104
competence-based management/
    competence-based
    competition approach 98
competence-creating subsidiary 91
competitive advantage
    Brazil 215–18
    country of origin differences 304–6
    country of origin similarities 306–7
    country-level variables 303–8
    and cross-border M&A 293, 301–3
    firm-level variables 308–12
    and innovation 291–2, 294–7
    and intangible assets 308–9
    and internationalisation 294–303

knowledge and learning 309–12
    role of governments 307–8
    and value-chain reconfiguration
        297–301
competitiveness sources
    134–5
configuration 114–15
core capability distribution 311
core competencies 98
Core Healthcare 142
core technological competencies 312
Corus 251
cost innovation 66–8, 76–9, 263–4,
    285–6, 296
Coteminas 105, 178
cross-border M&A *see* M&A
cross-border value-adding non-equity
    116
CSA (country-specific advantages) 1,
    5–6, 8, 27–8, 65, 84, 116–17,
    178, 181–6, 239–41, 249,
    253–5, 262–3, 280–1, 285,
    306
CSA/FSA framework 118–19, 239,
    246, 279, 308
(CSN) Companhia Siderurgica
    Nacional 17, 103
cultural differences 288
Cummins 93
currency valuation 206

Dabur Pharmaceuticals 142
Daksh e-Services 137–8
Delixi Group 72–3
demand-side market seeking 126–7,
    129, 181
development cycle, EMNEs 4
Digital Sky Technologies 72
Dionis Club 123
disaggregation 187
D'Long Group 268, 286
DMNE (developed market
    multinational enterprises) 1,
    4, 91–2, 174–6
domestic innovation-driven
    internationalisation
        37–40
domestic innovation-seeking
    internationalisation 38, 42–3
Dong Yi 72–3

double handspring 252, 271–5, 280, 286–7, 289, 312
double-layer acculturation 192
downstream integration 187
downstream investments 186
dragon multinationals 107, 180
DRF 145
Dr. Reddy's 60, 135, 140, 143–5, 147–8, 295
drug development/discovery 140–2, 145–6
Dunning, J. 118, 132–3, 242

economies of scale 6
Elbrus 123
Eli Lilly 145–6
Embraer 12, 15, 21–2, 107, 205–6, 209, 243, 295
Embrapa 15–16, 25–6
emerging market firms 89
Erber, F. 14
Essar 244
EuroChem 123
Eurofarma 204
Evraz 42, 123, 235, 296
exploitation vs. exploration 279–81

FACC (Fischer Advanced Composite Components) 272
Falconi, Vicente 23
FDI (foreign direct investments) 2–3, 116–17, 120, 132, 135–6, 245
    outward 34, 117, 142–4, 194–208, 221–2, 224, 241–6
    theory 117–19
Filippov, S. 82, 90
Fleury, A. 81–2, 90, 178
Fleury, M. T. L. 81–2, 90, 178
Ford Motor Company 48
foreign operation modes 120
Fortis Healthcare 57
four Ts 51
frugal engineering 133
FSA (firm-specific advantages) 5, 27–8, 65, 98, 117–19, 124, 183–6, 202, 239–41, 249–50, 253–5, 262–4, 275–6, 280–1

Galanz 64–5, 306
GAZ Group 235–6

Gazprom 35, 120, 229–33, 237, 282, 296
GBS (Gerdau Business System) 22–3
GCC (Guangzhou Cranes Corporation) 68
Geely 273
geographic clustering 151
Gerdau 13–15, 22–3, 103, 205, 243, 295
Glenmark Pharmaceuticals 143–4
global challengers 116–17
global competition 315
global consolidator strategy 39, 124, 205, 250–2, 286, 312, 318
global consolidators 42
global delivery model 58, 136, 249–50
global first-mover strategy 39, 124, 205–6, 252–3, 286–7
global industries, value-chain configuration in 121–3
global innovation-driven internationalisation 37–8, 40–1
global innovation-seeking internationalisation 42
global integration 4
Global Latinas 117
global location advantages 142
global outsourcing 151
global production networks 115
global R&D hubs 91
global R&D networks 89, 92
global suppliers 134–5
global value chain 316
    concept 121
    configuration 174–6
        EMNE brands/distribution 177
        EMNE customer responsiveness 177
        EMNE finance 176–7
        EMNE innovation 177
        EMNE strategies for 176–7
        EMNE technological base upgrading 177
globalisation
    MNCs 150–1
    use by EMNEs 8
globalisation flows 85
globalisation trends 116
GMR Planeta gostepriimstva 123

GMVN (global manufacturing virtual
	network) 151
go global (zou chuqu) policy 260, 282,
	284
Goldstein, A. 119
governance 6
government support 1
Governmental Commission on High
	Technologies (Russia) 32
Govindarajan, V. 79
GPNs (global production networks)
	104–5
Green Polymer project 15, 20
greenfield investments/projects 143, 181,
	183, 222, 225–6, 238, 289
GSA (government-specific advantages)
	239–41, 246, 249, 253–5,
	285, 309
Gui, L. 119
GVC (global value chains) 90–1

Haier 64–5
Hall, P. A. 49
Havaianas 18–19, 111
HCL (Hindustan Computers Limited)
	135–6
Hindalco 251
HISense 155
Holly 155
home government policies 6
home market development 305
host government policies 6
Huawei 2, 64–5, 75, 78, 288, 295

IB (international business) theory 116,
	118–19, 171–3, 185, 264
IBM 2, 41
InBev 205
incremental innovations 65
incremental internationalisation
	181, 184
India
	arbitrage-based internationalism
		47–53, 82, 90
	automobile industry 55–6, 60
	BPO (business process outsourcing)
		firms 47
	business focus 53
	business model innovation 51–2,
		54–5, 57, 63, 84

competitive advantage 239–55
competitiveness 59
country-specific advantages (CSAs)
	239–41, 249, 253–5, 280–1
cross-border M&A patterns 279
diamond industry 51–2, 57
drug development/discovery 140–2,
	145–6
economic development comparisons
	242
educational institutes 304
entrepreneurial firms 243–4, 296
FDI flows 135–6, 143–4, 241–6
firm-specific advantages (FSA)
	239–41, 246–55, 280–1
foreign exchange restrictions 143
four Ts 51
future research 86
global consolidator strategy 250–2
global delivery model 249–50
global first-mover strategy 252–3
governance improvements 59
government incompetence 239, 282,
	285
government licensing 48
government-specific advantages
	(GSAs) 239–41, 246, 249,
	253–5, 280–1
healthcare providers 57
host country knowledge 6
innovation
	and commercialisation 30
	for Indian market 52–6
	and internationalisation 46–62
	evolution since 1990 47–58
	phases in 46–7, 61–2
	as priority 35
innovation leveraging for
	international markets 50–1,
	56–8, 90
international acquisitions 241–6,
	256–9
international capital access 60, 63
internationalisation 241
IT sector 37, 47, 51, 54, 57, 92,
	248–50
labour cost-arbitrage strategy
	249–50
labour force 304–5
labour pools 135–8

India (cont.)
    labour-intensive skills 305–6
    liberalisation and international
        expansion 48, 59, 82
    license raj 48, 52
    local optimiser strategy 247–8
    low-cost partner strategy 248–50
    mergers and acquisitions 53,
        239–55
    MNEs 46–7
    natural resources 239, 304–5
    oligopolistic firms 48, 82
    opening markets 48
    organisational capability 84
    patents 146–7
    per capita income 242
    pharmaceutical sector 37, 53–4,
        57–9, 135, 139–48, 178,
        185, 300
    population 304–5
    process innovation 51, 54
    product-based innovation 50–1,
        53–4
    R&D investment 14, 35–7, 44–5,
        53–4, 60, 139, 141, 144, 178
    regulatory barriers 48, 82
    S&T (science and technology) 44–5
    skill gaps 144–5
    software sector 134–9, 178, 185
    sources of comparative advantage
        178, *see also* CSA
    subsidiary management and
        internationalisation 132–48
    subsidiary roles and software firms
        138–9
    technical skills 244
    TRIPS (trade-related intellectual
        property rights), and
        pharmaceutical industry 140
    value chains and internationalisation
        132–48
    value chains and software firms
        138–9
    wages 304–5
Indian Oil 46
Indian Patent Act (1970) 139, 141
industrial company acquisition 261
industry structures 50
industry voids 84
Infosys 2, 46, 60, 135–9, 249

innovation 291–2
    barriers to 297
    business model innovation 15, 21–3,
        51–2, 54–5, 57, 63, 66, 70–3,
        76–9, 84, 295
    and competitive advantage 291–2,
        294–7
    cost innovation 66–8, 76–9, 263–4,
        285–6, 296
    incremental innovations 65
    process innovation 16–17, 51, 54,
        74, 82–3, 295–6
    product innovation 17–19, 50, 74, 294
    reverse innovation 15–16, 24–6, 44,
        297
    shanzhai innovation 66, 73–4, 76, 84
        see also Brazil; China; India;
        Russia
innovation/output capabilities 92–3
institutional arbitrage 49
institutional context 6
institutional distance 49
institutional voids 49, 315
integrated operators 126
integration-responsiveness framework
    119
integrator companies 22
Intellect Telecom 41
international competitiveness 98
international operations expansion,
        psychic distances 4–5
international operations management
    181
international research networks 34
international supply-chain development
    114–15
internationalisation 37–43, 284–5
    accessing knowledge 291
    accessing resources 291
    arbitrage-based 47–53, 82, 90
    Brazil 115, 178, 183–4, 192, 209,
        211–14
    China 149–72, 183
    and competitive advantage 294–303
    incremental 181, 184
    India 46–62, 241
        pharmaceutical sector 142–8
        software sector 135–8
    investment motives 182
    of management 138

manufacturing process 171–3
product design 186
production 186
Russia 37–43, 122, 124–5, 130–1
strategies 115
sustainability 132
and value chains 132–48
waves of 99–101
investment development plan model
242
IPR (intellectual property rights)
tools 78
IVC (international value chain)
establishment 99–100

Jaguar 63, 244, 251
Japanese Production Model (JPM)
13–14, 22, 99–100, 104
JBS-Friboi 17, 103–4, 178, 205–8, 282
JFWTC (John F. Welch Technology
Center) 91, 93
joint ventures outward
investment 143
Jubilant Organosys 143–4

Kako 104–5
Kaspersky Lab 2, 41
knowledge industry 103, 112
knowledge-intensive industries 100
knowledge-seeking mandates 92
Kostova, T. 49

labour cost arbitrage strategy 249–50,
306
Land Rover 63, 244, 251
large-scale outsourced business
model 137
leapfrogging 221, 227, 237
Lenovo 64–5, 306
liability of foreignness 192
license raj 48, 52
Liu Chuanzhi 64
LLL (linkage, leverage, learning) model
133–4, 180
local implementers 106
local optimiser strategy 39, 124, 204,
247–8, 286
local serve mode 163
location economy 121
low-cost locations 307

low-cost partner strategy 39, 124,
248–50, 286, 305, 310
low value-added activities 92
Lukoil 35, 123, 126–7, 178, 233, 282,
289, 296

M&A (mergers and acquisitions) 2, 6,
181, 285
cross-border M&A
and competitive advantage 293,
301–3
and inovation 292–3
patterns 279
and R&D 301–2
and VCC 292
cultural differences 288
motivators for 201
national government policies 284–5
off-shore 7–8
outward 194–208
successful firm characteristics 201,
288–9 *see also* Brazil; China;
India; Russia
Mahindra and Mahindra 55–6, 93, 251
Mai 123
managerial implications 315–18
manufacturing capability development
310
manufacturing network, new 151
Marcopolo 204
market access 181
market-based environments 184
market power 6
market-seeking Russian MNEs 126–7,
129, 181, 301
maturity and configuration 114–15
Medvedev, Dmitry 30, 32–3
Megafon 39
Meng Xiangkai 272
Mercosur 101–2, 106
Microfinance 93
Microsoft 2, 41
Microsoft Research 93
mini-MNEs 123
Ministry of Foreign Trade and
Economic Cooperation
(MOFTEC) 266
Mittal 103
MNC future research 86–7
MNC globalisation 150–1

MNC theory 84–6
MNE industrial profile 119–21
MNE internal interactions 121–2
MNE theory 117–19
mobile telephony 39
Mobile TeleSystems 234
MTS 39–40, 123
multi-domestic model 99
Murray/D'Long Group case study 268

N-11 (Indonesia, Vietnam, Egypt,
    Turkey, Bangladesh, Iran,
    Mexico, Nigeria, Pakistan,
    Philippines and South Korea)
    313–15
Naresh Goyal 244
National Chemical Corporation
    (ChemChina) 274–5, 287
National Innovation Strategy (Russia)
    32
National Innovation System (Brazil) 11
Natura 15, 20, 111, 209
natural resource industries 300
natural resource vertical integrators 305
natural-sources vertical integrator
    strategy 124
network design 186
network dispersion 156
network efficiency 181
network joiners 122
Nevskiye Siri 123
Nicholas Piramal 140, 143–4
Nipuna 137–8
NLMK 42, 123, 126, 235
Norilsk Nickel 126–7, 178, 227, 289,
    296
Novolipetsk Steel 42
Novolipetsky 123
NRK 235

Odebrecht Group 15, 19–20, 24,
    106–7, 243
OET (Odebrecht Entrepreneurial
    Technology) 19–20, 24
off-shore model 138
off-shoring 90–2, 112, 184
OLI (ownership location
    internalisation) theory 132–4,
    180
Oliveira, Miranda 81–2, 90

O'Neill, Jim 5
operational excellence 13–14
output/innovation capabilities 92–3
outsourced business model 137
outsourcing 92, 105, 137–8, 151, 174,
    184
own value chains 134–5
ownership advantages 1, 133

parent company roles 128
part downstream integration 187
part upstream integration 187
patent reform 139–42
patents and innovation capability
    30, 65
Patni Computers 139
Pepsi 48
Petrobras (PB) 2, 13–17, 193, 203–4,
    296
policy implications 315–18
Polyus Gold 236
Porter, M. E. 99, 297
Premji, Azim 138
Presidential Commission for
    Modernisation and
    Technological Development
    (Russia) 32–3
privileged access to resources and
    markets 42
process innovation 16–17, 51, 54,
    74, 82–3, 295–6
product innovation 17–19, 50,
    74, 294
product life cycle theory 4, 247
production internationalisation 186
production and operational excellence
    42
Progeon 137–8
protectionist barriers 1, 4
psychic distances 4–5, 208
pull-oriented concept 153
push-pull international production
    171–3
Putin, Vladimir 32

R&D (research and development) 7, 11,
    14, 25–6, 29, 32–7, 40–1,
    44–5, 53–4, 60, 66–8, 75, 82,
    84, 86, 104–5, 139, 141, 144,
    178, 271–4, 301–2

R&D scoreboard (investments) results 35–7
Ramamurti, R. 79, 118–19
Ranbaxy 60, 135, 140, 142–7
Randon 111
redundancy level 115
regional serve mode 163
Reliance 53–5
Ren Jianxin 274
Renova 42
resource-seeking acquisitions 261–2
resources seekers 126, 181
reverse innovation 15–16, 24–6, 44, 297
Rosatom 32, 127–8
Rosnano 32
Rosneft 123, 126, 296
Rostekhnologii 32
Rugman, A. M. 118–19
RUSAL 42, 123
Russia
  capital flight 34
  competitive advantage 296
  competitiveness 223
  constraints on opportunities 120–1, 130
  cross-border M&A patterns 279
  economic diversification 30
  educational institutes 304
  efficiency providers 123
  FDI (foreign direct investment), outward 34, 221–2, 224, 243
  foreign acquisitions 220
    acquirer advantages 223
    importance of 222–3
    main industries 225
    medium-sized deals 228
    mega deals 227, 230–1
    number of 226
    patterns of 223–8
  foreign expansion 124–8, 220
  future research 86
  greenfield projects 226
  industry consolidation 223
  innovation
    and commercialisation 30
    and competitive advantage 29–45
    constraints on 82
    and internationalisation 37–43
    as priority 35

innovation-driven strategies 29
innovation rankings 14
innovation weaknesses 44–5, 82
integrated operators 126
internationalisation determinants 124–5, 130–1
internationalisation options 122
knowledge transfer 83
labour force 304–5
low-tech industries 44
market economy transition 31
market-seeking Russian MNEs 126–7
mobile telephony 39
natural resource-based growth 284
natural resources 304–5
outward FDI investor motivation 221–2, 236–7
operation sectors limits 120–1
organisational capability 83
population 304–5
public policy 31–3
R&D (research and development) 29, 32–7, 40–1, 44–5, 83
regulatory environment 82
resource suppliers 123
resources seekers 126
reverse innovation 44
S&T (science and technology) complex 29, 31, 33, 43–5
sources of comparative advantage 178, *see also* CSA
strategic company alliances 225–6
subsidiaries 124
  strategic role of 128–9
technology providers 123, 127
value-chain configuration (VCC) 116–25, 178, 299
  in global industries 121–3
value chains and resource endowments 6
wages 304–5
RUSTI (Reddy US Therapeutics Inc) 145

Sabo 15–16, 25, 104–5, 178, 204
Satyam 137–8
Sberbank 235–6
scale economy 121, 285–6 *see also* cost innovation

SciPhone 74
scope economy 121
Servestal 42
services industries 300
Settles, A. 82, 90
Severnoye Siyaniye 123
Severstal 233–4, 289, 296
Shanghai Automotive Industries
        Corporation (SAIC) 245,
        266–7, 286
Shanghai Zhenhua Port Machinery
        64–5
Sinopec 270
Sistema 40–1
Sitronics 35, 40
skill gaps 144–5
Skolkovo innovation centre (Russia) 32
SKS Microfinance 295
SM (strategic management) and
        EMNEs 116, 119–21, 130
SMAR 15–16, 26
soft infrastructure 317
Soskice, D. 49
springboard acquisitions 261
springboard theory 280
Ssang-Yong/SAIC case study 266–7,
        286–7
Stefanini solutions 204
strategic alliances 181
strategic business area 119
subsidiaries 7
    formation of goals 129
    and host country characteristics 129
    Indian pharmaceutical sector 142–8
    Indian software sector 138–9
    management of and
        internationalisation 132–48
    and MNE internal characteristics
        129
    resources and capabilities 129
    roles of 128–9, 181–3, 300
Sun Pharmaceutical 46, 142–4
Sunil Mittal 244
sunrise and sunset industries 100,
        103–4, 302
supply-side resource seeking 126, 181
Surgutneftegas 235
sustainable innovation 15, 19–20, 28
Suzano 26
Suzlon 55, 60, 252–3, 295

Swift 103–4, 205
system-escape motives 236

Tang brothers 268
Tanti, Tulsi 244, 252–3
Tata 46, 55–6, 60, 63, 103, 244,
        251–2
TCL 268–9
TCS (Tata Consultancy Services) 46,
        137–9, 249–50
technology providers 123, 127
technology as qualifier 27
technology seeking RMNEs 127
Tencent 71–2, 295
Thomson Electronics/TCL case study
        268–9
Tigre 18, 106, 204
TNI (transnationality indices) 101–2
Totvs 204
trade barriers 1–2, 288
triple bottom line principles 15, 20
TRIPS (trade-related intellectual
        property rights) 60, 140
Turris 123

Unipro 123
Uppsala model 181, 209
upstream integration 187
upstream supply integration 186

Vale 2, 13–15, 17, 106–8, 193, 203–4,
        296
value-added activities 128–9
value-chain builders 122, 299
value-chain choices 288
value-chain creators 316
value-chain joiners 299, 316
value-chain location 109–12
value-chain network design 186
value-chain optimisation 309
value chains
    and internationalisation 132–48
    and LLL (linkage, leverage, learning)
        paradigm 133–4
    set up preferences structure 111
value role–company size matrix 122
VCC (value-chain configurations) 5–7,
        97–111, 116–25, 181
    Brazil 107–14, 299
    China 149–72, 184–5

and competitive advantage 297–301
competitive conditions of countries
110
geographic regions 109
global 174–6
host country development stage
109–10
India 300
pharmaceutical sector 142–8
software sector 138–9, 300
and innovation 292
and internationalisation 293
patterns 186–7
Russia 116–25, 178, 299
Verizon 288
Vernon, R. 12, 247
Videocon 251
Vimpel 39–40, 123, 126–7, 234, 289
virtual laboratories 26
Votorantim 17, 104, 205
VSMPO Avisma 123

Wanhua Polyurethane 75
Wanxiang 64–5, 155, 245
Washington Consensus 13
WEG 13–16, 25, 204
Wen Jiabao 266
Wenzhou 72–3
white goods case study (China)
154–8
Wipro 2, 60, 137–9, 244, 250
Wockhardt 140, 143–4, 146

X'ian Aircraft International (XAC) 272,
282, 287

Yang, David 41
Yanzhou Coal 270

Zhang Yue 70
Zhongqlang 155
zou chuqu policy 260, 282
ZTE 155